FOOD LOVERS' SERIES

FOOD LOVERS'
GUIDE TO®
CHICAGO

The Best Restaurants, Markets
& Local Culinary Offerings

2nd Edition

Jennifer Olvera

Guilford, Connecticut

Editor: Amy Lyons
Project Editor: Lauren Brancato
Layout Artist: Mary Ballachino
Text Design: Sheryl Kober
Illustrations: Jill Butler with additional art by Carleen Moira Powell and MaryAnn Dubé
Map: Sue Murray © Morris Book Publishing, LLC

ISSN: 2164-9448
ISBN 978-0-7627-9202-3

Printed in the United States of America
10 9 8 7 6 5 4 3 2

I dedicate this book to my son, Hayden Greer, one of the smartest, coolest dudes I know. (Naturally, he's a great cooking, dining, and traveling companion, too.)

Contents

About the Author

Jennifer Olvera holds an English degree from DePaul University. She got her start in the food world as a restaurant reviewer for *Chicago* magazine. Jennifer went on to pen far-flung culinary travel stories for the *Los Angeles Times, Chicago Tribune,* and Frommers.com and is a regular contributor to the *Zagat Chicago Restaurants Survey*. She has regularly tested and developed recipes for the *Chicago Sun-Times,* and she writes and photographs a weekly recipe column called Sunday Supper for Serious Eats. Jennifer also oversees Midwest and Chicago dining for Gayot, and her work has appeared on both Orbitz and Priceline.

Jennifer lives in the Chicago suburbs with her son, Hayden Greer; three cool (but fairly aloof) cats; and her retired Greyhound, Stewball (Stew for short). When she's not plucking heirloom tomatoes from her backyard garden, you'll find her canning, sourcing ingredients from local farms, or relaxing on her deck, an ice-cold martini in hand.

Follow her edible adventures via Twitter @olverajennifer, and check out her recipes at seriouseats.com/sunday_supper.

Acknowledgments

I'm lucky to live in a great food city, one that offers inspiration at every turn. Some chefs set about shifting the culinary landscape. Others prepare humble, heartwarming meals without pretense or pomp. There's a place for both, and here they coexist and thrive in my city side-by-side.

It's not surprising, really, that many of my early memories involve food. I cultivated a garden as a tot and learned to eat ice-cream cones from the bottom up (sorry, Mom!). These days, I include my son in every food adventure I can; they're meaningful moments.

There are simple pleasures, like eating blueberries right off of the bush. Then there are ones that level you—meals made by people in places that alter the way you think. It's never too soon to develop an appreciation of food and a respect for those who produce what we eat.

I've traveled a great deal in my career, yet it doesn't change a simple fact: I am a Midwestern girl at heart. Chicago is home because of the people who inhabit it.

I therefore want to acknowledge those who believed in me through the years—my mom, sister Katie, and aunt Greta, especially. I also want to thank my editor, Amy Lyons, for giving me the chance to write in-depth about a place I hold dear.

Introduction

Somewhere along the line, Chicago got branded as a brawny, broad-shouldered place, its deep-dish-devouring types garbling the word "tree" (instead of "three") between bites of relish-slathered hot dogs and swigs of "pop."

Let me say, that's a disservice. Chicago is a food city—and it's a sophisticated, multifaceted one at that. It fosters a large immigrant population, whose culinary traditions arrived intact. The abundance of ethnic, mom-and-pop eateries, often tucked into strip malls or located off the beaten track, offer proof of that.

From Chicago's historic, defunct stockyards to its heyday as a candy-making juggernaut, food has been a strong, pervasive undercurrent. Flaming *saganaki,* chicken Vesuvio, and shrimp de Jonghe—not to mention the brownie—are said to have started right here.

From its beginnings on, Chicago attracted and retained talented chefs. Plenty of them are known the world over. Haute haunts, such as Alinea, Grace, and L20, offer proof of that. Perhaps more notably, though, chefs have chosen to open casual, cost-conscious spots. Paul Kahan, Bill Kim, Rick Bayless, and Stephanie Izard are among those leading the charge. Not one compromised culinary integrity to do so. Emphasizing quality ingredients—often local and sustainable—their menus are a revelation for the food-enthused.

There is one thing that proves problematic for Chicagoans, however: its growing season—or lack thereof. Thankfully, hoop houses (greenhouses) are sprouting up, extending the availability of farm-fresh fare. We've also seen the opening of **The Plant** (p. 308), a closed-loop farm-of-the-future, nestled into an old meatpacking facility.

Given its temperamental weather, Chicagoans are right to revel in the spring and summer seasons. (And, boy, do they ever!) Restaurants grow produce on rooftops; apiaries produce honey in the unlikeliest of places; and garden-flanked sidewalks and beer gardens emanate with the joviality winter inhibits.

In the pages that follow, I'll share the big-flavored, food-loving spirit of Chicago as I know it. Here, the classics appear alongside that which is lesser known. This is a guidebook—make no mistake—so you'll find greatest hits. But it also offers inspiration beyond roads well traveled.

This isn't a visitor's guide in the traditional sense—it's for the culinary community as a whole: curious, longtime residents; visiting families or couples; and the expense account–wielding business traveler. Simply put, it's for all those who share the love of good eating.

Most of all, though, this is a book for those respectful—and supportive—of small farms, appreciative of artisanal products, and intoxicated by the simple things, like a steaming bowl of morning *pho*.

Navigating the City

Exploring Chicago is relatively easy. The city's layout is based on a grid system, and its block numbers—increasing 100 per block—are generally uniform throughout. The origin is at the intersection of State Street (0W/E) and Madison Street (0N/S). In most cases, individual blocks are approximately an eighth of a mile long. A secondary street typically appears every four blocks, or half-mile. Even addresses are located on the north and west side of the street, while odd numbers are found on the south and east. Certain streets—such as Lincoln Avenue, Clark Street, and Milwaukee Avenue—run diagonally, but their addresses are numbered the same as north–south and east–west thoroughfares.

Chicago is serviced by two major airports: O'Hare International Airport and Midway Airport. The former is situated 17 miles northwest of downtown Chicago, while the latter is located approximately 10 miles southwest. O'Hare is far more frenetic, though it hosts the largest number of domestic and international carriers. Midway tends to experience fewer delays, but it doesn't serve as many airlines.

The easiest—and most cost-effective—way to get around Chicago is to take public transportation because garages, valet service, and, increasingly, metered parking are costly. The city's Regional Transportation Authority (RTA) encompasses the Chicago Transit Authority (CTA) bus and elevated rail systems (referred to locally as the "L") as well as Metra commuter trains and the Pace suburban bus system. Check out the online trip planner at rtachicago.com; alternately, plan itineraries by calling (312) 836-7000. The current CTA fare when paying cash is $2.25 per single ride; however, transit cards, purchased at transitchicago.com and at rail stations, allow for transfers and—in some cases—slightly reduced fares.

The CTA Blue Line runs between O'Hare and Chicago's epicenter, the Loop; it takes upward of an hour to get from point A to point B. The Orange Line connects Midway and the Loop, with a ride time ringing in at about 30 minutes one way.

Unfortunately, public transportation in the 'burbs as well as the city's outlying areas leaves something to be desired. If you're heading outside of the city proper, plan on driving or renting a car.

How to Use This Book

In the pages that follow, you'll find entries organized for easy navigation. The front half of the book is dedicated to restaurants, while the back highlights everything from gourmet shops and ethnic grocers to farms, farm stands, and cooking schools. Throughout the book, sidebars point to edibles of interest, growing trends, and tales of those doing interesting things in Chicago and beyond.

Organization

Each locale is followed by its address and designated neighborhood within the city of Chicago. The establishments in this book are categorized in chapters by proximity—**North, Near North, Mid City, Near South,** and **South**—and listed alphabetically within chapters to keep things tidy. To clarify the neighborhood division, communities are listed at the beginning of the chapters and are as follows:

North: Albany Park, Andersonville, Argyle Street, Devon Avenue, Edgebrook, Edgewater, Edison Park, Jefferson Park, Lincoln Square, North Park, Norwood Park, Ravenswood, Rogers Park, Sauganash, Uptown

Near North: Avondale, Belmont Cragin, Hamlin Park, Hermosa, Irving Park, Lakeview, Logan Square, North Center, Portage Park, Roscoe Village, Wrigleyville

Mid City: Bucktown, Gold Coast, Humboldt Park, Lincoln Park, Noble Square, Old Town, Streeterville, Ukrainian Village, Wicker Park

Near South: East Village, Fulton River District, Garfield Park, Greektown, Loop, Near West Side, River North, River West, West Loop, West Town

South: Archer Heights, Ashburn, Beverly, Bridgeport, Bronzeville, Chatham, Chinatown, Englewood, Far South Side, Greater Grand Crossing, Hyde Park, Lawndale, Little Italy, Little Village, Near South Side, Pilsen, Printer's Row, Roseland, South Deering, South Loop, University Village

Price Code

Restaurants follow a pricing guide so you have some idea of what to expect. Dollar signs point to the following price ranges for a dinner and single drink:

$	less than $10
$$	$10 to $30
$$$	$30 to $50
$$$$	$50 or more per plate

Suburban Stunners, Stalwarts & Surprises

Suburban restaurants appear in a separate but collective chapter and categorized by directional proximity to Chicago.

Cocktail Culture

Chicago's burgeoning cocktail and brewery culture continues to spark interest—with good reason. Within these pages, learn of sublime sips, hops havens, and lounges serving noshes of note.

Specialty Stores, Gourmet Shops & Purveyors

Purveyors, including gourmet grocers, specialty stores, butchers, and fishmongers, offer a food-shopping fix.

Sweet Treats

Sweet spots—bakeries, confectionaries, and ice cream, ice, and gelato shops—get a chapter all their own.

Farm Fresh

Farm-fresh locales abound in the Chicago area; page through to find an edited list of farmers' markets, local farms, and farm stands.

Culinary Instruction

Because many food enthusiasts don't just eat but also cook, there's a chapter dedicated to cooking schools and classes that help hone skills.

Food Fests & Events

It seems there's always something food-related happening in Chicagoland. Look to the chapter dedicated to food fêtes, including festivals and events.

Recipes

Before the feast winds down, peruse recipes from Chicago chefs (and the author), giving you something to savor—in hands-on fashion.

Keeping Up with Food News

In this city, food journalists and bloggers abound. Each covers Chicago's cuisine scene from a slightly different angle.

Edible Chicago (ediblechicago.com) is published four times a year and is available at farmers' markets and gourmet food stores, with the goal of connecting readers with their food, telling stories of local producers, and providing inspiration for those interested in sustainable living.

LTHForum.com is an Internet-based culinary chat site and virtual "dining society." It skews toward undiscovered, mom-and-pop destinations. A definitive resource for food lovers, LTHF's highly anticipated "Great Neighborhood Restaurants" guide is available in downloadable, pocketbook format.

The *Chicago Reader*—hipsters' alt weekly of note—covers Chicago's dining scene through Mike Sula's journalistic eye.

Sky Full of Bacon (skyfullofbacon.com/blog) is the launching pad for Michael Gebert's blog and thought-provoking food podcasts on Chicago and Midwestern food.

The Stew (chicagotribune.com/features/food/stew) is a blog penned by the *Chicago Tribune*'s Good Eating and Dining staffs, and it's loaded with timely food- and drink-related news. Its most interesting commentary comes from Monica Eng, an intrepid reporter whose pieces have stirred up many a spirited discussion. Phil Vettel is the *Chicago Tribune*'s respected dining critic.

If you eat and/or drink in the city, you're bound to encounter *Time Out Chicago* (timeoutchicago.com). Though it ceased publishing the print edition, the digital content remains source for restaurant reviews.

HELPFUL TIP

In the back of the book are appendices to help you find a restaurant by cuisine or a food purveyor by type.

Chicago magazine's **Dish** (chicagomag.com/Radar/Dish), overseen by Penny Pollack, is a weekly food newsletter that may be viewed online or delivered via e-mail. The food section in the magazine proper is worth a look, too.

Chicagoist (chicagoist.com) is a city-centric website and blog covering Chicago happenings, which includes food from Food and Drink Editor Anthony Todd.

CS, a publication from Modern Luxury, offers edible insight from dining critic and writer/eater extraordinaire Lisa Shames.

Steve Dolinsky (aka "The Hungry Hound," stevedolinsky.com) is a Chicago food-broadcaster-turned-avid-eater, occasional *Iron Chef* judge, and blogger covering the city's culinary scene.

Chicago Gapers Block: Drive Thru (gapersblock.com/drivethru) is the food and drink arm of the Chicago-minded web pub, delivering news and observations on Chicago food.

David Hammond, co-founder and lead moderator of LTHForum.com, is behind cable series "You Really Should Eat This," the food columnist for Oak Park's Wednesday Journal, and a welcome voice to many food pubs about town.

Nick Kindelsperger oversees Chicago's **Serious Eats** (chicago.serious eats.com), a go-to blog and "food community" for dining reviews and noteworthy tipples around town. It now offers a downloadable magazine as well.

Snarky offshoot of the national food blog, **Eater Chicago** (chicago .eater.com) provides food coverage, news niblets, and commentary.

Providing a wealth of information on restaurants and hotels both nationally and abroad, **Gayot.com** is packed with dining reviews, travel guides, and helpful themed best-of lists.

Metromix (chicago.metromix.com) is an online entertainment guide covering dining, nightlife, music, and events.

Red Eye's (redeyechicago.com) Michael Nagrant, a former Chicago Sun-Times and CS food critic, reviews eateries both obvious and off the beaten track.

312 Dining Diva (312diningdiva.com) is Audarshia Townsend's dining and drinking blog, a source for of-the-moment info on openings, closings, and happenings around town.

A free e-mail daily, **Tasting Table** (tastingtable.com) uncovers unique food, dining, and libations in Chicago.

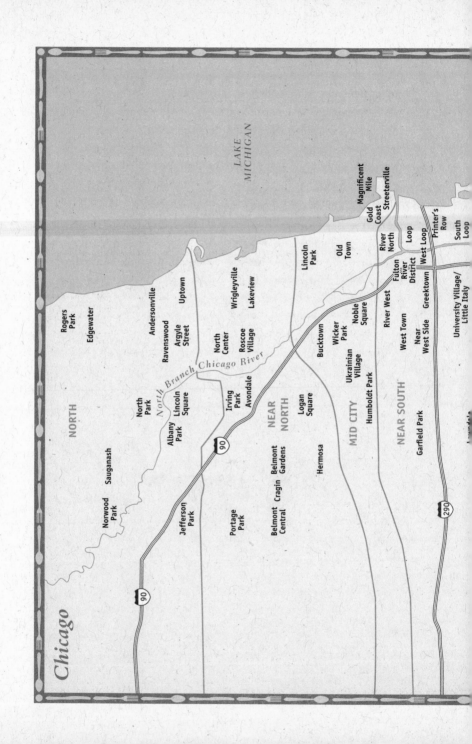

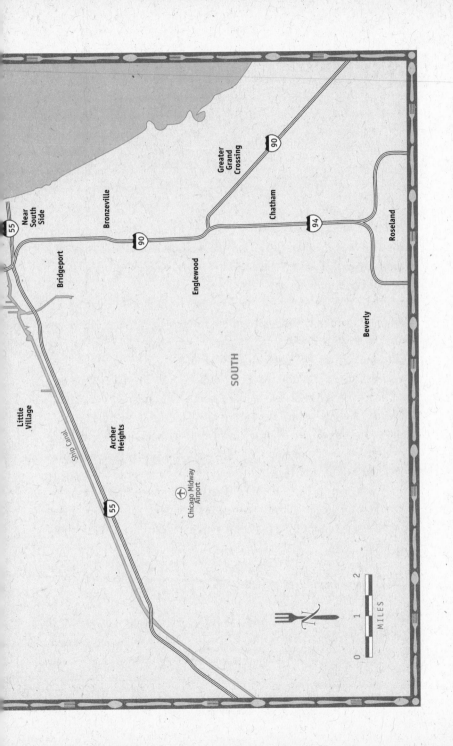

North

Albany Park, Andersonville, Argyle Street, Devon Avenue, Edgebrook, Edgewater, Edison Park, Jefferson Park, Lincoln Square, North Park, Norwood Park, Ravenswood, Rogers Park, Sauganash, Uptown

When embarking on a food adventure in Chicago, be aware there are over 200 neighborhoods and 75-plus communities (some of which, confusingly, share the same name). Boundaries are often open for interpretation, sometimes redefined and—admittedly—fluid.

The city's northern reaches are home to culinarily rich, ethnic enclaves. Among them: Devon Avenue—Chicago's so-called "Little India"—and Argyle Street in Uptown, with its bounty of Vietnamese foodstuffs. A portion of Lawrence Avenue in the Albany Park neighborhood houses Koreatown; watch for its sign on the inbound Kennedy Expressway. Not to be overlooked is charming Andersonville, once an epicenter of Swedish culture. These days its cheery, hip—not to mention, diverse—restaurants hold court with funky bars and LGBT-friendly businesses.

Whatever your speed—heartwarming Thai, glistening barbecue duck, or aromatic *chile en nogada*—find it right here.

Acre, 5308 N. Clark St., Andersonville, Chicago, IL 60640; (773) 334-7600; acrerestaurant.com; New American; $$. An impressive list of beers, turned from behind a Brunswick bar, pair with seasonal, farm-to-table fare at this comfortable spot from Marty Fosse and Tim Rasmussen (**Anteprima** [below], **Bar Ombra** [p. 220]). Look to the heartwarming, pickle-y deviled eggs and Berkshire pork burger, topped with house-cured bacon and blueberry jam if you're wise. Or just come during brunch, when wood-grilled calamari with orzo, fennel, and rapini in punchy chorizo vinaigrette offers a perfect pick-me-up.

Agami Contemporary Sushi, 4712 N. Broadway, Uptown, Chicago, IL 60640; (773) 506-1845; agamicontemporarysushi.com; Japanese/Sushi; $$$. Nestled in the historic Goldblatt's building, this thoroughly modern Japanese den turns out wacky rolls amid underwater-themed surrounds. Grab a curvaceous, semiprivate booth, and make short work of the Spicy Tuna Rice Crispy, crisped rice topped with tuna tartare and a shard of fresh jalapeño. Of the specialty maki, the Ocean Drive—spicy mayo-swathed tuna, yellowtail, avocado, cilantro, and peppers in cod sheets with chile oil and lime—shines. The kitchen turns out competent cooked dishes, too.

Anteprima, 5316 N. Clark St., Andersonville, Chicago, IL 60640; (773) 506-9990; anteprimachicago.net; Italian; $$$. Cute as a button, this rustic, regional Italian restaurant from Marty Fosse (ex-**Spiaggia** [p. 88], Carlucci) goes well beyond what's red-sauced to reveal sweetbreads with peas, spring onions and Vin Santo, and pancetta-wrapped Berkshire pork loin on a bed of Pinot Noir sauce. The comfort-driven, highly seasonal selections—tangy, thyme-scented sweet-and-sour cipollini; peppery *strascinati* amatriciana tossed with tomatoes, pancetta, and chiles; tender, roasted rabbit with pickled peppers, rabbit conserva, and shelly beans—are extra-enjoyable when eaten on the flower-filled patio. Many atypical, affordable—but topnotch—Italian wines are offered by the quartino. Also, check out sibs **Bar Ombra** (p. 220) and **Acre** (p. 2).

On the Road Again

Chicago has a fair share of food trucks, rambling around town to fulfill cravings of all types. Unfortunately, the application process is burdensome, the parking regulations rigid, and the rules for running them more stringent than in other cities. That puts purveyors at a disadvantage. Still, the hunger—and following—for them is clear. In fact, food trucks made their first appearance at Taste of Chicago in 2013.

Cupcakes prove particularly popular when eating on the fly. However, more interesting options can be found. Whether you seek mini doughnuts (@BeaversDonuts), modern Jamaican (@Jerk312), or a *luchadores*-inspired tamale (@tamalespace101), you'll find your match. Follow their whereabouts on Twitter or on websites such as chicagofoodtruckfinder.com, roaminghunger.com/chi, food truckfreak.com, and foodtruckcorner.com.

Aroy Thai, 4654 N. Damen Ave., Ravenswood, Chicago, IL 60625; (773) 275-8360; Thai; $$. Check out the Thai classics menu at this top-tier gem, tucked under the Brown Line tracks, then revel in the tangy, rice-specked Isaan-style sausage and curry-simmered ground pork, served atop a crispy fried omelet. But behold the impossibly rich, sour, insidious *tom yam* "beef ball and tender" soup with mushrooms. Get it with sunny, lime-blasted grilled pork salad, a textural triumph showered with toasted rice powder.

Arya Bhavan, 2508 W. Devon Ave., Rogers Park, Chicago, IL 60659; (773) 274-5800; aryabhavan.com; Indian/Pakistani; $$. Indian cuisine takes center stage at this vegetarian enclave, which features raw food on Monday evenings and a bountiful weekend buffet wafting with aromatic curries. On the menu, classic starters like samosas and cilantro-flecked *uthappam* team with paper-thin *dosa, jeera* rice, and fragrant, complexly flavored North and South Indian curries and lentils.

Ba Le, 5014 N. Broadway, Uptown, Chicago, IL 60640; (773) 561-4424; balesandwich.com; Vietnamese/Bakery; $. When ordering from the counter of this bustling, modern storefront, plan ahead—you'll long for leftovers. The *banh mi* sandwiches are in a league of their own. Go with the lemongrass-marinated barbecue pork, particularly when nestled into a still-warm, house-baked baguette. When the mood strikes, add on spring rolls and sweet, layered che (puddinglike sweets) or *rau câu* (coconut jelly). Remember to procure extra loaves of baked bread to go—they freeze beautifully. **Additional locations:** 166 W. Washington St., (312) 346-3971; 2141 S. Archer Ave., (312) 528-6967.

Big Jones, 5347 N. Clark St., Andersonville, Chicago, IL 60640; (773) 275-5725; bigjoneschicago.com; Regional American; $$. Urbane yet inviting, Paul Fehribach puts the cooking of Southern grandmas to shame. His coastal cuisine has farm-to-table leanings, and the quality ingredients show in the results. Benne-crusted crab cakes with pureed hearts of palm and spicy pineapple relish are not to be missed. Heirloom recipes—like wine butter–smothered crawfish étouffée a' la Breaux Bridge—recall simpler times. The legendary, family-style fried chicken dinner is not to be missed. End with a pot of flowering chrysanthemum tea and warm butter cake.

Bistro Campagne, 4518 N. Lincoln Ave., Lincoln Square, Chicago, IL 60625; (773) 271-6100; bistrocampagne.com; French; $$$. This Lincoln Square spot is committed to turning out dishes both classic and contemporary, crafted from seasonal, organic, and local ingredients. Whether your meal at this neighborhood bistro begins with escargots bathed in garlicky Pernod butter or ridiculously tender duck confit, beef short ribs with roasted bone marrow, or leg of lamb with flageolet beans and niçoise tapenade, the result is the same: comfort to the nth degree. When weather allows, ask for a seat on the lovely garden patio.

Blue Nile Ethiopian, 6118 N. Ravenswood Ave., Uptown, Chicago, IL 60660; (773) 465-6710; bluenilechicago.com; Ethiopian; $$. Blink and you'll overlook this simple strip-mall spot, where spongy, tangy *injera* "pancakes" stand in for silverware and service is well intentioned. Mouth-singeing *doro wat*—chicken stew with hard-boiled egg—is familiar and pleasing. *Yebeg alicha,* headily spiced, silken lamb stew redolent of garlic, and lentils simmered in fiery *berbere* sauce are soul-soothing, too.

bopNgrill, 6604 N. Sheridan Rd., Rogers Park, Chicago, IL 60626; (773) 654-3224; bngrill.com; Korean; $$. Sure, you'll find traditional Korean dishes (bibimbap, *bulgogi*), but the reality is it's the kimchi burger with a runny fried egg, sharp cheddar, and kimchi mayo or the umami burger—which resides beneath a heap of truffled mushroom duxelles, sun-dried tomato confit, *togarashi* mayo, bacon, and smoked Gouda—that you want. Oh, and the weirdly wonderful caramelized kimchi fries, buried in cheese sauce, bacon, scallions, and sesame seeds, too.

Broadway Cellars, 5900 N. Broadway, Edgewater, Chicago, IL 60660; (773) 944-1208; broadwaycellars.net; New American; $$. Date-perfect, this friendly eatery checks pretension at the door. Whether you sit in the dining room—all intimate with white-clothed tables—or on the outdoor patio, you'll be met with memorable, vino-minded dishes that are fairly priced. Get the yellowfin tuna *puttanesca,* its linguine studded with olives, capers, onions, and tomatoes. Likewise, the honey-brined pork chop is fine.

Cafe Hoang, 1010 W. Argyle St., Uptown, Chicago, IL 60640; (773) 878-9943; cafehoang.com; Vietnamese; $$. It's requisite to begin with salads—lemony, basil-laden chicken; chile oil–laced duck; spicy, gingery lemon beef—when dining at this Southeast Asian mainstay. The crispy pork, shrimp, and veg-flecked *ban xeo* pancake and a bowl of noodle soup—such as *bun bo hue,* a meaty, spicy beef and pork-hock concoction enlivened by lime—are smart successors. When you don't want to trek to the Argyle strip, visit its Chinatown location: 232 W. Cermak Rd., (312) 674-9610.

Cafe Selmarie, 4729 N. Lincoln Ave., Lincoln Square, Chicago, IL 60625; (773) 989-5595; cafeselmarie.com; Bakery/Cafe; $$. A neighborhood institution (circa 1983) for light bites and breakfast— not to mention afternoon tea and early dinner—this popular bakery dishes up house-made granola and brioche French toast with berry compote, moving on to the more substantial croque- monsieur and Hungarian goulash as the day progresses. Both the lofty dining room and chill patio are populated by neighborhood types, many of whom like to linger.

Ceres' Table, 4882 N. Clark St., Edgewater, Chicago, IL 60460; (773) 878-4882; cerestable.com; New American; $$$. Composed and inviting at once, this welcoming spot from Giuseppe Scurato (ex–**Topaz Cafe,** p. 194) is named for the Roman goddess of agriculture and har- vest. Appropriately, seasonality guides the contemporary—but never over-the-top—menu. Risotto *arancini* with a gooey Taleggio core is a standout. Ditto the deftly prepared, shaved artichoke–mushroom salad, gone luxe with nutty wisps of Parmesan and lemon-truffle vinai- grette. Whether followed by pheasant with eggplant caponata, beans, and salsa verde or lush goat cheese ravioli in tomato water, spot-on flavors prevail.

Chicago Brauhaus, 4732 N. Lincoln Ave., Lincoln Square, Chicago, IL 60625; (773) 784-4444; chicagobrauhaus.com; German; $$. It's always Oktoberfest at this buoyant *Biergarten,* one of the few remaining of its ilk. And while many of the Germans who settled in Lincoln Square are now gone, here at least the oompah lives on. Come famished and load up on rib-sticking fare, like onion-and-pickle-stuffed beef rouladen, wurst, schnitzel, and liver-dumpling soup. Expect free-flowing steins and plenty of kitsch—it all fuels the fun, especially when the Brauhaus Trio makes their nightly appearance, lederhosen and all.

Chopal Kabab & Steak, 2242 W. Devon Ave., Rogers Park, Chicago, IL 60659; (773) 338-4080; Pakistani; $. Artifacts and vibrant, intricately carved furniture adorn this Pakistani pad with a menu that yields grilled halal kebabs; spiced, yogurt-marinated lamb; and veal steaks. Buttery broccoli rabe and Chopal *lassi* are among the additional rewards.

Dak, 1104 W. Granville Ave., Edgewater, Chicago, IL 60660; (773) 754-0255; dakwings.com; Korean; $. Accolades go to the glistening, jumbo Korean fried chicken wings (*tong dak*) at this family-run quick-serve. Skip the barbecue-sauced ones in favor of those saturated with soy and sesame. They come with pickled daikon (*moo*), but you'll also want an Asian pear soda or bubbly, yogurt-based Milkis and a side of kimchi to go with. As for the bibimbap, it's a fine-enough rendition, but the *bulgogi* with toothsome *dukbokki* rice cakes fares better.

Dawali Mediterranean Kitchen, 4911 N. Kedzie Ave., Albany Park, Chicago, IL 60625; (773) 267-4200; dawalikitchen .com; Middle Eastern; $. Arabic for "grapevine," this quick-serve spot is a go-to for exemplary *shawarma,* its charred meat fatty enough to be flavorful—and extra-delish when fresh-carved from the spit. Tender, moist falafel and mint-flecked haloumi pies are tasty companions. Another location is at 1625 N. Halsted St., (312) 944-5800.

Demera Ethiopian, 4801 N. Broadway, Uptown, Chicago, IL 60640; (773) 334-8787; demeraethiopianrestaurant.com; Ethiopian; $$. This homey, casual Ethiopian eatery is a go-to for vegetarians and spice-seeking carnivores in equal parts. Start with crisp beef or spinach *sambussa*—both requisite precursors to communal platters (*messob*) of *doro wat,* wicked-hot, *berbere*-sauced chicken; *gomen* (greens); and *kitfo,* spiced beef tartare. Finish with house-roasted Ethiopian coffee—though not before sipping Demera's homemade honey wine.

Dong Ky, 4877 N. Broadway, Uptown, Chicago, IL 60640; (773) 989-5579; Vietnamese/Chinese; $. There's not much in the way of ambience at this hole-in-the-wall adjacent to Broadway Supermarket. Fortunately, the super-cheap, very fresh fare will leave you singing its praises right quick. Skip the *pho* in favor of *bun,* complex, salty-sweet—and, yes, a bit funky—rice-stick noodle dishes. Or, opt for the *quang,* a slightly brothy egg-noodle concoction. There are enough selections covering the rest of the Asian repertoire (Szechuan chicken, shrimp egg foo yong) to sate less adventuresome diners.

Elizabeth Restaurant, 4835 N. Western Ave., Lincoln Square, Chicago, IL 60625; (773) 681-0651; elizabeth-restaurant .com; New American; $$$$. Beautiful, hyper-seasonal, precious fare—that's what you'll encounter at Iliana Regan's ultra-tiny, by-ticket establishment. Mind you, eating here is a strange (though uniquely satisfying) journey for those willing to spend. Foraged ingredients—think Queen Anne's lace—become inspiring, strangely wonderful components to dishes (read: Queen Anne's lace gel). Not to mention confusing ones. Dining here is a nightlong affair, given the "Owl" menu is 8 to 10 courses, and the "Diamond" rings in at a lengthy 25 plates. With meal prices hovering on the high end, not including tax, tip, or wine, it's a hefty commitment for a mighty wild ride.

Ethiopian Diamond, 6120 N. Broadway, Edgewater, Chicago, IL 60660; (773) 338-6100; ethiopiandiamondcuisine.com; Ethiopian; $$. Bright, cheery, and authentic, this stew lover's paradise delivers Ethiopian classics, plenty of them vegetarian, which are scooped up with pleasantly sour *injera* flatbread. A safe, always satisfying bet are the *wats,* stews simmered in spicy sauce, or *tibs,* cubed meats burnished with pepper-and-onion-flecked sauce. There is also a location at 7537 N. Clark St., (773) 764-2200.

Gale Street Inn, 4914 N. Milwaukee Ave., Jefferson Park, Chicago, IL 60630; (773) 725-1300; galestreet.com; American; $$. For five decades this legendary joint has doled out trademark tender barbecue ribs alongside soul-satisfying jambalaya, traditional steaks, chops, and seafood. Midweek specials court budget-conscious diners of the silver-haired persuasion, a fact that's furthered by early bird specials on London broil and half racks of baby backs. Waits can be long on weekends, so belly up to the bar.

Gather, 4539 N. Lincoln Ave., Lincoln Square, Chicago, IL 60625; (773) 506-9300; gatherchicago.com; New American; $$. Group-friendly and shareable in spirit, this inviting New American from David Breo and Executive Chef Ken Carter (Charlie Trotter's) features airy, garlicky brandade, offset by lemon confit and served with a stack of potato blini; crispy pork belly with romesco sauce; and indulgent, caramel-glazed apple fritters with vanilla ice cream. Then there's the family-style Sunday supper menu—a steal for adults, since children under 10 eat for free. Sit at the kitchen counter to peer behind the scenes.

Glenn's Diner, 1820 W. Montrose Ave., Ravenswood, Chicago, IL 60613; (773) 506-1720; glennsdiner.com; American/Seafood; $$. A reimagined diner from a Davis Street Fishmarket vet proves an easy option for eggy eats and over two-dozen types of cereal, served all day. However, it's the crazy-fresh Alaskan king crab legs and dozen-plus simply prepared, fresh fish options daily that steal the show. Keep your eye on the specials, which may include a colossal prawn "cocktail," blue striped marlin, Idaho brook trout, or potato-crusted walleye.

Goosefoot, 2656 W. Lawrence Ave., Lincoln Square, Chicago, IL 60625; (773) 942-7547; goosefoot.net; New American; $$$$. Chris Nugent (ex–**Les Nomades,** p. 74) has gone it alone at this upper-echelon, contemporary American BYOB with seasonal prix-fixe menu, one that's always deftly prepared. Rich chestnut soup with Alba mushrooms and truffle essence and licorice-and-curry-scented lobster and scallops, anyone? Precise but unpretentious service is another plus. Watch for Nugent's soon-to-debut artisan chocolate line.

Hae Woon Dae, 6240 N. California Ave., Rogers Park, Chicago, IL 60659; (773) 764-8018; Korean; $$. Pay no mind to the strip-mall setting. This campfire-scented Korean barbecue has the requisites right. Snack on a bevy of *panchan,* from pickled turnips to kimchi. Then roll up your sleeves for a DIY approach, sizzling quality meats—soy and sesame oil–marinated *kalbi,* pork *bulgogi*—for mere seconds atop white-hot coals. Wrap the charred results in lettuce leaves, zapped with sauce and accompanied by *soju* to temper the heat.

Hai Yen, 1055 W. Argyle St., Uptown, Chicago, IL 60640, (773) 561-4077; haiyenrestaurant.com; Vietnamese; $$. If you only get one thing at this newbie-friendly Argyle Street eatery, make it the *bo* *la lot,* grilled beef sausages wrapped in betel leaves. Also a winner is the showy, lime-spurted *chao tom,* grilled, ground shrimp balls speared with sugarcane and served with a salt-pepper mix for dredging. Both the lotus root and banana blossom salads are sprightly and fresh, while roll-your-own rice paper dishes afford a customizable, DIY experience. Order a glass of *chanh,* bubbly lime soda, and finish with the sweet, battered bananas.

Heartland Cafe, 7000 N. Glenwood Ave., Rogers Park, Chicago, IL 60621; (773) 465-8005; heartlandcafe.com; Vegetarian/Eclectic; **$$.** On the scene since 1976, this community epicenter consists of a restaurant, bar, and general store stocked with kitschy, silly toys. Catering largely to vegetarians, though its repertoire extends well beyond, the restaurant's focus is kept organic and local. Turn to the specials; if you're lucky they will include phyllo-encased, double-cream Brie with brandy-fig compote or vegan pasta primavera. But you can do no wrong with the substantial black-bean burger and pecan-crusted ruby-red trout with fruit salsa. Live acts—from singer-songwriters to rockabilly musicians—perform regularly. Sibling Red Line Tap, 7006 N. Glenwood Ave., (773) 274-5463, is a prime place to watch games.

Hema's Kitchen, 2439 W. Devon Ave., Rogers Park, Chicago, IL 60659; (773) 338-1627; hemaskitchen.com; Indian/Pakistani; **$$.** Crowds flock to Hema Potla's inviting Indian BYOB, where flaky, cilantro-and-pea-spiked vegetable or ground-lamb samosas are an onslaught of flavor. Meanwhile, chickpea flour–battered potato chips go beyond the norm. Sizzling tandoori chicken, devilish vindaloo, and lentils fragrant with cumin follow suit. There is a second location at 2411 N. Clark St., (773) 527-1705.

Hon Kee, 1064 W. Argyle St., Uptown, Chicago, IL 60640; (773) 878-6650; Chinese; **$.** Lacquered barbecue ducks hang like beacons in the window, luring diners inside this bare-bones joint. Noodle-packed soups and crisp, roast pork with scrambled eggs are among the reasons to dawdle. Traditional dishes—from egg foo yong to lo mein, chop suey, and fried rice—are packed with flavor, though it's the ethereal shrimp dumpling soup that most likely demands seconds.

Huaraches Dona Chio, 1547 W. Elmdale Ave., Edgewater, Chicago, IL 60660; (773) 878-8470; Mexican; $. A handful of tables and nonexistent decor do little to sell this humble subterranean spot: It's the crisp, handmade, grilled-to-order huaraches (smoky chicken *tinga* and the *huitlacoche,* in particular) that get the job done. Mind you, they're massive, leaving little space for other lovelies: *picadillo*-stuffed gorditas and nopales tacos. Another outpost is at 3119 W. Lawrence Ave., (773) 353-5000.

Hyderabad House, 2225 W. Devon Ave., Rogers Park, Chicago, IL 60659; (773) 381-1230; Indian; $. Score meat-centric South Indian dishes around-the-clock at this cabbie favorite, which dishes up chicken masala, lamb *biryani,* and chicken *paratha* that challenge your flame threshold—along with beef *boti*—for near-cents. Shoot a game of pool before heading out the door.

Icosium Kafé, 5200 N. Clark St., Andersonville, Chicago, IL 60648; (773) 271-5233; icosiumkafechicago.com; African; $$. Don't pass on this Algerian creperie, where organic veggies and halal meats burst from their signature paper-thin confines. Get one jammed with toasted almonds, wilted spinach, raisins, caramelized onions, mint, sun-dried tomato tapenade, and a touch of cream cheese, adding some nicely spiced *merguez* into the mix. You may also customize your own, or get creations in salad form. Breakfast crepes—be they blueberry, rose petal jam, and Brie or pecan, fig jam, and feta—are tasty as well. Order honeyed mint tea or eye-popping Turkish coffee alongside.

Jamaica Jerk, 1631 W. Howard St., Rogers Park, Chicago, IL 60626; (773) 764-1546; jamaicajerk-il.com; Caribbean; $$. These West Indies wonders will warm you up—and tide you over until that island escape. Bring your own hooch to mix with pineapple sorrel or limeade, and settle in the ocean-toned, lattice-flanked dining room, which is presided over by a Cooking and Hospitality Institute of Chicago–trained chef. By the time the curry goat; tangy, pickled escov-eitched fish; and tolerably hot jerk chicken arrive, you'll have forgotten the outdoor temps. For a sweet finish, linger over homemade Grape-Nut or rum-raisin ice cream.

Jin Ju, 5203 N. Clark St., Andersonville, Chicago, IL 60640; (773) 334-6377; Korean; $$. The elevated, enjoyable fare served in these low-lit digs draws daters seeking a solid—albeit not particularly authentic—meal. This bodes well for those less than familiar with Korean cuisine. Still, the consensus agrees the *bulgogi,* bibimbap, and spirited *soju* cocktails are good.

Jin Thai Cuisine, 5458 N. Broadway, Edgewater, Chicago, IL 60640; (773) 681-0555; jinthaicuisine.com; Thai; $$. Modern with just a handful of tables, this stylish Edgewater Thai from a husband-and-wife team turns out addictive angel wings stuffed with bean thread noodles; soupy, curry-laced *khao soi* noodles; and crunchy, airy *khanom buang* crepes stuffed with shrimp, tofu, bean sprouts, and flecks of coconut. While you're at it, green papaya salad is a must.

J.K. Kabab House, 6412 N. Rockwell Ave., Rogers Park, Chicago, IL 60645; (773) 761-6089; jkkababhouse.com; Indian/Pakistani; $. Grilled kebabs in several forms (try the ground beef *seekh*), plus charcoal-grilled chicken tikka, lentils mingling with tender cubes of lamb, and roti attract a low-key clientele, both here and at 2402 W. Army Trail Rd., Hanover Park, (630) 830-6089.

Katsu, 2651 W. Peterson Ave., Rogers Park, Chicago, IL 60659; (773) 784-3383; Japanese; $$$. Standing head and shoulders above most sushi bars, this intimate eatery is a stalwart for staggeringly fresh sashimi platters, a deep-fried fish appetizer that is the stuff of dreams, and a generous sake selection perfect for pairing. Also memorable: the luxe super-white toro maki. Special touches, perhaps gold-leaf or flower garnishes, give dining an extra-special feel, despite straightforward surroundings.

Khan BBQ, 2401 W. Devon Ave., Rogers Park, Chicago, IL 60659; (773) 274-8600; khanbbq.net; Indian/Pakistani; $$. Cheap eats and casual environs benchmark this Indo-Pak, a go-to for incomparable kebabs and chicken *boti.* From the charcoal-grilled tandoori chicken to fish and stewy riches, the endlessly flavorful finds—though it hardly seems fair—cost next to nothing.

La Ciudad, 4515 N. Sheridan Rd., Uptown, Chicago, IL 60640; (773) 728-2887; laciudadgrill.com; Mexican; $$. If you came to this sleek, strip mall–centered Mexican for the *tres leches* cake alone, you'd leave happy. But that's not to say you should overlook the sultry mango-avocado salad, soulful *pollo en mole,* and peculiarly alluring, Mexico City–style *chilango* burger topped with ham and sliced frankfurters. Don't forget to BYO.

La Fonda Latino, 5350 N. Broadway, Edgewater, Chicago, IL 60640; (773) 271-3935; Colombian/Pan-Latin; $$. Colombian fare dominates the menu, though the flavors of Mexico and Argentina shine through at this chill spot, where killer margaritas meet a menu of beef empanadas dotted with plump raisins, a chimichurri-bolstered *churrasco,* and *sobrebarriga,* meltingly tender, slow-simmered flank steak with black beans and rice.

La Unica, 1515 W. Devon Ave., Rogers Park, Chicago, IL 60660; (773) 274-7788, **Cuban/Latin; $.** Stocked with Peruvian, Mexican, and Cuban necessities, this market also houses a hidden gem of a cafe in back. Line up for the mustard-kissed Cuban, which delivers a dose of piquant pickles, tender pork, melty Swiss, and ham perfectly sandwiched between crisped bread. Also winning are the garbanzo soup, flavorful black beans, and *arroz con pollo.* For a real bargain, sample the crazy-cheap snacks, including croquettes.

Marie's Pizza & Liquors, 4127 W. Lawrence Ave., Albany Park, Chicago, IL 60630; (773) 725-1812; **mariespizzachicago.com; Pizza/Italian; $$.** Dated and charming, this no-fuss neighborhood pizzeria and liquor store has been long adored for its crave-worthy, tavern-style, thin-crust pies; generous pours; and jazzy live acts. Then there's the stalwart red vinyl, wood-paneled setting; the heart-shaped Valentine's Day pizzas; and the ample array of hooch for on- or off-site consumption. The love only grows during the holiday season, thanks to over-the-top Santa decor.

m. henry, 5707 N. Clark St., Edgewater, Chicago, IL 60660; (773) 561-1600; **mhenry.net; New American; $$.** Modernized, organic-leaning a.m. eats—Dulce Banana Rumba French Toast with raisins and

EAT LOCAL, READ LOCAL

David Tamarkin, the former dining editor of *Time Out Chicago*, launched *Middlewest*, middlewestmag.com, an edgy, biannual recipe 'zine backed by Kickstarter. Unlike your average mag, this one consists of modern, photo-driven recipe cards with global, make-at-home edibles. Also, check out Ed Marszewski's (Maria's Packaged Goods & Community Bar) *Mash Tun*, mashtun journal.org, which is dedicated to craft beer.

toasted pecans, a heaping fried-egg sandwich with applewood bacon and Gorgonzola—attract loyalists to this sunlit daytime cafe. Later, opt for design-your-own grilled cheese (perhaps sour *boule*, stuffed with pears and walnut pesto) and consider grabbing pies, muffins, and savory flatbreads on the fly. Consider sibling m. henrietta, 1133 W. Granville Ave., (773) 761-9700, as well—it's open for dinner.

Merla's Kitchen, 5207 N. Kimball Ave., North Park, Chicago, IL 60625; (773) 539-2090; merlaskitchen.net; Filipino; $. From the granny-style chicken *adobado* and steamed *siopao* to empanadas and *pancit* infused with homemade stock, there's plenty to love about this humble haunt. A word to the wise: Get the signature platter for an ample taste, and cap off the experience with 11-ingredient halo-halo at meal's end.

Monti's, 4757 N. Talman Ave., Lincoln Square, Chicago, IL 60625; (773) 942-6012; ilovemontis.com; Sandwiches; $. Cheesesteak of the Philly variety—that's what's on tap at this off-the-beaten-path, regional joint from Philadelphia-born Jennifer Monti and James Gottwald. But don't come expecting some soggy, Whiz-drenched number; here, the sauce is crafted from Wisconsin cheddar, the griddled meat is rib eye, and the imported bread makes sussing out the hide-and-seek location worthwhile. For a city that grew up on Italian beef, that's saying something.

Moody's Pub, 5910 N. Broadway, Edgewater, Chicago, IL 60660; (773) 275-2696; moodyspub.com; Burgers; $$. Touted in equal parts are the burger and beer garden at this casual pub, where Goose Island flows from the taps, sides are customarily deep-fried, and peanuts top the candlelit tables inside. When it's cold, grab a bench by the flickering fireplaces, order your half-pounder with cheese, and soak up the dark-cozy setting and convivial scene.

Mysore Woodlands, 2548 W. Devon Ave., Rogers Park, Chicago, IL 60659; (773) 338-8160; mysorewoodlands.info; Indian/

Vegetarian; $$. Vegetarians dig the massive *dosa,* available in over a dozen varieties, plus other familiar vegetarian fare (think *saag paneer*). Nibble to your heart's content with combination plates, which come with a host of accoutrements and dessert. Check out the *payasam,* raisin-and-cashew-stippled vermicelli pudding.

Mythos, 2030 W. Montrose Ave., Lincoln Square, Chicago, IL 60618; (773) 334-2000; mythoschicago.com; Greek; $$$. Delivering a refreshing change of pace, one that deviates from Greektown shenanigans, this serene, sister-run taverna serves standbys. However, here the *saganaki* isn't flamed tableside; just-charred *loukaniko* (Greek sausage) is made for the restaurant by design; and the gently sauced pastitsio arrives in an individual crock.

Nha Hang Viet Nam, 1032 W. Argyle St., Uptown, Chicago, IL 60640; (773) 878-8895; Vietnamese; $$. If interactive eating is your thing, the wrap-your-own woven rice cake with grilled pork and meatballs is not to be missed. But you should scoop up rare beef salad with crackly, house-made shrimp chips; tackle the deep-fried garlic-butter frog legs; and succumb to the sticky, fish sauce–marinated chicken wings as well. Mind you, the menu runs deep, going well beyond the usual repertoire to include a goat and lotus root hot pot, mild *mi quang* noodles, and transcendent red crab bathed in sticky glaze.

Noon-O-Kabab, 4661 N. Kedzie Ave., Albany Park, Chicago, IL 60625; (773) 279-8899; noonokabab.com; Persian; $. This perpetually packed, authentic Persian restaurant is known for its tender, flame-grilled kebabs (it's but a fool who bypasses the chicken) as well as its downy, dilled long-grain basmati, studded with lima beans and garlic. Skewers of shrimp, steak, and ground beef are great alternatives; minted Persian salad, smoky baba ghannouj, and saffron-scented dolmades set the gold standard, too.

Pasteur, 5525 N. Broadway, Edgewater, Chicago, IL 60640; (773) 728-4800; pasteurrestaurantchicago.com; Vietnamese; $$. Beloved, closed, reopened, and (mostly) beloved again, this sophisticated Vietnamese turns out bright, crunchy shrimp-papaya salad; tender, complex curry beef; and heartwarming clay-pot salmon. The fine-dining setting beats its Argyle Street competitors, though authenticity is toned down as a result.

Pecking Order, 4416 N. Clark St., Ravenswood, Chicago, IL 60640; (773) 907-9900; peckingorderchicago.com; Filipino; $$. Kristine Subido opened this Filipino-style pad, an ode to poultry, with her mother, Melinda. The resulting labor of love serves twice-fried; lemongrass-ginger-stuffed, annatto-calamansi-butter-brushed rotisserie; and basted, grilled birds. Anything-but-boring sides—tomato-ginger *sofrito* green beans, garlic-fried rice, Sriracha slaw—are furthered by homey sandwiches, a chicken and egg-noodle bowl, and garlicky coconut adobo rice *arancini*. For dessert, nothing but halo-halo shaved ice will do. A popular weekend brunch—complete with coconut-laced chicken and waffles and chicken poutine hash—keeps the effects of overindulgence at bay.

Pho 777, 1065 W. Argyle St., Uptown, Chicago, IL 60640; (773) 561-9909; pho777chicago.com; Vietnamese; $. The anise-scented *pho* with all the trimmings is sustaining, filling, and incredibly satisfying, but it has nothing on the bright, minty beef salad, showered with peanuts and topped with cloudlike, crackling rice crackers. However, don't leave this endearing Argyle Street eatery without ordering the veggie-laden pan-fried noodles, slick with sweet-salty sauce and offset by barbecue pork, beef, and shrimp. It's the breakfast of champions.

Pho Xe Tang (aka Tank Noodle), 4953 N. Broadway, Uptown, Chicago, IL 60640; (773) 878-2253; tank-noodle.com; Vietnamese; $. The number of available options at this Argyle fave prove overwhelming. The good news is it provides the most reliable, point-and-pick experience on the Argyle strip. Start with the *banh xeo*, sizzling, crisped pancakes studded with shrimp, pork, and sprouts. Follow with a bowl of fragrant *pho*, the perfect restorative for winter chills, or tender beef and vegetables on a bed of wide, fried, crispy outside/ doughy within rice noodles.

Reza's, 5255 N. Clark St., Andersonvlle, Chicago, IL 60640; (773) 561-1898; rezasrestaurant.com; Persian; $$. This popular mini-empire with River North (432 W. Ontario St., 312-664-4500) and Oak Brook (40 N. Tower Rd., 630-424-9900) outposts serves no-brainer Persian plates, including many vegetarian options. Most memorable on the supersized menu: grilled, garlic-buttered mushrooms; ground beef *koobideh* and moist-but-charred chicken skewers; and fluffy, generously dilled rice.

Ruby's Fast Food, 3740 W. Montrose Ave., Albany Park, Chicago, IL 60618; (773) 539-2669; Filipino; $. Turo-turo-style dining dictates you literally point-and-pick fare from the homey lineup at this family-run haunt, where the name belies the experience. On rotation are some 120 dishes; luck is on your side if nubs of *lechon kawal* (fried pork belly); shatteringly crunchy, crispy *pata* (fried pork leg); and *tapsilog* (cured beef topped with a yolky egg) are among them. Get a side of garlic rice, and bliss will ensue.

Sahara Kabob, 6649 N. Clark St., Rogers Park, Chicago, IL 60618; (773) 262-2000; saharakabob.com; Middle Eastern/Assyrian; $. Smoky, chunky baba ghannouj; fall-apart, tender lamb shank; flavorful falafel; spicy, meat-topped *lahmim beajin*—they're all good at this simple Assyrian storefront with a serious following. Bountiful portions and budget-conscious prices make any question of dining here a done deal.

Salam, 4634 N. Kedzie Ave., Albany Park, Chicago, IL 60625; (773) 583-0776; salamchicago.com; **Middle Eastern; $.** Get the crunchy outside, crumbly inside falafel while it's hot and you'll be met with some of the best in town. The no-frills establishment also hits high notes for its silky hummus, sprightly *fattoush* and Jerusalem salads, and tasty kebabs and kofta.

San Soo Gab San, 5247 N. Western Ave., Lincoln Square, Chicago, IL 60625; (773) 334-1589; **Korean; $$.** Wildly popular with late-night boozehounds, this classic Korean barbecue allows you to sear your own grub on tabletop grills, munching on a generous array of *pan-chan* practically around the clock. Though you'll leave its wood confines smelling of smoke, the *kalbi* certainly is worth its weight in coals—even when served by a not-so-welcoming staff.

Semiramis, 4639 N. Kedzie Ave., Albany Park, Chicago, IL 60625; (773) 279-8900; semiramisrestaurant.com; **Lebanese; $$.** Airy and cheery, this cute, from-scratch cafe deserves accolades for its fresh salads (try the lemony, parsley-packed tabbouleh); meze (including the minty, slatherable fava mash called *foul*); and garlicky *toum*. The rotisserie chicken, which comes with *lavosh* and salad or rice, has its own fan club; then again, so does the lamb and beef *shawarma*, which is offset by hunks of eggplant and pickles. Be sure to order cinnamon-scented *maamoul,* too.

Silver Seafood, 4829 N. Broadway, Uptown, Chicago, IL 60640; (773) 784-0668; silverseafoodrestaurant.com; **Chinese/Seafood; $$.** Specializing, not surprisingly, in fare from the watery deep, this popular Cantonese kitchen delivers a spot-on experience, provided you order right. Regulars make fast tracks for the Chinese menu (translated), which bypasses Americanized standards in favor of the more exotic: shark's fin soup, pigeon with planks of green onion, and bird's nest. Once tried, though, it's hard to order beyond the salt-and-pepper squid, seafood hot-and-sour soup, or fried flounder.

Smak Tak, 5961 N. Elston Ave., Jefferson Park, Chicago, IL 60646; (773) 763-1123; smaktak.com; Polish; $$. An old-world vibe permeates this hidden-but-hyped Polish "lodge," where the hearty—and, yes, heavy—sustenance is downright sublime. No one can resist the glistening, lacy potato pancakes, which are garnished with sour cream and applesauce. Plump, perfect pierogi and meaty, vibrantly sauced cabbage rolls have no rival, while the Hungarian-style potato pancake—bursting with goulash goodness—justifies a bit of waistline expansion.

SP Kebab, 6808 N. Sheridan Rd., Rogers Park, Chicago, IL 60626; (773) 856-3755; spkebab.com; Middle Eastern/European; $. Encounter Euro-style kebabs—ridiculously massive, incredibly messy pork and chicken sandwiches, to be exact—and get yours spicy-sauced, veggie-loaded, and tucked into *lahmacun*-like flatbread. Better yet, split it with a dining companion, saving a smidge of room for garlicky *tzatziki* chicken salad or an order of Cajun fries. Vegetarian? You'll have no problem feeling the love.

Spacca Napoli, 1769 W. Sunnyside Ave., Ravenswood, Chicago, IL 60640; (773) 878-2420; spaccanapolipizzeria.com; Pizza; $$. Devotees can't get enough of the thin, oak-fired Neapolitan pizzas topped with quality ingredients. Running faves include the basil-flecked Margherita and Funghi e Salsiccia, crowned with Fior di Latte mozzarella, basil, mushrooms, and fennel-perfumed Italian sausage. Another showstopper is the sauceless Quattro Formaggi, topped with mozzarella, Danish blue, Emmental, and Fontina. The wine and beer list get the job done.

Spoon, 4608 N. Western Ave., Lincoln Square, Chicago, IL 60625; (773) 769-1173; spoonthai.com; Thai; $$. Go outside of your comfort zone at this authentic, top-tier restaurant with a traditional and translated Thai menu. Order some items from the latter, perhaps the Isaan-style pork-rice sausage and jerky with flaming, tangy tamarind sauce. From the fabulous fried chicken to bracing banana blossom salad; sour, spicy tamarind shrimp curry; and explosively flavorful *naem khao thawt*—rice salad dotted with ham—there are reasons for repeat visits.

Sun Wah Bar-B-Q Restaurant, 5041 N. Broadway, Uptown, Chicago, IL 60640; (773) 769-1254; sunwahbbq.com; Chinese/Barbecue; $. Get the duck—make that anything with duck or pork—at this stellar, Hong Kong–style Chinese barbecue, where you can customize your own brothy, chewy noodle-filled bowls. Roast duck on rice is eminently satisfying—likewise the duck with pan-fried noodles, the glimmering barbecued pork, and the barbecue duck. The setting is simple, but the food is anything but ho-hum.

Sunshine Cafe, 5449 N. Clark St., Andersonville, Chicago, IL 60640; (773) 334-6214; Japanese; $. As unassuming as a home-style Japanese kitchen, this quaint cafe isn't much to look at. However, the perfect sukiyaki, filled with glass noodles and shards of rib eye and topped with an optional cracked egg; crisp-skinned, flaky grilled mackerel; and *tonkatsu* command attention. Even the potato croquettes, *musubi,* and miso are more memorable than most.

Superdawg Drive-in, 6363 N. Milwaukee Ave., Norwood Park, Chicago, IL 60646; (773) 763-0660; superdawg.com; Hot Dogs; $. This neon-lit, carhop-equipped, red-hot stand—dating back to 1948—is larger than life. And while it holds court among Chicago-style dogs, here a pickled green tomato topper stands in for tomato. Add in crinkle-cut fries and straw-defying, pint-size milk shakes, and it's easy to see how the kitsch caught on. There is a second locale at 333 S. Milwaukee Ave., Wheeling, (847) 459-1900.

Taste of Lebanon, 1509 W. Foster Ave., Andersonville, Chicago, IL 60640; (773) 334-1600; Middle Eastern; $. There's no need for frills when everything—from the falafel to the *fattoush, shawarma,* and peppery lentil soup—is this good. But since the ambiance is next to nil, it's best to get these lovelies—and deftly prepared hummus or baba ghannouj—to go.

Thai Pastry, 4925 N. Broadway, Unit E, Uptown, Chicago, IL 60657; (773) 784-5399; thaipastry.com; Thai; $$. The desserts beckon diners to this low-key, highlighter-hued storefront, though the expertly prepared Thai classics keep them coming back. Go with the jerkylike seasoned dry beef or fresh spring rolls, followed by sweet pad thai when playing it safe, or choose curry-sauced frog's legs when an adventurous mood strikes. While you're at it, share the spicy, citrusy roasted duck salad showered with cilantro and chile, and finish with Thai custard. There's a second location at 7350 W. Lawrence Ave., Harwood Heights, (708) 867-8840.

Trattoria Trullo, 4767 N. Lincoln Ave., Lincoln Square, Chicago, IL 60625; (773) 506-0093; Italian/Deli; $$$. Fans of Puglian fare can't get enough of this quaint restaurant from Giovanni DeNigris, where

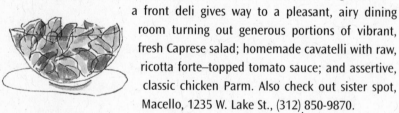

a front deli gives way to a pleasant, airy dining room turning out generous portions of vibrant, fresh Caprese salad; homemade cavatelli with raw, ricotta forte–topped tomato sauce; and assertive, classic chicken Parm. Also check out sister spot, Macello, 1235 W. Lake St., (312) 850-9870.

Tre Kronor, 3258 W. Foster Ave., Albany Park, Chicago, IL 60625; (773) 267-9888; trekronorrestaurant.com; Swedish; $$.

Scandinavian eats—served in a peculiarly muraled, cafelike setting—bring high-calorie comfort in the form of Danish cinnamon rolls, a dilled Oslo omelet with smoked salmon and cream cheese, and *falukorv* (veal sausage). But don't let that deter you from the killer vanilla-orange French toast. You may also be tempted to linger over gravlax, melon salad with Danish blue cheese, Swedish meatballs, and herbaceous fish plated with dilled sun-dried tomato rice and aquavit-pickled cucumber-egg salad.

Tweet, 5020 N. Sheridan Rd., Uptown, Chicago, IL 60640; (773) 728-5576; tweet.biz; New American; $$. Not exactly under the radar, this popular eatery is head of its class for breakfast—biscuits and gravy, fluffy pancakes, even fluffier omelets, and a host of breakfast burritos. Salads and sandwiches (especially the Reuben) successfully hold court midday. Don't forget to bring cash, as credit cards are not accepted.

Udupi Palace, 2543 W. Devon Ave., Rogers Park, Chicago, IL 60659; (773) 338-2152; udupipalacechicago.net; Indian/Vegetarian; $$. Most who dine at this satisfying South Indian vegetarian—believe it or not, many of them carnivores—begin with the oversize *masala dosa,* followed by any number of ubiquitous, hearty lentil dishes and spicy vegetable curries to collective joy.

Uru-Swati, 2629 W. Devon Ave., Rogers Park, Chicago, IL 60659; (773) 262-5280; uru-swati.net; Indian/Vegetarian; $$. Set apart by its solid chaat (snacks), lively vegetarian curries, and combustible, chile-dotted *uttapam* with veg "soup" for dipping—not to mention its hipper vibe—this vegetarian updates the Devon dining experience. Other items to sample amid its mock-skyline backdrop: doughnutlike, ground vegetable fritters; puffy *pani puri;* and the 2-foot-long paper *dosa.* Make it easy on yourself and ask for the translated menu.

Near North

Avondale, Belmont Cragin, Hamlin Park, Hermosa, Irving Park, Lakeview, Logan Square, North Center, Portage Park, Roscoe Village, Wrigleyville

From marvelous Macanese to buzz-worthy Lakeview Thai, Chicago's Near North communities have endless places to indulge. Get your fill of kosher barbecue, entertain an underground dining experience, or get down with a griddle-pressed Cuban—whatever you choose, there's a memorable meal waiting to be had.

Andy's Thai Kitchen, 946 W. Wellington Ave., Lakeview, Chicago, IL 60657; (773) 549-7821; Thai; andysthaikitchen.com; $$. Andy Aroonrasameruang (ex–**TAC Quick**, p. 50) is the force behind ATK, a bold, buzzy-but-small spot with an impressive lineup of lesser-knowns and perfectly prepped, Americanized standards. Fiery, lime-forward seafood *tom sab* gives way to crackly basil pork belly, funky basil preserved egg, and several riffs on papaya salad, including a notable tempura-battered take. From cashew-laced fish maw salad to braised pork leg and crispy curry catfish, firework flavors abound. In other words, don't expect anything dumbed down.

Ann Sather, 909 W. Belmont Ave., Lakeview, Chicago, IL 60657; (773) 348-2378; annsather.com; Swedish; $$. Though the original outpost, once a few doors down, is no more, tradition lives on at this

Swedish-American eatery, where folks gorge on sticky cinnamon rolls and Swedish pancakes, plus a hearty sampler of lingonberry-glazed roast duck, Swedish meatballs, potato sausage, spaetzle, kraut, and brown beans. **Additional locations:** 5207 N. Clark St., (773) 271-6677; 1147 W. Granville, (773) 274-0557; and 3411 N. Broadway, (773) 305-0024.

The Art of Chicken, 2041 N. Western Ave., Logan Square, Chicago, IL 60647; (773) 697-9266; Spanish; $. Choose from flame-broiled full, half, and quarter spicy, smoky-infused El Jefe or herb-marinated crazy Chico chickens, meant to be pulled from the bone and tucked—with salsa—into warm pita bread. Get yours with buttermilk-boiled *elotes* slathered with mayo, cheese, and chile.

The Art of Pizza, 3033 N. Ashland Ave., Lakeview, Chicago, IL 60657; (773) 327-5600; artofpizzainc.com; Pizza; $$. Carnivores, when going for broke, must veer toward the sausage, bacon, Italian beef, ground beef, and pepperoni-jammed rendition at this come-as-you-are pie purveyor. Though it's known for its sublimely sauced, deep-dish pizza, the other versions (pan and thin crust, though not par- ticularly thin at all)—plus passable pastas and chicken Parm—are serviceable.

Arun's, 4156 N. Kedzie Ave., Irving Park, Chicago, IL 60618; (773) 539-1909; arunsthai.com; Thai; $$$$. Fancy Thai from Arun Sampan-thavivat is served via a fixed-price tasting menu in a formal, gallerylike setting. Intricate dishes arrive as if they're presents, wrapped in deli-cate zucchini ribbons or topped with edible, carved roses or lacy but-terflies. The ever-changing preparations may include a roll of burdock, shiitake, and carrot-stuffed chicken, gilded with shiso leaf in sweet, caramelized soy sauce, or delicate steamed rice dumplings revealing a minced chicken, shrimp, and jicama interior. But ready yourself for the investment, knowing there are more interesting, if less prettily plated, options around town.

The Bad Apple, 4300 N. Lincoln Ave., North Center, Chicago, IL 60618; (773) 360-8406; badapplebar.com; Burgers; $$. The friendly bar with a "bad" attitude boasts serious, atypically topped burgers made from custom-ground beef. Take as examples the Lengua, which wears a crown of house-smoked calf tongue, pickled onion, salsa verde, and Chihuahua cheese, and the Elvis' Last Supper, a strangely appealing peanut butter–slathered version with bacon. Couple them with fancified, house-cut fries; homemade ketchup; and a large craft and import beer and cocktail selection, and it's easy to see why this spot is forever swamped.

Belly Shack, 1912 N. Western Ave., Logan Square, Chicago, IL 60647; (773) 252-1414; bellyshack.com; Pan-Asian/Latin; $$. Melding in harmony two seemingly dissimilar cuisines beneath the Blue Line, this BYOB achieves star status thanks to Bill Kim (also of **urbanbelly** [p. 52] and **bellyQ** [p. 96]) and his wife, Yvonne Cadiz-Kim. Don't be put off by the stark, urban space—you'll feel nothing but forgiveness when the *tostones* arrive, garlicky enough to ward off vampires in their cloak of chimichurri. Then, head straight for the *ssam kogi* and refreshing, noodle-y Asian meatball sandwich, saving room for softserve christened with huckleberry-lime topping.

Bolat African Cuisine, 3346 N. Clark St., Wrigleyville, Chicago, IL 60657; (773) 665-1100; bolatchicago.com; African; $$. It'd be easy to overlook this unassuming spot from the owners of Iyanze, located where the Brown and Red Lines converge. Don't, since dishes—when judiciously chosen—surprise. Emphasizing the cuisines of Nigeria and Ghana—as well as sub-Saharan Africa as a whole—the crowded but rarely disappointing dining room serves aromatic, saucy jerk chicken on a bed of cooling coconut rice; flavorful *jollof* rice; starchy *fufu* topped with spinach and scallops; and rousing, if tough, goat pepper stew. A selection of native beers, cocktails, and house-made ginger beer is available.

Bread & Wine, 3732 W. Irving Park Rd., Irving Park, Chicago, IL 60618; (773) 866-5266; breadandwinechicago.com; New American; $$$. Wine and dine at this cheery small-plates lounge, where glasses filled with globe-trotting wines join artisan cheeses and shareable plates—pork shank rillettes, flank steak with crispy semolina gnocchi and béarnaise—pave the way for indulgent finales, like Nutella mud pie and pink peppercorn–pineapple cake. Pick up some tipples and local and house-made pantry items for the road.

Bountiful Eatery, 3312 N. Broadway, Lakeview, Chicago, IL 60657; (773) 687-9811; bountifuleatery.com; Gluten-Free; $. The name lends insight into this healthy, gluten-free venture, an affordable option in Lakeview with something for all tastes. Help hangovers with an orange, banana, pineapple, and kale concoction. Or, snag a wheat-free pita wrap that's bursting with turkey, avocado, red onion, and romaine swathed in chipotle-lime vinaigrette; otherwise, try the hearty quinoa bowl that's loaded with toppings of your choice. Either way, the satisfying, filling finds leave you with bucks to spare.

The Brown Sack, 3581 W. Belden Ave., Logan Square, Chicago, IL 60647; (773) 661-0675; thebrownsack.com; Deli; $. Who needs to brown-bag it when you've got options like this cash-only sandwich shop with a cozy-food bent? Chipotle-warmed tortilla or creamy tomato soups complement a classic sandwich lineup, including a venerable BLT with avocado and shrimp; slow-roasted, paprika-kissed pork; and a many-napkins-required Reuben. Salads are packed with fresh ingredients. Meanwhile, fruit smoothies are available, too. When weather cooperates, snag a seat on the quaint back patio, a thick-churned peanut butter shake in hand.

Browntrout, 4111 N. Lincoln Ave., North Center, Chicago, IL 60618; (773) 472-4111; browntroutchicago.com; New American; $$$. Green-minded, sustainable, and communal in approach, this low-key, oft-changing modern American from Sean Sanders and his wife, Nadia, sources ingredients from local, organic, sustainable farms; seafood from natural waters; and grass-fed, free-range meat from nearby producers. The result may be Kennebec poutine with Nordic Creamery cheese curds, fried chicken sawmill gravy, and peperoncini, or seared Canadian walleye with chervil-specked littleneck clams, artichoke *barigoule,* lemon emulsion, pancetta, and sunflower seeds.

Cafe Marianao, 2246 N. Milwaukee Ave., Logan Square, Chicago, IL 60647; (773) 278-4533; Cuban; $. If you're willing to contend with the chaos (read: a standing-room setting), you'll be amply rewarded at this casual Cuban—namely when ordering its vinegary, mojo-steeped steak sandwich that's blanketed in cheese and onions and pressed until toasty. In the morning the ham and egg omelet sandwich is a must. Wash down whatever you order with a Materva or cup of *café con leche.*

Carnitas El Paisa, 3529 W. Fullerton Ave., Logan Square, Chicago, IL 60647; (866) 477-3037; carnitaselpaisa.com; Mexican; $. Saucy *cochinita pibil* is one of those things you can't help but love; here, it—and *carnitas* and *chicharrones*—is made with the utmost love. For that matter, the steamy *barbacoa* is, too.

Chalkboard, 4343 N. Lincoln Ave., North Center, Chicago, IL 60618; (773) 477-7144; chalkboardrestaurant.com; New American; $$$.

Underground Edibles

Chicago's no newcomer when it comes to underground, illicit behavior. (Remember Prohibition, Al Capone, et al?) Although they're hardly cut from the same cloth, dinner clubs offer an off-the-grid experience and mighty fine meals in return. Just be prepared to sign up "in secret," BYOB, and ready yourself for a off-kilter setting, such as an apartment or loft.

Sunday Dinner Club, (773) 878-2717, sundaydinnerclub.com, is a by-referral gathering, usually held at the owner's apartment. They occur between 5 and 10 times a month and accommodate no more than two-dozen guests, who are rewarded with the likes of halibut in bacon-ginger broth with asparagus, purple potatoes, and candied pork.

The Hearth, hearthunderground.com, is run by a student at the University of Chicago and held at ever-changing locations for 6 to 60 guests, depending. The menus change, too, with past offerings including short ribs with coffee, apricot orzo, and dark chocolate and poached prawns with calamari and potato gnocchi.

Yo Soy, yosoy.squarespace.com, hosts gay-friendly, Latin-leaning underground suppers and events, backed by seasonal, sometimes tongue-singeing, eats.

Gilbert Langlois (**SushiSamba Rio** [p. 130], Rushmore) is behind this cozy, conversation-friendly storefront with a Victorian vibe and an eponymous, frequently changing menu. Plump mussels, perhaps steamed in toasted curry-coriander-inflected beer, pave the way for interesting mains, from pork tenderloin with apple-potato confit and ancho-corn vinaigrette to peppery Southern fried chicken on a bed of mashed potatoes with white sausage gravy and comforting collard greens. Come for afternoon tea, or plan to brunch in style (you'll want the breakfast cassoulet).

Chicago Diner, 3411 N. Halsted St., Lakeview, Chicago, IL 60657; (773) 935-6696; veggiediner.com; Vegetarian; $$. Ingredients like seitan and tofu masquerade as meat at this come-as-you-are vegetarians' Eden. But those preferring to skip the vegan cheese can find merits, too, such as marinated portobello and quinoa salad, which is packed with veggies in basalmic vinaigrette. Always a hit: the Whopping Deluxe, an assertively seasoned, black bean–pepper burger with storied sweet-potato fries. Finish with a cookie dough–peanut butter or chocolate-banana-coffee shake. There's also an outpost at 2333 N. Milwaukee Ave., (773) 252-3211.

Chief O'Neill's Pub & Restaurant, 3471 N. Elston Ave., Avondale, Chicago, IL 60618; (773) 583-3066; chiefoneillspub.com; Irish; $$. A spacious, flower-filled beer garden is the lure of this Irishman come summer, though Emerald Isle mainstays—fish-and-chips, bangers-and-mash, slow-cooked corned beef with braised cabbage—enjoy a year-round fan club. Named for Chief Francis O'Neill, an Irish music archivist and former Chicago chief of police, its handsome wood dining room affords a respite from the cold, especially when rounds of single-malt scotch and suds come into play.

Chilam Balam, 3023 N. Broadway, Lakeview, Chicago, IL 60657; (773) 296-6901; chilambalamchicago.com; Mexican; $$$. There's zero pretension at this sustainable, upscale BYOB. Located below street level, it serves up fare in farm-to-table fashion. The complexly flavored, deeply satisfying creations may include grilled octopus tacos with roasted tomato salsa, olives, and *queso fresco* or achiote swordfish steamed in a banana leaf with black beans, pickled oranges, and Brussels sprout slaw. Hit the ATM first because it's cash only. Its sister spot, **Shaman** (p. 86), is in Noble Square.

Cho Sun Ok, 4200 N. Lincoln Ave., North Center, Chicago, IL 60618; (773) 549-5555; chosunokrestaurant.com; Korean; $$. An unassuming exterior belies the happenings inside this smoke-scented Korean barbecue, where some of the best things—*bulgogi, kalbi*—are cooked on the tabletop by you. But don't ignore the brow-mopping *yuk gae jang,* a flaming-hot soup teeming with beef, kimchi, sprouts, and egg, or the *mul-naeng myun,* cold beef broth with buckwheat noodles, pickled veggies, and hard-boiled egg—just asking for condiments.

D'Candela, 4053 N. Kedzie Ave., Irving Park, Chicago, IL 60618; (773) 478-0819; Peruvian; $. This family-run operation is the kind that warms you right up, especially when you order the juicy, sultry *pollo a la brasa,* charcoal-roasted chicken that positively must be slathered with creamy yellow *aji.* But don't overlook the tender *cordero con frijoles y arroz,* the *tostones,* or the raisin-studded picadillo empanadas, the latter plunked in a spicy, jalapeño-based hot sauce or salsa criolla. While you're at it, get some bright, acidic ceviche—several hauntingly good takes are on hand. And to drink? Give the purple corn number, *chicha morada,* a whirl.

Deleece, 3747 N. Southport Ave., Lakeview, Chicago, IL 60613; (773) 325-1710; deleece.com; New American; $$. This neighborhood spot is long on charm, in no small part due to its eclectic menu crammed with potstickers, Spanish rice–stuffed poblanos, and caramelized, pan-roasted salmon with sticky black rice and pear-ginger sauce. Its cost-conscious prix fixe is as popular as its brunch. Nearby sibling Deleece Grill Pub, 3313 N. Clark St., (773) 348-3313, serves comfort food and craft brews.

Dharma Garden, 3109 W. Irving Park Rd., Irving Park, Chicago, IL 60618; (773) 588-9140; dharmagardenchicago.com; Thai; $$. You won't spend a lot, but you'll get your fill at Vilairat Junthong's Southeast Asian, where in-the-know diners—plenty of them highly regarded, expat chefs—head for real-deal Thai. That's especially true of the lengthy, translated Thai-language menu, which houses Northern Thai specialties, like marinated beef jerky (*nua dad deaw*), comforting *khao tom* soup, and pickled bamboo shoot salad (*sup naw mai*).

DMK Burger Bar, 2954 N. Sheffield Ave., Lakeview, Chicago, IL 60657; (773) 360-8686; dmkburgerbar.com; Burgers; $$. Michael Kornick (**mk**, p. 118) and David Morton (**Morton's**, p. 79) elevate the humble burger at this wildly popular joint with an order-by-number approach and an impressive grass-fed lamb burger with sheep's milk feta, olive tapenade, Greek salad, and *tzatziki*. Faced with the griddled patty melt with smoked bacon, burnt onions, and Leroy's remoulade, however, choosing poses a challenge. Fried okra and pickles, gussied up hand-cut fries, and thick espresso shakes leave its coed clientele hankering for more. For fresh catches both raw and cooked, visit **Fish Bar** (p. 35) next door. Another location is at 2370 Fountain Square Dr., Lombard, (630) 705-9020.

El Cubanito, 2555 N. Pulaski Rd., Logan Square, Chicago, IL 60639; (773) 235-2555; Cuban; $. No-frills and tiny, this simple storefront can hardly keep up with the demand for its exemplary, jam-packed (if pickle-shy) Cuban sandwich. And the guava-cheese number and saucey chopped steak sandwiches? Goodness, they're tasty, too—not to mention rock-bottom-cheap.

El Rinconcito Cubano, 3238 W. Fullerton Ave., Logan Square, Chicago, IL 60647; (773) 489-4440; Cuban; $. When the vaca *frita*—shredded, fried beef—is available at this friendly Cuban, make it a double. But come with a crew: The ham *croquetas* and *ropa vieja* are winning, too.

Falafill, 3202 N. Broadway, Lakeview, Chicago, IL 60657; (773) 525-0052; eatfalafill.com; Middle Eastern; $. Wildly popular, the quick-serve namesake—and other protein-based varietals—get customized with 20-plus toppings, including spicy *zhoug* and fava-based *bissara*. Upping the ante, guest chefs design a monthly wrap, the proceeds of which go to charity. **Additional locations:** 72 E. Adams St., (312) 360-9400; 1053 Lake St., Oak Park, (708) 383-6900.

Fat Rice, 2957 W. Diversey Ave., Logan Square, Chicago, IL 60647; (773) 661-9170; eatfatrice.com; Portuguese; $$. Yep, everybody loves this Macanese joint—and for good reason. Many good reasons, in fact, starting with the over-the-top *arroz gordo,* a hodgepode of land and sea atop crispy, flavor-saturated sofrito rice. Get it, some bold pickles—sour chili cabbage, perhaps—and pineapple upside-down cake, and you're golden. A smart, edited wine, beer, and booze list is ready to pair.

Fish Bar, 2956 N. Sheffield Ave., Lakeview, Chicago, IL 60657; (773) 687-8177; fishbarchicago.com; Seafood; $$. Casual, compat, and approachable, this sustainably minded, admittedly shticky seafood house from **DMK Burger Bar** (p. 34) owners Michael Kornick (also of **mk,** p. 118) and David Morton (of **Morton's,** p. 79) is the sort where you sip sweet, boozy tea from Mason jars, slurp bivalves like there's no tomorrow, and dive into a surprising star of the show: best-ever, deep-fried onions, jalapeño coins, and lemon wheels. Come to think of it, the grilled, chile-flecked octopus with preserved lemon is memorable, too.

4 Suyos, 727 W. Fullerton Ave., Logan Square, Chicago, IL 60647; (773) 278-6525; 4suyos.com; Peruvian; $$. BYO to this low-key Incan in Logan Square, which is so tasty that it could convert even the most steadfast of *anticuchos* (beef heart) boycotters. After all, here the *aji panca* and vinegar-infused organs come from locally beloved Slagel Farm. You'll also want the beyond-fresh ceviche and the *ají amarillo*–kissed papas a *la Huancaína.* And because no meal is complete without sweets, make *alfajor*—dulce de leche–filled shortbreads—your go-to.

Frasca Pizzeria & Wine Bar, 3358 N. Paulina St., Lakeview, Chicago, IL 60657; (773) 248-5222; frascapizzeria.com; Italian; $$. You'll wind up wishing this laid-back, hip, and family-friendly spot from the **D.O.C. Wine Bar** (p. 221) crew was in your 'hood. Even if its entrees and pastas are fairly forgettable, the apps, wood-fired pizza, and afford-able wine list are of note. Make like the locals and snag wild mushroom risotto fritters and prosciutto-wrapped Fontina, drizzled with balsamic vinegar. Then, keep it simple with a classic Margherita pie, or get your roasted fingerling, onion, bacon, and three-cheese 'za adorned with an egg. On Wednesday, pizzas are buy one, get one free. Also, check out siblings Dunlays on Clark, 2600 N. Clark St., (773) 883-6000; Dunlays on the Square, 3137 W. Logan Blvd., (773) 227-2400; and **The Smoke Daddy** (p. 87).

Frog n Snail, 3124 N. Broadway, Lakeview, Chicago, IL 60657; (773) 661-9166; frognsnail.com; French/New American; $$$. Chef Dale Levitski does the Midwest proud at this regional bistro that's full of surprises. That includes use of its namesake ingredients, the first seen in a fried green tomato prep, the latter appearing in, perhaps, a mushroom-mingled *ragù*. There are plenty of comforting options, like the Kitchen Sink Cassoulet, brightened with cabbage-apple slaw, or braised short rib Stroganoff. But expect the unlikely from this near–*Top Chef* winner, too, like a peanut butter Monte Cristo with Honeycrisp pie filling during brunch.

Glunz Bavarian Haus, 4128 N. Lincoln Ave., North Center, Chicago, IL 60618; (773) 472-4287; glunzbavarianhaus.com; German/Austrian; $$. The German repertoire is well represented here thanks to the beer, wine, and spirit-distributing Glunz family (The House of Glunz), who crafted this schnitzel den with Stiegl-swillers in mind. Cheese and sausage platters are fit for a baron, and sauerbraten or roast pork with bread dumplings, kraut, and caraway jus are so welcoming—and filling. Before throwing in the towel, tack on some

Viennese strudel. Alternately, tip some back over a meal at Glunz Tavern, closed when Prohibition began and revived at 1202 N. Wells St., (312) 642-3001.

HB Home Bistro, 3404 N. Halsted St., Lakeview, Chicago, IL 60657; (773) 661-0299; homebistrochicago.com; New American; $$$. Victor Morenz lends inviting, seasonal appeal to this BYOB, which delivers knockout, homespun cuisine to a repeat clientele. Sunchoke and toasted almond bisque sets the tone; house-made fettuccine with lamb *ragù*, ramp greens, and an oozing fried egg follow suit. Also, visit its Euro-bent brother, Vincent, 1475 W. Balmoral Ave., (773) 334-7168.

Hearty, 3819 N. Broadway, Wrigleyville, Chicago, IL 60613; (773) 868-9866; heartyboys.com; New American; $$. Updated comfort food and great cocktails benchmark this Steve McDonagh and Dan Smith charmer, offering a solid, reliably satisfying experience time after time. If you can handle something so, well, hearty, start with the corn-battered rabbit sausage with ale syrup, and continue to chicken thigh smothered in lemon velouté and served with a cayenne–green onion beignet. And don't skip dessert—the root beer float cupcakes and lemon creamsicle can't be denied.

Hot Doug's, 3324 N. California Ave., Avondale, Chicago, IL 60618; (773) 279-9550; hotdougs .com; Hot Dogs; $. Yes, you can procure a classic, Chicago-style dog, but (good as it is) don't bother. The real reason to succumb to this serious stand is Doug Sohn's creative sausages, which vary by day. Be wooed by specials—maybe bacon sausage, christened with crème fraîche, caramelized onions, and double-cream Brie—and named-for-celebrity standbys like the Norm Crosby, a snappy, garnished-as-you-wish Thuringer.

Indie Burger, 1034 W. Belmont Ave., Lakeview, Chicago, IL 60657; (773) 857-7777; indieburger.com; American; $$. Organic patties—that's what you'll get at this convivial joint, specializing in grass-fed burgers and sandwiches on puffy buns. Get your beefy number dolled up with blue cheese and a yolky egg if you're wise. As for onion rings, well, you'll need an order of those airy beauties, too.

Irish Oak, 3511 N. Clark St., Wrigleyville, Chicago, IL 60657; (773) 935-6669; irishoak.com; Irish; $$. Kitted out with an Emerald Isle bar, this near-ballpark pub with a Cubs-loving, backwards-cap clientele exudes authentic charm. Fried food fans frequent the beer-battered pickles and wings, a precursor to standard sandwiches; shepherd's pie, fish-and-chips, and Guinness stew feel more true blue. Pints of beer, whiskey, and Irish-cream-based concoctions contribute to the convivial vibe.

Jam, 3057 W. Logan Blvd., Logan Square, Chicago, IL 60647; (773) 292-6011; jamrestaurant.com; American; $$. Chef Jeffrey Mauro (Charlie Trotter's, **North Pond** [p. 79]) spins inventive a.m. eats worth rising early for. Whether you come for malted custard French toast with macerated rhubarb, pink peppercorn, and lime-leaf cream or an egg sandwich stuffed with pork shoulder, ricotta salata, and plum preserves, return later for a corned beef sandwich, slathered with horseradish cream cheese on marble rye.

Kit Kat Lounge & Supper Club, 3700 N. Halsted St., Lakeview, Chicago, IL 60613; (773) 525-1111; kitkatchicago.com; New American; $$. There's a bawdy vibe: Therein lies the allure of this bachelorette party–populated locale, where cross-dressing divas perform and the updated American comfort food and martini-centric libations play a supporting role. However, its brunch menu, filled with cheekily named dishes, has an audience of its own. (In other words, leave the kiddos at home.)

Kitsch'n on Roscoe, 2005 W. Roscoe St., Roscoe Village, Chicago, IL 60618; (773) 248-7372; kitschn.com; Eclectic; $$. At this Naugahyde nook, adornments—bubbling lava lamps, vintage action figures, lunchboxes, and Formica-topped tables— meet a modernized menu crammed with comfort fare. Faves include fried chicken and waffles with ancho honey, meat loaf with port gravy, and chicken-fennel potpie. Then again, the mac and cheese—topped with bacon-flecked bread crumbs—always does the trick. There's barbecue, too, and a not-to-be-missed, Twinkie-fied take on tiramisu. Ask to sit in the tiki garden when it's warm, but expect a wait during brunch.

Kuma's Corner, 2900 W. Belmont Ave., Avondale, Chicago, IL 60618; (773) 604-8769; kumascorner.com; Burgers; $$. Burgers get top billing at this lodge-y, wood-trimmed tap. Settling on one is hard, but the namesake, topped with bacon, cheddar, and a fried egg, is classic; the Metallica, which drips with buffalo sauce and blue cheese, is hardcore; and the Black Sabbath, a blackened mess-maker with house-made chili, pepper jack, and red onion, proves gut-busting, to say the least. Diversions include chorizo-stuffed poppers with jalapeño-raspberry jam and slow-cooked pork on a pretzel roll. A just rough-and-tumble enough staff, pleasant patio, and extensive craft-beer selection are also attributes. A second installment, Kuma's Too, is at 666 W. Diversey Pkwy., (773) 472-2666.

La Bomba, 3221 W. Armitage Ave., Logan Square, Chicago, IL 60647; (773) 394-0106; labombaplace.com; Puerto Rican; $. Puerto Rican yummies abound at this quaint spot, a must for the crisp, plantain-sandwiched skirt steak *jibarito*; porky *mofongo*; and comforting sides such as *arroz con gandules* and starchy tostones. Homey, hearty soups and slick flan are also worthy of recognition.

La Oaxaqueña, 3382 N. Milwaukee Ave., Irving Park, Chicago, IL 60641; (773) 545-8585; laoaxaquenachicago.com; Mexican; $. This casual, pint-size Oaxacan taqueria turns out regional, mole-soused chicken and destination-worthy *camarones rellenos*; jam, bacon, and cheese-stuffed shrimp; tender, garlicky squid *al ajillo*; delish tortas; and warming *caldo* (soup).

Las Tablas, 2942 N. Lincoln Ave., Lakeview, Chicago, IL 60657; (773) 871-2414; lastablas.com; Colombian/Steak House; $$. Bring your appetite and prepare to loosen your belt—a meal at this hopping, meat-minded Colombian demands both. Sip a vodka-spiked *limonada* in wait of flaky beef empanadas pocked with hard-boiled egg. Next, turn to gut-busting meat and seafood combinations or *bandeja paisa*, sizzling rib eye piled with crisp pork belly, fried, yolky egg, rice, beans, plantains, and avocado.

Laschet's Inn, 2119 W. Irving Park Rd., North Center, Chicago, IL 60618; (773) 478-7915; laschetsinn.com; German; $$. Great German food and beer at prices that don't send you to the poorhouse—that's what you'll get at this wood-beamed, beer mug–adorned old-world pub, turning out artery-clogging classics to great success. It turns out the *rouladen* (beef rolls filled with pickles, bacon, and onions and blanketed in gravy), fantastically crisp potato pancakes, and wiener schnitzel do more than fill a niche. Consider starting with the *hackepeter*—steak tartare with capers and onions on rye—followed by fried chicken, goulash, or sauerbraten, savoring your Hirter and Hoegaarden before the food coma sets in and the apple schnapps, a meal-ending tradition, arrives.

Little Bucharest Bistro, 3661 N. Elston Ave., Irving Park, Chicago, IL 60618; (773) 604-8500; littlebucharestbistro.com; Eastern European/Romanian; $$. Branko Podrumedic resurrected his longtime eatery, which features stained-glass panels salvaged from a former address. From the kitchen comes vibrant borscht and roasted beet, artichoke, and Spanish onion salad, swathed with creamy garlic dressing. Rib-sticking mains—schnitzel, paprikash, and goulash, not to mention grilled Romanian sausages, which pair nicely with old-world vinos—more than suffice.

L'Patron, 2815 W. Diversey Pkwy., Logan Square, Chicago, IL 60647; (773) 252-6335; Mexican; $. Brothers Ernesto and Cesar Gonzalez run this unassuming taco stand, which appears ordinary—on paper. In reality, it's anything but. Ernesto's Kendall education and **Topolobampo** (p. 133) training are put to good use in the tender, rosy-pink *carne asada* tacos, quesadilla-meets-taco gringo, and excellent beer-battered fish tacos, all ramped up with a rotating lineup of expertly prepared salsas, served into the wee hours in close confines. But don't let the name fool you: You'll have to BYO.

Lula Cafe, 2537 N. Kedzie Ave., Logan Square, Chicago, IL 60647; (773) 489-9554; lulacafe.com; New American; $$$. This Midwest-leaning, globally inspired neighborhood gem leaves an impression with its purveyor-driven menu that's long on flavor but (relatively) easy on the wallet. Though dishes are ever-changing, expect to encounter things like prawns *a la plancha* with fried squash blossoms, garlic scapes, lime vinaigrette, and thyme aioli, or mortadella-stuffed rabbit saddle with wheat berries, creamed parsnips, hen-of-the-woods mushrooms, and sorrel. In the end, the eats are about as offbeat-cool as the crowd that frequents the funky digs. Brunch is a must, provided you can get a table.

Marco's Beef & Pizza, 6008 W. Fullerton Ave., Belmont Cragin, Chicago, IL 60639; (773) 745-1015; marcosbeef.com; American; $. Some things are worth going out of the way for. The Italian beef with its sloppy tangle of homemade, jus-soaked meat, tucked into pliant

TEAM EFFORT

Community gardens are popping up everywhere, thanks to not-for-profit **GreenNet** (greennetchicago.org). Currently the city of Chicago has over 600 active gardens in 50 wards, plus community gardens are cropping up in both urban and suburban areas. Some feature youth programs, while others have a beautification bent. Education is a component, too, as at the North Lawndale Green Youth Farm, a West Side initiative done in conjunction with the Chicago Botanic Garden and local chefs, schools, and community leaders. Visit the GreenNet site to unearth a public plot near you.

bread, is one such thing. The broasted chicken is accolade-worthy as well, and pizza by the slice isn't half bad either.

Masa Azul, 2901 W. Diversey Ave., Logan Square, Chicago, IL 60647; (773) 687-0300; masaazul.com; Regional American; $$. A Southwestern vibe pervades this Logan Square find from **Sepia** (p. 127) vet Jonathan Zaragoza (also of **Birrieria Zaragoza** [p. 139] fame). Memorable offerings include meltingly tender *cochinita pibil* that's christened with pickled onions; oven-roasted, mole-rubbed goat with arbol chile picante; and a soft-boiled, panko-crusted chorizo Scotch egg, enlivened with pickled jalapeño vinaigrette. Don't miss the superior, roasty *salsa de molcajete* and the thoughtful array of agave spirits.

Mia Francesca, 3311 N. Clark St., Lakeview, Chicago, IL 60657; (773) 281-3310; miafrancesca.com; Italian; $$. The flagship of the Francesca family, Scott Harris's loud, lively Italian *cucina* has an inviting, cobbled terrace and crazy-tight tables in a narrow dining room, where everyone eats while packed like sardines. Whether seated inside or out, the Northern Italian fare—carpaccio scattered with capers;

pancetta-studded linguine *all'amatriciana*; lemony, rosemary-scented roast chicken—is a recipe for success.

Milt's BBQ for the Perplexed, 3411 N. Broadway, Lakeview, Chicago, IL 60657; (773) 661-6384; miltsbbq.com; Barbecue; $$. This kosher entrant into the barbecue scene gives its profits to charity, whether you opt for fried okra, smoky brisket, or a grilled Romanian char-dog with a side of vinegar slaw. House-infused bourbon and specialty cocktails are handy companions.

Mirabell, 3454 W. Addison St., Irving Park, Chicago, IL 60618; (773) 463-1962; mirabellrestaurant.com; German; $$. This hardy German "lodge" is outfitted with the expected trappings (steins, beer signs), while offering a bygone menu of schnitzel preps, chill-abating goulash, smoky Thuringer with kraut, and zesty sauerbraten, accompanied by red cabbage and dumplings. Best of all, you can bust out your lederhosen—no one will bat an eye.

Mixteco Grill, 1601 W. Montrose Ave., Lakeview, Chicago, IL 60613; (773) 868-1601; mixtecogrill .com; Mexican; $$. Bring your own libations to this über-busy Mexican, where bespectacled hipsters chow down on mid-priced moles (including a deeply smoky version atop *sopes*) in a deceptively underwhelming setting. And while anything mole-sauced is a best bet, achiote-burnished *cochinita pibil*—topped with pickled onions and flaming habanero salsa—is amazing, too. Also, come for brunch.

Mr. D's Shish-Kabobs, 6656 W. Diversey Ave., Belmont Cragin, Chicago, IL 60707; (773) 637-0042; Middle Eastern; $. It may be off the beaten path, but, boy, do the marinated, grill-charred kebabs; juicy, gravy-soused steak sandwich; and fresh-cut fries at this cop-populated, family-run stand make jaunts worthwhile.

Mrs. Murphy & Sons Irish Bistro, 3905 N. Lincoln Ave., North Center, Chicago, IL 60613; (773) 248-3905; irishbistro.com; Irish; $$$. Quite the departure in more ways than one, this modern Irishman affords an upscale, if off-kilter, experience in the home of a former funeral parlor. Drawing inspiration from its Emerald Isle roots, boxty-style potato cakes are gussied up with smoked salmon and crème fraîche, and ribs are slathered with whiskey barbecue sauce and arrive with creamy Guinness mac and cheese. The place pays homage to the late, legendary Jim Murphy.

90 Miles Cuban Cafe, 3101 N. Clybourn Ave., Roscoe Village, Chicago, IL 60618; (773) 248-2822; 90milescubancafe.com; Cuban; $$. A taste of Cuba in an intimate shack adorned with vintage news clippings and reclaimed barn-wood details, Alberto and Christine Gonzalez's *ropa vieja*–fragranced cafe prepares crackly Cubano, *lechón,* and guava-Swiss sandwiches that are worth seeking out. A second location is at 2540 W. Armitage Ave., (773) 227-2822.

Olga's Deli, 3209 W. Irving Park Rd., Irving Park, Chicago, IL 60618; (773) 539-8038; Deli/German; $. Making mouths happy without an iota of pomp, this longstanding Irving Park deli serves several-stories-thick chicken schnitzel and pork tenderloin sandwiches that are simply, generously seasoned and moistened with mayo. You may wait for them—and the lacy potato pancakes or German potato salad—but, believe it or not, that's part of the charm.

Paladar Restaurant and Rum Bar, 2252 N. Western Ave., Chicago, IL 60647; (773) 252-4747; paladarchicago.com; Cuban; $$. Modeled after small, privately owned restaurants in Cuba, Jose Gonzolaz's delightful dining room turns out pitch-perfect Cuban sandwiches, soul-warming *ropa vieja,* and lovely mojitos sweetened with fresh-squeezed sugarcane. The ultra-fresh, spicy avocado salad is don't-miss, too.

Parson's Chicken & Fish, 2952 **Armitage Ave., Chicago, IL** 60647; (773) 384-3333; parsonschickenandfish.com; Seafood/New American; $$. The Longman and Eagle (p. 232) crew does it again with a killer, fried lineup of its namesake, plus fresh-shucked oysters and boozy slushies (most notably the Negroni) that are best sipped on its sun-stippled patio when it's warm. And, man, that salty michelada is good.

Penny's Noodle Shop, 3400 **N. Sheffield Ave., Lakeview, Chicago, IL** 60657; (773) 281-8222; **pennys noodleshop.com; Asian;** $$. You won't pay a lot but you'll get plenty at this likeable noodle house. Expect all the mainstays, including pad thai, chicken satay, and *lad nar*. However, soups—such as *tom yum,* greens-flecked barbecue pork, udon, and ramen—are its strength. There are multiple locations in the city and suburbs. **Additional locations:** Wicker Park, 1542 N. Damen Ave., (773) 394-0100; Oak Park, 1130 Chicago Ave., (708) 660-1300; and Northfield, 320 Happ Rd., (847) 446-4747.

Pide ve Lahmacun, 1812 **W. Irving Park Rd., North Center, Chicago, IL** 60613; (773) 248-6344; **Turkish;** $. Namesake calzones and flatbreads, eye-popping coffee, and *salep*—a hot orchid tuber beverage reminiscent of rice pudding—draw commuters in search of fresh, crazy-cheap Turkish eats. It's run by a husband-and-wife team, who also operate cabbie-populated I-Cafe next door, (773) 755-4022.

pingpong, 3322 **N. Broadway, Lakeview, Chicago, IL** 60657; (773) 281-7576; **pingpongrestaurant.com; Asian;** $$. The vibe—right down to the styling staff—is cool. The good news is, the fare—tempura fish tacos, crab Rangoon, curried Singapore noodles—is up to the task. And the salt-and-pepper shrimp? The *bulgogi* and the twice-cooked pork belly? Well, they're good, too.

Pollo Campero, The Brickyard, 2730 N. Narragansett Ave., **Hermosa, Chicago, IL 60639; (773) 622-6657; campero.com; Guatemalan; $$.** Visit once, and opine over the moist, crispy-skinned Guatemalan fried chicken. Torn from the bone, it possesses just the right kick when tucked into warm corn tortillas and topped with salsas, cilantro, and onions from the condiment bar. Throw in sides of bacon-flecked pinto beans and crunchy slaw, and you've got something akin to bliss. There is also an Albany Park location, 4830 N. Pulaski Rd., (773) 282-1966.

Real Kitchen, 1433 W. Montrose Ave., **Lakeview, Chicago, IL 60613; (773) 281-2888; realkitchenchicago.com; American; $$.** The oft-changing, chef-driven takeaway goes well beyond the basics. But it's no wonder, really, given Charlie Trotter's and El Bulli vets are the ones who turn out the peppered cauliflower-Parmesan soup, blue cheese–topped brisket sandwiches, and Key lime mousse. Be sure to check out the pantry items, house-made stocks, and cut-to-order fresh pasta as well.

Reno, 2607 N. Milwaukee Ave., **Logan Square, Chicago, IL 60647; (773) 697-4234; renochicago.com; American; $$.** Bagels and wood-fired pizza shine at this three-squares spot from the **Telegraph, Webster's Wine Bar,** and **Bluebird** crew (pp. 225, 226, and 221, respectively). The bagels—available in flavors like olive-herb—are Montreal in style, while the pizzas lean Neapolitan but feature inventive toppings like smoked chicken, arbol-peanut salsa, and smoked green onions. Equally enjoyable pastas and creative sandwiches are furthered by an affordable wine, craft beer, and whiskey-centric cocktail list.

Resi's Bierstube, 2034 W. Irving Park Rd., **North Center, Chicago, IL 60618; (773) 472-1749; German; $$.** They don't make them like this *Brauhaus* anymore, which may have something to do with why this holdout is so beloved. But credit also goes to the schnitzel, massive *weiss*-centric beer list, and inviting *Biergarten*, the perfect place to procure sausages—from liver to knackwurst, beerwurst, and bratwurst—with sides of sauerkraut and lacy potato pancakes.

Sabatino's, 4441 W. Irving Park Rd., Irving Park, Chicago, IL 60641; (773) 283-8331; sabatinoschicago.com; Italian/Pizza; $$. Fantastic, affordable Sinatra staples await at this low-lit Italian stalwart, where service is as back-in-the-day as the *puttanesca*-sauced tagliatelle, eggplant Parm, and seafood-packed *zuppa di mari*. And the veal saltimbocca? You'll be back for more, guaranteed. End the evening on a romantic note with a tableside flambé.

Senza, 2873 N. Broadway, Lakeview, Chicago, IL 60657; (773) 770-3527; senzachicago.com; Gluten-Free/New American; $$$. Who needs gluten when the food is this good? At least that's the thinking behind this casual, flavor-forward Lakeview eatery that does ingredient-minders a solid with a set-price experience. Luxurious soups, impressive pastas, and pampering proteins—think barramundi with hedgehog mushrooms and black garlic, or huckleberry-laced duck confit—merely happen to be gluten-free. Also on tap is brunch, be it Old Bay–accented shrimp and grits or crab cake Benedict with dill hollandaise.

Shokran, 4027 W. Irving Park Rd., Irving Park, Chicago, IL 60641; (773) 427-9130; shokranchicago.com; Moroccan; $$. Complex, exotic flavors abound at this out-of-the-way Moroccan gem, where diners are transported to Fez by way of headily spiced tagines, raisin-dotted couscous, and soothing mint tea. Not to be overlooked is the parsley and preserved-lemon-flecked carrot salad and the *zaalouk,* stewy roasted eggplant salad that's brightened with fresh cilantro.

Smoque BBQ, 3800 N. Pulaski Rd., Irving Park, Chicago, IL 60641; (773) 545-7427; smoquebbq.com; Barbecue; $$. Roll up your sleeves—this anything but low-key neighborhood BYOB with its own "meat manifesto" will leave you licking your fingers and clamoring for more. Choose between the long-smoked, crisp-edged Texas-style brisket—fantastic in sandwich form—rubbed and sauced spare ribs, or vinegary hunks of pulled pork. (Opt for taste portions if you're wise.) Sides, like creamy mac and cheese and slaw, are good but not the star of the show.

socca, 3301 N. Clark St., Lakeview, Chicago, IL 60657; (773) 248-1155; soccachicago.com; French/Italian; $$$. The affordable French- and Italian-inflected fare served here has earned a loyal following. Repeat diners make a beeline for the chickpea-flour crepe dish for which the restaurant is named. Also justifiably popular are the house-made pastas, cacciatore-style braised rabbit risotto, and comfort-minded hanger steak topped with melting herb butter. Then again, the pizzettes are quite good as well.

Sol de Mexico, 3018 N. Cicero Ave., Belmont Cragin, Chicago, IL 60641; (773) 282-4119; soldemexicochicago.com; Mexican; $$$. A bit off the beaten track, this impressive destination from Carlos Tello (brother-in-law of mole master Geno Bahena) has Clementina Flores (Bahena's mom) in the kitchen. There, she preserves the art of authentic, regional Mexican cooking using the freshest of ingredients. The flawless, complex moles—whether elevating ostrich or mussels, sea bass or scallops—are a revelation. Also celebratory: the sweet-savory *chiles en nogada,* poblanos brimming with fruit-flecked pork picadillo, sprinkled with pomegranate seeds, and finished in silky walnut sauce.

Sola, 3868 N. Lincoln Ave., North Center, Chicago, IL 60613; (773) 327-3868; sola-restaurant.com; Hawaiian/Asian; $$$. Carol Wallack's Hawaiian-bent spot is one to keep in your back pocket. Take note of the seasonal specials, which feature a themed ingredient—ramps, for example. From Kahlúa pork with banana bread and crispy onions to hoisin-mustard panko tuna with bamboo rice, avocado, and soy-wasabi *buerre blanc,* narrowing down options is an exercise in discipline. Come for the short ribs Benedict during brunch.

Southport Grocery, 3552 N. Southport Ave., Lakeview, Chicago, IL 60657; (773) 665-0100; southportgrocery.com; New American; $$. The stroller set loves this close-quarters storefront, though dining at this pint-size grocer and cafe is not always the pleasantest of experiences. However, the insanely good eats—a house-made, grown-up Pop Tart bursting with berry preserves and mascarpone cheese; scones that don't resemble a hockey puck; and moist cupcakes—are  a good reward for surviving close confines. Sandwiches, such as grilled Brie or house-made pastrami, are appealing at midday. Packaged goods—oils, sauces, cheeses, and pastas—are tempting at any hour. Watch for the restaurant's secret suppers, which offer a break from the breakfast and brunch it's known for.

Sticky Rice, 4018 N. Western Ave., North Center, Chicago, IL 60618; (773) 588-0120; stickyricethai.com; Thai; $$. Seriously, skip the pad thai. This vibrant, welcoming haunt serves some of, if not *the* best Thai citywide. (Ask for the translated Thai-language menu.) Then, go with the brow-moppingly hot, house-made sausage; tart-spicy *nam prik num* sauce with veggies and sticky rice; Thai *larb,* a commingling of ground pork and intestines; and tongue-singeing banana-blossom salad. Daring diners may also procure a handful of insect-based dishes.

Table, Donkey and Stick, 2728 W. Armitage Ave., Logan Square, Chicago, IL 60647; (773) 486-8525; tabledonkeyandstick .com; Modern European; $$$. After much ado went into finding its chef through pop-up dinners, Scott Manley (**Vie** [p. 195], **EL Ideas** [p. 144]) won out. Now, he turns out meat (pheasant galantine) and cheese (grassy Robiola Rocchetta) spreads; shareable black garlic–braised snails; and a *schweinekopf* sandwich blanketed in Taleggio with Dijon, pickled pear, and marinated kale, all in an Alpine-inspired space that once housed Bonsoirée.

TAC Quick, 3930 N. Sheridan Rd., Wrigleyville, Chicago, IL 60613; (773) 327-5253; tacquick.net; Thai; $$. Trim and stylish, locals look to this approachable spot for authentic Thai, namely items on its (translated) "secret" menu. Once it's in hand, order the bracing papaya salad with blue crab and Isaan-style pork and rice sausage, pronto. Follow with the fried chicken with scorching tamarind sauce—it'll haunt your dreams.

Tamales Garibay, 3859 N. Kedzie Ave., Chicago, IL 60618; (773) 267-6721; garibaytamales.com; Mexican; $. Alicia Romero's plump, ethereal tamales are a paragon of the form, particularly in the case of the pork verde and earthy chicken mole versions. A familiar list of (unnecessary) alternates includes tacos, tortas, burritos, and quesadillas.

Tango Sur, 3763 N. Southport Ave., Lakeview, Chicago, IL 60613; (773) 477-5466; Argentine/Steak House; $$. Carnivores—at least the ones patient enough to wait—descend on this lively BYOB, known for its empanadas, generously cut steak with chimichurri sauce, and slick, sweet flan—all of which benefit from a backing of live Latin guitar. Folklore, its similarly minded Argentine sib, is in Wicker Park at 2100 W. Division St., (773) 292-1600.

Taqueria Ricardo, 4429 W. Diversey Ave., Hermosa, Chicago, IL 60639; (773) 292-0400; Mexican; $. Hidden in a nondescript *supermercado* is this bright, jerry-built hole-in-the-wall, a pitch-perfect place for *tacos al pastor* (slightly charred and carved from a spit behind the counter) as well as juicy, wood-grilled chicken. Also solid is any-thing—including tacos and tortas—with grilled steak. Fantastic salsa verde brightens dishes, which arrive with grilled knob onions and jalapeños.

Thai Aree, 3592 N. Milwaukee Ave., North Center, Chicago, IL 60641; (773) 725-6751; Thai; $. A neighborhood gem in the truest sense, this authentic spot is a must for ginger-laced Thai sausage, supe-rior green curry, and grilled beef garlic salad. Add in some *nam sod,* ground pork with peanuts, or tear-inducing *tom kha gai* soup and rest assured: Bliss will ensue.

Thai Classic, 3332 N. Clark St., Lakeview, Chicago, IL 60657; (773) 404-2000; thaiclassicrestaurant.com; Thai; $$. Solid renditions of familiar Thai dishes and an extensive, rock-bottom weekend brunch featuring more than two-dozen dishes have earned a reputation for this reliable, casual institution. All the basics are covered and done well, from the *tom yum* soup and refreshing papaya and beef salads to the spicy, saucy drunken noodles.

Toons Bar & Grill, 3857 N. Southport Ave., Lakeview, Chicago, IL 60613; (773) 935-1919; chicagotoons.com; American; $$. There's more than meets the eye at this friendly Lakeview hang. Stop in for shuffleboard, but stay for KC-style ribs and pulled pork, hand-formed burgers, and crunchy, juicy jumbo wings with chunky blue cheese. Sides are also worth noting, including the hand-cut chili cheese fries and airy beer-battered onion rings. Watch for its annual all-you-can-eat crawfish bowl each spring.

Tropi Cuba, 3000 W. Lyndale St., Logan Square, Chicago, IL 60647; (773) 252-0230; tropicubachicago.com; Cuban; $. A classic case of "don't judge a book by its cover," this bitty bastion of Cuban flavors serves superb sandwiches, though its bar-stool seating is nestled into the back of a no-frills grocery store. If the black beans and rice don't tug at your heartstrings, odds are the guava and cheese *pastelito* or *lechón* will.

Turquoise, 2147 W. Roscoe St., Roscoe Village, Chicago, IL 60618; (773) 549-3523; turquoisedining.com; Mediterranean/ Turkish; $$$. Turkish cuisine, served in a wood-trimmed, white-tablecloth setting, gets a boost the moment a basket of warm, house-made bread arrives. Is it a bit spendy? Yes. But the expertly prepared, almost elegant *sogurme*—a creamy, garlicky mélange of smoked eggplant, yogurt, brown butter, and toasted walnuts—homemade *lahmacun* (meat-topped flatbread), and salt-crusted fish justify the mini-splurge.

Uncommon Ground, 3800 N. Clark St., Wrigleyville, Chicago, IL 60613; (773) 929-3680; uncommonground.com; Eclectic; $$$. Come as you are—this green-minded, kid-friendly coffeehouse welcomes it. Then, dig into dishes constructed from locally sourced ingredients. Generally the feel-good chopped salad and grown-up Butterkäse grilled cheese are enough to appease the carbon-offset crowd, though the roster of regular entertainment goes a long way to keep things interesting. The Edgewater location is at 1401 W. Devon Ave., (773) 465-9801, complete with certified organic rooftop garden.

urbanbelly, 3053 N. California Ave., Avondale, Chicago, IL 60618; (773) 583-0500; urbanbellychicago.com; Pan-Asian; $$. Gluttons flock to Bill Kim's tearfully good noodle shop, where the communal wood seating is ever-packed. It's understandable, since the *pho*-scented duck dumplings, chewy rice cake–chicken noodle bowl specked with mango, and uncommonly good short rib–scallion rice will leave you longing for seconds, thirds, and a visit the following day. Get sides of pungent kimchi and blistered green beans for full-on bliss. Best of all, you can afford it since the BYOB policy keeps prices down.

Victory's Banner, 2100 W. Roscoe St., Roscoe Village, Chicago, IL 60618; (773) 665-0227; victorysbanner.com; Vegetarian; $$. The eggs here are ethereal, and the French toast with real maple syrup is worth every calorie—just as the sari-wearing servers suggest. While taking in the spiritual vibe, order perfectly presentable cinnamon apple–topped oatmeal, or try the Indian *uppama*—a hot, cream of wheat–like porridge, dotted with peas, onions, and tomatoes alongside coconut chutney and tangy yogurt accompaniments. The fresh, light lunch fare—from wraps to sandwiches and salads—is good, though it never trumps the served-all-day a.m. eats.

Volo, 2008 W. Roscoe St., Roscoe Village, Chicago, IL 60618; (773) 348-4600; volorestaurant.com; American/Wine Bar; $$$. Wine enthusiasts unite at this small-plates gem with a picturesque garden patio. Although the selections alter by season, its artisan cheeses, luxurious bone-marrow starter, and brined, slow-simmered duck confit certainly are welcome finds. Add that to the fact that the sweet-pea flatbread is as fresh as can be.

Wood, 3335 N. Halsted St., Lakeview, Chicago, IL 60657; (773) 935-9663; woodchicago.com; Belgian; $. Wood-fired, seasonal small and large plates, flatbreads, cheeses, and charcuterie are the thrust at this thoughtful Boystown hang. Whether you settle on the classic steak tartare, oxtail sweet-potato ravioli, or clam-and-bacon-accented halibut, know it—and the chill, friendly vibe—will woo. Be sure to visit the take-out venture, Backwoods (in back), for frites. Pluck the twice-fried, grab-and-go beauties from their paper cones, choosing from noteworthy, if unneeded, dunking sauces, like luxe truffle aioli and malt vin aioli.

Yusho, 2853 N. Kedzie Ave., Avondale, Chicago, IL 60618; (773) 904-8558; Japanese; $$$. Matthias Merges, a Charlie Trotter's vet, goes casual-cool at this yakitori-inspired, small-plates spot with mismatched furnishings, draft cocktails, and a quirky lineup of drinking foods that deserve every bit of the buzz they receive. Expect a beautiful procession of plates, all with bright, balanced flavors, be it skewered, miso-accented leeks, topped with crispy shallots and Marcona almonds, or the tender wisps of horseradish-kissed beef tongue. For killer cocktails, check out sister property **Billy Sunday** (p. 227).

Mid City

Bucktown, Gold Coast, Humboldt Park, Lincoln Park, Noble Square, Old Town, Streeterville, Ukrainian Village, Wicker Park

Chicago is a city of distinct neighborhoods. Following its midsection from the lake outward, this is evidenced by Lincoln Park's tree-trimmed, brownstone-lined streets, posh Old Town, and funky Ukie Village, all offset by multicultural, working-class Humboldt Park and the buzzing tract of Bucktown and Wicker Park. Exploring its eateries reveals everything from molecular gastronomy to seasonally minded scenes and mom-and-pop shops. When craving hangover correctives, or swanky seafood in classic digs, look no further to fill the bill.

a tavola, 2148 W. Chicago Ave., Ukrainian Village, Chicago, IL 60622; (773) 276-7567; atavolachicago.com; Italian; $$$. This neighborhood charmer executes its rustic, handily sauced Northern Italian classics with might. Start with the lightly dressed, grilled duo of portobello and oyster mushrooms; bank on being wowed by the slow-simmered Bolognese and celestial, brown butter–kissed gnocchi; and never rule out the specials, perhaps spoon-tender short ribs beneath a confetti of gremolata. Cooking classes, which require advance reservations, are offered on select Monday evenings.

Ada St., 1664 N. Ada St., Noble Square, Chicago, IL 60642; (773) 697-7069; adastreetchicago.com; New American; $$$. Michael

Kornick and David Morton's Mediterranean-tinged boîte is nestled in an unlikely (read: desolate, industrial) address and reached through a labyrinth of hallways. Don't be deterred. Just pick out a record on your way in, and settle into the laid-back, rustic dining room for witty, balanced cocktails. They're just the ticket for pairing with Zoe Schor's polenta fries, brown butter–dressed strip steak, and airy brioche doughnuts with port wine caramel.

Adobo Grill, 1610 N. Wells St., Old Town, Chicago, IL 60614; (312) 266-7999; adobogrill.com; Mexican; $$. Tableside-prepped guac and 'ritas shaken before your eyes promise a festive experience at this tightly packed, upscale Mexican. It's hard to find fault with gooey, chorizo-studded *queso,* which arrives in an earthenware dish, though the lengthy list of starters—a hit with the after-work crowd—hosts plenty of other musts; try, for example, the achiote chicken *salbutes,* topped with pickled red onions. Oaxacan black mole, which sauces pork tenderloin, is rounded in flavor, while the simple-but-luxurious *cochinita pibil* is made for tucking in to warm tortillas.

Alinea, 1723 N. Halsted St., Lincoln Park, Chicago, IL 60614; (312) 867-0110; alinea-restaurant.com; New American; $$$$. Dining is a theatrical experience at this stunner from Grant Achatz, whose artful plates confound, demand instruction, and fool by way of deceptively simple menu descriptors. Nothing is what it appears to be—rather, the menu is a composite of ingredients, revealing little about the magic on plate. The set-price, sticker-shock adventure consists of a single, seasonal, constantly evolving 20-plus-course arrangement, served by a polished (some would say stoic) waitstaff. This is special-occasion dining in its truest, most destination-worthy form. But romantic it is not. Instead, it's legendary and gastronomic, and you may be left scratching your head. The extensive wine list is top-shelf. Achatz is also the force behind **Next,** a by-ticket-only restaurant (p. 120); **The Aviary,** a molecular cocktail lounge (p. 226); and exclusive **The Office** (p. 233).

Allium, Four Seasons Hotel, 120 E. Delaware St., 7th Fl., Gold Coast, Chicago, IL 60611; (312) 799-4900; alliumchicago.com; New American; $$. Don't be intimidated by the bougie backdrop—Kevin Hickey's regional, seasonal menu is as approachable as it is ambitious. While served in a gracious hotel setting, the menu is a farm-to-table affair, one rift with familiar flavors and chef-y takes on beloved dishes. In other words, don't be surprised when crackly cheese *lavosh* arrives dangling in the air; a Chicago-style hot dog comes garnished with homemade everything; and a can't-miss milk shake melds butterscotch and miso flavors. But old-schoolers won't be left in the cold, thanks to classics like beef tenderloin with bourbon-peppercorn sauce.

Aloha Eats, 2534 N. Clark St., Lincoln Park, Chicago, IL 60614; (773) 935-6828; alohaeats.com; Hawaiian; $. Enter beneath the surf-board sign and be transported to a balmier place, one where island eats—crisp, panko-breaded *katsu*; tender Kahlúa pork with crunchy cabbage; and Spam *musubi*—promote a beachy state of mind. Alternately, slurp your way through noodle-packed *saimin,* punched up with kimchi, knowing you'll be left with pocket change. Mix plates are key for indecisive types.

Antico, 1946 N. Leavitt St., Bucktown, Chicago, IL 60647; (773) 489-4895; anticochicago.com; Italian; $$. Simple and fresh Italian fare from Brad Schlieder (ex–**a tavola,** p. 55)—that's what you'll get at this cozy neighborhood gem. Start things off right with lush, earthy wild mushrooms, nestled into a bed of creamy saffron polenta, or, perhaps, fennel-stippled, house-made sausage, offset by braised red cabbage and mostarda. Save room for the knockout gnocchi, served three ways but hopefully in indulgent sage brown butter. Save—or make—room for the pillowy zeppole, tempting beneath a shower of powdered sugar.

Antique Taco, 1360 N. Milwaukee Ave., Chicago, IL 60622; (773) 687-8697; antiquetaco.com; Mexican; $$. Superlatives don't give this vintage-feeling stunner its due—cleaned plates (of which there are many) do. The atypical space, adorned with antiques and reclaimed materials, sets the tone, but sparkly flavors steal the show, starting with the tamarind-licked *carnitas* tacos with a spinach-bacon topper. Honestly, it's hard to go wrong, from the arugula-mushroom taco with crunchy *pepitas* to the vibrant fish version, christened with smoky cabbage and creamy Sriracha tartar sauce. Habanero popcorn and chorizo chili cheese curds make choosing sides a troublesome task. You'll want—make that *need*—a *horchata* milk shake to go with.

Arami, 1829 W. Chicago Ave., Ukrainian Village, Chicago, IL 60622; (312) 243-1535; aramichicago.com; Japanese; $$$. Few things are more satisfying than a bowl of ramen noodles—especially the porky namesake from this elegant, gardenlike respite. Of course, a satisfying meal can be made of nothing cooked, thanks to pristine sashimi, nigiri, and specialty maki that's made with restraint. Lovely veg preparations and items from a robata grill complete the experience.

Armitage Pizzeria, 711 W. Armitage Ave., Lincoln Park, Chicago, IL 60614; (312) 867-9111; Pizza; $$. Never mind frills—like comfortable seating, an array of choices, and snappy service. James Spillane (ex-**Coalfire,** p. 102) isn't having it; yet, he's an icon just the same. And while the chewy, charred East Coast–style pizzas are straightforward and the sparse space may be off-putting to some, most can't deny themselves of the "meat," topped with hot Calabrese salami, Italian sausage, and pepperoni, and the garlicky, oregano-scented "white" with basil, ricotta, and Romano cheeses.

Balena, 1633 N. Halsted St., Lincoln Park, Chicago, IL 60614; (312) 867-3888; balenachicago.com; Italian; $$$. The virtues of this expansive Lincoln Park Italian are many: Chris Pandel's carb-forward crowd-pleasers, the amari-based cocktails, and Amanda Rockman's creative, composed desserts, to start. Delve deeper and the *amore* grows, courtesy of the wood-burning-oven-singed mortadella and pistachio pizza, striking *tagliolini nero,* and pistachio gelato with crunchy nougat, orange confit, and burnt-orange caramel. The place—a partnership with BOKA Restaurant Group—gets packed, especially pre- and post-theater. Head to **The Bristol** (p. 63) when you'd rather chill.

Balsan, Waldorf Astoria, 11 E. Walton St., Gold Coast, Chicago, IL 60611; (312) 646-1400; balsanrestaurant.com; New American; $$$$. Head to the third floor of this tony hotel and be bowled over by what you encounter: a sleekly casual, seasonally informed respite serving house charcuterie. Start with the off-the-charts suckling pig terrine and torchon of *foie gras.* Do yourself a solid and get some briny oysters from the raw bar, too. Both the small and large plates continue the refined-yet-casual approach, be it bucatini with veal cheek Bolognese or wood-oven-fired tarte flambé. Desserts end on a high note.

Bar Toma, 110 E. Pearson St., Gold Coast, Chicago, IL 60611; (312) 266-3110; bartomachicago.com; Italian/Pizza; $$. Tony Mantuano's hopping pizzeria and wine bar offers more than a respite for Mag Mile tourists. In fact, it all begins with morning coffee and ricotta-filled cornetti. As the day wears on, antipasti, like Calabrian licorice chips and charred carrots with goat cheese, almonds, and aged balsamic vinegar, give way to puffy, crisp-crusted Roman-style pizza topped with the likes of merguez, olives, pistachios, and Manchego. Check out the action at the mozzarella bar, where hand-rolled orbs are plated with San Marzano tomatoes and basil. Finish with seasonal housemade gelati, which comes in both classic and fun (Cap'n Crunch Berries) flavors.

Barn & Company, 950 W. Wrightwood Ave., Lincoln Park, Chicago, IL 60614; (773) 832-4000; barnandcompany.com; Barbecue; $$. Amid reclaimed barn-wood decor and pig paintings, Chef Bob Zrenner and pitmaster Gary Wiviott kick out smokehouse classics: deeply smoky brisket and hunky pulled pork, plus a hefty pork, potato, green bean, and molten egg salad dressed with bourbon-barbecue vinaigrette. When it comes to drinks, stick with the Country Mary, pony up for some bourbon, or design your own bucket of beer. There's a pretty patio, plenty of flat-screens, and live acts to pass time.

The Bento Box, 2246 W. Armitage Ave., Bucktown, Chicago, IL 60647; (773) 278-3932; artisancateringchicago.com/box.html; Asian Fusion; $$. The frequently changing pan-Asian fare from Rick Spiros's pint-size BYO storefront is sparkling fresh, seasonal, and made-to-order, facts that show in spirited Jidori chicken and veg lime-leaf curry, a wonder swathed in bracing *nuoc cham* vinaigrette. Tender *bulgogi* with fiery, house-made kimchi is a people-pleaser, too.

Big Bowl, 6 E. Cedar St., Gold Coast, Chicago, IL 60611; (312) 640-8888; bigbowl.com; Chinese/Thai; $$. Bountiful, if standard, Asian faves comprise the menu at this Lettuce Entertain You eatery.

House-made ginger ale helps cool mouths fired up by wrinkled Szechuan green beans. Familiar, sweet-tart orange chicken and pad thai are also safe bets, though many prefer to design their own stir-fry creations. **Additional locations:** 60 E. Ohio St., (312) 951-1888; Lincolnshire, 215 Parkway Dr., (847) 808-8880; and Schaumburg, 1950 E. Higgins Rd., (847) 517-8881.

Big Star, 1531 N. Damen Ave., Wicker Park, Chicago, IL 60622; (773) 235-4039; bigstarchicago.com; Mexican; $$. At his taco bar with a mock dive-bar mentality, Paul Kahan crafts one amazing, carved-from-the-spit taco al pastor; studded with smoky pineapple bits and garnished with grilled onions and cilantro, it takes a rightful position this side of heaven. Diversions include grilled, salted jalapeño *toreados* and a bacon-wrapped Sonoran hot dog. Wash everything down with shot-ready whiskies and tequilas, and don't leave without getting a dulce de leche milk shake. Upping the cool factor are curated honky-tonk tunes.

Birchwood Kitchen, 2211 W. North Ave., Bucktown, Chicago, IL 60647; (773) 276-2100; birchwoodkitchen.com; Cafe; $$. When it's warm, hang out in the courtyard of this local food-centric, counter-service sandwich shop; when it's not, get cozy within the exposed brick storefront, which is perfumed with house-roasted meat. Other efforts that show in the final product include seasonal, house-made chutneys, jams, and pickles, which are used as garnishes. Try the turkey meat loaf with house-made mozzarella and tangy-sweet tomato jam, or the Spanish tuna melt with roasted tomato and Gruyère—or, maybe, the baguette stuffed with goat cheese, pickled beets, and walnut pesto. A notable brunch breaks the mold to include bacon bread pudding and the like.

Bistronomic, 840 N. Wabash Ave., Gold Coast, Chicago, IL 60610; (312) 944-8400; bistronomic.net; French; $$. Martial Noguier is behind this seasonal, rustic eatery, where artisanal charcuterie and cheeses; small, medium, and large plates; and cans and jars of olives to sardines find fans. A classy setting, complete with looming, architectural lighting and gray banquettes, lends a romantic edge.

Bistrot Zinc, 1131 N. State St., Gold Coast, Chicago, IL 60610; (312) 337-1131; bistrotzinc.com; French; $$. An authentic Left Bank feel permeates every nook of this neighborhood constant with State

Street views. Although it dishes up both the familiar—plump *moules frites* redolent of shallots and fines herbes—and contemporary, stick with the former. Steak frites, topped with requisite maître d'hôtel butter, for example, will not let you down. Finish with decadent chocolate-espresso *pot de crème*.

Black Bull, 1721 W. Division St., Ukrainian Village; Chicago, IL 60622; (773) 227-8600; blackbullchicago.com; Spanish/Tapas; $$. Inspired by the pintxos bars of Spain, this venture from the **Hubbard Inn** (p. 110) and **Barn & Company** (p. 60) crew stands out in a wave of like-minded spots. And while it doesn't stray far from the norm, gratifying meals can be made of Bob Zrenner's sweet-smoky, bacon-wrapped dates; extra-crunchy *patatas bravas*; and luxurious, if humble, braised Brussels sprouts offset by sweet caramelized onions, toasted chiles, punchy blue cheese, pine nuts, and a silken poached egg. A straightforward cocktail list and affordable wines lend hangout appeal.

BOKA, 1729 N. Halsted St., Lincoln Park, Chicago, IL 60614; (312) 337-6070; bokachicago.com; New American; $$$. As sexy as they come, this Kevin Boehm and Rob Katz–owned venture is a force to be reckoned with, thanks to Giuseppe Tentori's grown-up, Mediterranean-inflected cuisine. Begin, perhaps, with a refined, light starter of yellowfin tuna sashimi, accented by chermoula. By the time the Lucknow dusted quail arrives with mizuna gnocchi, black trumpet mushrooms, blood oranges, and sunchoke puree accompaniments, you'll find yourself making follow-up reservations on the spot.

Bongo Room, 1470 N. Milwaukee Ave., Wicker Park, Chicago, IL 60622; (773) 489-0690; thebongoroom.com; American; $$. A hit with the brunch bunch, this casual hangover-helper turns the greasy spoon on end with dessertlike red-velvet pancakes beneath cream-cheesy sauce; a breakfast burrito stuffed with eggs and taco accoutrements; and funky riffs on French toast. Numerous creative salads and sandwiches carry through the lunch hour. **Additional locations:** 1152 S. Wabash Ave., (312) 291-0100, and 5022 N. Clark St., Andersonville, (773) 728-7900.

The Bristol, 2152 N. Damen Ave., Bucktown, Chicago, IL 60647; (773) 862-5555; thebristolchicago.com; New American; $$$. Locavores converge at Chris Pandel's sustainably minded, exposed brick Midwestern, featuring a shareable daily menu and hipster clientele. Take in the indie tunes while inhaling head-on prawns *a la plancha* in anchovy butter and simply amazing crunchy snap peas with salty whipped feta. If the pork porterhouse with dried cherry-guanciale vinaigrette is available, give it a shot. Also worthy is the otherworldly raviolo; when popped, its silky egg-yolk interior melds into a pool of nutty brown-butter sauce. At meal's end, wrangle up Amanda Rockman's Basque cake with apple sabayon.

Cafe Absinthe, 1954 W. North Ave., Wicker Park, Chicago, IL 60622; (773) 278-4488; absinthechicago.com; French; $$$. Make your way to the alley entrance of this neighborhood Frenchie, popular for its seasonal cuisine. Check out the generously sized, bacon-accented ostrich wing starter or earthy, creamy mushroom risotto with mascarpone. And anytime crisp-skinned duck breast is available, do indulge. Also, check out the prix-fixe menu on Sunday and Tuesday—at $35, it's a pretty good deal.

Cafe Ba-Ba-Reeba!, 2024 N. Halsted St., Lincoln Park, Chicago, IL 60614; (773) 935-5000; cafebabareeba.com; Spanish/Tapas; $$. This Lettuce Entertain You joint helped make tapas a local household name. Happy-hour enticements—a pintxos menu with short rib–stuffed piquillo, for example—draw crowds. But anything on the menu tastes extra-enticing when you're passing the hours on the enclosed patio. Veer toward the small plates—the paella is just so-so—such as chorizo-wrapped Manchego dates, beef tenderloin brochettes with caramelized onions, or meatballs in sherry-accented tomato sauce. Come for brunch, when the bleary-eyed sip rounds of deceptively fruity sangria.

Cafe des Architectes, Sofitel Chicago Water Tower, 20 E. Chestnut St., Gold Coast, Chicago, IL 60611; (312) 324-4063; cafedes architectes.com; French; $$$$. Greg Biggers, a veteran of **Tru** (p. 91), shakes things up, beginning with Meyer lemon tortellini with Tasso ham, polenta, and heady Moroccan veal jus. The story continues with honey-miso halibut, spring onions, and duck confit Wellington, and butter-poached Maine lobster with lobster mousse and elderflower beurre blanc. For a finale, consider a cheese flight or whimsical rhubarb-raspberry vacherin with Greek yogurt cream, port wine reduction, and raspberry cotton candy.

Cafe Laguardia, 2111 W. Armitage Ave., Bucktown, Chicago, IL 60647; (773) 862-5996; cafelaguardia.com; Cuban; $$. There's no pretension at this family-run Cuban, dispensing dynamite ham croquettes. Among entrees, the crisp, fried pork chops are head and shoulders above all else, though it's rare to encounter a dud. Great mojitos and live music ratchet up the volume—but also heighten the fun factor.

Cafe Spiaggia, 980 N. Michigan Ave., Level Two, Gold Coast, Chicago, IL 60611; (312) 280-2750; spiaggiarestaurant.com; Italian; $$$. The (somewhat) more affordable sister to Tony Mantuano's nearby **Spiaggia** (p. 88) features rustic-chic, frescoed confines and intoxicating Italian eats. Nibble on house-cured sardines, topping crostini with bright salsa verde, raisins, and fennel; young goat's cheese with apple blossom honey; or barely there gnocchi with rich wild-boar *ragù*. Craving porchetta? This version, hit with Calabrian peppers, will ruin you for the rest.

Cape Cod Room, The Drake Hotel, 140 E. Walton Pl., Gold Coast, Chicago, IL 60611; (312) 787-2200; thedrakehotel.com; Seafood; $$$. Not as stodgy as its address would suggest, this circa-1933 blast from the past—decked in nautical trappings—keeps its menu true to form and its fabled carved-wood bar intact. You'll want to get the Dover sole, prepared tableside, and lobster thermidor (if money allows). There are more contemporary options, too, like salt-roasted prawns with dry-aged pork–studded collards, mascarpone grits, and lemon vinaigrette.

Carmine's, 1043 N. Rush St., Gold Coast, Chicago, IL 60611; (312) 988-7676; rosebudrestaurants.com; Italian; $$$. This Rush and Division mainstay, a member of the Rosebud family of restaurants, has a dark, clubby, and convivial feel and loyal, if aging, following. They come for Soprano-esque staples, like fried calamari, bruschetta, and clams baked in garlic butter as well as a hand-rolled meatball salad. There are requisites like chicken Parm and Milanese as well.

Carniceria y Taqueria Tierra Caliente, 1402 N. Ashland Ave., Wicker Park, Chicago, IL 60622; (773) 772-9804; Mexican; $. Fans of places within spaces will warm to this solid taqueria, set in a *supermercado*. Terrific tacos are the main draw, starting with gold-standard *al pastor*. Carved from the spit, they're juicy and charred on best days and prove well beyond average on the worst ones. And the *carne asada*? When it's right off the grill, it's outstanding. As for the unctuous *barbacoa*, pause only to zap it with superior salsa verde and a squirt of lime.

Carriage House, 1700 W. Division St., Wicker Park, Chicago, IL 60622; (773) 384-9700; carriagehousechicago.com; Regional American; $$$. Mark Steuer's special, skillful meals honor tradition and exhibit the new soul of the South in equal measure. The Old Bay–fragranced Low Country boil is a finger-licking affair, with each component prepared at its peak. Meanwhile, lush, lighter-than-expected she-crab soup gives way to a picnic board showcasing greatest hits: shaved country ham, shrimp remoulade, pimento cheese, bread and butter pickles, and pickled eggs. Pair any—or all—with complex, balanced cocktails that are worth the trip alone. Sister property The Bedford, where Steuer also chefs, is at 1612 W. Division St., (773) 235-8800.

Cemitas Puebla, 3619 W. North Ave., Humboldt Park, Chicago, IL 60647; (773) 772-8435; cemitaspuebla.com; Mexican; $. The foods of Puebla take center stage at this neighborhood joint with a cultlike following. Its namesake sandwich is an unequivocal must, its sesame-studded roll stocked with avocado, house-marinated chipotles, a sprinkle of Oaxacan cheese, *papalo* (seasonally), and a choice of meat. The *carne asada* and the gut-busting Atomica—Milanesa, guajillo pork enchilada, and ham—are masterpieces.

Chickpea, 2018 W. Chicago Ave., Ukrainian Village, Chicago, IL 60622; (773) 384-9930; chickpeaonthego.com; Middle Eastern; $. Jerry Suqi (Narcisse, Sugar, La Pomme Rouge) switched gears for this family affair: His mother turns out expertly prepared kibbe; tender, lemony *malfoof* (rice-and-lamb-filled cabbage rolls); and a tangy dip of homemade yogurt, zucchini, and mint to hipsters amid walls hung with import movie posters.

Cipollina, 1543 N. Damen Ave., Wicker Park, Chicago, IL 60622; (773) 227-6300; cipollinadeli.com; Deli; $$. Carol Watson (**Milk & Honey Cafe**, p. 78) is behind the enticing array of Italian preparations at this quaint, cool-kid carryout where panini are given the porchetta treatment. A palate-perking Italian sub—layered with wisps of imported meat and daubed with house-made giardiniera—is the standout handheld, along with a number donning prosciutto, Parmesan-truffle butter, Calabrian peppers, and arugula. Seasonal orange-lavender sandwich cookies and almond croissants address the sweeter side.

Coast Sushi, 2045 N. Damen Ave., Bucktown, Chicago, IL 60647; (773) 235-5775; coastsushi.net; Japanese; $$$. Downright sexy, this low-lit sashimi slinger is BYOB. Signature rolls like the White Dragon—spicy-sauced shrimp tempura, wasabi *tobiko,* cream cheese, and scallion with tempura crunch—may turn off purists, but that's beside the point. The kitchen also sees success with fiery orange-tamarind duck breast, its skin glistening and crisp. **Additional locations:** 1700 S. Michigan Ave., (312) 662-1700; 2545 Prairie Ave., Evanston, (847) 328-2221.

Coco Pazzo Cafe, 636 N. St. Clair St., Streeterville, Chicago, IL 60611; (312) 664-2777; cocopazzocafe.com; Italian; $$. The casual **Coco Pazzo** (p. 102) cousin is equally ingredient-driven, though more straightforward in its execution. Start with antipasti, perhaps *sfogliatelle,* stuffed with roasted mushrooms and asparagus. Then, choose appetizer portions of pasta—perhaps hand-cut chitarrine—saving room for Tuscan seafood stew. Dine alfresco when weather allows.

Covo Gyro Market, 1482 N. Milwaukee Ave., Wicker Park, Chicago, IL 60622; (312) 626-2660; covogyro.com; Greek; $. You can thank **Prasino** (p. 192) owners (also of Wild Monk) for this casual, counter-service concept, where gyros are built from beef-lamb, chicken, or standout pork. Choose your preferred style—puffy gyro, mini-gyro, or salad—and add vibrant toppings like roasted garlic–hot pepper aioli, *tzatziki,* red onion, and crumbled feta. Then, dig in at this hip, Edison bulb–illuminated spot.

Cumin, 1414 N. Milwaukee Ave., Wicker Park, Chicago, IL 60622; (773) 342-1414; cumin-chicago.com; Nepalese/Indian; $$. Rocking out aromatic dishes in a contemporary setting, this hip haunt has your standards: samosas, *biryani,* and chicken tikka masala. But it's the

Nepalese dishes—like chicken momo, steamed dumplings filled with herbaceous, minced chicken—you'll pine for. Don't pass go without ordering the *palungo ko saag,* wilted spinach, spruced up with mustard, cumin, and fenugreek seeds, plus roasted garlic and fiery chiles.

Da Lobsta, 12 E. Cedar St., Gold Coast, Chicago, IL 60611; (312) 929-2423; dalobstachicago.com; Seafood; $$. Take a trip to New England at this summery Gold Coast spot, where a classic tarragon-laced lobster roll gives way to ones with Greek or Indian flavors. Blue crab and shrimp are admirable stand-ins. Either way, clam chowder and Cape Cod chips are requisite accompaniments.

deca Restaurant + Bar, Ritz-Carlton Chicago, 160 E. Pearson St., Gold Coast, Chicago, IL 60611; (312) 573-5160; decarestaurant .com; French; $$$. Located on the 12th floor of the luxury Ritz-Carlton hotel, this casual, mid-priced brasserie appeals to modern-day diners with casual eats from Mark Payne. A highlight of the menu is the glorious seafood tower, chock-full of oysters and crab claws, plump shrimp, and Manila clams. Other options range from escargot with spring garlic to steak au poivre with mushroom gratin and beet jus.

Del Seoul, 2568 N. Clark St., Lincoln Park, Chicago, IL 60614; (773) 248-4227; delseoul.com; Korean; $. Drawing inspiration from Kogi trucks, this updated Korean tackles banh mi (*soju*-marinated *bulgogi,* smoky *gochujang* pork), *kalbi* tacos, bibimbap, and barbecue plates with sautéed onions, house kimchi, and baby bok choy—all on the cheap.

En Hakkore, 1840 N. Damen Ave., Bucktown, Chicago, IL 60647; (773) 772-9880; Korean; $$. As lovely to set eyes on as it is to indulge, the bibimbap features a rainbow's worth of fresh and pickled veg. Enjoy it—and pork, beef, and mushroom *paratha* tacos, drizzled with creamy *gochujang*—at this sweet spot's rustic, communal tables.

Enoteca Roma, 2146 W. Division St., Ukrainian Village, Chicago, IL 60622; (773) 342-1011; enotecaroma.com; Italian; $$. This rustic Italian wine bar—an offshoot of Letizia's Natural Bakery—has a not-so-secret weapon: a picturesque garden patio in back, where couples converse over mix-and-match bruschetta, antipasti, and cheese and salumi platters. Baked terrines, pastas, and pizzas offer something more substantial. A large vino and beer list is thrown in for good measure.

Etno Village Grill, 2580 N. Lincoln Ave., Lincoln Park, Chicago, IL 60614; (773) 698-8069; etnogrill.com; Eastern European; $. Perched at the crux of Lincoln, Sheffield, and Wrightwood, this casual, customizable *cevap* stop is a noteworthy, Balkans-tinged alternative to staid fast food—not to mention one with a hormone- and antibiotic-free approach. Zero in on the grilled beef-pork sausage, tucked into artisan bread and topped with a dizzying array of condiments. (Make sure the salty, signature feta spread is among them.) On your next visit, nothing but the Camembert, ginger-poached pear, and applewood smoked bacon–topped burger and a spicy, well-dressed *pleska* patty handheld will do. Always, Parmesan fries are the must-have accompaniment.

Flying Saucer, 1123 N. California Ave., Humboldt Park, Chicago, IL 60622; (773) 342-9076; flyingsaucerchicago.com; American; $. Enveloping in the way only a retro diner can be, this cash-only Humboldt Park haunt is a vegetarian-friendly daytime find for build-your-own omelets and Mexican-tinged eye-openers, like *huevos volando,* eggs set atop corn tortillas, smothered with guajillo, sour cream, and Chihuahua cheese and sidled by addictive black beans. Mind you, no one could call the brown rice La Bazza bowl boring, what with its commingling of tofu, kale, and a slew of south-of-the-border condiments.

For lunch, fill up on the "kitchen sink" salad or grilled rosemary chicken sandwich, topped with bacon and basil aioli.

Franks 'N' Dawgs, 1863 N. Clybourn Ave., Lincoln Park, Chicago, IL 60614; (312) 281-5187; franksndawgs.com; Hot Dogs; $. Aussie Alexander Brunacci is behind this ramped-up stand with a formula that works. Some of the encased meats are made in-house; the artisanal ingredients are stuffed into French-style *pain de mie* buns; and local chefs are enlisted to create signature, gourmet sausages. Try the brat corn dog coated in Anson Mills polenta batter—you'll never go state fair again. Whether you settle on a the Muscles from Brussels (smoked garlic sausage with crispy Brussels sprout leaves, rendered pancetta, pickled carrots, onions, fennel, and horseradish, zapped with black pepper mayo, white balsamic reduction, and a sprinkle of pretzel crumbs) or the Tur-Doggin (turkey-date sausage with crispy duck confit, herb-garlic aioli, pickled onion relish, and pickled carrots), it's a revelatory experience that won't bust your budget.

Geja's Cafe, 340 W. Armitage Ave., Lincoln Park, Chicago, IL 60614; (773) 281-9101; gejascafe.com; Fondue; $$$. Romance is in the air at this intimate subterranean den, an anniversary-appropriate fondue destination. Plunk pumpernickel into a cauldron of melty, kirsch-infused Gruyère; place beef tenderloin, lobster, and shrimp in bubbling oil, dunking the results in an array of sauces once cooked; and finish with a flaming chocolate finale. A large wine list and live flamenco guitar are added appeals.

Gemini Bistro, 2075 N. Lincoln Ave., Lincoln Park, Chicago, IL 60614; (773) 525-2522; geminibistrochicago.com; American; $$$. Jason Paskewitz is onto something at this inviting, contemporary bistro with a roster of comforting, by-the-books small, medium, and large plates built from familiar ingredients. Robust, creamless tomato soup with grilled cheese and a filler-light jumbo lump crab cake with

Tabasco aioli are strengths. But the prime burger—served on a potato roll that barely contains the juices—is nothing to sniff at.

Gibsons Bar & Steakhouse, 1028 N. Rush St., Gold Coast, Chicago, IL 60611; (312) 266-8999; gibsonssteakhouse.com; Steak House; $$$. A gold-standard steak house, this joint serves expense-account steaks, chops, and sweet, football-size lobster tail in the heart of the so-called Viagra Triangle. Start with the fantastic shrimp cocktail, served on a bed of ice with nose-clearing cocktail sauce. Or, grab some jumbo crab claws with Dijon dipping sauce and slurp an oversize, ice-cold martini. Clear room for the nicely marbled Chicago cut (a bone-in rib eye) with a brittle pepper crust. Sides—like the double-baked potato—and ridiculously large desserts are meant to be shared. **Additional locations:** 5464 N. River Rd., Rosemont, (847) 928-9900; 2105 S. Spring Rd., Oak Brook, (630) 954-0000.

Green Zebra, 1460 W. Chicago Ave., Noble Square, Chicago, IL 60642; (312) 243-7100; greenzebrachicago.com; Vegetarian; $$$. This dazzler is beloved for its deceptively straightforward menu of largely vegetarian small plates. Things that are the stuff of dreams: creamy sunchoke soup with hints of Granny Smith apple, preserved lemon, pine nuts, and German thyme; artfully plated hen-of-the-woods mushroom pâté, with Vidalia onion marmalade and herb-flecked butter; and an organic farm egg, offset by smoked potato purée with country sourdough for sopping up the yolky goodness.

Honey 1 BBQ, 2241 N. Western Ave., Bucktown, Chicago, IL 60647; (773) 227-5130; honey1bbq.com; Barbecue; $$. Roll up your sleeves and prepare to pig out—pitmaster Robert Adams's wood-smoked barbecue is the real deal. Chewy, full-flavored rib tips; spicy, spurting hot links; and sauced sparerib racks—all worthy of a detour—team with addictive, fried, sauce-free wings just begging to be dunked in house-made sauce.

Howells & Hood, 435 N. Michigan Ave., Streeterville, Chicago, IL 60611; (312) 262-5310; howellsandhood.com; American; $$$. Scott Walton (Markethouse) has taken his locavore-leaning skills to this vast, Tribune Tower–centered dining room, a former press room named for the building's neo-Gothic architects, John Howells and Raymond Hood. An insane number of taps (114) are meant for pairing with Walton's refined eats and storied charcuterie. Begin with smoked, potted Berkshire pork with braised mustard seeds, sour green apple, and apple-cider mustard, or splurge on the towering lobster shortcake with spicy sherry cream. When it's warm, enjoy candied bacon, stout, and pecan pie with bourbon sabayon on the expansive patio.

HotChocolate, 1747 N. Damen Ave., Bucktown, Chicago, IL 60647; (773) 489-1747; hotchocolatechicago.com; American; $$. At Mindy Segal's solid, market-driven restaurant, it's true that the desserts shine. However, the pastry chef's savory side conjures up "oohs" and "ahhs," too. That's especially true with Dennis Stover (ex–**Longman & Eagle,** p. 232) in the kitchen, crafting pan-seared barramundi with rhubarb, house-made pickles, and creamed ramp and dandelion greens, as well as house-ground lamb sausage flatbread with Carr Valley Creama Kasa cheese, arugula, oregano oil, and pickled beets. But don't feel bad coming for the over-the-top finales alone: Warm Québécoise pie, made with Burton's maple syrup, is worth the trip.

Hugo's Frog Bar & Fish House, 1024 N. Rush St., Gold Coast, Chicago, IL 60611; (312) 640-0999; hugosfrogbar.com; Seafood; $$$$. This clubby adjunct to **Gibsons Bar & Steakhouse** (p. 71) shares a kitchen and offers the same superior steaks, while emphasizing super-fresh catches and its namesake amphibian in garlic butter. Great beginnings include the shrimp cocktail, king crab fingers, and lump crab cake. From there, it's on to Alaskan halibut *en papillote,* pan-seared scallops with truffle butter, or lobster tail with lemon butter. Desserts are sized for sharing—with a crowd. **Additional locations:** 55 S. Main St., Naperville, (630) 548-3764; 3300 S. River Rd., Des Plaines, (847) 768-5200.

Irazu, 1865 N. Milwaukee Ave., Bucktown, Chicago, IL 60647; (773) 252-5687; irazuchicago.com; Costa Rican; $$. Providing a reliable entry point for those unfamiliar with the food of Central America, this welcoming, cash-only eatery kicks things off with fried plantains topped with roasted garlic oil. Another dish you'll be smitten with is the *casado,* rib eye with rice, beans, plantains, and an over-easy egg alongside cabbage salad. And don't miss the *pepito* sandwich, steak with onions and cheese, as well as the oatmeal shake.

Kai Zan, 2557 W. Chicago Ave., Humboldt Park, Chicago, IL 60622; (773) 278-5776; eatatkaizan.com; Japanese; $$$. Unconventional only begins to describe this petite, modern sushi bar from brothers Melvin and Carlo Vizconde. And while you'll find more familiar and immensely enjoyable dishes in sushi, noodle, lava rock–charred, and teppanyaki form, the real magic happens when you choose the chef-designed *omakase* menu. Breathtaking presentation aside, balanced, well-conceived dishes—enoki bacon or a wasabi taco, perhaps—surprise. However, so do the specials, be it pristine, whole sea urchin or an *unagi* popper with cream cheese and jalapeño. Tabs stay relatively low, thanks to an affordable $5 corkage fee for BYO.

Las Manas Tamales, Green City Market, Clark Street and Stockton Drive, Lincoln Park, Chicago, IL 60614; (773) 860-0832; green citymarket.org; lasmanastamales.com; Mexican; $. Tamale vendor

Amber Romo Wojcinski appears at the Green City Market year-round, hawking her hyper-local green chile chicken, red chile pork, and black bean–studded veggie chili versions, augmented by a lineup of seasonal fillings, perhaps chicken with peach-jalapeño salsa or roasted butternut squash with bacon and tomatillo. Find her indoors at the Peggy Notebaert Nature Museum, 2430 N. Cannon Dr., (773) 755-5100, when the deep freeze sets in, November through March.

Las Palmas, 1835 W. North Ave., Wicker Park, Chicago, IL 60622; (773) 289-4991; laspalmaschicago.com; Mexican; $$. This vibrant, artsy neighborhood gem—a creative, Frida Kahlo–hung offshoot of the same-named mini-chain—has it going on. The menu takes a turn for the inventive, with options like pineapple and tequila-marinated skirt steak, served atop rum-spiked plantains with *papas fritas* with mango pico de gallo, and orange-blackberry-glazed roast duck with grilled peach and goat cheese salad. Don't miss the creative cocktails, such as a refreshing cucumber margarita, but do grab a perch on the secluded patio when weather allows.

Le Bouchon, 1958 N. Damen Ave., Bucktown, Chicago, IL 60647; (773) 862-6600; lebouchonofchicago.com; French; $$$. Petite, loud, and pleasing, Le Sardine's sibling serves a similar spread. Make a meal of steamed mussels and an onion tart, or begin with house-made pâté, followed by robust grilled hanger steak with red-wine sauce, slow-simmered beef Bourguignon, or roast duck *à l'orange*. Ubiquitous as it may be, the silky crème brûlée is a must.

Les Nomades, 222 E. Ontario St., Streeterville, Chicago, IL 60611; (312) 649-9010; lesnomades.net; French; $$$$. Harking back to another time and place, this sophisticate with an elegant, tucked away town-house setting, winning wine list, and haute French fare is as special occasion—and solid—as ever. Here, Roland Liccioni quietly and skillfully crafts what few in the city do anymore: *très chic,* technique-driven French cuisine. Sit pretty over a lobe of seared *foie gras*, its creative companions banana water, tart apple puree and fig confit, or Alaskan halibut with trofie pasta, in sorrel sauce with carrot hollandaise. Otherwise, skip the guesswork and opt for the spendy tasting menu.

Lillie's Q, 1856 W. North Ave., Bucktown, Chicago, IL 60622; (773) 772-5500; lilliesq.com; Barbecue; $$. After a devastating fire that totaled his original location, Charlie McKenna and his bastion for competition-winning barbecue are back. Rejoice over beer-battered, fried pickles and oysters with North Carolina-style vinegar sauce, stunning pulled pork, and indulgent mac and cheese. If you happen to be at the Chicago French Market, 131 N. Clinton St., (773) 772-5500, it's another way to get your fill.

Lito's Empanadas, 2566 N. Clark St., Lincoln Park, Chicago, IL 60614; (773) 857-1337; litosempanadas.com; Colombian; $. Snack on piping-hot, savory pockets without throwing your budget. The classic beef, studded with briny olives and sweet raisins, is a go-to. Less traditional—but still standout—is the ham-and-pineapple-inflected Hawaiian and heaven-sent Nutella number. Another outpost is at 1437 W. Taylor St., (312) 846-6216.

Little Market Brasserie, Talbott Hotel, 10 E. Delaware Pl., Gold Coast, Chicago, IL 60611; (312) 640-8141; littlemarket brasserie.com; American; $$. Big-name Chef Ryan Poli (**Tavernita**, p. 131) handles the crowds at this moody, cocktail-centric Mercadito Hospitality venture. Get interactive with an order of pull-apart monkey bread, or dig into a mound of short rib, gravy, and cheese curd–topped poutine. The catch-all menu has something for everyone, whether it's oysters, a South Side–inspired Big Baby burger, or grilled cheese with a fried egg, bacon, avocado, and Sriracha sauce. Tippling

Bros.' design-your-own charged cocktails, made with house sodas, share space with other inventive libations and a large boutique wine and craft beer list.

L2O, Belden-Stratford Hotel, 2300 N. Lincoln Park West, Lincoln Park, Chicago, IL 60614; (773) 868-0002; l2orestaurant.com; Seafood; $$$$. Everything about this Lettuce Entertain You marvel—the austere, spa-y setting, the masterful tasting and prix-fixe menus, the carefully curated wine list—flies in the face of the prevailing, modern-day sentiment: that dining should be accessible, affordable, and local. But this superlative seafooder does what it wants and does so with swagger. About all that's heard in response is a collective "ooooh." From start to finish, dining here is a rarefied experience, one in which flavor pairings—Scottish blue lobster with romaine, mussels, and apples, or a lime parfait paired with unlikely avocado, tarragon, and Cara Cara oranges, for example—transport and transform those who splurge.

LuxBar, 18 E. Bellevue Pl., Gold Coast, Chicago, IL 60611; (312) 642-3400; luxbar.com; American; $$$. Set amid a sea of pricier picks, this wood-paneled place is refreshing. Serving savory staples—tomato soup, sliders, buttermilk fried chicken—to all manner of diners, it also serves the big brother Gibsons' steaks, only at a less frenetic pace. Come on Friday and Saturday nights for prime rib, or tumble out of bed for weekend brunch.

M Burger, 161 E. Huron St., Streeterville, Chicago, IL 60611; (312) 254-8500; mburgerchicago.com; Burgers; $. This Rich Melman-backed, secret-sauced burger and shake shack presents an affordable choice amid a backdrop of Mag Mile excess. The thing is, the other options—an all-natural chicken Nurse Betty with tomatoes, avocado, and pepper jack; the chopped chicken salad—are good as well.

Additional locations: 5 W. Ontario St., (312) 428-3548; Thompson Center, 100 W. Randolph St., (312) 578-1478; and Water Tower Place, 835 N. Michigan Ave., (312) 867-1549.

MANA Food Bar, 1742 W. Division St., Wicker Park, Chicago, IL 60622; (773) 342-1742; manafoodbar.com; Vegetarian; $$. One of the most exciting vegetarian places to open in years comes from veterans of Sushi Wabi and **De Cero** (p. 103). The multiculti results—served in a trim, minimalist setting—range from wakame-cucumber salad with daikon sprouts in lemon-sesame dressing to tofu *bulgogi* with shiitake to a blue-cheese tart with caramelized onions. Stay and sip sake cocktails, or grab grub from the pickup window on Division when dining (oh-so-virtuously) on the fly.

Masaki, 990 Mies Van Der Rohe Way, Streeterville, Chicago, IL 60611; (312) 280-9100; masakichicago.com; Japanese/Sushi; $$$$. Gracious dining awaits for a price at this stunning prix-fixe Japanese, where *omakase* menus focus varyingly on raw and cooked preparations. Whatever you decide, sensational sushi and perfectly cooked treasures of the sea—steamed miso black cod, pan-seared scallops atop cha-soba and asparagus—await. Expert sommelier pairings further elevate the experience, which can easily ring in at $500 for two. Its dissimilar sibling is **Pelago Ristorante** (p. 81) in the Rafaello Hotel.

Michael Jordan's Steakhouse, InterContinental Chicago, 505 N. Michigan Ave., Gold Coast, Chicago, IL 60611; (312) 321-8823; mjshchicago.com; Steak House; $$$$. A showy setting and even showier steak-house fare are the draw at this Michael Jordan namesake, with locations in New York and Connecticut. Interestingly, some of the most memorable options don't contain beef at all. The extravagant shellfish platter brims with shrimp, lobster, crab, and oysters; the tower of garlic bread gets blanketed Roth Käse blue cheese fondue; and the colossal crab cake with Meyer lemon aioli stands as yet another perfect example. But that's not to say the 32-ounce tomahawk rib eye for two is anything other than a sight to behold. Pair selections with wine from the impressive cellar.

Mike Ditka's, The Tremont Hotel, 100 E. Chestnut St., Gold Coast, Chicago, IL 60611; (312) 587-8989; mikeditkaschicago.com; Steak House; $$$$. Da coach's quintessential Chicago steak house serves a mighty juicy pork chop, noteworthy half-pound burger, and self-professed "kick-ass" 30-ounce paddle steak, as well as sustainable seafood. Par for the course, it all takes place in a manly, memorabilia-filled setting. There is also a location at 2 Mid America Plaza, Oakbrook Terrace, (630) 572-2200.

Milk & Honey Cafe, 1920 W. Division St., Wicker Park, Chicago, IL 60622; (773) 395-9434; milkandhoneycafe.com; Cafe; $. The masses descend on weekends, but it's understandable given this cheery storefront serves reputable, brunch-y bites, like orange brioche French toast and trademark granola. During calmer times, sandwiches—from a smoked turkey Reuben to a BLT with thick slabs of bacon—suffice. When seating is at a premium, consider stopping by its counterpart, Italian-style deli **Cipollina** (p. 66).

Mirai Sushi, 2020 W. Division St., Wicker Park, Chicago, IL 60622; (773) 862-8500; miraisushi.com; Japanese/Sushi; $$$. Oozing style—sans airs—Miae Lim's upscale, bi-level sushi and sake bar strikes a balance between classic and global-leaning flavors. Take the *sakana* carpaccio—tuna, salmon, and whitefish with cilantro, capers, and sesame oil—as an example. When dining here, get the Bin Cho, citrus-dressed baby tuna with arugula, too, and the Spicy Mono, octopus topped with spicy tuna and sweet *unagi* sauce.

Mon Ami Gabi, Belden-Stratford Hotel, 2300 N. Lincoln Park West, Lincoln Park, Chicago, IL 60614; (773) 348-8886; monamigabi

.com; French; $$$. Consistency reigns at this Lettuce Entertain You bistro, where the steak frites—sauced with maître d'hôtel butter or prepared au poivre style—and lemony chicken paillard win every time. Then again, the skate wing shellacked with caper–brown butter doesn't exactly falter. Grab a seat on the patio when it's warm. There's also a location at 260 Oakbrook Center, Oak Brook, (630) 472-1900.

Morton's The Steakhouse, 1050 N. State St., Gold Coast, Chicago, IL 60610; (312) 266-4820; mortons.com; Steak House; $$$$. This original outpost—which spawned a national chain—exudes clubby charm with service, complete with tableside presentation, to match. Prime steaks (especially the bone-in rib eye) are really the way to go, though its lobster tail, crab cakes, and chocolate cake appease its suited-up clientele as well. **Additional locations:** 65 E. Wacker Pl., (312) 201-0410; Schaumburg, 1470 McConnor Pkwy., (847) 413-8771; Rosemont, 9525 W. Bryn Mawr Ave., (847) 678-5155; Northbrook, 699 Skokie Blvd., (847) 205-5111; and Naperville, 1751 Freedom Dr., (630) 577-1372.

North Pond, 2610 N. Cannon Dr., Lincoln Park, Chicago, IL 60614; (773) 477-5845; northpondrestaurant.com; New American; $$$$. Bruce Sherman's arts and crafts–style dining room—set so picturesquely within Lincoln Park proper—takes a farm-to-table to approach to dishes, be it warm, cinnamon-scented carrot soup with smoky, charred squid, chorizo, and carrot "caviar" or herbaceous, pancetta-wrapped rabbit saddle with rhubarb jam, green garlic, and a hazelnut-rabbit "truffle." Provided everyone concurs (it's a full-table affair), the tasting menu is a wise choice.

NYC Bagel Deli, 1001 W. North Ave., Lincoln Park, Chicago, IL 60642; (312) 274-1278; nycbd.com; Bagels; $. Corey Kaplan's pleasantly chewy, kettle-boiled bagels are the vessel for sandwiches, including a delish Reuben, built from Boar's Head meats. But you can also enjoy them lox-style or smeared with jalapeño or artichoke-Parmesan cream cheese. New York pizza and fresh salads play a supporting role. **Additional locations:** 300 S. Wacker Dr., (312) 922-7500; and 515 N. Dearborn St., (312) 923-9999.

Oiistar, 1385 N. Milwaukee Ave., Wicker Park, Chicago, IL 60622; (773) 360-8791; oiistar.com; Asian Fusion; $$. Ramen stars at this birchwood kitchen, where most versions are made with a rich, porky, 18-hour simmer. The signature *tonkotsu*-style version features pork loin or pork belly, tree ear mushrooms, a soft-boiled egg, garlic, and a drizzle of spicy oil. By contrast, the spicy Pozolmen bowl—a pozole and ramen hybrid—bobs with hunks of pork, pico de gallo, and a tangle of toothsome noodles. Focus on them, and maybe an accompanying *bao,* rather than apps. If you're daring, consider the aggressively seasoned French kimchi soup with andouille sausage and a swath of Provolone.

Orange, 2413 N. Clark St., Lincoln Park, Chicago, IL 60614; (773) 549-7833; orangerestaurantchicago.com; New American; $$. Earning fame for "fruishi"—fruit sushi—and creative pancake flights, brunch lovers wait endlessly for a table at this trusty joint. Coconut-infused French toast skewers and pesto green eggs and ham further clarify why. Another location is at 2011 W. Roscoe St., (773) 248-0999.

The Original Gino's East Pizza, 162 E. Superior St., Gold Coast, Chicago, IL 60611; (312) 266-3337; ginoseast.com; Pizza; $. Tourists (and enough locals) don't mind waiting for seats at this legend, famous for it brightly sauced, cornmeal-crusted deep-dish delights. Sausage is a safe bet, though many a hard-core carnivore gorges on the Meaty Legend, a gut-expander loaded with bacon, Canadian bacon, pepperoni, and sausage. There are numerous city and suburban locations, including at 633 N. Wells St., (312) 988-4200; 521 S. Dearborn St., (312) 939-1818; and 2801 N. Lincoln Ave., (773) 327-3737.

Papa's Cache Sabroso, 2517 W. Division St., Humboldt Park, Chicago, IL 60622; (773) 862-8313; papascachesabroso.com; Puerto Rican; $. Yep, you'll want the solid steak *jibarito* from this BYO. Sandwiched between slices of smashed, fried, garlicky plantains, its transcendent. However, you'd also be wise to order the garlic-bathed *tostones* and *pollo chon,* chicken lacquered with garlic mojo and glistened in the rotisserie.

The Peasantry, 2723 N. Clark St., Lincoln Park, Chicago, IL 60614; (773) 868-4888; thepeasantry.com; New American; $$. Gussied-up street food is the focus at this **Franks 'N' Dawgs** (p. 70) follow-up, which delivers some of the time. And while over-the-top preparations are hit-or-miss, more straightforward choices—the hanger steak and bone marrow burger with triple truffle fries, christened with truffle butter, salt, and oil, for example—justify the trip. For dessert, keep it simple with a scoop of local Black Dog gelato.

Pelago Ristorante, Rafaello Hotel, 201 E. Delaware Pl., Gold Coast, Chicago, IL 60611; (312) 280-0700; pelagorestaurant.com; Italian; $$$. Mauro Mafrici (**Masaki,** p. 77) serves three squares daily at this serene spot in a boutique hotel, where riffs on routine Italian entice. Perfect veal ravioli get a boost from pistachio sauce, while pesto-sauced *trofie* lounges with string beans and potatoes. Meanwhile, gremolata-showered monkfish takes an osso bucco approach, and rolled, duck-filled pork arrives redolent of marjoram. Desserts—like lemon cake with grapefruit salad and orange sorbet—sweeten the pot.

Perennial Virant, 1800 N. Lincoln Ave., Lincoln Park, Chicago, IL 60614; (312) 981-7070; perennialchicago.com; New American; $$$. Rob Katz and Kevin Boehm of **BOKA** (p. 62) back this inviting, sustainably minded American bistro with a fab patio; rustic-chic, wood-trimmed dining room; and Paul Virant (**Vie,** 195) is in the kitchen, whipping up stuff inspired by nearby Green City Market. Expect dishes that make the most of the season's bounty (and, often, the bounty preserved): deviled eggs with seasonal giardiniera; crispy carnaroli rice with cheese curds, pea shoots, smoked spring-onion vinaigrette, and pickled summer beans; and grilled Illinois venison loin, plated with hummus, wilted spinach, garlic-mustard chimichurri, and preserved eggplant, to name a few. For dessert, get the chèvre fritters, paired with seasonal jam and the chef's hive honey.

Phil's Last Stand, 2258 W. Chicago Ave., Ukrainian Village, Chicago, IL 60622; (773) 245-3287; philslaststand.com; Hot Dogs; $. Helmed by its ever-present namesake, this stand's high-quality, charred dogs are of the natural-casing Vienna variety. Almost as wow-inducing are the killer fried shrimp and signature Fatso cheeseburger that's all redolent of grill smoke. Perhaps the biggest sur-prise, though, comes in the form of a veggie dog, a cylindrical, fried sweet-potato mixture garnished with all the Chicago-style fixings. That and the excellent char-grilled salami with grilled onion, cheddar, and mustard.

Pizzeria da Nella, 1443 W. Fullerton Ave., Lincoln Park, IL 60614; (773) 281-6600; pizzeriadanella.com; Pizza; $$. In a city filled with great pizza joints, Nella Grassano's is unquestionably one of, if not *the* most authentic in the Neapolitan department. The sparse space is an appropriate place to enjoy dishes—white balsamic-marinated salmon, burrata with prosciutto, and garlicky tomato bruschetta—prepared with a light but expert hand, allowing the ingredients to shine. As for those wood-fired pies, well, they're about as close to perfection as you're going to get.

Podhalanka, 1549 W. Division St., Wicker Park, Chicago, IL 60622; (773) 486-6655; Polish; $. There's no vibe to speak of at this dank, old-school gem, where cold-weather Polish comforts—tangy white borscht with sausage, pierogi generously topped with sour cream, stuffed cabbage—fortify. Bar stools are the seat of choice, but it's fruity *kompot,* rather than booze, that's dispensed.

Pozoleria San Juan, 1523 N. Pulaski Rd., Humboldt Park, Chicago, IL 60651; (773) 276-5825; pozoleriasanjuan.com; Mexican; $$. Restorative hominy soup is the heart of this soulful Mexican diner. Choose from *roja, verde,* and *blanco* broths, all of them arriving with umpteen add-ins, including nubs of pork, crackly *chicharrones,* radish coins, onions, slivers of cabbage, avocados, and lime. Tacos, tortas, and burritos are available as well.

The Pump Room, Public Hotel, 1301 N. State Pkwy., Gold Coast, Chicago, IL 60610; (312) 601-2970; pumproom.com; New American; $$$. This historic dining room is nothing if not popular. Thanks to a slick, cool-hued rehab, it's gorgeous, too. But the truth is, in Chicago, serious food lovers don't have much tolerance for out-of-town star chefs. Here, Jean-Georges Vongerichten designed a fatigue-inducing lineup for the masses, who clamor to sit in legendary Booth One. If you find yourself among them, get the fried chicken, popcorn-topped salted caramel ice-cream sundae, and plenty of cocktails so you can watch the scene unfold.

The Purple Pig, 500 N. Michigan Ave., Gold Coast, Chicago, IL 60611; (312) 464-1744; thepurplepigchicago.com; Small Plates; $$$. It's all about the swine and wine at this buzzing Scott Harris, Jimmy Bannos Sr., Tony Mantuano, and Chef Jimmy Bannos Jr.

collaboration, which quickly rose to acclaim for its pig ear with crispy kale, piquant cherry peppers, and fried egg. Cured meat, schmears, and heftier plates—including meltingly tender, milk-braised pork shoulder—attract an after-hours crowd, a fact that's furthered by the affordable import wine list.

Ripasso, 1619 N. Damen Ave., Wicker Park, Chicago, IL 60622; (773) 342-8799; ripassochicago.com; Italian; $$$. Theo Gilbert is a master of his craft, turning out fresh, house-made pastas, some of them carryovers from his late, great Terragusto. Of note is the truffle-scented pappardelle topped with four-meat sauce and the three-squash cappellacci in nutty sage brown butter with amaretti crumbles. Get either—and the savory, flanlike onion *sformato* (custard)—and you'll undoubtedly be pleased.

Riva, Navy Pier, 700 E. Grand Ave., Streeterville, Chicago, IL 60611; (312) 644-7482; rivanavypier.com; Seafood; $$$. Phil Stefani's stylish catch—a getaway for the tourist-weary traveler—has an amazing Lake Michigan view, coupled with pristine seafood-centric eats. Indulge in the platter of oysters, chilled shrimp, jumbo lump crab, and tuna tartare or rich lobster bisque, followed by Pacific halibut with sweet-corn essence. Plan ahead and dine when there's a fireworks display.

Roots Handmade Pizza, 1924 W. Chicago Ave., Ukrainian Village, Chicago, IL 60622; (773) 645-4949; rootspizza.com; Pizza; $$. Iowa ex-pats and pizza enthusiasts rub elbows at this Quad Cities–style pie hole from the owners of Fifty/50, where sweet, malted crust, made-in-house sausage, a distinct mozzarella-cheddar cheese mix, and a long, rectangular pizza-cut set the tone. Like anyone who has been to an Iowa joint knows, the taco pizza arrives heaped with boldly seasoned, crumbled sausage, lettuce, tomatoes, taco-seasoned chips, and sour cream as well as packets of taco sauce meant to be spurted on top. Excellent, customizable salads include every option under the sun. Made-from-scratch mozzarella sticks (cheese included) elevate the ordinary. A great beer list with many Midwesterners ties everything together.

Rustic House, 1967 N. Halsted St., Lincoln Park, Chicago, IL 60614; (312) 929-3227; rustichousechicago.com; American; $$$. A familiar feel pervades the menu at Jason Paskewitz's likeable haunt, a sibling to **Gemini Bistro** (p. 70). Steadies include the rotisserie chicken and duck à l'orange, the rich veal ragù on a nest of pappardelle, and the pancetta-studded Brussels spouts. A nightly prix fixe is a steal, even when you opt to add on three wine pairings for $25. Then again, you could always just come for the wine and the snack trio of duck fat–fried Marcona almonds, honey-peppered bacon, and marinated olives alone.

Ruxbin, 851 N. Ashland Ave., Ukrainian Village, Chicago, IL 60622; (312) 624-8509; ruxbinchicago.com; New American; $$$. Small and off-kilter, this modern American BYO from Per Se vet Edward Kim breaks the ice with conversation-starting, repurposed decor (church pew seating, a cookbook page ceiling). After an assured wait, the dialogue continues over a meal of atypical, though not totally out-there, eats: house-cut garlic fries with chipotle aioli, egg-yolk raviolo filled with house ricotta in shiitake broth, and hanger steak with chimichurri and candied bacon, for example. Craving something sweet? Brownies with smoked cherries and juniper ice cream should do the trick.

The Savoy, 1408 N. Milwaukee Ave., Wicker Park, Chicago, IL 60622; (773) 698-6925; savoychicago.com; Seafood; $$$. A nautical vibe envelops this stylish seafooder, which forgoes the obvious in favor of Sunray Venus clams with chorizo, piquillo peppers, and basil-laced absinthe broth; crispy whole fish dressed with wilted chard, Brussels sprout leaves, olives, and salsa romesco; and a surf 'n' turf of pork belly confit and seared scallops with Door County cherry mojo and cider-braised kale. There's also a lineup of absinthe cocktails, though be forewarned they're potentially palette-numbing.

Sayat Nova, 157 E. Ohio St., Streeterville, Chicago, IL 60611; (312) 644-9159; sayatnovachicago.com; Armenian; $$. Lanterns cast a moody, low glow at this quiet, all-but-hidden Armenian surprise just off of the Mag Mile. It's a pleasant pit stop for kebabs, broiled lamb chops, and tangy *labneh.* No meal is complete without a finisher of *mahalabiya,* comforting milk pudding topped with walnuts.

Schwa, 1466 N. Ashland Ave., Wicker Park, Chicago, IL 60622; (773) 252-1466; schwarestaurant.com; New American; $$$$. Michael Carlson's casual-haute BYOB defies categorization—but, really, that's the point. Dining at the restaurant, located along a dreary stretch of Ashland, is an experience, one where chefs themselves serve intricate, fantastical tasting menus to those who are privileged enough to have reservations, left on the notoriously full voicemail, confirmed. Provided you can see through the foams (and don't mind dining to the not-so-occasional hip-hop beat), Carlson's wizardry—honed alongside Grant Achatz—shines bright.

Shaman, 1438 W. Chicago Ave., Noble Square, Chicago, IL 60642; (312) 226-4175; shamanchicago.com; Mexican/Small Plates; $$. Call it some kind of a trade-off: This follow-up to **Chilam Balam** (p. 32) lets you BYO for free, but you'll have to pay in cash for your small-plates Mexican, be it a proper guac, habanero-spiked *cochinita pibil,* or wild mushroom flautas with roasted poblano sauce and pea-shoot salad. You'll be in good company if you finish with Creamsicle *tres leches.*

Signature Room at the 95th, John Hancock Center, 875 N. Michigan Ave., Streeterville, Chicago, IL 60611; (312) 787-9596; signatureroom.com; American; $$$$. Admittedly, this panoramic dining room, with its 96th-floor companion lounge, is known foremost for its pretty face. However, it challenges diners to tear their eyes from the view. The reward for doing so is seasonally driven dishes such as spring vegetable potpie with braised rabbit, a chorizo-stuffed pork chop with ancho sauce and roasted corn relish, and slow-roasted short ribs, offset by herbed polenta, braised leeks, and wild mushrooms. While taking in the glittery skyline, do peruse the extensive, global wine list.

Silom 12, 1846 N. Milwaukee Ave., Bucktown, Chicago, IL 60647; (773) 489-1212; silom12chicago.com; Thai; $$. For the most part, the menu reads like a familiar formula, but a sleek setting adds to the appeal of this stylish Bucktown Thai. Peer closer and find above-and-beyond dishes like green curry–braised osso buco and crisp outside, tender within pork shank with marinated red cabbage and sweet chile sauce. Both are ideal alternatives to the properly prepared crab Rangoon, drunken noodles, and handful of ramen soups.

Simply It, 2269 N. Lincoln Ave., Lincoln Park, Chicago, IL 60614; (773) 248-0884; simplyitrestaurant.com; Vietnamese; $$. Affordable and stylish, Tuan Nguyen's BYOB storefront puts fresh flavors at the forefront. More mainstream than its Argyle street counterparts, this menu provides an entry point to Vietnamese cuisine by way of lemongrass beef with rice-paper wrappers, Saigonese crepes, and sticky rice cakes wrapped in banana leaves and stuffed with chicken, mung beans, and shiitakes. Clay-pot and noodle dishes are among the entrees, though coconut-mango beef—showily served in a coconut shell—is too appealing to pass by.

The Smoke Daddy, 1804 W. Division St., Wicker Park, Chicago, IL 60622; (773) 772-6656; thesmokedaddy.com; Barbecue; $$. A retro feel pervades this down-home 'cue shack, ignited with smoked-until-pink ribs, brisket, and pulled pork. Sides, including delish sweet-potato fries, and finales—fried apple pie, a skillet cookie—aren't just afterthoughts. Live music, typically of the blues and jazz persuasion, ups the lively vibe.

Sono Wood Fired, 1582 N. Clybourn Ave., Lincoln Park, Chicago, IL 60642; (312) 255-1122; sonowoodfired.com; Pizza; $$. Daters dig this Lincoln Park pizzeria, next door to fellow Urban Burger Bar. The thrust of the menu is creatively topped, red or white, wood-fired pies. Try the one donning spicy soppressata, buffalo mozzarella, tomatoes, and charred onions with basil. Bruschetta, salads, and pastas are among the added options.

Spiaggia, 980 N. Michigan Ave., Gold Coast, Chicago, IL 60611; (312) 280-2750; spiaggiarestaurant.com; Italian; $$$$. Tony Mantuano's staggering, ostentatiously adorned (and priced), multilevel dining room is as special occasion as the buzz suggests. From the jaw-dropping cheeses—kept in a climate-controlled cave—to pastas that bring diners to their knees, this is mind-blowing dining at its best. For something more down to earth, try the regional Italian at casual-chic **Cafe Spiaggia** (p. 64), or head to **Terzo Piano** (p. 131), located in the Modern Wing of the Art Institute.

Sprout, 1417 W. Fullerton Ave., Lincoln Park, Chicago, IL 60614; (773) 348-0706; sproutrestaurant.com; New American/French; $$$. There's little other than praise for Dale Levitski's inventive, enchanting haute cuisine at this offbeat, DePaul-area eatery. Among the most memorable dishes—if you're going a la carte, that is—is the unbelievably tender veal cheek with lardons, carrots, mushrooms, and Ossau-Iraty cheese and the pitch-perfect salmon, with blood oranges, turnips, squash, and buerre blanc. Also try Levitski's **Frog n Snail** (p. 36).

Storefront Company, 1941 W. North Ave., Wicker Park, Chicago, IL 60622; (773) 661-2609; thestorefrontcompany.com; New American; $$$. Belly up to the kitchen counter of Bryan Moscatello's aptly named spot for a close-up and experimental six-course chef's tasting, no doubt highlighting animals' forgotten parts. Set within Wicker Park's Flat Iron Arts Building, its meals for mortals are every bit as composed—starting with lamb meatballs with goat ricotta, currants, and pine nuts in red pepper sauce, and rosy, lightly smoky venison, seared and served with huckleberries, pumpernickel, and rye dumplings. Whimsical sweets—among them chocolate several ways—don't disappoint. Neither do the balanced "kitchen cocktails," like the simply named Ginger with ginger-laced gin.

TABLE fifty-two, 52 W. Elm St., Gold Coast, Chicago, IL 60610; (312) 573-4000; tablefifty-two.com; Regional American; $$$. Art Smith, Oprah's personal chef, had tongues wagging from the moment he opened these doors. However, it's safe to say his food is what earned adherents (the Obamas included). Join the fan club in enjoying well-wrought Southern classics, such as fried green tomatoes with hot-sauce aioli and tomato jam, or cornmeal-crusted catfish with cheesy grits and bacon-braised collards. Don't leave without some goat-cheese biscuits—or the coconut-y pineapple hummingbird cake at meal's end.

Takashi, 1952 N. Damen Ave., Bucktown, Chicago, IL 60647; (773) 772-6170; takashichicago.com; Asian/French; $$$. Star chef Takashi Yagihashi crafts brilliant fare in an elegant, Zenlike space. Combining his French training with Japanese-accented, American ingredients, Yagihashi turns out a striking trio of pâté and terrine; practically meltable, caramelized pork-belly steamed buns offset by pickled daikon; and grilled bobwhite quail with roasted apples and quince, sauced with port-balsamic reduction. Choose the multicourse *omakase* or seven-course *kaiseki* menus, and see what he really can do. Also consider visiting fast-serve Noodles by Takashi, located in Macy's on State Street, (312) 781-4483, or **Slurping Turtle** (p. 129) in River North.

Toast, 746 W. Webster Ave., Lincoln Park, Chicago, IL 60614; (773) 935-5600; toast-chicago.com; American; $$. Crowds swell from this petite, contemporary spot, its solid, affordable brunch accruing waits. From classic and tweaked Benedict preparations, scrambles, and omelets to a hyped French toast "orgy"—a trio stuffed with fresh strawberries, Mexican chocolate, and mascarpone—the bevy of bites delights. Later, come for sandwiches, buffalo sliders, or a croquemonsieur. There's also a location at 2046 N. Damen Ave., (773) 772-5600.

Tocco, 1266 N. Milwaukee Ave., Wicker Park, Chicago, IL 60622; (773) 687-8895; toccochicago.com; Italian; $$. Owner Bruno Abate is the kind of consummate host you can't help but feel an affinity toward; the same is true of the space-age boîte he oversees alongside his wife, Melissa. It churns out crackly pizzas and calzones from a wood-burning oven and antipasti and salads brimming with fresh, honest ingredients. Pair them with smoky carbonara and *scottata con rucola,* seared, thinly sliced strip steak topped with arugula and shards of nutty Parmesan. There's an affordable wine list to match.

Tozi, 1265 N. Milwaukee Ave., Wicker Park, Chicago, IL 60611; (773) 252-2020; Korean; $$. If you get only one thing at this Korean barbecue, make it the *japchae,* its jiggly glass noodles saturated with sweet-savory soy sauce and interspersed with umpteen vegetables and smoky beef. Get it—and the knockout *mandoo* dumplings and bottle of shochu or sake—and leave happy, without ever igniting the gas-fueled tabletop grill. Still, who wants to miss the procession of *panchan,* brought to complement tender, tasty *bulgogi* and *kalbi*?

Trenchermen, 2039 W. North Ave., Wicker Park, Chicago, IL 60647; (773) 661-1540; trenchermen.com; New American; $$$. Genre-bending plates come courtesy of Patrick Sheerin (formerly **Signature Room at the 95th**, p. 86), at this below-street-level spot, set within a former Turkish bathhouse. Requisite are the dill-pickle-stuffed tots with cured chicken bresaola and vibrant red onion yogurt. Pleasing follow-ups include potato gnocchi in ricotta cream with black truffles and house ham, and comforting fried chicken thighs with popcorn grits and mushrooms. The creative cocktail program is also worth paying mind. Brunch, not surprisingly, is the place to be.

Tru, 676 N. St. Clair St., Streeterville, Chicago, IL 60611; (312) 202-0001; trurestaurant.com; French; $$$$. Break out the suit and tie (it's a must) at this luxe, expense-account restaurant, serving caviar on crystal steps and ever-changing tastings—aka "collections"—that are almost too artsy to eat. Thank Executive Chef Anthony Martin (Joël Robuchon) for that. Iconic caviar service comes perched on coral, with selections from the world-over; splurge, if you can. The set-price meal that follows will dazzle, from the arrival of the long carrot soup with glacial orange cardamom to the Duroc pork belly with compressed black plum and onions three ways. Inspired desserts, as one would expect, hold their own. The wine list is, as one would also expect, superior; the gallerylike dining room is a sight for sore eyes.

Twin Anchors, 1655 N. Sedgwick St., Old Town, Chicago, IL 60614; (312) 266-1616; twinanchorsribs.com; Barbecue; $$. Chicagoans either love or are ambivalent toward this barbecue joint. Those in the former camp tout the old-school tavern's zestily sauced, fall-apart baby backs and porky beans, served where *Return to Me* and a scene from *The Dark Knight* was filmed. The pretension-free setting—much the same as it ever was with checked floors, leather books, and Sinatra on the juke—is half the charm.

2 Sparrows, 553 W. Diversey Pkwy., Lincoln Park, Chicago, IL 60614; (773) 234-2320; 2sparrowschicago.com; New American; $$. The brunch bunch digs Gregory Ellis's daytime dishes. The hip, compact, LEED-certified setting, too. One bite of the blackened pork belly sandwich in a house-made biscuit, maple-bacon doughnut, or spiced Nutella-orange pop tart and you'll be a believer, too. Throw in a house soda or Earl Grey gin fizz, and linger until lunchtime, when the tarragon vinaigrette–dressed market salad comes into play.

Volare, 201 E. Grand Ave., Streeterville, Chicago, IL 60611; (312) 410-9900; volarerestaurant.com; Italian; $$. This perpetually packed, carb-heavy Venetian presents bruschetta and carpaccio, minestrone and veal Milanese, in high-decibel surroundings. Fans of its vodka sauce may find the suburban ristorante, 1919 S. Meyers Rd., Oakbrook Terrace, (630) 495-0200, more conversation-friendly.

WAVE, W Hotel–Lakeshore, 644 N. Lake Shore Dr., Streeterville, Chicago, IL 60611; (312) 255-4460; waverestaurant.com; Mediterranean; $$. Gregory Elliott's French-Italian small plates stand out despite glittering Lake Michigan views from within the hip W Hotel. Expect noshes like roasted bone marrow with red wine–shallot jam, house-made garganelli tossed with suckling pig and caramelized onions in pork sugo, and braised, espresso-sauced short ribs with sweet-potato gratin. A restorative weekend brunch menu helps with after-effects.

The Wieners Circle, 2622 N. Clark St., Lincoln Park, Chicago, IL 60614; (773) 477-7444; Hot Dogs; $. The off-color banter is half the charm of this Chicago-style dog stand, an institution where char-dogs are forked out with insults on the side. Expect a rowdy (read: drunk) late-night crowd that spews plenty of f-bombs. In other words, keep the kiddos at home as the evening wears on.

Near South

East Village, Fulton River District, Garfield Park, Greektown, Loop, Near West Side, River North, River West, West Loop, West Town

It's hard to find spots in the pedestrian-populated city center and its surrounds, so public transportation or valet parking are the way to go. Brave the traffic, accept the crowds, and revel in the palpable pulse only these 'hoods provide. There's something for all kinds—restaurants and lounges with panoramic views, umpteen spots from storied chefs—making these stomping grounds a hungry belly's best friend.

Ai Sushi Lounge, 358 Ontario St., River North, Chicago, IL 60610; (312) 335-9888; aichicago.us; Japanese/Sushi; $$$. Thank the folks behind Ringo and Tsuki for this trendy, loungelike spot, where the contemporary menu encourages grazing, the results occasionally surprise, and meals most often deliver. Among the rolls that stand out is the volcano; full of contrasts, it melds crunch (cucumber, soft-shell crab, and tempura) with buttery avocado and spicy mayo. But watch out when ordering maki—like the tempura-fried habanero lobster with spicy caper-inflected ceviche—because tabs quickly add up. Competent dishes from the kitchen make meals pleasing, even for the sushi-shy. And if you're adventuresome? You can have a whole Fugu blowfish meal; a la carte preparations are available, too.

aria, Fairmont Chicago, 200 N. Columbus Dr., Loop, Chicago, IL 60601; (312) 444-9494; Pan-Asian/Eclectic; $$$. The menu defies tradition at this hotel dining room, though you can look to dishes like duck confit Treviso with pickled cherries, Brie, and Champagne vinaigrette; habanero crab cakes with mango salsa and lemon sabayon; and pan-seared scallops with hard cider–lacquered pork belly and a shishito pepper–mushroom *ragù* in sweet corn sauce. Conversation-friendly and curtain-swathed with low lighting, this is a smart choice for a tête-à-tête.

Artopolis Bakery, Cafe & Agora, 306 S. Halsted St., Greektown, Chicago, IL 60661; (312) 559-9000; artopolis chicago.com; Greek/Mediterranean; $$. Affordable Mediterranean fare—*artopitas,* puff pastries stuffed with *kasseri,* feta, and mint; lemony avgolemono; wood-fired pizzas; sandwiches on hearth-baked bread—lend this popular Greektown spot plenty of charm. Roasted leg of lamb—heady with scents of oregano and rosemary—and specials such as pastitsio are offset by European-style bakery creations. The agora (market) brims with tempting imports, from jam and honey to olive oil and Greek wine.

Athena, 212 S. Halsted St., Greektown, Chicago, IL 60661; (312) 655-0000; athenarestaurantchicago.com; Greek/Mediterranean; $$. There are few better places to hang out on a summer evening than this garden patio, even if the cozy, date-appropriate dining room is welcoming in its own right. It's not just the setting that will grab you, however: spicy *tirokafteri* (feta spread); savory feta-stuffed, roasted red peppers; and charbroiled *loukaniko* sausage seal the deal. Hearty, traditional dishes, such as roast leg of lamb and moussaka, also are attention-getters.

Atwood Cafe, Hotel Burnham, 1 W. Washington St., Loop, Chicago, IL 60602; (312) 368-1900; atwoodcafe.com; New American; $$$. Nestled quite comfortably in a historic building along bustling State Street, this intimate, Art Deco dining room received a proverbial shot in the arm when Derek Simcik graced its kitchen, bringing with him a world of tasty travels and plenty of pastry cred. Count yourself lucky if the following appear on the menu: sweetbreads and chive waffles with bourbon-spiked strawberries and maple gastrique; pork belly–squash hash; or persimmon bread pudding with savory black pepper brittle and Chantilly cream.

Au Cheval, 800 W. Randolph St., West Loop, Chicago, IL 60607; (312) 929-4580; auchevalchicago.com; New American; $$. Brendan Sodikoff's European diner is worlds away from your average greasy spoon. Filling and over-the-top in the best way, it's a prime perch for sticky chile-sesame fried chicken; rich, roasted bone marrow with beef cheek marmalade; and a belt-busting, house-made, fried bologna sandwich (preferably with a runny fried egg on top). Even the potato hash smothered with duck heart gravy seems right when served in a moody, narrow space that's friendlier than its hipness suggests.

avec, 615 W. Randolph St., West Loop, Chicago, IL 60606; (312) 377-2002; avecrestaurant.com; Mediterranean/Small Plates/Wine Bar; $$. Paul Kahan's beloved eatery, a Mediterranean mob scene adjacent to **Blackbird** (p. 221), is the kind of place where you compose a meal from cheese cave selections; Fermin Serrano *jamón* with persimmons, fresh mint, lime, and Catalan *picada;* and, the perennial favorite, chorizo-stuffed Medjool dates, wrapped in smoked bacon and served with piquillo pepper– tomato sauce. On the sweeter side, expect closers like toasted ricotta pound cake, gussied up with candied

Meyer lemon, blueberry gelato, and lemon crunch. The notable wine list highlights boutique labels from Portugal, Italy, France, and Spain.

BadHappy Poutine, 939 N. Orleans St., River North, Chicago, IL 60610; (312) 890-2165; badhappypoutineshop.com; New American; $$. This fry-themed quick-fix carries on the gluttonous *Québécois* tradition of poutine. Keep it classic and get sturdy frites topped with standard cheese curds and gravy. Or, veer into uncharted waters with pork belly, truffle mayo, and *foie gras* mousse. Otherwise, "opa!" your way through a pile topped with gyro meat, feta, *tzatziki,* kalamata tapenade, and (curiously) curry gravy. Then, go home and take a nap. On Sundays, make like a local and bring your own vodka to brunch.

Bavette's Bar & Boeuf, 218 W. Kinzie St., River North, Chicago, IL 60654; (312) 624-8154; Steak House; $$$. Brendan Sodikoff's Euro steak house puts most city meateries to shame with perfectly executed fare that goes beyond the regular repertoire. Amazing steak aside, it's the other things—a boulder-size meatball and pasta, short rib Stroganoff with caramelized creminis, meat loaf with mushroom jus—that'll have you begging (or budgeting) for more. Meanwhile, the sultry setting—all done up in red leather booths, exposed brick, and antique mirrors—enchants. Pass some time sipping superior classic cocktails in the lower-level lounge.

bellyQ, 1400 W. Randolph St., West Loop, Chicago, IL 60607; (312) 563-1010; bellyqchicago.com; Asian Fusion; $$$. Chef Bill Kim (**urbanbelly** [p. 52], **Belly Shack** [p. 28]) is the man with the plan at this expansive Michael Jordan and Cornerstone Restaurant Group collab, a scene-y Asian barbecue with a handful of DIY infrared grills and a menu of hot pots, crunchy kimchi, and marinated meats, the standout of which is the namesake beef. Tea-smoked duck arrives tasty, if lightly flavored, a fact that's all-but-forgotten if Thai fried chicken or the double-smoked bacon-kimchi pancake is at play. Keg wines and soft-serve ice cream topped, perhaps, with passion fruit ice and coconut jelly, foster the love.

BenjYehuda, 212 W. Van Buren St., Loop, Chicago, IL 60607; (312) 408-2365; benjyehuda.com; Middle Eastern; $. Score spit-carved chicken *shawarma* in pita or *laffa* bread, topped with shredded cucumbers, tahini, and tart pickles. Better yet, sample the menu with a Yehuda flight of generously topped mini falafel, mini chicken, and mini steak pitas, plus fries. And speaking of fries, get yours with a cup of Merkts cheddar—your mouth will thank you. A second outpost is at 10 S. LaSalle St., (312) 726-9653.

Benny's Chop House, 444 N. Wabash St., River North, Chicago, IL 60611; (312) 626-2444; bennyschophouse.com; Steak/Seafood; $$$$. Any cues to a budgetary crunch are checked at the door of this modern throwback,  where the steaks are cooked to order, the oysters are way-fresh, and there's enough dark wood details to take out a small forest. Beyond prime, dry-aged steaks, turn to the Kurobuta pork chop, red wine–braised short ribs, or sweet Maine lobster.

The Berghoff, 17 W. Adams St., Loop, Chicago, IL 60603; (312) 427-3170; theberghoff.com; German; $$. An institution with wood-paneled walls, checkered floors, and a bar that fills with business types and tourists 10 deep, its hefty menu holds formulaic dishes, like crisp wiener schnitzel, tangy sauerbraten, and creamed spinach. Everything benefits from a round of house brews or Berghoff-label root beer.

BIG & little's, 860 N. Orleans St., River North, Chicago, IL 60610; (312) 943-0000; bigandlittleschicago.com; New American; $. *Hell's Kitchen* contestant Tony D'Alessandro earned a cult following for skillful, golden-battered fish-and-chips and top-tier fish tacos, served

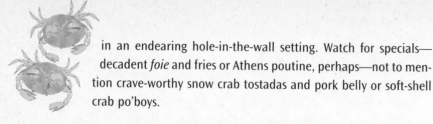

in an endearing hole-in-the-wall setting. Watch for specials—decadent *foie* and fries or Athens poutine, perhaps—not to mention crave-worthy snow crab tostadas and pork belly or soft-shell crab po'boys.

Billy Goat Tavern, 430 N. Michigan Ave., Lower Level, River North, Chicago, IL 60611; (312) 222-1525; billygoattavern.com; Pub/Burgers; $. This subterranean tavern—made famous by the SNL "cheezborger" skit—pays homage to reporters past, while luring the average working man and tourist for a quick, cheap meal. Are its burgers the best in the city? Not by a long shot, but traditions run deep. Just remember: no Coke, Pepsi. There are seven other area locations (see website for information).

Bin 36, 339 N. Dearborn St., River North, Chicago, IL 60654; (312) 755-9463; bin36.com; New American/Wine Bar; $$$. With more than a decade under its belt, this deservedly popular wine bar and bistro from Dan Sachs, Executive Chef William Hewitt, and Wine Director Brian Duncan thrives. So, come for the excellent cheese selection or warm ricotta fritters, taking advice on suggested pairings. Then, snag a bottle or two from the wine shop on the way out for a rainy day.

Blackbird, 619 W. Randolph St., West Loop, Chicago, IL 60611; (312) 715-0708; blackbirdrestaurant.com; New American; $$$$. Paul Kahan carries on at this loved hot-spot, its eco-friendly, minimalist dining room still among the hippest in town. With CIA-trained **Alinea** (p. 56) vet David Posey at his side, it continues to craft brilliant, surprising dishes from local products: fried suckling pig with wild garbanzos, candied turnip, and a soft-boiled quail egg, and roasted rabbit loin and *lap chong* with celtuce, candied onion, cashews, and tart-sweet tamarind, for example. Finales, whether a cheese course or a cardamom-scented, roasted rhubarb Danish, also deliver. Kahan also owns adjacent wine bar, **avec** (p. 95); rustic, beer-and-pork-bent

The Publican (p. 124); budget-friendly taqueria **Big Star** (p. 60); and butcher-meets-deli **Publican Quality Meats** (p. 267).

The Boarding House, 720 N. Wells St., River North, Chicago, IL 60654; (312) 280-0720; boardinghousechicago.com; New American; $$$. Proprietor and Master Sommelier Alpana Singh, a former *Check, Please!* host, oversees the impressive wine program at this vast venture, set within a 19th-century boardinghouse. Grape-friendly nibbles—think crispy chicken thighs with green garlic pistou—are handy companions.

Bombon Cafe, 36 S. Ashland Ave., West Loop, Chicago, IL 60607; (312) 733-8717; chicagobestcakes.com; Mexican/Bakery; $$. Sweet and savory collide at this sunny cafe from husband-and-wife team Laura Cid-Perea and Luis Perea. The authentic Mexican *tortas* are a specialty, and they're loaded with big, bold flavors—no surprise since Rick Bayless is Cid-Perea's former boss. This is true whether you opt for the Sonora—layered with marinated skirt steak, caramelized onions, roasted peppers, jalapeños, and avocado—or the Toluca with spicy chorizo, avocado, pickled red onions, Oaxaca cheese, and a slather of beans. Save room for the sweets, especially the sinful *tres leches*. Nearby, **La Lagartija** (p. 149) turns out Mexican and Tex-Mex dishes, while Bombon Cake Gallery, 3748 W. 26th St., (773) 277-8777, tempts commuters ever-so-sweetly from the second floor of Ogilvie Transportation Center.

Branch 27, 1371 W. Chicago Ave., West Town, Chicago, IL 60642; (312) 850-2700; branch27.com; New American; $$$. Located in a former branch of the Chicago Public Library with coveted atrium seating, this rustic American bistro dispenses Thai chile–glazed wings; house-made fettuccine with braised kale, tomatoes, and lamb *ragù;* and steak frites, alongside Burgundy mushrooms and hand-cut fries.

Brindille, 534 N. Clark St., River North, Chicago, IL 50654; (312) 595-1616; brindille-chicago.com; French; $$$$. You'll fall immediately, madly in love with Carrie Nahabedian's **Naha** (p. 119) follow-up, a refined, sedate spot for sorrel-scented steak tartare; edible flower–gilded lobster with black trumpet mushrooms and cocoa beans; and warm, baked cherry-almond clafoutis, made all the more lovely when paired with vintage French cocktails.

Bub City, 435 N. Clark St., River North, Chicago, IL 60654; (312) 610-4200; bubcitychicago.com; Barbecue; $$. The Melman sibs

are at it again, this time resurrecting Weed Street's long-defunct Bub City Crabshack and Bar-B-Q (likewise a Lettuce spot)—only this time with a country-western concept and Doug Psaltis's cheddar and pulled pork–topped Giddy Up Fries, rockin' chili, and spicy fried chicken with Alabama white sauce. Shockingly fresh seafood platters aside, barbecue—namely Kansas City–style burnt ends—take center stage. Nonetheless, Paul McGee's whiskey-spiked cocktails threaten to steal the show. Finish meals with a nightcap in the subterranean tiki bar, **Three Dots and a Dash** (p. 236).

Cafe Iberico, 737 N. La Salle St., River North, Chicago, IL 60610; (312) 573-1510; cafeiberico.com; Spanish/Tapas; $$. Start with sangria at this tapas veteran, a deafening outpost with a crowd-minded—okay, cattle-call—feel. Then, nosh on marinated olives, ubiquitous *tortilla española,* and spicy-sauced *patatas bravas.* There's a large wine list and decent sangria—sip some while you wait for a table.

Carnivale, 702 W. Fulton Market, West Loop, Chicago, IL 60661; (312) 850-5005; carnivalechicago.com; Nuevo Latino; $$$. This boisterous, kaleidoscopic modern Latin hot-spot has a menu that's as showy as its setting. Standouts are the starters, including a ceviche sampler that includes lively Ecuadorian shrimp with rooftop chiles, tomatoes, red onion, cilantro, and creamy-fresh avocado-cucumber sorbet. Another winning dish is the tender, flavorful *ropa vieja*, perfect with a mojito or two.

Carson's Ribs, 612 N. Wells St., River North, Chicago, IL 60612; (312) 280-9200; ribs.com; Barbecue; $$. Barbecue is a hotly contested category in Chicago—especially these days—yet this dimly lit tourist trap marches on, serving its signature, sweetly sauced racks with mounds of slaw and au gratin potatoes. Boneless, center-cut pork chops are a decent alternative. There's also a location at 200 N. Waukegan Rd., Deerfield, (847) 374-8500.

Chicago Chop House, 60 W. Ontario St., River North, Chicago, IL 60654; (312) 787-7100; chicagochophouse.com; Steak House; $$$$. Located in a picturesque Victorian brownstone, this classic chophouse—adorned with vintage Chicago photos—baits carnivores with classic cuts. A 20-ounce, bone-in strip and prime rib, served traditionally or charred, hold court with a frenched bone-in veal chop, swordfish with sherry butter, and beer-battered shrimp. Signature potato pancakes with applesauce and sour cream and American fries are go-to, a la carte sides. A piano player performs nightly.

Chicago Cut Steakhouse, 300 N. LaSalle Blvd., River North, Chicago, IL 60654; (312) 329-1800; chicagocutsteakhouse.com; Steak House; $$$$. Decadence knows no bounds at this manly, suit-friendly meat-house, from the red velvet trim to the oversize windows framing Chicago River views. Then there's the focal dry-aged on premises, house-butchered steaks. However, the jury is still out on the iPad wine list and tightly packed (read: cramped) seating.

Coalfire, 1321 W. Grand Ave., West Town, Chicago, IL 60622; (312) 226-2625; coalfirechicago.com; Pizza; $$. Crackly, blazing-coal-fired Neapolitan pies have telltale charred crusts and come in versions both classic (Margherita) and creative (ricotta-topped pesto with black olives). A handful of salads—such as Caesar and Caprese—provide a counterpart to the creations, which also may be customized. Expect a wait during peak times, as the oven can't always keep up with demand.

Coco Pazzo, 300 W. Hubbard St., River North, Chicago, IL 60654; (312) 836-0900; cocopazzochicago.com; Italian; $$$. Still plating some of the best Tuscan cuisine in the city, this loftlike, house-made pasta purveyor has earned its cred. Incorporating seasonal ingredients with a contemporary eye, Federico Comacchio's cuisine is spirited, whether it's a tangle of striking squid ink tagliolini or pappardelle with slow-simmered rabbit *ragù*. The unfussy, expertly prepared entrees—grilled chicken under a brick; crisp pork Milanese; whole, wood-roasted sea bass—are equally prized.

Crepe Bistro, 186 N. Wells St., Loop, Chicago, IL 60606; (312) 269-0300; crepebistro.net; French; $$. This quiet, candlelit dining room and martini bar—popular with the pre-theater set—encases eclectic, savory, and sweet fillings within paper-thin crepes. The coq au vin features Mornay-licked chicken and mushrooms; the Tahiti sports ham, cheese, and hunks of pineapple; and the Kathmandu—cheesy, chicken and mushroom curry with mango chutney—provides a departure from the norm. Dessert crepes, including one oozing Nutella, sate sweet tooths.

Cyrano's Farm Kitchen, 546 N. Wells St., River North, Chicago, IL 60654; (312) 467-0546; French; $$. A master of traditional French fare, Didier Durand—the restaurant's ever-present chef/owner—re-concepted his longtime bistro into a rustic, locavore-friendly farm-to-table restaurant for French onion soup, jarred pâté, and beef

Bourguignon. For a tranquil alternative, visit Cyrano's Cafe & Wine Bar on the River Walk, 233 E. Lower Wacker Dr., (312) 616-1400. In summer, its riverside patio, ice-cream parlor, and crepe stand is the place to be.

David Burke's Prime Steakhouse, The James, 616 N. Rush St., River North, Chicago, IL 60611; (312) 660-6000; david burkesprimehouse.com; Steak House; $$$$. Manned by Executive Chef Rick Gresh, this meatery dry-ages its beef on-site in a room flanked by Himalayan salt and has a penchant for using locally sourced, seasonal ingredients. Start with the Wagyu beef sashimi with earthy mushroom chips and truffle mayo, or the rich, silky lobster bisque, punched up with green-apple essence. Splurge on the marbled, 55-day rib eye, a bone-in masterpiece. When dining with a crowd, sample the difference between 28- and 75-day aged cuts.

De Cero, 814 W. Randolph St., West Loop, Chicago, IL 60607; (312) 455-8114; decerotaqueria.com; Latin; $$. Nestled along Restaurant Row, this modern taqueria promotes sharing with snacks and customizable taco platters—beer-battered shrimp, chipotle-braised beef with pickled red onions, and chorizo-potato with Applewood bacon versions among them. But odds are, you won't want to share the duck confit nachos at all.

Del Frisco's Double Eagle Steakhouse, 58 E. Oak St., River North, Chicago, IL 60611; (312) 888-2499; delfriscos.com/chicago; Steak House; $$$. Chicagoans flock to this chain for Texas excess. Plump, fresh oysters on the half shell and nicely charred, wet-aged steaks make for a satisfying, if spendy, meal, especially when paired with bottles from its 1,500-bottle-strong cellar.

Embeya, 564 W. Randolph St., Chicago, IL 60661; (312) 612-5640; embeya.com; Modern Asian; $$$. The austere dining room may draw you in, but the progressive Asian plates from fine-dining vet Thai Dang (**L20**, p. 76) linger. That's true from the crisp, jolting papaya salad, which arrives flecked with culantro and toothsome beef jerky, to the garlicky, tamarind-glazed ribs and soulful *thit heo kho,* slow-cooked pork belly with quail eggs in caramel sauce. Tabs can easily soar, except on Sundays when a steal of a three-course tasting is $29 per person or $50 if you spring for wine.

Epic, 112 W. Hubbard St., River North, Chicago, IL 60654; (312) 222-4940; epicrestaurantchicago.com; American; $$$. All things to well-heeled people, this expense account–worthy River North restau-lounge—its rooftop patio perched above Hubbard—attracts its share of scene-seekers. Turns out, Matthew Pollock's creative cuisine—tuna tartare with guacamole and barbecue pappadums; grouper with 12-hour *puttanesca*; braised short ribs with cheddar grits—keeps them coming back. The soaring, two-floor industrial space—and impressive desserts, like huckleberry crostata—are further fineries.

Everest, 440 S. LaSalle St., 40th Fl., Loop, Chicago, IL 60605; (312) 663-8920; everestrestaurant.com; French; $$$$. Hovering 40 floors above street level with staggering skyline views, this Chicago Stock Exchange–housed, gallerylike gem—a Lettuce Entertain You venture with Jean Joho—remains at the top of its game. Though you may order a la carte—crusted Berkshire pork cheeks and poached veal tongue with *choucroute salade* is one reason—it's preferable to go the degustation route. It yields incentives, such as a dish of olive oil–poached Alaskan halibut, braised artichokes, and fiddlehead ferns.

Flo, 1434 W. Chicago Ave., West Town, Chicago, IL 60642; (312) 243-0477; eatatflo.com; Regional American; $$. Southwestern comfort is the name of the game at this cozy cafe, which gets its chiles from Hatch, NM. From grilled shrimp and grits with roasted poblano sauce to chicken-fried steak with creamy, roasted garlic–chipotle gravy and Frito pie, the guilty pleasures abound. But be forewarned: The crowds are crazy during breakfast—especially weekend brunch.

The Florentine, JW Marriott, 151 W. Adams St., Loop, Chicago, IL 60603; (312) 660-8866; the-florentine.net; Italian; $$$. Located in a Daniel Burnham–designed building, this second-floor dining room has a corporate, mock-library feel, albeit one with gauzy curtains and endless wood details. More attention-grabbing is the get-anything menu of modern Italian fare, like ravioli *en brodo* with black cabbage or whole-roasted sea bream, enlivened with salsa verde.

Fogo de Chão, 611 N. LaSalle Blvd., River North, Chicago, IL 60654; (312) 932-9330; fogodechao.com; Brazilian/Steak House; $$$. Come hungry, leave stuffed—that's the mantra at this all-you-can-eat *churrascaria,* where the salad bar is as diet-defying as the garlicky, gaucho-carved *picanha,* bacon-wrapped filet, and juicy, salty rib eye. Starchy sides, including warm cheese bread and caramelized bananas, are included. However, desserts—including papaya cream—will set you back extra cash.

Frontera Grill, 445 N. Clark St., River North, Chicago, IL 60654; (312) 661-1434; rickbayless.com; Mexican; $$$. Rick Bayless's wildly popular, casual counterpart to **Topolobampo** (p. 133) lives up to the hype. The sustainable ceviche and seasonal, revelatory creations—served in a folk art–adorned dining room—change often but may include a sashimi-style Mazatlan blue shrimp, dashed with serrano-lime juice, jicama, cucumbers, red onions, and micro-cilantro; *carnitas* tamales, steamed in a banana leaf; or serrano-marinated chicken with mezcal-infused roasted tomatillo sauce. If achiote-marinated *cochinita pibil* is available, make it your main meal. When in the mood for a sandwich and soup, however, head to Bayless's ultra-tasty **XOCO** (p. 136).

The Gage, 24 S. Michigan Ave., Loop, Chicago, IL 60603; (312) 372-4243; thegagechicago.com; Gastropub; $$$. Located across from Millennium Park, this noisy, fancified tavern is a must for hearty fare. Dive in with the Scotch egg with spicy mustard; poutine topped with smoked pork confit, pickled red onions, and cheese curds; or barbecue-glazed bison short ribs. Plenty come for the fish-and-chips but end up ordering the prime burger, topped with local Camembert and melted onion marmalade, instead. See how the team handles French fare at refined follow-up **Henri** (p. 110).

g.e.b., 841 W. Randolph St., West Town, Chicago, IL 60607; (312) 888-2258; gebistro.com; New American; $$$. *MasterChef* judge Graham Elliot's rockin' bistro announces itself with a Marshall stacks host stand, chef-inspired saint candles, and repurposed LP menus, all of them backdrops for dishes classic—pork schnitzel with rye spaetzle and braised apples—and whimsical, as in bacon-studded beer-cheddar risotto. Everything—beignets included—tastes best when enjoyed on the large, lively patio.

Giordano's, 135 E. Lake St., Loop, Chicago, IL 60601; (312) 616-1200; giordanos.com; Pizza; $$. This now-national, deep-dish destination, a Chicago original, has been serving pies alongside red-sauce standbys since the '70s. There are many locations scattered throughout Chicagoland (see website for information).

Girl & the Goat, 809 W. Randolph St., West Loop, Chicago, IL 60607; (312) 492-6262; girlandthegoat.com; New American; $$$. Topping the list of good things in life is Stephanie Izard's inventive, modern American—the epitome of the Chicago dining aesthetic. Izard, a *Top Chef* winner, crafts risky, hyper-local small plates, where her bravado sees equal success in the vegetable and atypical surf 'n' turf realm. The menu changes often, but you can expect turn-tos like wood-grilled broccoli with Rogue Creamery smoky blue cheese and spiced crispies; grilled baby octopus with guanciale, favas, and pistachios in lemon vinaigrette; and ham frites, gone luxe with smoked tomato aioli and cheddar-beer sauce. Izard—and her fans—also dig animals' forgotten parts, so check out the "pig face," bedecked with a sunny-side egg. She's also the force behind **Little Goat Diner** (p. 116), a three-meal affair with a classic aesthetic.

Gold Coast Dogs, 159 N. Wabash Ave., Loop, Chicago, IL 60601; (312) 917-1677; goldcoastdogs.net; Hot Dogs; $. This Chicago stalwart made its name with a signature char dog—a singed, split beef frank, tucked into a poppy-seed bun and topped with mustard, relish, onions, sport peppers, celery salt, tomato, and a pickle. There are outposts at both Midway and O'Hare airports, as well as Union Station, 225 S. Canal St., (312) 258-8585.

Grace, 652 W. Randolph St., West Loop, Chicago, IL 60661; (312) 234-9494; grace-restaurant.com; New American; $$$$. In the event you have hundreds lying around, play dress-up because Curtis Duffy's destination dining room is a worthy way to spend them. The beautiful, painstaking plates are as breathtaking to eat as they are to behold, whether you choose the flora or fauna menu. The latter may yield Osetra caviar with Meyer lemon *gelée* and kumquat jam, or Scottish salmon amid a poof of foam with spicy red cabbage, citrus pudding, and marigolds. The former may host befuddling, meaty maitake, preserved daikon, and finger lime with striking, coffee-spiked potato puree. Michael Muser's French-leaning wine list is picked— and priced—to match.

graham elliot, 217 W. Huron St., River North, Chicago, IL 60610; (312) 624-9975; grahamelliot.com; New American; $$$$. On the short list of Chicago chefs who spark dissenting opinions: Graham Elliot. His "bistronomic" eatery, having a penchant for cranked-up tunes and a middle-finger-to-convention mentality, is as much about the experience as it is about the chef's science-project cooking techniques, seen in tasting and chef's menu form. For more of a bistro experience, check out **g.e.b.** (p. 106).

Grange Hall Burger Bar, 844 W. Randolph St., West Loop, Chicago, IL 60607; (312) 491-0844; grangehallburgerbar.com; Burgers; $$. A farm-to-table sensibility informs the menu at this super-cute spot from husband-and-wife team Angela Hepler-Lee and Chris Lee (**De Cero**, p. 103). Choose between chef or self-designed grass-fed beef or free-range, sage-scented turkey burgers. Then, share a seasonal salad, super blue cheese and hot-sauced fries, or beer-battered pickles. Throw in a few craft beers or cocktails spiked with local spirits, and finish with house-made salted caramel-banana ice cream or a slice of pie.

Greek Islands, 200 S. Halsted St., Greektown, Chicago, IL 60661; (312) 782-9855; greekislands.net; Greek/Mediterranean; $$. Always festive and packed to the rafters, this veteran churns out venerable Greek dishes (flaming *saganaki, tzatziki,* and tender char-broiled baby octopus). The lengthy menu, filled with dolmades, gyros, and chicken *riganati,* includes a family-style component that begs for Sunday suppers or festive, late-night feasts. There is a suburban counterpart at 300 E. 22nd St., Lombard, (630) 932-4545.

GT Fish & Oyster, 531 N. Wells St., River North, Chicago, IL 60654; (312) 929-3501; gt oyster.com; Seafood; $$$. You'll fall hard for this Giuseppe Tentori and BOKA Restaurant Group catch, a sleek, surf-inspired hot-spot for just-plucked oysters, budget-busting caviar service, and lobster rolls stuffed with a full-pound of Maine lobster. More humble but no less accolade-worthy are its bright sunfish ceviche, shrimp bruschetta with avocado and grapefruit, and fish-and-chips, meant to be dunked in dill pickle remoulade. Benjamin Schiller's cocktails have a following of their own.

Habana Libre, 1440 W. Chicago Ave., West Town, Chicago, IL 60642; (312) 243-3303; habanalibrerestaurant.com; Cuban; $$. There's much to love about this cheery neighborhood Cuban: the flaky guava-cheese empanadas, the garlic-laden *tostones,* the really good *ropa vieja,* and the even better *pollo frito.* And the *jibarito?* It'll leave you wanting another. Then there's the BYOB policy, which keeps the cost factor down.

Halo Asian Mix, 29 E. Adams St., Loop, Chicago, IL 60603; (312) 360-1111; haloasianmix.com; Asian Fusion/Hawaiian; $. Filipino and Hawaiian offerings outshine the Ameri-Chinese, Thai, and Japanese selections at this fast-casual concept, where you'll easily get with sloppy, artery-clogging *loco moco,* sweet-salty *tocilog,* and pork adobo, sidled by a mountain of garlic fried rice.

Hannah's Bretzel, 180 W. Washington Blvd., Loop, Chicago, IL 60602; (312) 621-1111; hannahsbretzel.com; Cafe; $$. The organic bread, baked on-site, has everything to do with the success of this sandwich spot. Make short work of the serrano-Manchego sammie with fig chutney and shards of fennel. The vegetarian options are noteworthy, too; try one with Brie, apples, caramelized onions, and apple-thyme yogurt tucked in a whole-grain baguette. **Additional locations:** 131 S. Dearborn St., (312) 269-5550; 233 N. Michigan Ave., (312) 621-1111; 400 N. LaSalle St., (312) 621-1111; and 555 W. Monroe St., (312) 621-1111.

Harry Caray's, 33 W. Kinzie St., River North, Chicago, IL 60654; (312) 828-0966; harrycarays.com; Steak House/Italian; $$$$. This nod to the legendary late announcer serves one of the biggest and best shrimp cocktails in town. The memorabilia-laden confines may have something to do with the allure, though the Vesuvio-style prime steaks and standard pasta preparations have accrued a justified fan base. There are outposts and offshoots in the city and suburbs; see the website for information.

Heaven on Seven, 111 N. Wabash Ave., 7th Fl., Loop, Chicago, IL 60602; (312) 263-6443; heavenonseven.com; Cajun/Creole; $$. Spice-seekers flock to Jimmy Bannos's cash-only lunchbreakers' Eden, where the gumbo, po'boys, and andouille with jalapeño-cheddar corn muffins are tops. A wall of hot sauce allows for customization. There are follow-ups at 600 N. Michigan Ave., 2nd Fl., (312) 280-7774, and 224 S. Main St., Naperville, (630) 717-0777.

Henri, 18 S. Michigan Ave., Loop, Chicago, IL 60603; (312) 578-0763; henrichicago.com; French/New American; $$$$. This hushed expense-accounter, kin to **The Gage** (p. 106), is heavy on indulgent French classics, though atypical options are in the mix. Whether you start with the Brussels sprouts *pissaladière* with mushrooms, Gouda, and cured *foie gras* or head straight for the rack of lamb with cognac prunes, save room for the *mille-feuille,* a napoleon layered with vanilla crème. And do peruse the biodynamic wine and craft cocktail lists.

HUB 51, 51 W. Hubbard St., River North, Chicago, IL 60654; (312) 828-0051; hub51chicago.com; New American; $$. Rich Melman's "kids" are behind this trendy pleasure den. The all-encompassing menu hosts everything from maki to tacos, house-made jerky, and oversize sandwiches (try the knife-and-fork-required open-face BLT), with plenty of shareable plates—dry-rubbed ribs, pulled-chicken nachos—for tipplers.

Hubbard Inn, 110 W. Hubbard St., River North, Chicago, IL 60654; (312) 222-1331; hubbardinn.com; Gastropub; $$. A worldly collection of artifacts sets the tone at this communal, bi-level boîte serving sensible-but-stylish bar snacks, flatbreads, sandwiches, and small plates from Bob Zrenner (**North Pond** [p. 79]). Nibbles range from rabbit rilletes salad with cashews and date puree to standout crispy duck confit, accented with lavender. Also solid are the fall-apart-tender, whiskey-braised short ribs and Hampshire pork with sweet-savory grape sauce and pickled grapes. Siblings include **Barn & Company** (p. 60), English, and **Black Bull** (p. 62).

I Dream of Falafel, 331 S. Franklin St., Loop, Chicago, IL 60606; (312) 913-9660; idreamoffalafel.com; Middle Eastern; **$.** If you like Chipotle and **Roti Mediterranean Grill** (p. 125), you'll be smitten with this Middle Eastern mainstay, regardless of whether you choose the falafel *laffa,* spit-roasted chicken *shawarma,* or doner kebab. Top yours with smoky baba ghannouj, garlicky *toum,* or pickled turnips with a pleasant vinegar tang, and you'll be longing for more. **Additional locations:** 112 W. Monrose St., (312) 263-4363; 555 W. Monroe St., (312) 559-3333; 18W066 22nd St., Oak Brook Terrace, (630) 468-2606.

Ina's, 1235 W. Randolph St., West Loop, Chicago, IL 60607; (312) 226-8227; breakfastqueen.com; American; **$$.** Ina Pinkney's breakfast institution is adorned with iconic, off-the-wall salt and pepper shakers, and it's all about the morning eats. Faves include scrapple—a commingling of eggs, cornmeal, black beans, and cheddar—and "heavenly hots," thin pancakes with peach, raspberry, and blueberry compote. Linger through lunch and find curried chicken salad, chicken potpie, and house-made meat loaf.

India House, 59 W. Grand Ave., River North, Chicago, IL 60654; (312) 645-9500; indiahousechicago.com; Indian; **$$.** The consistent, moderately priced Indian fare—served in sedate, exposed-brick environs—leaves spice-lovers smitten. Though there is a large selection of vegetarian dishes, from aromatic lentils to delish *palak paneer,* it's the royally sauced lamb and chicken creations that provide a true palate-perk. *Gulab jamun* and refreshing mango *kulfi* are finales of note. Its original location is in Schaumburg; other outposts are in Hoffman Estates, 721 W. Golf Rd (847) 278-0760; and Buffalo Grove, 228 McHenry Rd., (847) 520-5569.

The Italian Village, 71 W. Monroe St., Loop, Chicago, IL 60603; (312) 332-7005; italianvillage-chicago.com; Italian; $$. A contrary commingling of romantics and suits patronize this old-school, upper-level spot with intimate, semiprivate booths. Serving fare from the boot without fanfare inside the family-run Italian Village complex, its frequented dishes include grilled calamari, many classic chicken and veal preparations, and lasagna.

Japonais, 600 W. Chicago Ave., River North, Chicago, IL 60610; (312) 822-9600; japonaischicago.com; Japanese; $$$. Pretty people are an extension of this sultry hot-spot, which spans contemporary and classic Japanese cuisines. After indulging in lobster teriyaki or sake-spiked pear-plum-glazed short ribs, you'll want to head downstairs to the romantic riverside lounge.

Joe's Seafood, Prime Steak & Stone Crab, 60 E. Grand Ave., River North, Chicago, IL 60611; (312) 379-5637; joes.net; Seafood/Steak House; $$$$. People come to this pricey seafooder, a Miami original that partnered with Lettuce Entertain You, for solid renditions of its namesakes. Begin with as much of the chilled stone crab as you can afford, later opting for mushroom-stuffed sole with butter-poached lobster. The bone-in steaks—rib eye, strip, filet—are a decadent, artery-clogging alternative. Finish with pie: The Key lime and banana cream are noteworthy.

Kabocha, 952 W. Lake St., West Loop, Chicago, IL 60607; (312) 666-6214; kabochachicago.com; Japanese/French; $$$. Executive Chef Shin Thompson (Bonsoirée) teams with Ryan O'Donnell (Gemini Bistro, Rustic House) at this pleasant Japanese brasserie, where a "seafood aquarium" serves as edible art and the chef's storied scallop motoyaki—singed crab and scallop on the half shell, bathed in creamy ponzu aioli—makes a comeback. From the duck confit pot stickers to the Wagyu beef tartare, there's nary a flop.

Kan Zaman, 617 N. Wells St., River North, Chicago, IL 60610; (312) 751-9600; kanzamanchicago.com; Lebanese; $$. Settle in at low-slung, pillow-strewn tables, and seek solace in hearty lentil soup, silky hummus, and tender dolmades. On weekends, watch belly dancers while munching on rotisserie-cooked *shawarma* and moist, charbroiled kebabs.

Karyn's Cooked, 738 N. Wells St., River North, Chicago, IL 60614; (312) 587-1050; karynraw.com; Vegetarian/Vegan; $$$. Karyn Calabrese (Karyn's Fresh Corner), a raw foodist, caters to veg loyalists with an upscale take on adventurous cuisine. However, it's doubtful stand-ins, from grilled seitan to ground-soy tacos, fool most carnivores.

Keefer's Restaurant, 20 W. Kinzie St., River North, Chicago, IL 60654; (312) 467-9525; keefersrestaurant.com; Steak House; $$$. Chef John Hogan fashions fine steak-house variants in a sweeping dining room. Sure, you'll find the classics—crab cakes, lobster bisque, steak, and more steak—but you'll also encounter French-inflected favorites, including steak Diane, Dover sole meunière, and duck liver terrine accompanied by fruit compote, brioche, toast points, and some sauterne.

Kiki's Bistro, 900 N. Franklin St., River North, Chicago, IL 60610; (312) 335-5454; kikisbistro.com; French; $$$. Located just enough off the beaten path to feel secret, this longtime, intimate bistro belonging to its eponymous owner is Francophiles' regular haunt. Tucking into the *magret de canard*—duck breast and leg confit with braised red cabbage, wild rice, and green-peppercorn sauce—it's easy to see why. Contemplate ordering the *plat du jour,* be it skate wing in caper–brown butter sauce or steak frites.

Kinzie Chophouse, 400 N. Wells St., River North, Chicago, IL 60654; (312) 822-0191; kinziechophouse.com; Steak House; $$. One of the most understated steak houses around, this handsome spot near the Merchandise Mart is popular with suits and out-of-towners, who converge over hefty salads, competent prime rib, or wild-mushroom and steak risotto, and a large array of steaks and chops.

La Madia, 59 W. Grand Ave., River North, Chicago, IL 60654; (312) 329-0400; dinelamadia.com; Italian/Pizza; $$. Thin, crackly crust 'zas, topped with local and artisanal ingredients, are popular with a midday and late-night crowd. Warm, foil-wrapped olives and Marsala-glazed wild mushroom bruschetta are good for grazing. Whenever you dine, plan on keeping the white-sauced Taleggio and slow-roasted grape pie to yourself. A late-night prix fixe includes salad, a pizza, and indulgent Wisconsin electric cookies for two—and wine, to boot. There's an

To the Market—For Meat

Gregory Laketek learned his craft in Italy, and we thank him for that—and his **West Loop Salumi,** westloopsalumi.com, is an Old World ode to charcuterie, like garlicky, spreadable *ciauscolo,* made from whole, raw milk–fed Berkshire hogs. Watch for house-made *culatello,* too.

interactive chef's table where cooking classes regularly take place. Owner Jonathan Fox is also behind mad-popular **Firecakes Donuts** (p. 276).

La Sardine, 111 N. Carpenter St., West Loop, Chicago, IL 60607; (312) 421-2800; lasardine.com; French; $$$. This prototypical bistro, **Le Bouchon**'s (p. 74) bro, executes the classics—codfish *brandade,* salade Lyonnaise, beef Bourguignon—with panache. As for Jean Claude Poilevey's seafood-stocked bouilla-baisse, it's simply the best. Linger over a cheese plate and a gravity-defying chocolate soufflé, too.

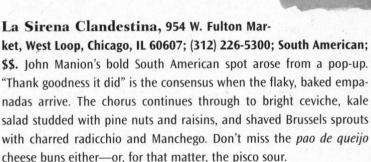

La Sirena Clandestina, 954 W. Fulton Market, West Loop, Chicago, IL 60607; (312) 226-5300; South American; $$. John Manion's bold South American spot arose from a pop-up. "Thank goodness it did" is the consensus when the flaky, baked empanadas arrive. The chorus continues through to bright ceviche, kale salad studded with pine nuts and raisins, and shaved Brussels sprouts with charred radicchio and Manchego. Don't miss the *pao de queijo* cheese buns either—or, for that matter, the pisco sour.

La Scarola, 721 W. Grand Ave., River West, Chicago, IL 60610; (312) 243-1740; lascarola.com; Italian; $$. People can't get enough of this joint's Italian-American classics, served in an unassuming storefront setting. Though nothing—from the spaghetti to the meat lasagna—charts new territory, the commonplace preparations suit ever-present diners just fine.

Lawry's the Prime Rib, 100 E. Ontario St., River North, Chicago, IL 60611; (312) 787-5000; lawrysonline.com; Steak House; $$$$. Silver carts, wafting with the scent of prime rib, rove through this dramatic, multiroom Italian Renaissance–style mansion, which houses this Beverly Hills–based standby. Carved tableside—after its signature "spinning" salad bowl is served—the beef isn't something to balk at.

Little Goat Diner, 820 W. Randolph St., West Loop, Chicago, IL 60607; (312) 888-3455; littlegoatchicago.com; New American; $$. What Stephanie Izard touches turns to gold—that includes this reimagined West Loop diner, where creative plates include savory pork belly–scallion pancakes and breakfast spaghetti 'n' clams. Some of the best dishes, though, are simple and straightforward. In that camp: the all-American burger with "secret sauce" on a sesame-seed bun. Note, too, the open-face Horseshoe, a Springfield, IL, original, gone glam with goat-chili cheese fries. Toss back some house sodas, and share the goat's milk caramel sundae if you dare. Then, carb up with carryout from adjacent **Little Goat Bread** (p. 282).

Lockwood, Palmer House Hilton, 17 E. Monroe St., Loop, Chicago, IL 60603; (312) 726-7500; lockwoodrestaurant.com; New American; $$$$. Situated off the lobby of the soaring, historic Palmer House Hilton hotel, this class act attracts guests and tourists alike with mildly esoteric American fare from Joseph Rose (**Sixteen** [p. 129], **The Pump Room** [p. 83]) served in a swanky, contemporary setting. A standout, when available, is the lightly smoky wild sockeye salmon with morels.

Lou Malnati's, 439 N. Wells St., River North, Chicago, IL 60654; (312) 828-9800; loumalnatis.com; Pizza; $$. The flagship Lincolnwood location, which opened in 1971, spawned spin-offs throughout Chicagoland. These days, its deep-dish wonders can be shipped nationwide. Does it live up to the hype? Let's just say these cheese-laden, butter-crusted pies aren't just for tourists. There's thin-crust, too, but it—and the rest of the menu—are by no means in a starring role. There are many additional area locations; see the website for information.

Lou Mitchell's, 565 W. Jackson Blvd., West Loop, Chicago, IL 60661; (312) 939-3111; loumitchellsrestaurant.com; American; $$. This charming breakfast institution began serving consistent, perfectly fluffy omelets; crisp 'browns; and thick, buttered Greek toast in 1923, and it's still going strong. Though you may have to wait for a table—the malted Belgium waffles are worth it—freebie doughnut holes and Milk Duds, doled out to patrons by the friendly staff, keep hunger pangs at bay until your time arrives.

Mariscos El Veneno, 1024 N. Ashland Ave., East Village, Chicago, IL 60622; (773) 252-7200; Mexican/Seafood; $$. Always packed and never disappointing, this Mexican seafooder (aka Restaurant Veneno de Nayarit) serves up bracing marlin ceviche tostadas and fresh *crema*-drizzled shrimp tacos. BYO and prepare to put out the flames when house salsa verde comes into play. Another location is at 6651 S. Pulaski Rd., (773) 582-5576.

Mastro's Steakhouse, 520 N. Dearborn St., River North, Chicago, IL 60654; (312) 521-5100; mastrosrestaurants.com; Steak House; $$$$. This posh chain joins the city's long list of steak joints, proffering design-your-own seafood towers; large, spendy steaks and chops; fresher-than-fresh seafood; and a lengthy lineup of familiar sides. Butter cake is a best bet for dessert.

Mercadito, 108 W. Kinzie St., River North, Chicago, IL 60610; (312) 329-9555; mercaditorestaurants.com; Latin; $$$. This casually cool New York import attracts limelighters with ceviche, tacos, and *botanas,* served into the wee hours. Creative cocktails and an extensive tequila selection are a great team. Instead of calling it a night postnosh, descend to thwump-thwumping **Double A** (p. 230), an intimate lounge where an A-list crowd scores libations, prepared tableside. Cure your hangover on weekends, when *huevos* goes haute. Other ventures include **Tavernita** (p. 131) and **Little Market Brasserie** (p. 75).

Mexique, 1529 W. Chicago Ave., West Town, Chicago, IL 60642; (312) 850-0288; mexiquechicago.com; Mexican/French; $$$.

Speaking the language of two quite different cuisines—Mexican and French—Executive Chef Carlos Gaytan's off-the-beaten-path eatery is quite the wild ride. Just hop aboard, deciding between hibiscus-braised pork belly and chipotle-temple tamarind-glazed duck breast with chard and a corn-cranberry tamal. Another temptation: cocoa nib–adorned, roasted pork tenderloin with mole Teloloapan, spicy-sweet potato puree, and ratatouille.

mk, **868 N. Franklin St., River North, Chicago, IL 60610; (312) 482-9179; mkchicago.com; New American; $$$$.** Michael Kornick's bricked-out, two-tiered restaurant may have received a facelift, but it hasn't detracted from the deftly prepared, farm-driven tastings and a la carte offerings—prosciutto with melon and Ruby Red grapefruit, watermelon radish, pistachios, and mint, or wood-fired veal tenderloin with spaetzle and fragrant cumin-veal jus—that show both restraint and swagger. Remember, though, that the whimsical desserts—perhaps chicory churros with lemony rice pudding, raisins, espresso toffee, and hibiscus jam—are integral to the experience.

Moon's Sandwich Shop, **16 S. Western Ave., Near West Side, Chicago, IL 60612; (312) 226-5094; American/Sandwiches; $.** This bare-bones institution is a showstopper for homespun sandwiches, like mounded, mustard-slathered corned beef (also available in dinner form) or tomato-, mayo-, and lettuce-topped meat loaf served on rye. Almost as endearing, though, is the way in which servers present—with flourish—grits and eggs, chopped steak, and roast pork to a roster of regulars.

Moto, **945 W. Fulton Market, West Loop, Chicago, IL 60607; (312) 491-0058; motorestaurant.com; New American; $$$$.** This is the kind of bait-and-switch experience people either dig or detest. Mad scientist Homaro Cantu's den of molecular gastronomy turns out strange, theatrical tastings that rarely resemble food as we know it. Moto has a less tricked-out West Loop sibling, iNG, 951 W. Fulton Market, (855) 834-6464.

Mr. Beef, 666 N. Orleans St., River North, Chicago, IL 60610; (312) 337-8500; American; $. About the only reason to come to this quintessential stand—and a good reason it is—is to procure shards of Italian beef, stuffed into a jus-dipped roll piled with crunchy, spicy giardiniera. But the combo—Italian beef with the addition of snappy Italian sausage—is a work of art, too. To the joy of ex-pats (and chagrin of locals), a branch opened on California's Venice Beach boardwalk.

Naha, 500 N. Clark St., River North, Chicago, IL 60654; (312) 321-6242; naha-chicago.com; New American; $$$$. Carrie Nahabedian's elegantly unfussy ode to seasonal cuisine reinvents its menu often. However, expect inspiration from her Armenian roots and a West Coast sensibility to inform what appears. Stunning starters may include an artful meze platter or an intricate salad of hoop-house greens. From there, it's on to griddled English muffin sandwich with whiskey-cured pork jowl, a yolky fried duck egg, Taleggio, crunchy kohlrabi, and dill pickle remoulade. Both the dessert menu and the sophisticated wine list play a supporting role. **Additional location:** 534 N. Clark St., (312) 595-1616.

Nellcôte, 833 W. Randolph St., West Town, Chicago, IL 60607; (312) 432-0500; nellcoterestaurant.com; New American; $$$. More than a pretty face, Jared Van Camp's posh, chandelier-strung pad is named for a Côte d'Azur mansion that hosted the Rolling Stones. Living up to the hype are locally focused dishes, made from house-milled flour:

pillowy bread; plush, wood-fired pizza gilded with truffles, roasted red grapes, and Taleggio; and chestnut agnolotti with braised duck, butternut squash, Brussels sprouts, and Gouda. Seasonal house-made gelato is a fine finale, though you'll want to swig a few sweet cocktails, too. Sibling **Old Town Social** (p. 233) is not to be missed.

Next, 953 W. Fulton Market, West Loop, Chicago, IL 60607; (312) 226-0858; nextrestaurant.com; New American; $$$$. Grant Achatz's oft-changing, buy-in-advance dining establishment is—literally—the hottest ticket in town. Thematic menus, which waffle between historic, nostalgic, and cuisine-specific, incorporate the modern molecular style you've come to expect. Whether wondrous, precise, or downright peculiar, one thing is certain: Culinary conversations ensue. Conceptual cocktails await next door at **The Aviary** (p. 226) and exclusive, subterranean **The Office** (p. 233). Achatz's **Alinea** (p. 56) is in Lincoln Park.

9 Muses, 315 N. Halsted St., Greektown, Chicago, IL 60661; (312) 902-9922; 9museschicago.com; Greek/Mediterranean; $$. A bit of a secret—if there is such a thing—along the Halsted strip, this clublike haunt is favored by Mediterranean imports, who come to gobble up broiled, feta-stuffed florina peppers, feta-topped fries showered with oregano, and generously piled gyros.

Osteria Via Stato, 620 N. State St., River North, Chicago, IL 60654; (312) 642-8450; osteriaviastato.com; Italian/Pizza; $$$. Affordable shared plates, served family-style, are the main attraction at this Lettuce Entertain You osteria. When opting to dine this way, with an array of antipasti, two pastas, and a main course (perhaps lemony chicken Mario), diners most definitely leave full. There are a la carte options as well. Pizzeria Via Stato, located within, turns out artisanal, Roman-style pizzas and offers a hundreds-strong selection of Italian wines.

Paramount Room, 415 N. Milwaukee Ave., River West, Chicago, IL 60654; (312) 829-6300; paramountroom.com; American; $$. This late-night gastro-lounge sports a great Belgian and craft beer selection and noshes that go above and beyond. Raves go to the tempura-fried green beans served with spicy lime-chile dipping sauce, the juicy Wagyu burger, and the black-and-tan float with Guinness ice cream. The bi-level, vintage speakeasy setting is likeable, too.

Paris Club, 59 W. Hubbard St., River North, Chicago, IL 60654; (312) 595-0800; parisclubchicago.com; French; $$. This Melman venture ushers in affordable French dining, in a hot-spot setting. Focusing on shareable plates, options include lobster and truffled scrambled egg crostini and chilled shellfish platters as well as short rib Bourguignon, steak frites, and charcuterie boards with house-made pâtés and terrines. Consider the plat du jour, especially when Dover sole meunière is on it. Pair everything with house tap wines.

Park Grill, 11 N. Michigan Ave., Loop, Chicago, IL 60602; (312) 521-7275; parkgrillchicago.com; New American; $$$. At this Millennium Park eatery, it's about location, location, location—that and views of the skaters when weather permits. Thankfully, the food is decent as well. Score wild mushroom flatbread, topped with truffled ricotta and preserved lemon, or short ribs with caraway spaetzle and rainbow chard. Afterward, ogle "the Bean," a gleaming public sculpture nearby.

The Parthenon, 314 S. Halsted St., Greektown, Chicago, IL 60661; (312) 726-2407; theparthenon.com; Greek/Mediterranean; $$. Claiming to have invented *saganaki,* the Parthenon sure does serve a mean block of gooey, flamed cheese. Spit-roasted gyros, pork souvlaki skewers, and many lamb preparations are among the generously sized main courses, though a satisfying meal can be had from appetizers alone.

Pegasus Restaurant & Taverna, 130 S. Halsted St., Greektown, Chicago, IL 60661; (312) 226-3377; pegasuschicago.com; Greek/Mediterranean; $$. Take a trip to the Mediterranean seashore at this mainstay, its pitch-perfect rooftop patio framed by expansive skyline views. There, a meze-style menu—garlicky *skordalia* with marinated beets, tomato-sauced meatballs, baked baby eggplant—encourages sharing. But you'll find plenty of people-pleasers on the main menu, be it spanakopita, moussaka, or pastitsio—including in family-style form.

Perry's Deli, 174 N. Franklin St., Loop, Chicago, IL 60606; (312) 372-7557; perrysdeli.com; Deli; $. It's a feeding frenzy in the truest sense at this Financial District sandwich slinger, where triple deckers—layer upon layer of corned beef and spicy salami, stuffed into mustard-and-mayo-slicked rye bread, for example—meet classics like a sugar-cured bacon BLT and corned beef–pastrami blend smeared with Russian dressing. Not surprisingly, it's a mob scene during lunch.

Petterino's, 150 N. Dearborn St., Loop, Chicago, IL 60601; (312) 422-0150; petterinos.com; Italian; $$. Here's why you should head to Rich Melman's 1940s throwback: the garlicky "rack" of shrimp de Jonghe. The Goodman Theatre–bound crowd flocks to the caricature-adorned dining room for other dishes, too, such as skirt steak topped with melted maître d'hôtel butter and frosty martinis, enjoying them while perched upon rich rouge banquettes.

Philly's Best, 769 W. Jackson Blvd., Greektown, Chicago, IL 60661; (312) 715-9800; phillysbest.com; American/Sandwiches; $. There's limited competition, but that that doesn't diminish the draw of this longtime spot for cheesesteak, where ingredients are imported from out east. One thing's for sure: Brotherly love abounds when it comes to its Whized wonder. The large menu holds many likeable alternatives—oven-baked grinders, stromboli, and Tastykakes, to name a few. **Additional locations:** 907 W. Belmont Ave., (773) 525-7900; 2436 N. Milwaukee Ave., (773) 276-1900; and Evanston, 815 Emerson St., (847) 733-9000.

Piccolo Sogno, 464 N. Halsted St., West Loop, Chicago, IL 60642; (312) 421-0077; piccolosognorestaurant.com; Italian; $$$. Home to one of the loveliest patios in town, this inviting trattoria—a venture from Tony Priolo and Ciro Longobardo—serves rustic, regional Italian dishes with consistently tasty results. When in need of comfort, twice-cooked bread and vegetable soup can't be beat—that is, until you bite into the selection of antipasti and pleasantly chewy pasta dishes, including wood-fired, mushroom-ricotta-stuffed *cannelloni d'ortica* with spring nettles. Sib Piccolo Sogno Due is at 340 N. Clark St., (312) 822-0077.

Pierogi Heaven, 169 N. Wells St., Loop, Chicago, IL 60606; (312) 263-9305; pierogiheaven.com; Polish; $. Don't count calories at this dumpling destination, where plush pillows are filled with mushrooms and kraut, potato and cheddar, or meat; all come with fried onions, bacon, and sour cream. Sweet cheese or fruit-filled versions lend credence to dessert. Supplant your selections with borscht or stuffed cabbage when the mood strikes.

Pizzeria Uno, 29 E. Ohio St., River North, Chicago, IL 60611; (312) 321-1000; unos.com; Pizza; $$. Laying claim to Chicago's original deep-dish pizza, this small, tourist-riddled eatery can handle some overflow at roomier Pizzeria Due, 619 N. Wabash Ave., (312) 943-2400, nearby. Nothing here is going to knock locals' socks off, but for a hefty slice of Windy City history, this pizza purveyor won't be outdone. There are numerous, less jammed locations in the city and suburbs.

Prosecco, 710 N. Wells St., River North, Chicago, IL 60654; (312) 951-9500; ristoranteprosecco.com; Italian; $$$. When in need of a romantic rendezvous, this polished Italian eatery delivers. Serving dishes both rustic and refined—all with an eye toward its noteworthy wine list—meals may begin with slivers of bresaola topped with arugula and Parmesan shards; a commingling of avocados, grilled and diced baby lobster tail, and prawns; followed by orecchiette with wild mushroom and sun-dried-tomato-dotted black truffle cream sauce.

Province, 161 N. Jefferson St., West Loop, Chicago, IL 60661; (312) 669-9900; provincerestaurant.com; New American; $$$. Rooted in from-the-farm, American cuisine, Randy Zweiban (ex-**Nacional 27,** p. 233) nods to Latin flavors at his LEED-certified, fuchsia-hued spot, where citrusy bass ceviche starts things off right. Soft-shell crab with grilled tomatoes and guajillo vinaigrette exudes the punchy flavors he's known for. Among small, big, and bigger plates, the chipotle-infused shrimp carbonara with house-cured bacon stands out, as does skirt steak with herbaceous chimichurri, horseradish *crema,* and a potato-mushroom cake. Seats on the patio are coveted when warm weather arrives.

The Publican, 837 W. Fulton Market, West Loop, Chicago, IL 60607; (312) 733-9555; thepublicanrestaurant.com; New American/Pub; $$$. Modeled after a beer hall, Paul Kahan's rustic ode to Belgian brews, heirloom pork, and sustainable seafood kicks things off with a dazzling selection of oysters, varying in profile from brackish to crisp. Do order the spicy pork rinds (in fact, make it a double). From less common parts (beef heart tartare) to charcuterie plates with pork pie, head cheese, and harissa-date pâté to fish stew primavera in green garlic–saffron broth or Cajun boudin with mustard greens and sweet pepper soubise, ingredients themselves prove so fundamental.

Rockit Bar & Grill, 22 W. Hubbard St., River North, Chicago, IL 60654; (312) 645-6000; rockitbarandgrill.com; American; $$. Contemporary bar food served in a Nate Berkus–designed, wood-beam dining room—what's not to like? But blame the tuna tartare, the Kobe burger topped with melted Brie, and the truffle fries for why it's always packed to the gills. Head upstairs for a late-night scene, and consider coming for weekend brunch. Rockit Burger Bar is at 3700 N. Clark St., Wrigleyville, (773) 645-4400.

Roditys, 222 S. Halsted St., Greektown, Chicago, IL 60661; (312) 454-0800; roditys.com; Greek/Mediterranean; $$. There's a celebratory air to this Halsted Street staple, and comfort in knowing what to expect: friendly, genuine service; heaping portions; and a convivial, cheery feel. Whether you start with *saganaki* dotted with shrimp or go for dolmades, one of the many lamb configurations, herbaceous Greek chicken, or comforting pastitsio, it's rare to leave disappointed.

Roka Akor, 456 N. Clark St., River North, Chicago, IL 60654; (312) 477-7652; rokaakor.com; Japanese; $$$. Solid sushi, sashimi, and small plates draw droves to this upscale, contemporary Japanese chain. Make like the masses and order the hamachi-serrano chili roll, Wagyu-kimchi dumplings, and yuzu-laced butterfish tataki. Continue with robata-grilled shishito peppers with ponzu and bonito flakes or splurge-worthy steaks. Then again, you could go with the *omakase* menu instead. A second location is in Skokie at Old Orchard, 4999 Old Orchard Center, (847) 329-7650. Sibling Bombay Spice Grill & Wine offers light takes on Indian faves at 450 N. Clark St., (312) 477-7657.

Roti Mediterranean Grill, 10 S. Riverside Plaza, Loop, Chicago, IL 60606; (312) 775-7000; roti.com; Mediterranean; $. The Mediterranean answer to Chipotle, this health-conscious quick-serve allows diners to design their own creations with a vast array of fresh, flavorful ingredients. Get a wrap (it holds more of the good stuff), loading it with assertively seasoned chicken, pearls of Israeli couscous, tangy cucumber-tomato salad, and feta, all dabbed with spicy hot sauce and baba ghannouj. Just thank your lucky stars if lines don't stretch down the block. **Additional locations:** 310 W. Adams St., (312) 236-3500; 33 N. Dearborn St., (312) 263-9000; 200 W. Randolph St., (312) 332-6013; Northbrook, 984 Willow Rd., (847) 418-2400; and Vernon Hills, 1240 E. Route 45, (847) 883-8800. Plus, Schaumburg and Oak Brook locations are in the works.

RPM Italian, 52 W. Illinois St., River North, Chicago, IL 60654; (312) 222-1888; rpmitalian.com; Italian; $$$. The Melmans teamed with reality TV darlings Giuliana and Bill Rancic, the result being this swanky hub, where Doug Psaltis crafts crowd-pleasers like truffled garlic bread, short rib pappardelle, and wood oven–fired pizzettes. Mama DePandi's bucatini pomodoro, too. Nonetheless, there's the potential for Paul McGee's balanced cocktails to upstage.

Ruby's Restaurant, 3175 W. Madison St., Garfield Park, Chicago, IL 60612; (773) 638-5875; Regional American; $$. This homage to the late Edna Stewart (Edna's) continues tradition with Southern staples—buttery biscuits, golden fried chicken, blackened catfish—served by the same staff in precisely the same way.

Russian Tea Time, 77 E. Adams St., Loop, Chicago, IL 60603; (312) 360-0000; russianteatime.com; Russian; $$$. Symphony-goers appreciate the old-world ambience of this czar-worthy affair, a landmark for heavy Russian and Eastern European cuisine, including rich, creamy beef Stroganoff, potato-filled dumplings, and caviar-topped blini. Many get tipsy on flights of house-infused vodka.

Sable Kitchen & Bar, Hotel Palomar, 505 N. State St., River North, Chicago, IL 60654; (312) 755-9704; sablechicago.com; New American; $$$. There's more than meets the eye at this stylish Kimpton gastro-lounge with Heather Terhune (**Atwood Cafe** [p. 95], **312 Chicago** [p. 132]) in the kitchen; updated, classic cocktails from Mike Ryan (**The Violet Hour** [p. 237]); and master sommelier Emily Wines tending to the vino. A simple bowl of warm olives, house-made jerky, and bacon jam aren't over the top, but they're plain tasty. Many plates, poised for sharing, are available in two sizes, though it's hard to do anything but keep the buttermilk fried chicken and waffles with bourbon-infused syrup to oneself.

Santorini, 800 W. Adams St., Greektown, Chicago, IL 60607; (312) 829-8820; santorinichicago.com; Greek/Mediterranean; $$. Seafood is the specialty at this hopping Greektown lair, so have your way with the fire-grilled calamari and octopus, whole sea bass, and red snapper. Thankfully, the dubious will also find everything from the village salad to the citrus-kissed dandelion greens super-fresh. Daily specials expand on the classics, so partake while basking in the comfort of the rustic, hearth-lit dining room.

Sepia, 123 N. Jefferson St., West Loop, Chicago, IL 60661; (312) 441-1920; sepiachicago.com; New American; $$$. Eats from Andrew Zimmerman (ex-NoMI), coupled with standout cocktails and a comfortably sultry setting, make this mid-priced, rustic-contemporary Obama fave an all-around hit. Riffs on American classics ooze with sophistication, be it the otherworldly crispy, soft-cooked egg with morels, ramps, and asparagus, or the Wagyu bavette pastrami, teamed with onion jam and bordelaise. Swanky box lunches and too-cool desserts—marshmallow mousse, for example—complete the package.

Shanghai Terrace, Peninsula Chicago, 108 E. Superior St., River North, Chicago, IL 60611; (312) 573-6744; peninsula.com; Chinese; $$$.

Come with an expense account—you'll need it. This elevated dim sum experience, set in a regal, Asian supper club–inspired space overlooking the historic Water Tower, features duck prominently. It appears in a special salad with tangerines, toasted almonds, and truffle-peanut dressing. Meanwhile, a multicourse splurge of crisp, lacquered Peking duck proves delicious, with the bird carved and served with Mandarin pancakes, turned into elegant salad, and as an inclusion in hot and sour soup. Alternatives include a casserole of braised eggplant with salty fish, chicken, and lemongrass and steamed giant tiger prawns.

Shaw's Crab House, 21 E. Hubbard St., River North, Chicago, IL 60611; (312) 527-2722; shawscrabhouse.com; Seafood; $$$$. Seasonal and sustainable seafood is the bait at this clubby, Art Deco–style dining room, where showstoppers include plump king crab "bites" and briny, shucked-to-order bivalves. From the shellfish platters—popular in its adjacent, casual oyster bar—to the superb sushi, lobster, and prime steaks, there's plenty to choose from. Since the bounty comes at a cost, many frequent this Lettuce Entertain You venture come happy hour, when specials woo. And the seafood-heavy brunch? It's oyster-filled-amazing. There's another location at 1900 E. Higgins Rd., Schaumburg, (847) 517-2722.

Sinha Elegant Brazilian Cuisine, 2018 W. Adams Ave., Near West Side, Chicago, IL 60612; (312) 491-8200; sinhaelegantcuisine .com; Brazilian; $$. Offering a break from *churrascaria* overkill is Jorgina Pereira's authentic, all-your-can-eat Brazilian BYO, where homey shrimp *bobó, acarajé* (black-eyed pea fritters), and tasty top sirloin are bestowed upon in-the-know diners. Plan ahead and make reservations—they're requisite, especially during weekend brunch.

Siena Tavern, 51 W. Kinzie St., River North Chicago, IL 60612; (312) 595-1322; ssienatavern.com; Italian; $$. Fabio Viviani's rustic

Italian haunt hits all the high notes in an expansive space anchored by a wood-burning oven. Whether you settle on the ridiculously rich, house-made gnocchi in truffle cream; coccoli, doughy pillows stuffed with stracchino cheese and prosciutto; or "burnt" pepperoni pizza with pleasantly chewy crust, save room for balsamic-glazed sea bass with charred tomato-olive salsa and, at meal's end, bomboloni with whiskey-caramel, raspberry-Chianti, and chocolate-hazelnut sauces.

Sixteen, Trump International Hotel & Tower, 401 N. Wabash Ave, 16th Fl., River North, Chicago, IL 60611; (312) 588-8000; sixteen chicago.com; New American; $$$$. Suits with big budgets divert to The Donald's sweeping, window-walled dining room, situated on the 16th floor of the hotel with a spacious, seasonal patio. Executive Chef Thomas Lents crafts cuisine that competes with—if not outshines— the Swarovski chandelier–lit space. Dishes, which change often, may include crispy pig's head and *foie gras* with horseradish gremolata or Wagyu with caramelized cauliflower. There's also the option of field-, stream-, and pasture-themed tasting menus, each one more luxurious than the last. Many an oenophile has been smitten with the glass-enclosed wine gallery, stocked with stratospherically priced, special sips. Likewise, desserts from Patrick Fahy delight.

Slurping Turtle, 116 W. Hubbard St., River North, Chicago, IL 60654; (312) 464-0466; slurpingturtle.com; Asian; $$. Get with the porky *tan tan men* ramen, bincho-grilled short ribs, and addictive duck fat–fried chicken at Takashi Yagihashi's casual, bi-level izakaya. Caramel-soy macaroons are the perfect post-meal indulgence, including on Sundays during bento brunch.

South Water Kitchen, Hotel Monaco, 225 N. Wabash Ave., Loop, Chicago, IL 60601; (312) 236-9300; southwaterkitchen.com; American; $$. Familiar-but-updated comfort food—seared scallops with pea-bacon hash and carrot-ginger purée—define this casual, centrally located standby. It has an interesting tavern menu, too—a fact that's enough to bait tipplers during happy hour.

Sumi Robata Bar, 702 N. Wells St., River North, Chicago, IL 60654; (312) 988-7864; sumirobatabar.com; Japanese; $$$. Gene Kato (**Japonais** [p. 112]) shows such restraint at this open-kitchen concept, anchored by a sumi-burning robata grill. Get the peppery pork jowl, salty beef tongue, and buttery Australian lobster tail, and feel your fondness grow. Get adventurous with charcoal-kissed organ meats, or play it safe with stunningly simple tofu, served chilled with caviar and crisped ginger. Either way, this intimate spot provides a breath of fresh air.

Sunda, 110 W. Illinois St., River North, Chicago, IL 60654; (312) 644-0500; sundachicago.com; Asian; $$$. The name of this New Asian hot-spot nods to Southeast Asia's Sunda Shelf, its menu rife with home runs. Sweet-spicy Brussels sprout salad, crisped-rice sushi topped with spicy tuna and jalapeño, and steamed pork belly buns are just a few you can't miss. Throw in a few of the expertly prepared cocktails, too.

Sushi Dokku, 823 W. Randolph St., West Loop, Chicago, IL 60607; (312) 455-8238; sushidokku.com; Japanese; $$. This reincarnation of Sushi Wabi is a familiar formula, from the Hot Daisy maki with albacore, spicy mayo, and cucumber in a soy-paper wrapper to the small plates like tuna tataki with spicy mustard, tempura, and chewy udon in light soy broth. Sake cocktails are another plus.

SushiSamba Rio, 504 N. Wells St., River North, Chicago, IL 60610; (312) 595-2300; sushisamba.com/location/chicagorio; Japanese/South American; $$$. A sweeping, theatrical dining room and prime rooftop patio are the eye candy; flavor-packed Japanese, Peruvian, and Brazilian eats that the pretty people adore are the hook. The shareable noshes—heirloom tomato–seaweed salad, *chicharrón* calamari, rock shrimp tempura— are most always on point. There's whole crispy snapper, raw bar selections, and sushi as well, but customizable yaki platters—simple and non-convoluted—stand out. For dessert, the Samba split is pretty sweet.

Tavern at the Park, 130 E. Randolph St., Loop, Chicago, IL 60601; (312) 552-0070; tavernatthepark.com; New American; $$. Sometimes location is everything, but thankfully the food at this Millennium Park adjacent is beyond average as well. Settle in the handsome, wood-trimmed dining room for crunchy Parmesan-coated meatballs with vinegar peppers; five-cheese fondue; or a loaded, chopped salad. When prime rib is available, get it; alternately, the lobster mac and cheese, peppered with applewood bacon, wins out.

Tavernita, 151 W. Erie St., River North, Chicago, IL 60654; (312) 274-1111; tavernita.com; Spanish; $$$. Boisterous, scene-y, and tightly packed, this Mercadito-run haunt specializes in spirited small plates from Ryan Poli, the most notable of which include pork belly *bocadillos* topped with pickled red onions; Wagyu meatballs on a bed of hazelnut romesco; and a sublime, simple artichoke-beet salad with blue cheese and artichoke chips. Throw in some tap cocktails—the green tea–infused Booty Collins, perhaps. Also, consider pintxos from Barcito, a concept within.

Terzo Piano, Modern Wing, The Art Institute of Chicago, 159 E. Monroe St., Loop, Chicago, IL 60603; (312) 443-8650; terzopiano chicago.com; Italian; $$$. Sit on the spacious patio overlooking Millennium Park or in the stark, white, sunlit dining room filled with mod bucket seats. Either way, you'll be wooed by Tony Mantuano's modern Italian eats. Fortify with the lovely antipasto selection, and sip balanced seasonal cocktails, like blood orange–bourbon punch. Then, pick from the likes of applewood-smoked trout, plated with a poached egg, creamy spinach, and goat's milk cheese. This museum adjunct only serves lunch, with the exception of Thursday evenings. Also, look to Piano Terra in the tranquil north garden, a great option for fresh salads made from local ingredients.

Tesori, 65 E. Adams St., Loop, Chicago, IL 60603; (312) 786-9911; tesorichicago.com; Italian; $$$. A Symphony Center location means built-in clientele for this likeable Italian, which serves rich, truffle-buttered duck agnolotti with *foie gras,* pistachio-crusted lamb loin, and pappardelle crowned with rabbit ragù. An express menu gets diners in and out fast, while a one-ingredient menu shines the spotlight on an accolade-worthy item.

Texas de Brazil, 51 E. Ohio St., River North, Chicago, IL 60611; (312) 670-1006; texasdebrazil.com; Brazilian/Steak House; $$$. As with any fixed-price *churrascaria,* the table is set for a meat overload experience. Here, though, an aerial steward fetches bottles from a two-story wine cellar. Before the gauchos begin their onslaught, hit the positively luxurious salad bar, which swells with Manchego, hearts of palm, and shrimp salad. (It's also where you'll want to grab vinaigrette and chimichurri to garnish the main event.) Meats, which arrive in endless procession until you flip your disk from green to red, include snappy-skinned sausages, garlicky sirloin, and flank steak. Garlic mashed potatoes and caramelized bananas come with; dessert costs extra.

312 Chicago, Hotel Allegro, 136 N. LaSalle St., Loop, Chicago, IL 60602; (312) 696-2420; 312chicago.com; Italian; $$. Padova, Italy, native Luca Corazzina (**Prosecco** [p. 124]) plates rustic, regional dishes with a green-market sensibility in a softly lit, wood-heavy dining room outfitted with an exhibition kitchen. Start with sautéed shrimp, accompanied by caramelized radicchio, peach balsamic, and braised lentils. Savor house-made butternut squash tortellini with brown butter and sage, or warm up to beautifully prepared Skuna Bay salmon, which arrives with black kale, cippolini onions, and pleasantly chewy farro. The large but thoughtful wine list is loaded with affordable pairings.

Topolobampo, 445 N. Clark St., River North, Chicago, IL 60654; (312) 661-1434; rickbayless.com; Mexican; $$$$. As popular as it ever was, Rick Bayless's world-class, fine-dining destination represents his commitment to sustainable, small-farm ingredients—some custom grown and produced. The artwork-adorned dining room features ever-changing upscale, inventive takes on regional Mexican dishes. Swagger appears in the form of *esquites,* a salad of preserved Nichols Farm field corn, with guajillo chile, creamy black garlic, wisps of cincho cheese, nettles, lovage, and pickled king trumpet mushrooms, or wood-roasted 28-day-aged prime rib eye with 29-ingredient Oaxacan black mole. Is it really as good as the buzz suggests? You bet. But for a more affordable, casual, though no less eye-popping experience, try counterparts **Frontera Grill** (p. 105) or **XOCO** (p. 136). Also meriting consideration are Frontera Fresco at both Macy's on State Street, (312) 781-4483, and Northwestern University, Norris University Center in Evanston, (847) 491-3741; and Tortas Frontera at O'Hare Airport, (773) 686-6180.

Trattoria No. 10, 10 N. Dearborn St., Loop, Chicago, IL 60602; (312) 984-1718; trattoriaten.com; Italian; $$$. The raison d'être of this tucked-away subterranean Italian—convenient, near-theater address aside—is its house-made ravioli. The arrabbiata-sauced, spicy sausage–stuffed version is plain delicious. Still, you'll also be satisfied by the beef carpaccio with Gorgonzola dolce, the fresh-as-can-be Caprese, and the duck confit farfalle studded with pine nuts.

Uncle Mike's Place, 1700 W. Grand Ave., West Town, Chicago, IL 60622; (312) 226-5318; unclemikesplace.com; Filipino; $. Not to say the omelets don't rank, but the Filipino breakfast is the hook at this West Town diner, a destination for spicy Spam, charred *tocino* with garlic rice and eggs, and chubby *longanisa,* bolstered by tomato-onion salsa. The congeelike porridge has a deserved following, too.

Union Sushi + Barbeque Bar, 230 W Erie St., River North, Chicago, IL 60654; (312) 662-4888; eatatunion.com; Japanese; $$$. This graffiti-splashed River Norther from Mike Schatzman and Worachai Thapthimkuna (Sushi Wabi) is as popular a spot for robata-grilled gator and curry chicken thigh as it is for dumplings, noodles, and convoluted maki. More memorable, though, are surprises like the sweet-potato tots swimming in dashi.

Viand Bar & Kitchen, Marriott Courtyard, 155 E. Ontario St., River North, Chicago, IL 60611; (312) 255-8505; viandchicago.com; New American; $$$. Contemporary, approachable comfort food is the draw at this handsome, hotel-adjacent space. Design your own meat preparation, choosing between rib eye, filet, and flatiron steak, with accompanying sauces. But do this after having classic French onion soup. Beyond, ubiquitous dishes—osso bucco, roast chicken—meet more surprising alternatives, such as beef medallions with purple Peruvian potatoes.

Vivere, 71 W. Monroe St., Loop, Chicago, IL 60603; (312) 332-4040; vivere-chicago.com; Italian; $$$. The finest of the Italian Village eateries is also popular with the CSO- and theater-bound set, its dramatic, Jordan Mozer–designed dining room an ideal place to enjoy pheasant-filled agnolotti and semolina gnocchi with hen-of-the-woods 'shrooms and selections from the winning wine list. Going well beyond the red-sauce repertoire, there's also a Wagyu rib eye with whipped Parmesan potatoes and truffle-infused poached eggs of note.

Weber Grill, Hilton Garden Inn, 539 N. State St., River North, Chicago, IL 60654; (312) 467-9696; webergrillrestaurant.com; American; $$$. There's no way to keep the crowds at bay—the signature kettle-cooked creations have what it takes. So, get with the program and sneak peeks of the grilling action. Meanwhile, munch on decent steaks, burgers, and grill-fired pizzas. The mound of onion straws is a perfect match for beer-can chicken, brisket, and barbecue ribs. And the warm Dutch apple pie with Maker's Mark caramel sauce? It's kind of worth the wait. **Additional locations:** 2331 Fountain Sq., Lombard, (630) 953-8880; 1010 N. Meacham Rd., Schaumburg, (847) 413-0800.

Wildfire, 159 W. Erie St., River North, Chicago, IL 60654; (312) 787-9000; wildfirerestaurant.com; American; $$$. This haunt proves Rich Melman has the Midas touch. A throwback for steak, chops, and seafood, it's a preferred place to pony up for chopped salads, enjoyable Romanian skirt steak, and passable filets. **Additional locations:** Schaumburg, 1250 E. Higgins Rd., (847) 995-0100; Oak Brook, 232 Oakbrook Center, (630) 586-9000; Lincolnshire, 235 Parkway Dr., (847) 279-7900; and Glenview, 1300 Patriot Blvd., (847) 657-6363.

Vera, 1023 W. Lake St., West Loop, Chicago, IL 60607; (312) 243-9770; verachicago.com; Spanish; $$. Mark and Elizabeth Mendez, former chef and sommelier at **Carnivale** (p. 100), opened this sweet little Spaniard with ingredient-driven shareable plates and pintxos, an old-meets-new wine list, and a large, thoughtful sherry selection. Bread service is storied (and comes at a fee); get it and bacon-wrapped dates with blue cheese fondue, halibut with green romesco, and some paella to share. For a more intimate experience, dine at Otro Bar, the five-seat chef's table, for a special season-specific meal.

Wishbone, 1001 W. Washington Blvd., West Loop, Chicago, IL 60607; (312) 850-2663; wishbonechicago.com; Regional American; $$. Delivering Southern comfort—especially during breakfast and brunch—this casual kitchen causes cravings for creamy, bacon-flecked shrimp and grits, blackened tilapia, and red beans and rice. A second outpost is at 3300 N. Lincoln Ave., (773) 549-2663.

XOCO, 449 N. Clark St., River North, Chicago, IL 60654; (312) 334-3688; rickbayless.com; Mexican; $$. While you'd think the lines, awkward configuration, and uncomfortable seating of Rick Bayless's street food–inspired, counter-service Mexican would prove disconcerting, the wood-burning-oven-warmed *pibil torta*—stuffed with meltingly tender, achiote suckling pig, black beans, and pickled onion with a side of brow-mopping habanero salsa—knows only forgiveness. *Caldos,* served after 3 p.m., are equally endearing, especially the short rib version built from a brooding red chile broth and farm-to-table ingredients. Pastries—try the churros—plus fresh-roasted cacao-bean-to-cup hot chocolate and *agua fresca* are ideal accompaniments.

ZED451, 739 N. Clark St., River North, Chicago, IL 60610; (312) 266-6691; zed451.com; Eclectic/Steak House; $$$. This stylish, updated *churrascaria* has the same all-you-can-eat bent, but the harvest salads, tableside-carved proteins, and trendy-Zen scene—not to mention the gorgeous rooftop patio—add up to a superior experience. Although availability of soups and composed salads changes, they're always long on flavor. Be seduced by salty, buttermilk-herb bottom sirloin, fire-grilled rib eye, and seasoned rump roast. Proceed to New Zealand red deer and Amaretto-pistachio duck breast. Consider coming for brunch—it provides the perfect balance of sweet (cinnamon rolls) and savory (thick, pleasantly chewy maple bacon and carved meats).

Zocalo Restaurant and Tequila Bar, 358 W. Ontario St., River North, Chicago, IL 60654; (312) 302-9977; zocalochicago.com; Mexican; $$. An after-office crowd clocks in at this popular cantina, sought out for its guac trios, perky ceviche, and elotes (loaded corn-off-the-cob) as well as house-made tamales and shredded beef tostadas zapped with sherry-chipotle vinaigrette. Platters encourage sharing—especially when tequila flights and agave-inspired cocktails come into play. Its offshoot is Taco Joint, 158 W. Ontario St., (312) 337-8226.

South

Archer Heights, Ashburn, Beverly, Bridgeport, Bronzeville, Chatham, Chinatown, Englewood, Far South Side, Greater Grand Crossing, Hyde Park, Lawndale, Little Italy, Little Village, Near South Side, Pilsen, Printer's Row, Roseland, South Deering, South Loop, University Village

Largely less explored, Chicago's South Side covers more than half of the city's land. Filled with historic landmarks and museums, it leaves a lot to be discovered by food-minded passersby. Looking beyond burgeoning Little Italy, Chinatown, and the beloved taquerias of Pilsen, you'll find jerk pits, shrimp shacks, and diners worth detouring for. Come for kebabs, settle in for comfort-driven cuisine, and return (often) for the barbecue of champions.

Acadia, 1639 S. Wabash Ave., South Loop, Chicago, IL 60616; (312) 360-9500; acadiachicago.com; New American; $$$$. The menu at this tranquil South Loop dining room recollects summers Chef/Owner Ryan McCaskey spent in Maine. One look at the menu and you'll assume he ate well. Proof comes in the form of elegant Stonington lobster pie, swathed in sour cream pastry with black trumpet mushrooms; black cod, accompanied by caponata and squid ink vinaigrette; and seasonal, entire-table chef's tasting menus. Sommelier Jason Prah's wine list brims with all-budget finds, but creative craft cocktails will woo you, too.

Al's #1 Italian Beef, 1079 W. Taylor St., Little Italy, Chicago, IL 60607; (312) 226-4017; alsbeef.com; American; $. People go nuts for the shredded, giardiniera-topped Italian beef served here, even if there is an odd, nutmeglike quality to it. Get it dipped ("juicy" or "wet") and "hot" (with spicy, crushed red pepper–flecked pickled vegetables), or try it "sweet" (with roasted bell peppers). Then, roll up your sleeves and indulge in its sloppy glory while standing or sitting at picnic tables outside. Mind you, the fresh-cut, skin-on fries might just steal the show. There are seven other locations throughout Chicagoland (see the website for information).

Barbara Ann's BBQ, 7617 S. Cottage Grove Ave., Greater Grand Crossing, Chicago, IL 60619; (773) 651-5300; Barbecue; $$. Real, down-home 'cue is dreamy enough to have you breaking appointments in favor of a trek to this cash-only carryout, which exhibits the smokiness aficionados crave. However, the custom-made links may mean you forget about slabs and plump, juicy rib tips entirely.

Birrieria Reyes de Ocotlán, 1322 W. 18th St., Pilsen, Chicago, IL 60608; (312) 733-2613; Mexican; $. A shining example of its kind, this humble spot does goat proud—its birria a steaming, restorative consommé mounded with tender hunks of goat, onions, chile arbol, and cilantro spurted with lime. If the mood strikes, work your way through some goat tacos, while eyeing the comically tragic goat head adorning the wall.

Birrieria Zaragoza, 4852 S. Pulaski Rd., Archer Heights, Chicago, IL 60632; (773) 523-3700; Mexican; $$. There are excuses to eat out, and then there are things that *necessitate* a meal out. A visit to this *birrieria* falls squarely in the latter camp, a fact made clear when smoldering goat stew arrives. The *molcajates* of fresh-made salsa, handmade tortillas that are good enough to eat solo, and peerless goat tacos brightened with lime all pop with flavor.

Brasserie by LM, Essex Inn, 800 S. Michigan Ave., South Loop, Chicago, IL 60605; (312) 431-1788; brasseriebylm.com; French; $$$. The South Loop may not be a major dining destination, but this hotel-centered restaurant is helping to change that with an all-day menu of French classics: French onion soup gratinée; mussels steeped in fennel, curry, and cream; and comforting coq au vin. There are a couple of *croque* variations, too. Check out the $25 three-course prix-fixe menu for the best deal. Its sister properties are LM Bistro, 111 W. Huron St., (312) 202-9900; Brasserie 54 by LM, 5420 N. Clark St., (773) 334-9463; and Troquet, 1834 W. Montrose Ave., (773) 334-5664.

Cafe Bionda, 1924 S. State St., South Loop, Chicago, IL 60616; (312) 326-9800; cafebionda.com; Italian; $$. Lovers of red sauce find much to like in the bounteous portions of Old Country standbys (fried calamari, antipasto salad, spaghetti and meatballs). Other rib-stickers include rigatoni with slow-simmered, pot roast–infused "gravy"; jumbo shells cloaked in vodka tomato cream; and crisp-skinned, boneless brick chicken with rosemary potatoes.

Cafe Trinidad, 557 E. 75th St., Greater Grand Crossing, Chicago, IL 60619; (773) 846-8081; cafetrinidad.com; Caribbean; $. Munch on curry goat, hell-fire jerk chicken with pea-studded rice, and potato and *chana* (curried potatoes and chickpeas) while island beats and a friendly environ transport you someplace else. Roti wraps—great stuffed with the aforementioned jerk chicken—require hibiscus-esque sorrel to quell the habaneros' burn.

Cafecito, 26 E. Congress Pkwy., South Loop, Chicago, IL 60605; (312) 922-2233; cafecitochicago.com; Deli/Cuban; $. Be forewarned: These pressed sandwiches—some simple, others stylin'—result in post-visit cravings. The crusty Cubano strikes the perfect balance between porky goodness, briny pickles, piquant mustard, and heaven-sent

Fresh Tortillas

Few things are better than a warm, pliant pack of fresh-made tortillas. Thankfully, Chicago has these artisanal riches in plenty, in some cases available right from the source.

Atotonilco Tortilleria, 1707 W. 47th St., Chicago, IL 60609, sells theirs still warm at grocery stores like **Carniceria Jimenez** (p. 241) and Berwyn Fruit Market.

El Milagro Tortillas, 2919 S. Western Ave., Chicago, IL 60608; (773) 650-1614; el-milagro.com; are pretty much the crème de la crème. Get them at its stores and taquerias, 3050 W. 26th St., (773) 579-6120, and 1927 S. Blue Island Ave., (312) 421-7443. You can also procure its fresh *maíz* at some Mexican grocers, such as Berwyn Fruit Market.

Sabinas Food Products, 1509 W. 18th St., Pilsen, Chicago, IL 60608; (312) 738-2412; is a tarty tortilleria that sells its wares on-site.

---

cheesiness, while the Provoleta is a griddled marvel of provolone, roasted red pepper, and garlic-laden chimichurri. Sip eye-popping Cuban espresso while making room for round two: a meltingly tender *ropa vieja* sammie with black beans and sweet plantains. A second location is at 7 N. Wells St., (312) 263-4750.

Cai, 2100 S. Archer Ave., Chinatown, Chicago, IL 60616; (312) 326-6888; caichicago.com; Chinese; $$. Dim sum like you mean it at this bustling behemoth, an ornate option for sugary egg custard buns and flaky egg tarts, never mind delicate, translucent dumplings and a tasty pan-fried turnip cake, served until 4 p.m. When the Cantonese menu kicks in, duck—prepared a myriad of ways—shines.

Carnitas Uruapan, 1725 W. 18th St., Pilsen, Chicago, IL 60608; (312) 226-2654; Mexican; $. Light on frills but long on flavor are the *carnitas* served here—available in by-the-pound, moist, straight-up pork or whole-hog configurations. They arrive with warm corn tortillas, pickled jalapeños, and salsa verde for build-your-own fun. You'd be wise to get some *chicharrones* (fried pork rinds) and nopales to go with. And—if it's the weekend—go all-out with an order of hangover-helping menudo.

Cedars Mediterranean Kitchen, 1206 E. 53rd St., Hyde Park, Chicago, IL 60615; (773) 324-6227; eatcedars.com; Mediterranean/Middle Eastern; $$. You'll find all the Med stalwarts—gently spiced lentil soup, standout falafel, kebabs—at this sleek, strip-mall dining room. Yet it's the tender hunks of slow-braised lamb in garlicky yogurt sauce and the well-wrought stews and sandwiches that are most memorable.

Chicago's Home of Chicken and Waffles, 3947 S. King Dr., Bronzeville, Chicago, IL 60653; (773) 536-3300; Regional American; $$. Crunchy, salty chicken and sweet, syrup-doused waffles are the benchmark of this soul-food spot. Nonetheless, there are other finds for the after-church crowd, including smothered gizzards, red beans and rice, and gooey mac and cheese. It has a suburban sibling in Oak Park at 543 Madison St., (708) 524-3300.

City Tavern, 1416 S. Michigan Ave., South Loop, Chicago, IL 60605; (312) 663-1278; New American; citytavernchicago.com; $$. Take a step back in time at this South Loop watering hole, which grew into its own after a series of chef shake-ups. The menu is replete with classics (brandade) and updated American dishes, such as duck fat popcorn with blue cheese powder and smoked paprika, and vanilla-infused corn soup with pickled corn and ancho oil. Refined-yet-comforting entrees continue the theme, be it braised beef cheek and pickled tongue with mustard spaetzle or braised rabbit leg with egg noodles and wild mushrooms. Tweaked cocktails and an impressive beer list are welcome companions.

Couscous, 1445 W. Taylor St., University Village, Chicago, IL 60607; (312) 226-2408; couscousrestaurant.com; African/Middle Eastern; $. Coeds and post-op docs from the nearby medical campus rub elbows here over Maghrebin cuisine. Turn to the tagines and meaty soufflélike creations, which go down well with house-made lemonade. Don't discount the more familiar fare, though, be it hummus or falafel.

Daddy-O's Jerk Pit, 7518 S. Cottage Grove Ave., Chatham, Chicago, IL 60619; (773) 651-7355; Caribbean; $. Expert jerk preparations are dished out by an affable pitmaster in a cheery, no-frills, mostly carryout storefront, which emanates with reggae beats. The butterflied birds—set aflame by a Scotch bonnet and allspice-based rub—get tempered by plantain and rice and bean accompaniments. Braised oxtail and curry goat are enviable alternatives.

Davanti Enoteca, 1359 W. Taylor St., Little Italy, Chicago, IL 60607; (312) 226-5550; davantichicago.com; Italian/Small Plates/ Wine Bar; $$. Scott Harris's rustic, cavernous-feeling Little Italy wine bar—across from the Taylor Street **Mia Francesca** (p. 42)—is a happening joint for brick oven–fired pizza topped with pork belly, potato, and a farm egg; charcuterie and cheese spreads; tastily topped polenta boards; and smearable snacks like ricotta and honeycomb, served in Mason jars with crostini. Wines by the glass and quartino, coupled with an affordable price point, heighten its appeal.

Don Pedro Carnitas, 1113 W. 18th St., Pilsen, Chicago, IL 60608; (312) 829-4757; Mexican; $. If it's Sunday, come early—this spot does a brisk business with the post-mass crowd. A bit confusing unless you know the drill, there are two counters serving various wonderments: *barbacoa, birria,* nopales, and chorizo, plus *chicharrones* and *carnitas* sold by the pound and chopped to order. Step up and order to go, or wait for a table in the bare-bones dining room in back. Then, customize with green and red salsas, onions, cilantro, and lime to your heart's content (and tune of a mariachi serenade).

Double Li, 228 W. Cermak Rd., Chinatown, Chicago, IL 60616; (312) 842-7818; Chinese; $$. Serious Szechuan-style eats, courtesy of Ben Li, bypass all that has given Americanized Chinese a bad name. Rather, the bold, deeply nuanced, fiery, and intricate dishes set tongues tingling. Take the dry chile chicken, its crisply fried nubs of meat wok-tossed with scallions and dry chile; the cumin-scented lamb; and the rich, brow-mopping battered fish swimming in brick-red chile broth as examples. Not oversights are dishes such as sweet-savory, garlicky black-pepper beef; hoisin-glazed, house-made "bacon"; dumplings; and excellent twice-cooked pork.

EL Ideas, 2419 W. 14th St., Lawndale, Chicago, IL 60608; (312) 226-8144; elideas.com; New American; $$$$. Phillip Foss's culinary playground bestows a multicourse prix-fixe menu on a handful of diners, a few nights a week. But whether it's marrow-accented Osetra caviar with verjus or intricately plated black cod with hints of allium, rye, and turmeric, this destination on an easy-to-miss dead-end street won't fail to wow. Best of all, it's fine dining enjoyed approachably and presented by expert servers. That said, you'll pay in kind ($145 per person); however, the BYO policy sure helps.

Eleven City Diner, 1112 S. Wabash Ave., South Loop, Chicago, IL 60605; (312) 212-1112; elevencitydiner.com; Deli; $$. The food at Brad Rubin's retro-chic South Loop diner is on the pricy side, yet the Jewish staples do the trick when cravings hit. Best are the oversize sandwiches, like the Woody Allen, a double-decker corned beef and pastrami number. Melts on challah and brisket with potatoes and carrots are tempting, too. If none of these seem worthy of a mini-splurge, phosphates, floats, and egg creams prepared by an in-house soda jerk just might.

Epic Burger, 517 S. State St., South Loop, Chicago, IL 60605; (312) 913-1373; epicburger.com; Burgers; $. For fast food of another variety, head to this environmentally conscious joint serving burgers packed from pasture-fed, antibiotic- and hormone-free beef topped with low-mileage ingredients (cage-free eggs, Wisconsin cheese) alongside hand-cut, skin-on fries crisped in trans fat–free oil. Likewise, chicken sandwiches are for those with a conscience. Thick shakes and a fab lemon-squeeze smoothie are among the added perks. There are several other locations; see the website for info.

5 Loaves Eatery, 405 E. 75th St., Greater Grand Crossing, Chicago, IL 60619; (773) 891-2889; 5loaveseatery.com; American; $$. Big breakfasts, including fluffy omelets, powdered sugar–dusted Belgium waffles, and thick-cut French toast, give way to po'boys, stuffed baked potatoes, and satisfying salads with a loyal following. The quaint cafe also features all-you-can-eat "soulful" Saturdays and Sundays, when down-home Southern fare can be had on the cheap.

Flo & Santos, 1310 S. Wabash Ave., South Loop, Chicago, IL 60605; (312) 566-9817; floandsantos.com; Italian/Polish; $$. The folks behind Zapatista offer up this nostalgic ode to contrasting Polish and Italian cuisines. Here, pierogi and pizza exist in harmony, and families of South Siders even tolerate a touch of Cubbie Blue. The garlicky kielbasa—served in sandwich form and as a pizza topper with kraut—is a standout, and the lacy potato pancakes are good, especially when accompanied by a few brews or Polish vodka.

Go 4 Food, 212 W. 23rd St., Chinatown, Chicago, IL 60616; (312) 842-8688; go4foodusa.com; Chinese; $$. Although it's set off of the main drag, this contemporary Chinatown spot is a pleasing option for simple, well-prepared classics, plus a few surprises. Among them, count the *kalbi*-eqsue French beef tenderloin, addictive fried silverfish, and crisp, head-on salt-and-pepper shrimp as musts. Need a dose of comfort? E-fu noodles and an order of minced beef with egg yolk should do the trick.

Grant's Wonderburger Grill, 11045 S. Kedzie Ave., Beverly, Chicago, IL 60655; (773) 238-7200; American; $. For an endearing throwback experience; cheesy, griddled, "wonder"-sauced burgers; and loaded, skin-on, spiral-cut fries, make fast tracks for this 1954 diner that time forgot. Respectable chili, true cherry Cokes, and dinner-size sundaes have devotees, too.

Han 202, 605 W. 31st St., Bridgeport, Chicago, IL 60616; (312) 949-1314; han202.com; Chinese; $$. When en route to The Cell—or, frankly, just because—consider this exceptionally affordable diversion, a BYOB beacon of fine Asian fusion from Guan Chen. Hunker down and choose your own adventure with a five-course prix fixe ($25), opting for beef-lemongrass salad with tart matchsticks of Granny Smith, and blazing miso soup with contrasting bits of sweet king crab. Also worthy of consideration is the dish of clams with white truffle sauce and the expertly prepared shrimp-scallop red curry, which smacks of a five-star affair.

Harold's Chicken Shack No. 2, 6419 S. Cottage Grove Ave., South Side, Chicago, IL 60637; (773) 363-9586; American; $. It's impossible to single out one of the countless, mostly South Side institutions, which vary in quality, have slightly different menus, and waver in terms of environment. Some are too rough around the edges to be called charming. However, one thing is certain: When Harold's is good, it's so fine. Just look for the sign emblazoned with a crazed, chicken-chasing cook, cleaver in hand. Then, order a crackly-skinned, half chicken mix, fried "hard" and peppery, with juicy white and dark meat. It'll arrive cloaked in piquant hot sauce, atop fries and slices of white bread. Naturally, there's fried fish, shrimp, and by-the-books sides as well.

Honky Tonk BBQ, 1213 W. 18th St., Pilsen, Chicago, IL 60608; (312) 226-7427; honkytonkbbqchicago.com; Barbecue; $$. Owner Willie Wagner got his start as a man about town, setting up his smoker at outdoor festivals and neighborhood events. Now, his Memphis-style smoke shack turns out some amazing pulled pork, flavorful lightly charred brisket, and fried green tomatoes that down-right deserve a championship win. The properly chewy baby backs, with a side of bracing slaw, likewise will not let you down. Weekly specials—perhaps candied bacon or Manchego-and-shiitake-stuffed empanadas—deviate from the norm.

I-57 Rib House, 1524 E. 115th St., Far South Side, Chicago, IL 60643; (773) 429-1111; Barbecue; $$. For real-deal carryout on the far South Side, this beaut is hard to beat—especially when you order the charred, sage-scented hot links and slow-cooked ribs sauced hot, or ordered 50-50-style by those who can't handle heat.

Jamaica Jerk Villa, 8 E. 22nd St., South Loop, Chicago, IL 60616; (312) 225-0983; jamaicajerkvilla.com; Caribbean; $$. Marinated and rubbed, grilled jerk chicken will set your lips to tingling, building heat with each chomp. Biting callaloo helps to cool the burn ever so slightly. Alternatives such as stewed or curry chicken and oxtails can be had at a second location, 737 W. 79th St., (773) 651-2240, as well.

Joy Yee's Noodle Shop, 2139 S. China Pl., Chinatown, Chicago, IL 60616; (312) 328-0001; joyyee.com; Pan-Asian; $. Starch-seekers swoon over this one-stop noodle shop, which serves everything from wontons and udon to chow mein and Korean-style seafood soup. There are locations in Naperville, 1163 E. Ogden Ave., (630) 579-6800; Evanston, 521 Davis St., (847) 733-1900; 1135 S. Halsted St., (312) 997-2128; and 1465 Irving Park Rd., (773) 281-2318. Nearby, Joy Yee Plus, 2159 S. China Pl., (312) 842-8928, expands upon the concept with sushi, sukiyaki, and shabu-shabu. The restaurants also have a great selection of fruity drinks and bubble tea.

Koda Bistro, 10352 S. Western Ave., Beverly, Chicago, IL 60643; (773) 445-5632; kodabistro.com; French; $$$. Executive Chef Aaron Browning (**Everest,** p. 104) brings a change of pace to the Far South Side with this sleek, contemporary Frenchie with a seasonal mindset. Sip pours from the LED-lit bar before kicking back in the dim dining room for tarte flambées and produce-driven follow-ups, such as duck confit with spaghetti squash, duck fat–fried fingerlings, and cranberry gastrique.

La Casa de Samuel, 2834 W. Cermak Rd., Little Village, Chicago, IL 60623; (773) 376-7474; lacasadesamuelchicago.com; Mexican; $. The food of Guerrero informs the cooking at this Little Village taqueria, which serves vegetarian's nightmares (baby eel, grilled bull's testicles, rattlesnake) as well as truly special venison *cecina* with blistered handmade tortillas, silky guac, and acidic pico de gallo. Baked, grilled baby goat with beans and *chiles en nogada* are other house specialties.

La Chaparrita, 2500 S. Whipple St., Little Village, Chicago, IL 60623; (773) 247-1402; Mexican; $. Tucked within a *supermercado* is a gem of a find, serving top-tier tacos of many kinds. Whether you succumb to the beef *carnitas*-like *suadero,* pleasingly subtle chorizo, crispy tripe, or superior achiote-tinted *al pastor,* you'll want a fruity *agua fresca* alongside.

La Lagartija, 132 S. Ashland Ave., West Loop, Chicago, IL 60607; (312) 733-7772; lalagartijataqueria.com; Mexican; $$. "Little lizards" are a running theme at this Tex-Mex hot-spot, the creation of Laura Cid-Perea, a Bayless protégé, and her husband, Luis Perea. Groove on the noteworthy battered, chipotle-dressed shrimp and brick-red, caramelized *pastor* tacos, both tucked into piping hot, house-made tortillas. Its compadre, **Bombon Cafe** (p. 99), is just down the block; likewise, sweets-focused Bombon Cake Gallery, 3748 W. 26th St., (773) 277-8777, is nearby.

La Petite Folie, Hyde Park Shopping Center, 1504 E. 55th St., Hyde Park, Chicago, IL 60615; (773) 493-1394; lapetitefolie.com; French; $$$. Cordon Bleu–trained Executive Chef/Owner Mary Mastricola opened this pleasant neighborhood bistro with an all-French wine list to great neighborhood success. Tweaked seasonally, the classic and affordable fixed-price menus feature dishes like an Alsatian tart with Gruyère, smoked duck salad, and braised chicken, served in a quiet, date-appropriate dining room.

Lao Beijing, 2138 S. Archer Ave., Chinatown, Chicago, IL 60616; (312) 881-0168; Chinese; $$. Tony Hu's Chinatown hub emphasizes the cuisine of its namesake city, with options that include crispy eggplant, shrimp-pork dumplings with black vinegar for dunking, and a three-course meal of Beijing duck, which appears shredded, as soup, and as a mélange of crisped skin and scallions, scooped into pancakes and daubed with hoisin.

Lao Hunan, 2230 S. Wentworth Ave., Chinatown, Chicago, IL 60616; (312) 842-7888; laohunanonline.com; Chinese; $$. Tony Hu's empire is better for dishes like moist, battered dry-chile fish fillet; fragrant, broth-blasted Hunan-style tofu; and brow-mopping Hunan-style crispy eggplant, its creamy-inside, tempura-battered planks piled high with dried chiles and shards of green onion. But only a fool would miss the gingery, wok-blistered green chiles with black bean sauce and garlic chips.

Lao Ma La, 2017 S. Wells St., Chinatown; (312) 225-8989; tony gourmetgroup.com; Chinese; $$. Mouth-numbing Szechuan fare is the focus at this Tony Hu knockout, where everyone who's anyone gets the bubbling "house special grilled fish in spicy pan." Presented on a portable burner, this fiery beast is torn from the bone, then the remaining broth becomes a base for add-ins of your choice. Although the menu houses a conglomeration of Hu hits, save them for another day, opting instead a hot pot with skewers—like spice-sprinkled lamb—for your added enjoyment.

Lao Shanghai, 2163 S. China Pl., Chinatown, Chicago, IL 60616; (312) 808-0830; Chinese; $$. Speaking the Shanghainese dialect, this Tony Hu venture offers *xiao long bao*—broth- and pork-filled dumplings—and tender, braised pork belly in preserved bean curd, but you'll also find showier preps, like a platter of sizzling, spicy lamb and shredded deep-fried fish.

Lao Sze Chuan, 2172 S. Archer Ave., Chinatown, Chicago, IL 60616; (312) 326-5040; Chinese; $$. Tony Hu's beloved Chinatown fixture, popular with the hot pot–seekers, is every bit as pleasing for the gluttonous solo diner, who will be tempted to keep raging-hot three-chile chicken, cumin lamb, chile oil–drizzled Chengdu dumplings, and the wontons to himself. To eat one's way through the lengthy menu takes time, but it's a commitment that reaps rewards. Its suburban companion is at 1331 Ogden Ave., Downers Grove, (630) 663-0303.

Lao Yunnan, 2109 S. China Pl., Chinatown, Chicago, IL 60616; (312) 326-9966; tonygourmetgroup.com; Chinese; $$. Tucked within Chinatown Square Mall in the space that once housed Spring World, this Tony Hu venture proves good things sometimes do come in small packages, especially when a point-and-pick cold appetizer combo (get the pickled green beans), fiery cumin-scented Yunannese spare ribs, and Cross Bridge noodles in spicy broth are part of the equation.

Lem's Bar-B-Q, 311 E. 75th St., Greater Grand Crossing, Chicago, IL 60619; (773) 994-2428; Barbecue; $$. These chewy, caramelized, tangily sauced ribs; glistening, smoky tips; and flavorful, fat-riddled links are a gold standard, and they rope in diners who spot the glowing neon sign. It may not win any decorative awards, but this place is long on charm.

Little Three Happiness, 209 W. Cermak Rd., Chinatown, Chicago, IL 60616; (312) 842-1964; Chinese; $. Significant enough that its initials inspired the "LTH" in culinary chat site LTHForum.com, this Cantonese-style juggernaut dishes up a massive, highlights-heavy menu, ranging from spicy string beans with XO sauce and pork to dry pan-fried noodles with barbecue pork and roast duck. Black bean–sauced clams; head-on or -off salt-and-pepper shrimp; and fried chicken, accompanied by a pepper-salt blend, cilantro, and lemon, also spell bliss.

Ma Gong La Po, 2215 S. Wentworth Ave., Chinatown, Chicago, IL 60616; Chinese; $$. Don't get distracted by the lengthy menu—it's the grilled (but in actuality fried-crispy) fish hot pot you must have. The insanely spicy broth bubbles away on a burner before you. Laced with whole garlic cloves, it is a fantastic vehicle for your additions, like sweet-potato noodles and mushrooms. Beef with pickled cabbage and Northern-style shredded pancakes are other options that pack a flavorful punch.

Whatever you order, plan ahead with iced herbal tea—it'll temper the flames.

Manny's Coffee Shop & Deli, 1141 S. Jefferson St., University Village, Chicago, IL 60607; (312) 939-2855; mannysdeli .com; Deli; $$. A workingman's slice of life, Manny's has been serving its famed, high-piled corned beef, brisket, and pastrami on caraway-specked rye since 1942. Blue-plate specials—Salisbury steak on Monday, oxtail on Thursday—and cold-be-gone matzoh are among the other common denominators among the blue- and white-collar clientele.

May St. Cafe, 1146 W. Cermak Rd., Pilsen, Chicago, IL 60608; (312) 421-4442; maystcafe.com; Nuevo Latino; $$. Tweaked Latin fare—*mojo criollo*–marinated *lechón,* double-cream Brie and winter-pear quesadillas with chipotle sauce, chicken in Michoacan-style mole—enlivens this dreary stretch of Cermak. So, too, does Mario Santiago's spicy *sopa de tortilla* with grilled chicken, avocado, and sour cream garnishes.

Medici on 57th, 1327 E. 57th St., Hyde Park, Chicago, IL 60637; (773) 667-7394; medici57.com; American; $$. Folks come to this University of Chicago hang because they can count on it for solid sandwiches, burgers, and thin or pan pizza, which leave them with money to bank. The funky, historic BYOB—outfitted with carved and graffitied seating—also has an adjunct artisan bakery, located at 1331 E. 57th St., (773) 667-7394.

Mercat a la Planxa, Blackstone Hotel, 638 S. Michigan Ave., South Loop, Chicago, IL 60605; (312) 765-0524; mercatchicago.com; Spanish; $$. Jose Garces's Catalan cuisine is enough to make the gracious Grant Park view, not to mention the soaring, sensory overload space, fade into the background. Nibble on cured meat and *queso* with interesting accompaniments while considering the bold options to follow: melty, cider-glazed pork belly with green apples and truffle; comforting but chic house-made pork-apple sausage with truffled white beans and carrot escabeche; and perfectly seared *a la plancha* preparations. Try the seasonal sangria and a stylish cocktail or two.

MingHin, 2168 S Archer Ave., Chinatown, Chicago, IL 60616; (312) 808-1999; minghincuisine.com; Chinese/Seafood; $$. Make a blissful meal of glistening, crisp roast duck; chewy pan-fried noodle rolls with XO sauce; and crackly skinned, meltingly fatty Macau-style pork belly, taking care not to overdo its sugar accompaniment.

Moon Palace, 216 W. Cermak Rd., Chinatown, Chicago, IL 60616; (312) 225-4081; moonpalacerestaurant.com; Chinatown; $$. Shang-hainese fare, including plump xiao long bao (soup dumplings) and sweet, *shu mai*–style sticky rice, is served in a sedate, contemporary setting that's a notch above its Chinatown counterparts. Safe bets include the tender black-pepper beef and spicy fish. But consider calling ahead to order the pork shoulder, a glistening, group-friendly hunk of heaven. Alternately, take the plunge and dive into the eel preparations.

Morrie O'Malley's Hot Dogs, 3501 S. Union Ave., Bridge-port, Chicago, IL 60609; (773) 247-2700; morrieomalleys35.com; Hot Dogs; $. Sox fans storm this cash-only South Side institution pre- and post-Cell, choosing between charred or steamed Chicago-style hot dogs, jus-soaked gravy bread, excellent cheese fries, and tamale boats.

Morry's Deli, 5500 S. Cornell Ave., Hyde Park, Chicago, IL 60637; (773) 363-3800; Deli; $. This decades-old destination is a no-brainer when it comes to sky-high corned beef and/or pastrami on rye. That said, the pastrami-packed egg McMorry, topped with salami and cheese and tucked into a bagel, is an ideal a.m. alternative.

Mr. Spanky's, 335 W. 31st St., Bridgeport Chicago, IL 60616; (312) 450-3069; mrspankys.com; New American; $. Expect a fusion of flavors, be it pot roast with giardiniera or the Badass BLT with house applewood-smoked bacon, both tucked into steamed, slightly sweet Chinatown bakery buns. Ponder sides, like mac and cheese or root beer–baked beans, and snag house-made bangers, chorizo, and applewood-smoked pork by the pound for the road.

Nana, 3267 S. Halsted St., Bridgeport, Chicago, IL 60608; (312) 929-2486; nanaorganic.com; American; $. A welcome addition to the neighborhood, this cheery, exposed-brick cafe melds a menu of American and Mexican-inflected dishes, while incorporating organic and sustainable ingredients to great success. Jump-start the morning with a house-made chorizo, *pupusa,* and poblano cream riff on eggs Benedict. Whether it's the classic burger or smoked pork *torta* swathed in jalapeño jam, its apparent quality ingredients make all the difference in the world. Even the pimento cheese board is a revelation when seasonal, house-made pickles are part of the mix.

Nightwood, 2119 S. Halsted St., Pilsen, Chicago, IL 60608; (312) 526-3385; nightwoodrestaurant.com; New American; $$$. The offerings are ever-changing at this **Lula Cafe** (p. 41) sib, where an open kitchen turns out unfussy, farm-to-table dishes with oodles of crowd appeal. Depending on when you dine, that may mean burrata ravioli with Butcher & Larder sausage, hearth-roasted veal sweetbreads with complex black mole, or a two-patty burger finished with "special sauce." Nightwood is also a popular destination for brunch, given offerings like a wood-grilled goat quesadilla with warm local vegetables, *pepitas,* and a runny egg.

Nuevo Leon, 1515 W. 18th St., Pilsen, Chicago, IL 60608; (312) 421-1517; nuevoleonrestaurant.com; Mexican; $$. The nachos—oh, the individually constructed nachos. They are all the incentive you need to visit this all-around reliable institution with fantastic flour torti-llas, genuine service, and a come-casual vibe. The *guisado* (pork or beef stew) takes the nip out of the chilliest day, and the chicken swathed in mole is a stalwart that is hard to beat.

Parrot Cage, South Shore Cultural Center, 7059 S. South Shore Dr., Far South Side, Chicago, IL 60649; (773) 602-5333; apps.ccc .edu/parrotcage; New American; $$. Lovely lake views frame this genteel Washburne Culinary Institute student dining room in the architecturally stunning South Shore Cultural Center. Wednesday and Thursday evenings usher in affordable, choose-your-own, set-price meals; otherwise, snag braised lamb shank or seared salmon, prepared by chefs in training and served a la carte.

Pearl's Place, 3901 S. Michigan Ave., Bronzeville, Chicago, IL 60653; (773) 285-1700; Regional American; $$. Dishing out more Southern comforts than you can shake a stick at—juicy fried chicken, catfish, mac and cheese—this simple fixture oozes octogenarian appeal, though its down-home peach cobbler shows nothing short of all-ages charm.

Phoenix, 2131 S. Archer Ave., Chinatown, Chicago, IL 60616; (312) 328-0848; chinatownphoenix.com; Chinese; $$. Come early to avoid the crowds that flock to this popular dim-sum destination. Expansive windows overlooking Chinatown Square are built for people-watching from the comfort of the upscale, banquetlike space. When roving carts reveal sweet, flaky barbecue pork buns; shrimp dumplings; curried baby octopus; and toothsome, pork-filled *bao,* snag them. When order-ing off the menu, splurge on succulent Peking duck, dipping it—and all else—in the superb oily, spicy chile sauce that tops tables.

Pl-zen, 1519 W. 18th St., Pilsen, Chicago, IL 60608; (312) 733-0248; Gastropub; $$. Forgive this gastropub's phonetic spelling to find wild boar meatballs dotted with raisins and pine nuts; a lamb burger slathered with *tzatziki*-feta sauce; and—more surprising—porter-spiked "beeramisu," fashioned by a former Gioco chef.

Pompei Little Italy, 1531 W. Taylor St., Little Italy, Chicago, IL 60607; (312) 421-5179; pompeipizza.com; Italian; $$. Blocks of doughy pizza, baked in sheet pans, have lured loyalists to this bakery since 1909. It's true the cafeteria-style place, named in homage to Our Lady of Pompeii church, is a fuss-free and generally likeable option when in the neighborhood. Consider the strombolilike pizza strudel and the Italian sandwiches, perhaps pepper and egg, when deviating. Another outpost is in Orland Park at 8801 W. 143rd St., (708) 403-8900.

Potsticker House, 3139 S. Halsted St., Bridgeport, Chicago, IL 60608; (312) 326-6898; potstickerhouse.com; Chinese; $$. In-the-know diners ask for the translated Chinese-language menu. Items that woo include *xiao long bao* (pork-filled soup dumplings); "cigar" potstickers; a sweet, smoky, scallion-flecked pork cake; glazed, garlicky eggplant; and flaming-hot, aromatic cumin lamb.

Ribs 'N' Bibs, 5300 S. Dorchester Ave., Hyde Park, Chicago, IL 60615; (773) 493-0400; Barbecue; $. The hickory-smoked ribs may warrant, well, bib-wearing when visiting this South Side pit. Hokily named western dinners and "chuck wagon" combos with all the fixings appease 'cue-seekers, who also secure oddities like the char-crusted Bronco Burger and the Gunslinger, a drinker's delight of a sausage sandwich with fries.

The Rosebud, 1500 W. Taylor St., Little Italy, Chicago, IL 60607; (312) 942-1117; rosebudrestaurants.com; Italian; $$. This is where the Rosebud empire began, and it remains a force to be reckoned with still. Yes, more serious Italian dining destinations exist, but it's safe to assume the standards—stuffed artichokes, minestrone, chicken Vesuvio—won't lack crowd appeal or scrimp on portion size. There are numerous outposts, with varying bents, scattered about town.

Saint's Alp Teahouse, 2131 S. Archer Ave., Chinatown, Chicago, IL 60686; (312) 842-1886; saints-alp.com.hk; Taiwanese; $. As the name implies, tea of many stripes is the emphasis at this Hong Kong transplant, which most notably serves Taiwanese-style, milk shake–like bubble tea dotted with tapioca pearls. Quick bites (*yakitori*, spicy vermicelli, sweet milk toast)—though not the main draw—serve a purpose.

Soul Vegetarian East, 205 E. 75th St., Greater Grand Crossing, Chicago, IL 60619; (773) 224-0104; Vegetarian/Vegan; $$. Those with vegan and vegetarian leanings find a lot to like in the food from this mainstay, where options such as the mock-meat BBQ Twist are something a meat-eater could endure—even enjoy. What sets this place apart, though, is its flavor-driven dishes, such as chickenlike "protein tidbits." Maybe it's because they're not always as straight-up-healthy as the concept suggests.

Stax Cafe, 1401 W. Taylor St., Little Italy, Chicago, IL 60607; (312) 733-9871; American; $$. Stacks of pancakes—ricotta topped with rhubarb compote, butterscotch, upside-down pineapple—are the specialty at this modern daytime diner, though it makes sense to take your time with the braised-brisket hash, French toast, and eggs Sardou, too. When the hours wane, expect a fresh, affordable selection of soups, salads, and sandwiches to come into play.

SEAFOOD SHACKS

Chicago and fried shrimp: While seemingly disparate, the two are inextricably linked. Remnants of these Prohibition-era seafood shacks (aka fisheries) can be seen citywide, and they build upon George Troha's "French-fried" tradition.

Calumet Fisheries, 3259 E. 95th St., South Deering, Chicago, IL 60617; (773) 933-9855; calumetfisheries.com; Seafood; $$. The buxom, smoky, peel-and-eat crustaceans from this circa-1928 shrimp shack will steal your heart. Strictly takeout, cash only, and located near the famed "Blues Brothers bridge," it's where you'll see patrons—parked in cars—plucking chubs, fried oysters, and fried shrimp from paper sacks. Call ahead to special order its stellar smoked fish.

Hagen's Fish Market, 5635 W. Montrose Ave., Portage Park, Chicago, IL 60634; (773) 283-1944; hagensfishmarket.com; Seafood; $. Fresh, fried, and smoked seafood is the focus of this institution, which also will smoke what you've plunked with rod and reel. Don't expect a lot of fuss—it's not a sit-down kind of a place—however, the end result is priceless. Stop by for live shellfish as well as scrod, herring, smoked sable bellies, chubs, and lox. Fortunately, there's no reason to leave hungry since the fryer turns out an Alaskan pollack sandwich, cod sticks, and spicy popcorn shrimp, which you'll want to splash with malt vinegar or dunk into zesty tartar sauce.

Haire's Gulf Shrimp, 8112 S. Vincennes Ave., Chatham, Chicago, IL 60620; (773) 783-1818; Seafood; $$. To know them is to love them—that's what adherants of these bags of plump, lightly breaded beauties say. It's a good thing, since they are the draw—the only focus, in fact—at this South Side staple.

Johnson's Door County Fish, 908 E. Roosevelt Rd., Lombard, IL 60148; (630) 629-6520; Seafood; $. This nostalgic, Wisconsin-style seafood shack is the kind of mom-and-pop spot where you order at the counter and have magically delicious, fried fare brought to your table. Extra-crunchy, batter-encased shrimp and lake perch are standouts, splashed with lemon from squeeze bottles and dunked into mild cocktail sauce. There's also a passable selection of bottled beer.

Lawrence's Fisheries, 2120 S. Canal St., Chinatown, Chicago, IL 60616; (312) 225-2113; lawrencesfisheries.com; Seafood; $$. At one time a commercial fishing business, this casual, around-the-clock seafood operation—located along the river, steps from Chinatown's dim sum houses—serves thickly battered fried shrimp, fish-and-chips, wings, and by-the-pound seafood dinners, all of which benefit from a plunk in hot sauce.

Troha's Shrimp & Chicken, 4151 W. 26th St., Little Village, Chicago, IL 60623; (773) 521-7847; chicagoshrimphouse.com; Seafood; $. Lightly breaded, nicely spiced crustaceans are the main attraction at this circa-1920 seafood house, which claims to be the original of its (nearly extinct) kind. You'll find plenty of other artery-clogging fry-daddy delights as well, including near-perfect chicken, frog's legs, and smelt.

Take Me Out, 1502 W. 18th St., Pilsen, Chicago, IL 60608; (312) 929-2509; takemeouthotties.com; Chinese; $. Affording a break from the Mexican-heavy cuisine populating the 'hood, this destination showcases the soy-chile-lacquered Chinese chicken wings made famous at Great Sea on Lawrence Avenue. Nai Tiao's daughter, Karen Lim, decided to serve the fabled "hotties" in hipper digs, along with shrimp-topped fried rice and crab Rangoon.

Taqueria El Milagro, 1923 S. Blue Island Ave., Pilsen, Chicago, IL 60608; (312) 433-7620; el-milagro.com; Mexican; $. This taqueria adjunct of the beloved, local tortilla producer serves fab tamales of several stripes, crafted from fresh masa, plus tacos, chiles rellenos, and chicken swathed in mole at rock-bottom prices. Afterward, head to the store to pick up tortillas and chips for the road. Additional locations are in the Little Village neighborhood, 3050 W. 26th St., (773) 579-6120; and suburban North Riverside, 7501 W. Cermak Rd., (708) 447-5442.

Taqueria Tayahua, 2411 S. Western Ave., Little Village, Chicago, IL 60608; (773) 247-3183; Mexican; $. You don't have to spend a lot to reap the rewards of this off-the-beaten-track taqueria, outfitted with a telltale spit for roasting *carne al pastor*. Feel confident in ordering the comforting *carne en su jugo*, which arrives with a bevy of lively accompaniments—limes, cilantro, radishes, chiles—or settle on the *huitlacoche* quesadillas.

That's-a-Burger, 2134 E. 71st St., South Side, Chicago, IL 60649; (773) 493-2080; Burgers; $. Although service lags—and lags—people are willing to wait for what this exclusively carryout operation, bulletproof glass and all, has to offer: two-fisted, five-napkin burgers both classic and—at least in the case of the cheesy, split Polish-topped Whammy burger—tricked out. Also good: the TAB, topped with a fried egg, sport peppers, onions, and chili. A rarity, the turkey burger is fantastic. So are the superior hand-cut fries.

Top Notch Beefburgers, 2116 W. 95th St., Beverly, Chicago, IL 60643; (773) 445-7218; Burgers; $. For a real-deal diner experience, visit this throwback, a landmark burger joint owned by Diran Soulian; it has griddled up house-ground round patties with beef-tallow fries since 1954. Get yours topped with American and grilled onions, adding on some onion rings and a thick, indulgent shake. Then, bask in the simple deliciousness amid a beige, wood-paneled dining room hung with landscape paintings.

Tufano's Vernon Park Tap, 1073 W. Vernon Park Pl., University Village, Chicago, IL 60607; (312) 733-3393; tufanosrestaurant .com; Italian; $$. Looking as though it's from a mobster movie set, this cash-only 1930s relic—famous for its sprightly lemon chicken—exudes a back-in-the-day vibe. It's the sort of place where families celebrate landmarks over shared spaghetti *aglio e olio* and linguine with red or white clam sauce, presented by a veteran waitstaff. It's not particularly polished and certainly not trendy, but no one comes here looking for that.

Uncle Joe's Tropical Dining, 1461 E. Hyde Park Blvd., Hyde Park, Chicago, IL 60615; (773) 241-5550; unclejoesjerk.com; Caribbean; $$. Whole-bird, wood-smoked Jamaican jerk—loaded with habanero heat—begs for sides of plantains and red beans and rice to deliver relief. Jerk also appears on shrimp and fish. Meanwhile, standards like stewed chicken, oxtail, and curry goat, as well as locally made beef patties, foster the islandlike feel. **Additional location:** 4655 S. King Dr., (773) 855-8457.

Uncle John's, 337 E. 69th St., Greater Grand Crossing, Chicago, IL 60637; (773) 892-1233; Barbecue; $. You'll want the deeply smoky, surprisingly moist rib tips and breakfast sausage-y links combo from this carryout pit, where the magic happens behind glass and the results are just this side of hog heaven. There's only one drawback, really, and it's that you'll have to eat these babies in the car.

Valois, 1518 E. 53rd St., Hyde Park, Chicago, IL 60615; (773) 667-0647; valoisrestaurant.com; American; $. U of C coeds, profs, and neighborhood types can't get enough of this casual, landmark cafeteria, and it takes but a visit to agree. As the line snakes around the counter, options such as a Denver omelet or French toast reveal themselves in the morning. Later, roast pork doused with gravy, baked chicken, and hot sandwiches, plus fruit and cream pies, cobblers, and Jell-O, replicate what Mom makes.

Vito & Nick's, 8433 S. Pulaski Rd., Ashburn, Chicago, IL 60652; (773) 735-2050; vitoandnicks.com; Pizza; $. What may be the best cracker-thin pizza in the city is found at this institution, which got its start in 1923. Kitted out with carpeted walls, it attracts a blue-collar crowd that knows bright-sauced sausage pies are the boss. Though it serves a roster of sandwiches, pastas, and fried pub grub, plus all-you-can-eat smelt on Friday, it's doubtful anyone notices.

White Palace Grill, 1159 S. Canal St., University Village, Chicago, IL 60607; (312) 939-7167; whitepalacegrill.com; American; $. When cravings set in during the wee hours, this classic, all-hours diner has your back. Its diverse menu, available anytime, ranges from corned beef hash crowned with sunny-side up eggs and biscuits and gravy to standard sandwiches, south-of-the-border specialties (enchiladas, burritos), and fried fish or chicken dinners.

Wings Around the World, 510 E. 75th St., Greater Grand Crossing, Chicago, IL 60616; (773) 483-9120; flavorstoinfinity.com; Eclectic; $. A dizzying number of globally inspired hot wings—maple-glazed

Canadians, Indian curry, Szechuan-style—ensure you'll never tire of this take-out joint. In the event you do, fried fish and shrimp are options as well.

Yolk, 1120 S. Michigan Ave., South Loop, Chicago, IL 60605; (312) 789-9655; eatyolk.com; American; $$. The masses wait in anticipation for eye-openers such as pot roast eggs Benedict and *huevos rancheros* as well as skillets, frittatas, and fresh fruit and granola–topped oatmeal. However, it doesn't end there, what with all the banana-nut French toast, crepes, and fresh, chock-full salads. Look for its breakfast brethren at 747 N. Wells St., (312) 787-2277, and 355 E. Ohio St., (312) 822-9655.

Zaleski & Horvath Market Cafe, 1126 E. 47th St., Kenwood, Chicago, IL 60653; (773) 538-7372; zhmarketcafe.com; Deli; $. Locals swing by this charming specialty cafe and international gourmet grocer for its attractive selection of cheeses. They also seek sustenance from the chalkboard menu touting panini and cold sandwiches, plus daily soups (try the rustic garlic). Its pastries are perfect for pairing with *macchiato con panna,* espresso, and café au lait. There's also an outpost at 1323 E. 57th St., (773) 538-7372.

Zaytune Mediterranean Grill, 3129 S. Morgan St., Bridgeport, Chicago, IL 60608; (773) 254-6300; zaytunegrill.com; Mediterranean/Middle Eastern; $. You've got to hand it to a from-scratch place, especially when the results are this good. The brainchild of Kendall College grad Daniel Sarkiss, the spot's fresh, quality ingredients and made-to-order approach shine in flavorful grilled kebabs; crisp outside, downy inside falafel; and rosemary- and garlic-marinated chicken *shawarma.* An added advantage is that the food—free of trans fats and preservatives—is healthy.

Suburban Stunners, Stalwarts & Surprises

City-dwellers—at least those not already in the know—call the suburbs a wasteland. That's just fine with outlying addressees, who happily keep their hidden riches hush-hush. Look beyond low-lying, indistinguishable office complexes and uncover communities ripe with culinary aplomb, restaurants quaint and cultured, and plenty of jaunting material.

North & Northwest

Al's Deli, 914 Noyes St., Evanston, IL 60201; (847) 475-9400; als-deli.com; Deli/French; $. Two brothers run this pint-size, pitch-perfect sandwich shop with a Northwestern following, where quality ingredients and friendly service seem of another time and (European) place. And while the thick-cut turkey and Brie baguette and the generously sauced, chunky blue cheese roast beef sandwich are charmers, even the chewy, iced butter cookies and daily handcrafted soups deliver all the comfort one needs.

Avli Estiatorio, 566 Chestnut St., Winnetka, IL 60093; (847) 446-9300; avli.us; Greek; $$. It's no surprise to learn cookbook author Diane Kochilas is consulting chef at this vibrant North Shore Hellenic, where so-tender charred octopus, lively gigantes, and staggeringly fresh, minted lentils transport you to the Aegean right quick. Complete the journey with *horta* (dandelion greens), broiled whole fish with oregano and lemon, and bread pudding that's stippled with currants, figs, and orange peel preserves.

Barrington Country Bistro, Foundry Shopping Center, 718 W. Northwest Hwy., Barrington, IL 60010; (847) 842-01300; barringtonbistro.com; French; $$$. A charming locale for a romantic night out, this snug French bistro has a comfy country interior, with warm-weather seating outdoors. The seasonal menu changes often but usually includes bubbly, gratinéed French onion soup topped with Raclette; garlic-forward escargots; charcuterie plates; and twice-cooked, apple-glazed duck leg with celery remoulade.

Burt's Place, 8541 Ferris Ave., Morton Grove, IL 60053; (847) 965-7997; Pizza; $$. This is a destination unto itself, thanks to the cheesy, caramelized—okay, charred—mid-weight pizzas from owners Burt and Sharon Katz (Gullivers, Inferno, Pequod's), served at a leisurely pace in a space adorned with antique tchotchkes. A word to the wise: Get your fresh, tangy-sauced pie topped with sweet peppers and aromatic coins of Italian sausage. The restaurant is cash only.

Cafe Pyrenees, 1762 N. Milwaukee Ave., Libertyville, IL 60048; (847) 362-2233; cafepyrenees.com; French; $$. Some come to sip wine from the thoughtful list, though few leave without engaging in country French meals: a selection of sausages atop white-bean cassoulet, braised beef Bourguignon, a duo of sliced duck breast and crispy leg confit on a bed of mascarpone polenta with lingonberry sauce. Ask about its fixed-price retro menu, which features prices on par with their 1990 originals. Also, grab a bottle of vino from the wine shop for another day.

Campagnola, 815 Chicago Ave., Evanston, IL 60202; (847) 475-6100; campagnolarestaurant.com; Italian; $$$. Daters have long adored the dignified simplicity of this Italian in Evanston, its rustic dishes—made from locally procured ingredients—endlessly charming. Begin with a bruschetta of roasted tomato marmalade and whipped feta; bacon-wrapped, wood-fired radicchio with goat cheese and basil aioli; or pillows of ricotta with fragrant wild-boar *ragù,* saving room for brick-roasted chicken or smoky pheasant with bacon, Delicata squash, and cipollini. Its owners are also behind **Union Pizzeria** (p. 178) and mobile Hummingbird Kitchen, (847) 475-6680.

Captain Porky's, 38995 US 41, Wadsworth, IL 60083; (847) 360-7460; captainporky.com; Seafood/Barbecue; $$. Not far from the tranquil, rocky shores of Illinois State Beach Park, this relocated, scratch-cooking, smoked meat and fried seafood shack shows attention to detail. As a result, much shines: organic, locally grown produce; its own wild-caught fish; and quality imported ingredients, including olive oil from the family's own fields in Sparta, Greece. Ribs, infused with woody flavor, give way to perch, crawfish tails, and gator as well as a lobster roll po'boy and pulled-pork-shoulder sandwich. Adjacent The Shanty, 38985 N. US 41, (847) 336-0262, is its seafood-centric cohort.

Chaihanna, 19 E. Dundee Rd., Buffalo Grove, IL 60089; (847) 215-5044; chaihanna.com; Uzbek; $$. Set in a nondescript strip mall, this Uzbek is a gem of a joint loaded with foods unfamiliar to the large collective. Crisp, five-alarm pickled vegetables; dumplinglike, meat-filled *manti*; moist, flavorful skewers; and baked, samosa-esque *samsas* give way to something not to be missed at meal's end: *chak-chak,* a fried, honeyed dough dessert. The laid-back setting is offset by upscale touches, like lovely place settings.

Charlie Beinlich's, 290 Skokie Blvd., Northbrook, IL 60062; (847) 714-9375; charliebeinlichs.com; American; $$. The chin-dribbling cheeseburgers from this wood-paneled tap get props, though the shrimp cocktail has a fan base as well. The edited menu has a handful of other options—grilled ham and cheese, chili, a tuna salad sandwich—but no one pays them much mind.

Chef's Station, 915 Davis St., Evanston, IL 60201; (847) 570-9821; chefs-station.com; New American; $$$. The warehouse ring to its name is a misnomer. Rather, this funky, anything-but-institutional Euro bistro is set in the Davis Street Metra station. Raves go to the American eats, six-course tasting menu, and winning selection of over 350 wines. Cuddle up to a Manchego-caramelized Vidalia tart with 25-year aged balsamic; seared duck breast with mushroom bread pudding and red-wine reduction; and a turtle sundae topped with shaved chocolate, caramel sauce, and whipped cream.

Cho Jung Restaurant, 952 Harlem Ave., Glenview IL 60025; (847) 724-1111; Korean; $$. Come for the judiciously prepared *panchan* (behold the pickled apple); fresh, pancakelike *pajeon* specked with green onion and seafood; fried, dumplinglike *mandu*; and restorative *sundubu jjigae* (steaming, spicy stew). You'll also get a taste of the good life in vibrant, heartwarming *dolsot* bibimbap, christened with a yolky fried egg.

Colombian's Taste, 5n105 Rte. 53, Itasca, IL 60143; (847) 250-5366; colombianstaste.com; Colombian; $. This small but stellar spot, tucked into a shady strip mall, is an excellent option for empanadas as well as *pandebono* (poofs of savory cheese bread) and *buñuelo* (fried bread). Dunk your tostada *con todo* into guac, addictive *hogao* (tangy-sweet tomato-onion relish), and garlicky, briny green *aji*; seek solace in the gigantic, banana leaf–steamed tamal; and return—again and again—for the Beef Passion, grilled, cheese-stuffed skirt steak with bacon, cheese, mushrooms, and onions. Don't overlook the fried potatoes or fried pork rinds either.

Crêperie Saint Germain, 1512 Sherman Ave., Evanston, IL 60201; (847) 859-2647; creperiestgermain.com; French; $$. This tiny, endearing cafe concocts crepes both sweet (seasonal fruits *des bois*) and savory (duck confit with bacon lardon), using organic buckwheat and wheat flours. Supplement them with classic chicken liver terrine, plated with all the fixings, or a mini caramelized onion puff pastry *tout de suite.*

Cross-Rhodes, 913 Chicago Ave., Evanston, IL 60202; (847) 475-4475; crossrhodes.biz; Greek; $. On the surface, this is just another Greek diner—that is, until a plate of über-crisp, feta-showered fries bathed in lemony, white wine–herb sauce is placed before you. Round out your diet with avgolemono soup, accolade-worthy gyros, and deeply flavorful, Rhodes-style skirt steak.

D&J Bistro, 466 S. Rand Rd., Lake Zurich, IL 60047; (847) 438-8001; dj-bistro.com; French; $$. A hidden, though always bustling, crowd-pleaser, this chef-owned bistro does the standards and does them well, be it cheesy French onion soup, chicken braised in white wine with earthy root vegetables, or steak frites with shallot butter. This is a labor of love, so expect ground-to-order steak tartare and elaborate tarts and cakes for carryout. Menus catering to vegetarians and children are available.

Da Kao, 632 E. St. Charles Rd., Carol Stream, IL 60188; (630) 933-9110; Vietnamese; $$. Endure slow-mo service and a non-ambient setting and reap addictive rewards: puffed, pan-fried rice noodles; DIY betel leaf–wrapped rice paper rolls; and fine *pho* with all the fixings at this off-the-radar Vietnamese. Come during lunch for rock-bottom prices. Want to feel in-the-know? Order glistening, hacked-to-order duck from the illuminated case by the register.

Dung Gia - Annam, 1436 Miner St., Des Plaines, IL 60016; (847) 803-4402; dunggiarestaurant.com; Vietnamese; $$. David Tran relocated his popular Vietnamese from Evanston, and the fans followed, ordering sizzling *banh xeo* (a shrimp and veggie crepe); customizable *pho* and acidic *canh chua tom* (shrimp-tamarind soup); and garlicky beef skewers. The lunch menu is a steal.

Earth + Ocean, 125 Randhurst Village Dr., Mount Prospect, IL 60056; (847) 398-3636; eofoodanddrink.com; New American; $$. Rodelio Aglibot's vast, urban-feeling eatery is hard to forget. That's saying something given the Sunda vet's large, globetrotting menu has suburban sensibility and catchall appeal. Sift through selections and score lollipop chicken wings with "Buddha dust," adobo pork belly, sushi, and pappardelle with short rib ragu that's worth writing home about. Even the brunch — with its banana fritters and Hawaiian-style doughnuts—justifies the scene.

Edzo's Burger Shop, 1571 Sherman Ave., Evanston, IL 60201; (847) 864-3396; edzos.com; Burgers; $. Culinary-school graduate Eddie Lakin (Spruce, **Tru** [p. 91]) is among the contingent of chefs gone casual (but still mindful of quality). His house-ground chuck burgers—available in charred, pink-centered half-pound; flat-griddled; and patty melt configurations—don't need much gussying up. Yet, it's futile to resist garlic butter and giardiniera, let alone versions using Dietzler Farm meat. For a lesson in discipline, try bypassing the double-fried, Merkts-topped fries and the shakes, which range from Nutella to Mexican chocolate with a kick. There's also an Edzo's at 2218 N. Lincoln Ave., (773) 697-9909.

Evanston Chicken Shack, 1925 Ridge Ave., Evanston, IL 60201; (847) 328-9360; evanstonchickenshack.com; American; $. It is a shack, and it does serve chicken—stellar flour-dredged chicken, in fact. Order your assertively peppered bird with mashed potatoes and gravy, or dunk yours in sweet barbecue or Trappey's-type hot sauce. Then, dine on your dash in the parking lot or at one of a handful of red-checkered tables in the small, bare-bones space.

Found Kitchen & Social House, 1631 Chicago Ave., Evanston, IL 60201; (847) 868-8945; foundkitchen.com; New American; $$. Amy Morton's eclectic, happening gathering place proves some things run in the family, as her father, Arnie Morton, founded **Morton's** (p. 79) and she's the sister of **DMK Burger Bar** (p. 34) co-owner David Morton. Clearly, though, she has followed a different path, one made clear when Nicole Pederson's juicy lamb meatballs on a bed of yogurt and chimichurri, harrissa-spiced Brussels sprouts, and whole Rushing Waters trout with green goddess aioli arrive at mismatched tables. Following suit, chocolate pot *de crème* and the brown butter caramel–drizzled coffee gelato sundae don't disappoint. See something you like, decoratively speaking? Name your price, since pretty much everything decorative is for sale.

Francesco's Hole in the Wall, 254 Skokie Blvd., Northbrook, IL 60062; (847) 272-0155; francescosholeinthewall.com; Italian; $$. Enjoying a cult following, this North Shore Southern Italian with distressed walls, a markerboard menu, and handful of perpetually packed tables wafts with scents of snapper Vesuvio and Bolognese-sauced tortellini.

Frank's Karma Cafe, 203 S. Main St., Wauconda, IL 60084; (847) 487-2037; frankskarma.com; Deli; $. Named for a German shepherd with purportedly good luck, this ambitious deli specializes in seasonal soups, substantial salads, and sandwiches made from fresh ingredients. Adding interest are daily specials, available in limited quantities. Come on Monday, when Mediterranean meat loaf may appear, or on Thursday, when bacon-and-egg salad sandwiches take center stage. Real fruit smoothies, fresh-baked desserts, and afternoon-to-evening tea service—not to mention a back-door drop-off service geared toward harried moms—are added charms.

Gene & Jude's Red Hot Stand,

2720 River Rd., River Grove, IL 60171; (708) 452-7634; Hot Dogs; $. A major flood couldn't dampen the spirits of—or the enthusiasm for—this true-blue stand, which went about a rehab out of necessity. Lines continue to snake out the door for the snappy, Chicago-style dog, topped with sweet relish, mustard, onions, and sport peppers, tucked into a steamed bun and served with hand-cut fries. There's not much else in the way of pomp, save the option of a simple, steamed tamale.

Hackney's on Harms, 1241 Harms Rd., Glenview, IL 60025;

(847) 724-5577; hackneys.net; American; $$. The history is interesting: Founder Jack Hackney began selling these trademark burgers from the back porch of his Glenview home during Prohibition. The family tradition lives on here with the fresh-ground Hackneyburger on dark rye, served on a pretty patio shaded by silver poplars when it's warm. Be sure to get the fried onion rings, too. **Additional locations:** Chicago, 733 Dearborn St., (312) 461-1116; Glenview, 1514 E. Lake Ave., (847) 724-7171; Lake Zurich, 880 N. Old Rand Rd., (847) 438-2103; and Palos Park, 9550 W. 123rd St., (708) 448-8300.

Himalayan Restaurant, 8265 W. Golf Rd., Niles, IL 60714;

(847) 324-4150; himalayanrestaurant.com; Indian/Nepalese; $$. Serving a popular, varied lunch buffet in comfortably casual digs, this place provides an alternative to Devon Avenue (and the parking conundrum that goes with visits). Start with the ginger-flecked *momo* (dumplings) and masala chicken wings, which arrive sputtering atop herbaceous onions. And while tandoori dishes are downright commonplace, here they taste better—smokier, in fact. But that's not to say *ko masu,* stewlike goat or chicken fragranced with Nepalese spices, falls flat. Others are at 398 Army Trail Rd., Bloomingdale, (630) 523-5100, and 3747 Gran Ave., Gurnee, (224) 637-3000.

Inovasi, 28 E. Center Ave., Lake Bluff, IL 60044; (847) 295-1000; inovasi.us; New American; $$$. John des Rosiers (formerly of Bank Lane Bistro) has his way with food in an off-the-beaten-path, blue-hued storefront where it seems anything can happen. Known for off-the-cuff flavor profiles, des Rosiers concocts fleeting dishes, 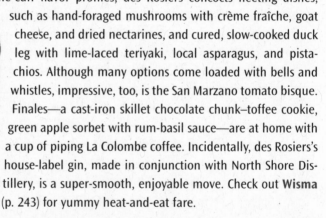 such as hand-foraged mushrooms with crème fraîche, goat cheese, and dried nectarines, and cured, slow-cooked duck leg with lime-laced teriyaki, local asparagus, and pistachios. Although many options come loaded with bells and whistles, impressive, too, is the San Marzano tomato bisque. Finales—a cast-iron skillet chocolate chunk–toffee cookie, green apple sorbet with rum-basil sauce—are at home with a cup of piping La Colombe coffee. Incidentally, des Rosiers's house-label gin, made in conjunction with North Shore Distillery, is a super-smooth, enjoyable move. Check out **Wisma** (p. 243) for yummy heat-and-eat fare.

Kabul House, 4949 Oakton St., Skokie, IL 60077; (847) 674-3830; kabulhouse.com; Afghan; $. Reliable Afghan eats are the focus at this affable, flavor-forward spot. Come for the thick, warming lentil soup; raviolilike *aushak* on a bed of mint yogurt and tomato sauce; and spiced beef-filled *mantoo.* Continue your education with a lineup of kebabs, namely standout *koobideh* (ground sirloin), as well as *kabuli pulao,* tender, braised lamb shank.

La Casa de Isaac, 431 Temple Ave., Highland Park, IL 60035; (847) 433-5550; lacasadeisaac.com; Mexican; $$. This North Shore hacienda serves a stable of familiar, traditional Mexican meals during breakfast, lunch, and dinner, including fresh-hewn salsas and guacamole, comforting *caldo de pollo* (chicken soup), *posole*, and chicken sauced with rich, traditional red mole. Take note that the restaurant closes for the Jewish Sabbath after Friday lunch service, reopening after sunset on Saturday.

Libertad, 7931 Lincoln Ave., Skokie, IL 60077; (847) 674-8100; libertad7931.com; Nuevo Latino; $$. Explosive Latin small plates come from the kitchen of this North Shore gem, the brainchild of Armando Gonzalez (Mas, **Bin 36** [p. 98], **mk** [p. 118]) and Marcos Rivera (**Las Palmas,** p. 74). Scoop up chipotle hummus with chapati tortillas, and chase it with perfectly seared, yuzu-accented scallops, plated with black rice, long beans, and habanero butter sauce. The *carne asada* is excellent, too, as is the skirt steak ramped up with chipotle goat cheese, chimichurri, and yucca fries. Hum-centric cocktails from Adam Seger make great bedfellows.

The Lucky Monk, 105 Hollywood Blvd., South Barrington, IL 60010; (847) 898-0500; theluckymonk.com; American; $$. With a name that nods to Trappist monks, whose dedication inspires its house-crafted ales and lagers, this buzzing suburbanite serves a prime, bigger-than-mouth-size burger with hand-cut fries; soupy poblano chili verde; and crisp, hand-stretched pizzas adorned with béchamel, mozzarella, and Fontina, or a trio of button, cremini, and oyster mushrooms. Then again, it's the fried pickle chips that may make it worth the haul.

Michael, 64 Green Bay Rd., Winnetka, IL 60093; (847) 441-3100; restaurantmichael.com; French; $$$. Michael Lachowicz (Le Français, Les Deux Gros) has culinary kahunas to name his "personal creation" as such. Fortunately, it's swagger you can count on. Confirmation arrives with a duo of two-way tuna, Thai-style tartare, and five-spiced loin; roasted *foie gras*–stuffed hen with leek-confit cabbage tart and truffle game jus; and hot strawberry soufflé with candied kumquat crème anglaise.

Mizrahi Grill, Crossroads Shopping Center, 215 Skokie Valley Rd., Highland Park, IL 60035; (847) 831-1400; mizrahigrill.com; Israeli; $$. Whether you order the crisp-crumbly falafel; the marinated, spit-carved turkey-lamb *shawarma*; or the bright cabbage, diced Israeli, or *matbucha* (tomato and roasted pepper) salads, expect that they're fresher than fresh. Moist kebabs and *sufganiyots* (fried jelly doughnuts) are further pleasures to succumb to.

Mustard's Last Stand, 1613 Central St., Evanston, IL 60201; (847) 864-2700; Hot Dogs; $. Most people come for the properly topped Vienna Beef dogs at this Chicago-style stand, popular for pre- and post-game nourishment near the Northwestern campus. However, others know the flame-grilled Wildcat burger is where it's at. Crowned with cheese sauce, caramelized onions, and barbecue sauce, it's nearly as endearing as the energetic crowd.

Myron & Phil's, 3900 W. Devon Ave., Lincolnwood, IL 60712; (847) 677-6663; myronandphil.com; Steak House; $$$$. This dark, moody steak house of yore has a tried-and-true formula that includes relish trays with pickled green tomatoes and chopped liver, flavorful Romanian skirt steak, super-garlicky shrimp de Jonghe, and lightly breaded lake perch. Entrees may be customized, so try your meat with burnt onions or a Parmesan crust, and opt for creamed spinach on the side.

Oceanique, 505 Main St., Evanston, IL 60202; (847) 864-3435; oceanique.com; Seafood/French; $$$$. Mark Grosz makes a solid case for seafood in Middle America with French-influenced fins, presented in a fancy-schmancy setting. The menu changes often, but opting for the three- or seven-course tasting menus is always prudent. It may yield a plate of day-boat scallops with cabbage kimchi and soy-lobster broth or lemongrass-fragranced Holland turbot with pea tips. A wine cellar 900-labels-strong houses rare Champagne, Bordeaux, and Burgundy. Keep an eye out for occasional wine dinners.

Paradise Pup, 1724 S. River Rd., Des Plaines, IL 60018; (847) 699-8590; Burgers; $. It's no wonder lines swell beyond the walls of this matchbox-size stand, run by two ever-present brothers. Once bitten, the legendary char-burgers cause cravings. Get yours slathered with Merkts cheddar and a nest of sweet, grilled onions. Complete with experience with artery-clogging three-layer fries, mounded with cheese, bacon, and sour cream, and a mighty fresh raspberry shake. Bring cash, and expect to eat in your car—or at an outdoor picnic table when it's warm.

Pho Ha, 1971 Bloomingdale Rd., Glendale Heights, IL 60139; (630) 894-4000; phohaglendaleheights.com; Vietnamese; $. Small in stature but big on flavor, this bare-bones Vietnamese makes a fresh, crusty *banh mi* as well as lip-smackingly good *pho* in several configurations. Get a fruit smoothie with tapioca pearls as well.

Pho Le, 541 S. Schmale Rd., Carol Stream, IL 60188; (630) 588-8299; Vietnamese; $. There's no ambience to speak of, but the brothy, meat- and noodle-packed bowls of *pho*—as well as the fried pork chop piled with shredded pork skin and an egg cake—are enough to endure a penchant for slow delivery.

Pita House, 365 S. Roselle Rd., Schaumburg, IL 60193; (847) 352-4750; pitahouse.com; Middle Eastern; $. A generic facade gives way to someplace where Middle Eastern flavors sparkle. That's true from the zucchini-based mama ghannouj to the lemon-zapped *fattoush* salad and decent *shawarma* and falafel sandwiches. There's also a location at 340 E. Roosevelt Rd., Lombard, (630) 576-5060.

Poochie's, 3832 W. Dempster St., Skokie, IL 60076; (847) 673-0100; poochieshotdogs.com; Hot Dogs; $. Few things in life are as satisfying as this charred (or steamed) Chicago-style red hot, dressed in onion, a generous squeeze of mustard, sweet neon relish, tomato, a pickle, and a shower of celery salt on a plush, steamed poppy-seed bun. But to ignore the other attributes of this straightforward stand would be a disservice. The hand-cut fries and cheddar burger are five-star, as is the char salami spurted with mustard and dressed with onions—grilled and raw.

Prairie Grass Cafe, 601 Skokie Blvd., Northbrook, IL 60062; (847) 205-4433; prairiegrasscafe.com; New American; $$. Disproving the notion that the suburbs suck: Ritz-Carlton Chicago vets Sarah Stegner and George Bumbaris, whose seasonal, stone and wood–hewn dining room drew city slickers until a mate opened in the West Loop. It's still worth the drive, with a menu that holds baked feta with spicy banana peppers and tomatoes; ancho-marinated skirt steak with white bean–Swiss chard *ragù* and grilled onions; and crispy half-duck with braised greens, quince jam, and crunchy beet slaw.

Quince at the Homestead, Homestead Hotel, 1625 Hinman Ave., Evanston, IL 60201; (847) 570-8400; quincerestaurant.net; New American; $$$. Sedate and romantic, this is dining for grown-ups. Featuring a la carte, tasting, and bar menus minded by Andy Motto (Le Lan), its offerings rove from goat cheese accented by pine nuts, romenesco, and olives to barramundi teamed with garbanzo beans, fennel, oranges, and chard. Composed desserts are hard to resist, especially when the minty s'more is available. Selections from the large, tended wine and creative cocktail lists should be savored before the roaring fireplace.

Renga-Tei, 3956 W. Touhy Ave., Lincolnwood, IL 60712; (847) 675-5177; Japanese; $$. Sashimi seekers succumb to this humble hang for Japan's kitchen comforts, such as *tonkatsu, goma-ae,* and *agedashi* tofu, served in a simple setting that is welcoming and warm.

Schnitzel Platz, 729 North Ave., Glendale Heights, IL 60139; (630) 942-9900; schnitzelplatz.com; German; $$. Tip back some *bier* at this beloved Bavarian, long plating caloric platters for the restraint-challenged. Tackle one with fried pork cutlets, *frikadelle* (German chopped steak), sausages, home fries, red cabbage, and sauerkraut. The massive menu also hosts dumplings, spaetzle, sauerbraten, and its namesake, prepared endless ways. Come during Oktoberfest for its legendary pig roast.

Soulwich, 1634 Orrington Ave., Evanston, IL 60201; (847) 328-2222; soulwich.com; Asian/Sandwiches; $. The Southeast Asian sammiches from this pint-size storefront aren't short on flavor, be it the signature Burmese coconut pork curry, the sweet fig paneer, or the Indonesian ginger barbecue beef, all topped with pickled veg and served with house-fried chips.

Tramonto's Steak & Seafood, 601 N. Milwaukee Ave., Wheeling, IL 60090; (847) 777-6575; westinnorthshore.com; Steak House/Seafood; $$$$. Although namesake Rick Tramonto has left for other pastures, this steak-and-seafood expert forges on with a menu of prime steaks with customizable sauces and toppers, butter-poached Maine lobster, and wood-fired fish. Sushi, a larger selection of which is available upstairs in the RT

Lounge, is on hand as well, and prime rib is served Thursday through Saturday. The large, affordable cellar stocks some serious wine finds.

Union Pizzeria, 1245 Chicago Ave., Evanston, IL 60202; (847) 475-2400; unionevanston.com; Pizza/Italian; $$. Creative Tuscan pizzas are cooked in a wood-fired oven and served alongside an array of Italian small plates, microbrews, and vino. Meanwhile, daily specials—such as herb-roasted Amish chicken or ziti with meaty, braised Sunday gravy—add to the mix. Its more upscale cuz, **Campagnola** (p. 166), is at 815 Chicago Ave. There's also a mobile kin, Hummingbird Kitchen, (847) 475-6680.

Wiener and Still Champion, 802 Dempster St., Evanston, IL 60202; (847) 869-0100; wienerandstillchampion.com; Hot Dogs; $. This red-hot stand doesn't reinvent the wheel, but it does tackle convention head-on. Hand-breaded corn dogs take festival food to the next level, while burgers dolloped with Merkts cheese are impossible to ignore. Still, missing fried pickles, country-fried bacon with Argentine garlic and herb sauce, and country-fried gyros would be a shame. Then there's the Chicago-style hot dog, presented as it is intended to be.

West & Far West

Al Bawadi Grill, 7216 W. 87th St., Bridgeview, IL 60455; (708) 599-1999; albawadigrill.com; Middle Eastern; $$. There are reasons to zero in on this neighborhood jewel, located on the outskirts of a strip mall amid a number of like-minded destinations. Among them: the sprightly pickles that arrive when you're seated; the charred, moist, wood-fired kebabs; the creamy hummus. Get some garlicky *motawma* (pureed potato dip) or *foul* (tahini-spiked fava bean dip) to slather on everything, and consider the *arayes*—pita stuffed with a minced lamb mixture or Syrian cheese—and rustic, chopped Arabic salad. Or, take stock in the homey *kufta* casserole.

Al Mawal, 10718 S. Harlem Ave., Worth, IL 60482; (708) 361-5100; Middle Eastern; $. Set amid an enclave of Middle Eastern eateries, this standout serves a lineup of hardwood-grilled meats, smoky baba ghannouj, and chunky *musabaha* to a satisfied collective.

Alex & Aldo's, 720 E. 31st St., La Grange Park, IL 60526; (708) 354-1390; Pizza; $$. Dark and dive-y, this petite pizza palace has made a name for itself with cracker-crust pies, homespun Italian dishes (veal Parmesan, various pasta preps ladled with "gravy"), and crostini with liver spread. Couple any with crumbly, breading-encased green olives and a finisher of homemade carrot cake, when it's available.

Alfie's Inn, 425 Roosevelt Rd., Glen Ellyn, IL 60137; (630) 858-2506; alfiesinn.com; American; $$. Low-lit and decked in stained glass and suits of armor for a medieval feel, this steady supplies baskets of battered mushrooms and onion rings, juicy chuck loinburgers with grilled (or raw) onions, and really cheap drinks.

Amber Cafe, 13 N. Cass Ave., Westmont, IL 60559; (630) 515-8080; ambercafe.net; New American; $$$. A relatively affordable choice for upscale eats in comfortable environs, this gem plies diners with seasonal, contemporary American fare, like warm Brie and pear salad, butternut squash ravioli, and crisp whitefish with pearls of couscous and lemon beurre blanc. Ask to be seated on the picturesque enclosed patio when it's warm. Its sibling, **Topaz Cafe** (p. 194), is in the Burr Ridge Village Center.

Aripo's Venezuelan Arepa House, 118 N. Marion St., Oak Park, IL 60301; (708) 386-1313; aripos.com; Latin; $. Cozy up to this cheery storefront, an ode to arepas (get the signature beef La Nuestra). Diversions, by no means less appealing, include creamy ham and cheese empanadas and a lineup Venezuelan classics, like *pabellón criollo*, shredded beef, chicken, or slow-roasted pork with fried plantains, black beans, and white rice. While you're at it, plunk some fine *boliqueso* (fried cornmeal balls) into garlicky *guasacaca*.

Autre Monde Cafe & Spirits, 6727 Roosevelt Rd., Berwyn, IL 60402; (708) 775-8122; autremondecafe.net; Italian/Mediterranean; $$$. Fall immediately in love with this Mediterranean maven from Beth Partridge and Dan Pancake, a must for bacalao-stuffed piquillos, smoked lamb shank atop white corn polenta, and soul-satisfying wild boar pappardelle. Pleasures are also abundant during brunch, with offerings like burrata and caviar with grilled bread and eggs poached in San Marzano tomatoes. An adjunct greenhouse ensures an infusion of fresh flavors, while a quirky wine list and extensive spirits selection—punctuated by riffs on the gin and tonic—only heighten the appeal.

Back Alley Burger, 1 S. La Grange Rd., La Grange, IL 60525; (708) 482-7909; backalleyburger.com; Burgers; $. Tucked into downtown La Grange, this counter-service nook fills a niche with funky, messy offerings like the Most Insane-est, a half-pound patty topped with habanero jam, scorpion sauce, Bhut Jolokia flakes, fried jalapeños, red onion, and Thai chili cream cheese on a cayenne-spiced Kaiser bun. Whether you opt for the more classic Coca Cola–sauced burger or a Merkts-slathered number, consider chili-cheese onion rings and fried pickles your go-to sides. Other pluses include fresh salads, homemade pie, and a handful of craft beers. Another location is at 609 W. St. Charles Rd., Elmhurst, (630) 516-1755.

Benjarong, 2138-B S. Mannheim Rd., Westchester, IL 60154; (708) 409-0339; benjarong.us; Thai; $$. Blink and you'll miss this cozy, tiny Thai in a strip mall adjacent to a grocery store. Although it does a brisk lunch and carryout business, the petite, artifact-adorned dining room is a respite come evening, making it the perfect time for coarse-ground beef basil with vibrant peppers; devilish, lime-blasted *yum nue* (beef salad); and expertly prepared *pad kee mao*.

Bodhi Thai, 6211 W. Roosevelt Rd., Berwyn, IL 60402; (708) 484-9250; bodhithaibistro.com; Thai; $$. To order off the menu at this stellar spot is to miss the point. What you really want to do is ask for the secret menu, or challenge the kitchen to prepare custom, "free-style" dishes just for you. Get the garlicky *sai oua* sausage, an Issan standby; fiery fried chicken (*kai thawt*); and insidious, citrus-y *nam tok* beef salad sprinkled with toasted rice powder, knowing you'll need dense sticky rice to temper the heat.

Burger Boss, 7512 W. North Ave., Elmwood Park, IL 60707; (708) 452-7288; theburgerboss.com; Burgers; $. Serious burgers—that's what wows at this west suburbanite from brothers Anthony and Nick Gambino (also of Cucina Paradiso). Design your own, choosing from a slew of free toppings, or opt for specialty versions, like the 8 a.m., topped with a cage-free egg. The sweet-potato fries really rock, especially with a spicy chipotle dipper; real-deal shakes warrant a look-see, too.

Chef Amaury's Epicurean Affair, 33 W. New York St., Aurora, IL 60506; (630) 375-0426; chefamaury.com; New American; $$$. Chef/ Owner Amaury Rosado quietly crafts sophisti-cated, modern American plates, steps from the Fox River in downtown Aurora. Invest in the five-course dinner, which may include escolar with grilled leeks, Israeli couscous, and silky avocado mousse. And be sure to get the rosemary-orange crème brûlée when it's on offer. There's a nice wine list as well, and cooking classes are offered.

Chef Paul's Bavarian Lodge, 1800 Ogden Ave., Lisle, IL 60532; (630) 241-4701; bavarian-lodge.com; German; $$. Although it isn't inexpensive, this Deutsche delivers what few do by offering an old-world experience and nearly 200 draft and bottle beers, many of them of German and Belgian descent. It's hard to go wrong with classics, like the basket of Bavarian pretzels or griddled potato pancakes with sour cream and applesauce. The same is true when it comes to entrees, namely the crisp schnitzels, sauced or unadorned; hearty rouladen; and caraway-scented roast pork loin. You may also design your own combinations, adding in smoked sausage for good measure.

Chicago Burgerwurks, 8819 W. Ogden Ave., Brookfield, IL 60513; (708) 387-2333; chicagoburgerwurks.com; Burgers; $. It'd be easy to blow past this ketchup and mustard–hued stand, but then you'd miss the dizzying roster of gourmet burgers and corresponding chicken sandwiches, each given its own hand-hewn sauce. It would also mean you'd never meet the full-flavored flank steak sandwich or the brooding cup of chili, made from meat scraps. Running faves include the Lucifurger topped with pepper jack cheese, sweet onions, and chipotle relish and the Au Poivre, finished in black-peppercorn gravy. There's a design-your-own sandwich option as well as *poutine*-inspired fresh-cut fries. Soups are superior, too; get the smoked tomato bisque when it's available.

Chinese Kitchen, 6551 S. Cass Ave., Westmont, IL 60559; (630) 968-3828; chinesekitchenwestmont.com; Chinese; $. What this quick-serve Cantonese lacks in ambience, it more than makes up for in flavor—a fact that is immediately apparent in fried, onion-flecked

Japanese tofu salt and spice, which is liberally sprinkled with jalapeños. Reliably tasty hot-and-sour soup, tender Mongolian beef, and fried chicken wings with spicy salt are met by more ambitious options, like crisp Dover sole and braised sea cucumber.

Chinn's 34th St. Fishery, 3011 W. Ogden Ave., Lisle, IL 60532; (630) 637-1777; chinnsfishery.com; Seafood; $$. It's less about the experience and more about the freshly sourced seafood at this crowd-thronged stalwart, where meals begin with rolls bathed in garlic and proceed to feature some of the best crab legs in town. Additional lures include potent mai tais and a retail market selling seasoned and straight-up selections to prepare at home.

Czech Plaza, 7016 W. Cermak Rd., Berwyn, IL 60402; (708) 795-6555; czechplaza.com; Czech; $$. The silver-haired set flocks to this authentic Czech eatery where little has changed—huge portions of crisp-skinned duck, breaded pork tenderloin, and Bohemian-style meat loaf included. Comforting liver-dumpling soup, fruit dumplings, and daily specials—such as Hungarian goulash—are attractive extras.

Dell Rhea's Chicken Basket, 645 Joliet Rd., Willowbrook, IL 60527; (630) 325-0780; chickenbasket.com; American; $$. Serving up road food in the truest sense, this restaurant and cocktail lounge—marked by a vintage neon sign—has been making mouths happy since 1938. Located at mile marker 274 on Historic Route 66, its setting is of another era, and its food—especially the cornmeal-fried chicken it's known for—is as satisfying as ever. Soul-soothing mac and cheese, homemade chicken noodle soup, and a salad bar where cheesy vegetable spread is king complete the throwback experience.

El Pollo Giro, 991 N. Aurora Ave., Aurora, IL 60505; (630) 896-0755; Mexican; $$. The flavorful, charcoal-grilled chicken—served with smoky jalapeños, knob onions, and bright salsa fresca—calls for visits to this casual quick-serve with a second outpost at 817 Montgomery Rd., Montgomery, (630) 898-5143.

Emilio's Tapas, 4100 Roosevelt Rd., Hillside, IL 60162; (708) 547-7177; emiliostapas.com; Spanish/Tapas; $$. The garlic potato salad could ward off vampires; the bacon-wrapped dates are at an avenue where sweet and savory collide. Get both with a pitcher of sangria, and make your way through shareable plates both hot and cold, including tuna-filled cannelloni topped with creamy white-wine vinaigrette and grilled, pepper-crusted beef tenderloin with onions, peppers, and sherry sauce. Its downtown companion, Sol y Nieve, is at 215 E. Ohio St., Chicago, (312) 467-7177.

Fabulous Noodles, 4663 Old Tavern Rd., Lisle, IL 60532; (630) 305-8868; fabulousnoodles.com; Chinese; $$. Its name doesn't lie: These soup noodles are a testament to how good Chinese food really can be. Get them in a spicy slurry with tender beef, Indonesian-style, or bolstered by sweet, caramelized barbecue pork. Noodles also come braised and pan-fried, with *yu* noodles a forerunner among the latter.

Freddy's Pizza, 1600 S. 61st Ave., Cicero, IL 60804; (708) 863-9289; freddyspizza.com; Italian/Pizza; $. At this ambitious from-scratch corner store, you must choose between steaming plates of chicken Parm, stacks of mozzarella Caprese, and platters of hot Italian sausage hidden in a tangle of sweet, sautéed peppers and potatoes—all placed lovingly atop and behind a glass counter. Peer behind the shelf piled with fresh-baked bread, too; you'll see the makings of outstanding, chewy Italian subs with imported meats and cheeses, house-label giardiniera, tomatoes, and lettuce. Order one, along with a side salad or two. Consider adding on a slice of sheet pizza and ultra-creamy limoncello or fruits of the forest gelato. A small selection of import goods and a case filled with frozen, homemade pasta leads to wise impulse buys, so bring enough cash since credit cards are not accepted. There's a small, enclosed room adjacent to the restaurant for dining in.

Gaetano's, 7636 Madison St., Forest Park, IL 60130; (708) 366-4010; gaetanos.us; Italian; $$$. Don't come looking for your nonna's Italian—Gaetano Di Benedetto's *cucina* serves anything but. The always changing, sometime impromptu approach keeps things interesting, resulting in a dish of Gulf shrimp in puff pastry with caramelized garlic and Gorgonzola fondue or crab cakes with roasted red peppers singed in a wood-burning oven. One visit may mean spicy shrimp bisque with house-made Italian sausage, another spaghetti *chitarra alla sorrentina*, "guitar-string" pasta tossed with tomatoes, olive oil, basil, and home-made mozzarella. True flavor-seekers should order the personalized, free-style dinner, served in four-course, family-style fashion at the chef's counter.

Ginger & Garlic, 1633 N. Naper Blvd., Naperville, IL 60563; (630) 799-3888; gingerandgarlicrestaurant .com; Chinese; $$. Ignore the adobe exterior: Inside a stylish dining room and impressive Chinese lineup await. Get in the spirit with blistered string beans, sizzling black pepper beef, and communal whole Peking duck, meant to be scooped into buns and topped with scallions and duck sauce. Also of note: the lobster noodles.

Golden Steer, 7635 W. Roosevelt Rd., Forest Park, IL 60130; (708) 771-7798; goldensteersteakhouse.com; Steak House; $$. Make no mistake: This dark, mirrored meat-house is of another era, one in which brassy servers deliver food on rolling metal carts, drinks are stiff, and no-fuss food is matter-of-fact good. Stubbornly steadfast, this haunt does that and more, prepping the best, bubbly crocks of French onion soup, salads with flavor-saturated croutons, and affordable steaks with heavily condimented baked potatoes wrapped in aluminum foil. Get a side of the weirdly wonderful mushrooms, and consider the moist, herb-swathed Grecian chicken as a red-meat alternative. The burger—served on dark rye—is tasty as well.

Grand Dukes Eatery & Deli, 6312 S. Harlem Ave., Summit, IL 60501; (708) 594-5622; granddukesrestaurant.com; Eastern European; $$. Uncommon decor—suits of armor, medieval-looking artwork—paves the way for hearty dishes, many Lithuanian, at this unassuming eatery. That means sauerkraut soup, *cepelinai* (potato zeppelins), and bacon-wrapped boar in tangy paprika-cream sauce. Be sure to visit the deli in back—it's packed to the gills with made-on-site meats, salads, and dumplings as well as condiments and breads.

Il Poggiolo, 8 E. First St., Hinsdale, IL 60521; (630) 734-9400; ilpoggiolohinsdale.com; Italian; $$$. This ever-crowded, artifact-filled dining room—located in a onetime silent-movie house—is as vibrant as any of the restaurateur's ventures, and the modern take on Italian fare generally delivers. Get seated on the balcony for a bird's-eye view, and begin with carpaccio or Taleggio-and-mushroom-filled *arancini*. Then move onward to the handmade *chitarra* topped with Bolognese or the pappardelle with red wine–braised duck *ragù*. Among the comforting mains: pork shoulder with creamy polenta and sautéed rapini in apple-cider reduction. Co-owners Peter and Dana Burdi are partners at **Nabuki** (p. 190) down the street.

International Mall, 665 Pasquinelli Dr., Westmont, IL 60559; Asian; $. This dingy food court next to Asian grocer **Whole Grain Fresh Market** (p. 261) features a handful of booths, brimming with varied Chinese nibbles (pork dumplings, swimming in spicy chile sauce) and soups (spicy-sweet beef noodle). Take note that it gets crowded on weekends, and you should be sure to bring cash.

Johnnie's Beef, 7500 W. North Ave., Elmwood Park, IL 60707; (708) 452-6000; American; $. Surly staffers expect you know your order in advance. Here's what to get: boldly seasoned Italian beef or a combo sandwich (Italian beef and Italian sausage). Order it juicy with hot peppers and a side of Italian ice. When it's warm out, sit at one of the picnic tables; otherwise, eat in your car, an exercise that necessitates a bib. Arrive early on weekends, as this standing-room spot sees lines before doors ever open. There is a second location at 1935 S. Arlington Heights Rd., Arlington Heights, (847) 357-8100.

Kama Indian Bistro, 8 W. Burlington Ave., La Grange, IL 60525; (708) 352-3300; kamabistro.com; Indian; $$. Talk about a pleasant surprise. Located in a narrow storefront across from the Metra station, this pillow-strewn, stylishly lit Indian exhibits the kind of dedication few do. Everything is made from scratch, including the spice blends and sauces; the ingredients are quality; and the heat is no-holds-barred. Planks of crispy, "chilly" potatoes and elegant, delicately flavored shrimp Sunnaina in white-wine garlic-tomato concassé are hits. However, nothing can prepare you for the complex chicken or lamb Kama-Kaze vindaloo set ablaze with ghost peppers—except, perhaps, a gallon of water to tame the flames. Consider, too, the dishes that employ a slow-fired house blend of 18 pickled spices, incorporated into a gentle tomato, onion, and garlic sauce. Numerous vegetarian and gluten-free dishes are available.

Katy's Dumpling House, 665 N. Cass Ave., Westmont, IL 60559; (630) 323-9393; katysdumpling.com; Chinese; $. If you're looking to be coddled—heck, even treated with civility—this may not be your place. However, if you're a lover of hand-pulled noodles and house-made dumplings, see past the service and spartan setting of this strip-mall Chinese. Witness the artistry in action beyond the counter, and focus on dishes that utilize its strong suit: spicy dan-dan noodles and oily, chile-flecked Szechuan cold noodles dotted with nubs of ground pork and cooling cucumber. All manner of oddities are in the carryout case, but you'll want to grab handmade, frozen pork-and-chive dumplings for later. A second location is at 790 Royal Saint George Dr., Ste. 115, Naperville, (630) 416-1188.

Klas Restaurant, 5734 W. Cermak Rd., Cicero, IL 60804; (708) 652-0795; klasrestaurant.com; Czech; $$. Part of a dying breed, this old-world Czech is both strange and wondrous—not to mention a criminal bargain. The setting—all castlelike with vaulted archways and weird-looking chandeliers—is a focal point. However, the Bohemian-style eats are easy to love, if treacherous on the waistline. Whether you get the paprika chicken, pilsner-simmered goulash, or wiener schnitzel a la Holstein crowned with anchovies, capers, and a fried egg, belt-loosening is sure to ensue. Dishes come with soup or salad, bread or potato dumplings, boiled or mashed potatoes and sauerkraut, sweet-sour cabbage or a daily veg, plus a homemade *kolacky*. Let the food coma settle in over a beer at the oddly outfitted bar, or take a peek at the ornate banquet space upstairs.

La France Cafe & Crêpes, 939 S. Main St., Lombard, IL 60148; (630) 613-9511; lafrancecafe.com; French; $$. Take to the Left Bank at this cozy spot for sweet (lemon curd and Chantilly) and savory crepes, the latter including olive-studded ratatouille niçoise or chicken curry with fig. Seek, too, the specials of the day—if beef Bourguignon happens to be among them, don't miss out.

Los Dos, 2251 Maple Ave., Downers Grove, IL 60515; (630) 297-8337; losdosrestaurant.com; Mexican; $$. It's little things that make a difference at this ambitious storefront for spot-on tacos, *salbutes,* and tostadas, things like chewy house-made tortillas, bracing salsa verde, and ultra-fresh shrimp ceviche. Then there's the handwritten specials—*bistec a la Mexicana,* citrus-blasted *poc chuc,* or tender pork ribs simmered in salsa verde, perhaps—not to mention the slick flan, which could make a believer out of anyone.

Macarena Tapas, 618 S. Rte. 59, Naperville, IL 60540; (630) 420-8995; macarenatapasnaperville.com; Tapas; $$. Don't let its suburban-sprawl setting deter you—this Nuevo Spaniard deserves more than a passing glance. Executive Chef John Borras, who trained with Ferran Adrià, prepares what's sought after (rustic bread brushed with tomatoes and olive oil and topped with *jamon*; *croquetas*; garlic shrimp). He also fashions more modern Catalan-type fare, like grilled chicken with avocado salsa verde, bacon-wrapped scallops atop romesco sauce, and tilapia with artichoke-spinach sauce. Gluttons will appreciate the availability of a varied, all-you-can-eat menu.

Marion Street Cheese Market, 100 S. Marion St., Oak Park, IL 60302; (708) 725-7200; marionstreetcheesemarket.com; New American; $$. A paradise for food lovers, this market, cafe, and wine shop emphasizes products from local purveyors, while featuring small plates inspired by those procurements. Nosh on cheese and charcuterie, design your own cheese flight, or tuck into a Berkshire pork chop with sweet-potato grits and bacon jam. You'll also find a shareable bison carpaccio and sunchoke *arancini* with hazelnut chimichurri. Wine and beer dinners are offered regularly, and brunch is served on Saturday and Sunday.

Mrs. T's Pizza, 4246 Main St., Downers Grove, IL 60515; (630) 963-0800; mrstpizza.com; Pizza/Italian; $$. There are pizzas, and then there is Mrs. T's whisper-thin, earthy mushroom pizza, a tavern-style marvel deserving of accolades. (Mind you, the sausage is superior, too.) Standard Italian alternatives like baked mostaccioli join mainstays such fried chicken and ribs, but honestly, why bother?

Nabuki, 18 E. First St., Hinsdale, IL 60521; (630) 654-8880; nabukihinsdale.com; Japanese; $$$. This venture from Peter and Dana Burdi (also of **Il Poggiolo** [p. 186] a few doors down and CiNe across the street) rolls out a menu of specialty maki in a setting rife with undulating, modern details. Get in the spirit with the Japanic roll, maki built from spicy tuna, cream cheese, avocado, and Japanese mint, topped with black and red *tobiko*. Or, see what the kitchen can do with glazed, Asian-style ribs. There's also a menu for kids that includes fan favorites, like panko-crusted chicken fingers.

Naf Naf Grill, Freedom Commons, 1739 Freedom Dr., Ste. 109, Naperville, IL 60563; (630) 904-7200; nafnafgrill.com; Middle Eastern; $. It's impossible to be ambivalent about Naf Naf's pillowlike, homemade pita. Use it to cradle freshly carved chicken *shawarma*, *kifta* kebabs, and falafel, or plunk it in creamy hummus or baba ghannouj loaded with chunks of char-grilled eggplant.

You may also grab stacks of pitas by the steaming bagful to go. Look for a handful of authentic Israeli offerings, including a light salad of cucumbers, tomatoes, cilantro, and onions. Find additional locations in Chicago, 309 W Washington St., (312) 251-9000, and 326 N. Michigan  Ave., (312) 263-0019; Niles, 5716 W. Touhy Ave., (847) 588-1500; Aurora, 4430 Fox Valley Center Dr., Ste. 101, (630) 499-1700; and Rosemont, 10433 Touhy Ave., (847) 294-0700. Evanston and Orland Park locations are also in the works.

New Rebozo, 1116 Madison St., Oak Park, IL 60302; (708) 445-0370; newrebozo.com; Mexican; $$. On top of having a consummate host—one with a trademark tagline, no less—this intimate mole and margarita master offers an authentic, *madre*-inspired menu made with love. Kick back in the vibrant space and be wowed by both the familiar and painstaking preparations, from skirt steak topped with mole poblano or mole pipian to 42-ingredient Pueblan mole-sauced chicken and straight-up, Americanized chimichangas.

Niche, 14 S. Third St., Geneva IL 60134; (630) 262-1000; niche geneva.com; New American; $$$$. This stylish suburbanite takes a lighthearted approach to American cuisine, teaming its Madeira-and-Mirin-lacquered pork belly with forbidden rice, its cheese plates with Honeycrisp apples, and its beech and maitake mushroom risotto with creamy mascarpone. Seared duck breast may be chaperoned by roasted Brussels sprouts, rutabaga, walnut sable cookie, and sour-cherry jus, while monkfish is at one with tomato confit, kalamatas, capers, and garlic puree. Desserts toe the line between being comforting and serious, as in butterscotch pudding or roasted pineapple tart with a pine-nut crust, coconut rum cream, and licorice-y basil sorbet.

Nickson's, 30 S. La Grange Rd., La Grange, IL 60525; (708) 354-4995; nicksonseatery.com; New American; $$. This rustic wood dining room is rooted in a familiar-but-tweaked menu of greatest hits: fried green tomatoes, chile-braised brisket tacos topped with corn relish, and a pepper-crusted elk burger gilded with aged white cheddar and a fried duck egg. American craft beers and girly cocktails encourage you to take your time, through the crowd with cranky kids does not. Gluten-free and children's menus are available.

Parkers' Restaurant & Bar, 1000 31st St., Downers Grove, IL 60515; (630) 960-5700; selectrestaurants.com/parkersamerican; Seafood/Pizza; $$$. This clubby spot earned a following for fresh seafood—the crispy Stevens Point lager-battered cod sandwich with slaw, green goddess dressing, and house-pickled vegetables alone tells

you why. The other story—authentic, Vera Pizza Napole-tana–certified pies with chewy, blistered crusts—seal the deal. Simply topped with quality ingredients like bright San Marzano tomatoes, fresh mozzarella, and basil leaves, don't bet against them stealing the show.

Porterhouse Steaks & Seafood, 15W776 N. Frontage Rd., **Burr Ridge, IL 60527; (630) 850-9999; porterhouse-ss.com; Steak House/Seafood; $$$.** This supper clubby, roadside spot remains in full effect with tasty bread service, saganaki, and dynamite steaks (get the Renee-style filet, blanketed in blue cheese and red wine bordelaise), brought by old-school servers for a fraction of what you'd expect.

Prasino, 93 S. La Grange Ave., La Grange, IL 60525; (708) 469-**7058; prasino.com; New American; $$.** Appealing to those with eco-conscious sensibilities, this spacious, sleek catchall serves three squares, global bevs, and organic smoothies to a crowd with tots in tow. Start mornings with carrot-cake pancakes stippled with plump raisins; meet midday for a black-bean burger injected with Southwest flavors; and unwind over cocktails and sustainable seafood when daylight wanes. There's a second installment at 1846 W. Division St., (312) 878-1212, and an upcoming location at 5220 Fashion Outlet Way, Rosemont. The same owners are also behind gastropub Wild Monk, 88 S. La Grange Rd., (708) 255-2337, and **Covo Gyro Market** (p. 67).

Priscilla's Ultimate Soul Food, 4330 W. Roosevelt Rd., **Hillside, IL 60162; (708) 544-6230; priscillasultimatesoulfood.com; Regional American; $$.** Give this cozy cafeteria a wide berth if you're watching your waistline, as generously smothered pork chops; mounds of moist, kicking fried chicken; and gooey pie, cake, and cobbler wreak havoc. On second thought, scrap the diet altogether and just go for broke.

Q BBQ, 70 S. La Grange Rd., La Grange, IL 60525; (708) 482-8700; q-bbq.com; Barbecue; $. The interior of this popular, pint-size store-front isn't especially smoky. Come to think of it, neither is its name-sake 'cue. Still, the pulled-pork and brisket sandwiches—garnished with slaw, crumbled blue cheese, and tangy Carolina-style sauce—are satisfying specimens when coupled with toasted cheddar mac and cheese and greasy-good hush puppies. **Additional location:** 103 S. Main St., Naperville, (630) 637-6400.

Riverside Family Restaurant, 3422 S. Harlem Ave., River-side, IL 60546; (708) 442-0434; Czech; $$. Offering plenty of bang for your buck, this geezer-favored locale has things going for it, namely crispy duck and breaded pork tenderloin. Prepare for the after-church masses—though trade-offs whenever you dine include superior liver-dumpling soup, bread dumplings, and other lovingly rendered classics, like *svickova*. Remember to bring cash.

Schmaltz, 1512 N. Naper Blvd., Ste. 152, Naperville, IL 60563; (630) 245-7595; schmaltzdeli.com; Deli; $. The cases of this Jewish delicatessen brim with possibility, from the broccoli-cheddar knishes to the lacy latkes and house-made salads. Moving beyond matzoh ball and other fine soups, you'll find the meat of the mat-ter: overstuffed sandwiches on plush marble rye. Not to be missed is the Reubenlike Sloppy Paul, a warm number with layer upon layer of pastrami or custom-cured corned beef, Swiss, kraut, and Russian dressing. Equally gut-busting good is the cold pastrami and corned beef–mounded Adams sandwich, which is smeared with spicy mustard.

Taco Grill & Salsa Bar, 111 W. Ogden Ave., Westmont, IL 60559; (630) 353-0964; Mexican; $. Even a fire hydrant's worth of water won't suppress the flames ignited by this taqueria's condiment bar; *horchata* at least helps. Contend with the full-flavored skirt steak, cone-carved *al pastor,* and *carnitas* tacos, helping yourself amply to the peppery, pickled radishes and carrot-jalapeño toppings, which are in endless supply when dining within the counter-service digs. The *tortas* and burritos are pretty fantastic, too.

Tamale Hut Cafe, 8300 W. Cermak Rd., Riverside, IL 60546; (708) 442-0948; tamalehutcafe.com; Mexican; $. This unassuming tamale stand packs a flavorful punch. Whether you order the pork verde, chipotle-sauced chicken *tinga,* or mushroom-filled masa, corn-on-the-cob *elotes* positively must go with. A writing and reading series—held on-site—lends a communal feel.

Taste of Himalayas, 110 N. Third St., St. Charles, IL 60174; (630) 444-1575; tasteofhimalayas.com; Indian/ Nepalese; $$. In an area not exactly flush with exotic offerings, this place stands out. But that's not to diminish the good stuff at play: clay oven–roasted garlic and ginger-spiked chicken *chhola;* dry chile chicken; and aromatic "village-style" goat stew. There is a lineup of Indian stalwarts and a lunch buffet that is hard to beat when maintaining a budget.

Topaz Cafe, Burr Ridge Village Center, 780 Village Center Dr., Burr Ridge, IL 60527; (630) 654-1616; topazcafe.com; New American; $$$. It's not just seasonal fare for tame palates coming from this stylish, modern American, where you can look to grilled calamari with garbanzo beans, pickled peppers, and punchy chorizo vinaigrette, and whitefish with toasted Sardinian couscous, roasted mushrooms, and lemon buerre blanc. Its predecessor, **Amber Cafe** (p. 179), is in Westmont.

Uncle Bub's, 132 S. Cass Ave., Westmont, IL 60559; (630) 493-9000; unclebubs.com; Barbecue; $$. This roadhouse shack, outfitted with farm-tool decor, sets a gold standard for so many reasons: its pulled pork with caramelized bits, deeply smoky brisket, positively addictive rib tips, and moist barbecue chicken. Risking sacrilege, though, you may find singular slaw and fried mac and cheese shine almost as brightly. Its regular pig roasts can go mobile. Also, during the holidays Bub's smokes turkeys and hams for at-home use.

Vie, 4471 Lawn Ave., Western Springs, IL 60558; (708) 246-2082; vierestaurant.com; New American; $$$$. Superlatives fail to describe Paul Virant's sedate, hyper-seasonal destination, where intricate dishes pay homage to the local farmers supplying ingredients. Having clocked time at **Blackbird** (p. 98), Charlie Trotter's, and **Everest** (p. 104), Virant (also of **Perennial Virant** downtown [p. 82]) wields enough house-pickled produce to rocket American cuisine to new heights. Sit at the bar for cocktails laced with house syrup, or settle comfortably into the black-and-white dining room punctuated by Mies van der Rohe chairs and tufted banquettes. Then revel in plates of dill-accented roasted duck sausage with mustard-braised kraut, pickled carrots, and wood-grilled onions; pan-seared halibut with wood-grilled leeks, slow-cooked hearts of palm, and Manila clam vinaigrette; and local sweet corn ravioli that's smoky from grilled Irish bacon. Later, you'll realize gooey butter cake—served with spiced carrot jam—never had it so good. Cooking classes are offered. Bring the kiddos along for Sunday suppers; if they're under 11, they pay their age.

Villa Nova, 6821 Pershing Rd., Stickney, IL 60402; (708) 788-2944; Pizza; $$. Fitting into the category of things so simple but sublime, words don't do justice: this thin-crust pie with a perfect sauce, bubbly brown cheese, and paper-thin crust ratio. And while the fennel-flecked sausage is worth touting, better yet is the plain-Jane cheese, which revels in simplicity. Nothing else on the menu is worth a hoot at the mostly carryout joint, so you need not look further. Other locations are in Lockport, 874 N. State St., (815) 838-6682, and New Buffalo, MI.

Westchester Inn, Westbrook Commons Shopping Center, 3069 Wolf Rd., Westchester, IL 60154; (708) 409-1313; Czech; $$. Tucked in a strip mall at the corner of Wolf and 31st, this old-world European cafe doles out bountiful portions of Bohemian staples, complete with soup or tomato juice, dumplings or potatoes, sauerkraut or cabbage, and dessert. Topping the list of choices: rich roasted duck, fruit dumplings, and breaded pork tenderloin—all of which allow for leftovers in abundance.

Zenwich, 416 N. York St., Ste. B, Elmhurst, IL 60126; (630) 359-5234; eatmyzenwich.com; Asian/Sandwiches; $. Terrific Asian-eqsue sandwiches star at this creative, top-tier haunt, which dishes up napkins-required panko-crusted pork *katsu,* moistened by Japanese barbecue and mustard; *bahn mi*–inspired grilled, caramelized pork; and *bulgogi*-style beef with crisp house-made chips to a come-casual crowd, most of whom add on bright, crunchy cucumber salad as a side.

South & Southwest

Aurelio's Pizza, 18162 Harwood Ave., Homewood, IL 60430; (708) 798-4548; aureliospizza.com; Pizza; $$. Located in the town where it all began, this pizza place has stood at its current address since 1977, dishing up signature, sweetly sauced pizzas to the generations. Come hungry and get the Super Six, a thin-crust version loaded with sausage, ham, pepperoni, mushrooms, and green peppers—or have it shipped overnight throughout the US.

Chuck's Southern Comfort Cafe, 6501 W. 79th St., Burbank, IL 60459; (708) 229-8700; chuckscafe .com; Barbecue; $$. There's a bit of an identity crisis going on at this barbecue-themed, down-home cafe, serving everything from pulled pork, hot links, and a heaping plate of barbecue nachos to *huevos* or *chorizo rancheros, pain perdu,* and a daily lineup of specials that may include a Taylor Street sub, smoked corned-beef dinner, Cajun meat loaf, or *camarones en mojo de ajo* (shrimp in garlic sauce). When *cochinita pibil* is available, give it due diligence. A second location is in Darien, 8025 S. Cass Ave., (331) 431-4000.

Cooper's Hawk Winery, 15690 S. Harlem Ave., Orland Park, IL 60462; (708) 633-0200; coopershawkwinery.com; New American/ Wine Bar; $$. Gussied-up American—served in a working winery—is what you'll get from this mid-priced, family-friendly eatery with never-fails like drunken bacon-wrapped shrimp, Thai chicken flatbread, and rich crab and lobster bisque. Pair them with its house vinos, bottles of which may be purchased from its retail store. Offshoots are in Burr Ridge, 510 Village Center Dr., (630) 887-0123; Naperville, 1740 Freedom Dr., (630) 245- 8000; Wheeling, 583 N. Milwaukee Ave., (847) 215-1200; Arlington Heights, 798 W. Algonquin Rd., (847) 981-0900; and South Barrington, 100 W. Higgins Road, Ste. V-1, (847) 836-9463.

Courtright's, 8989 S. Archer Ave., Willow Springs, IL 60480; (708) 839-8000; courtrights.com; New American; $$$$. Fringed by the forest preserve, this idyllic, upscale fine-dining destination is a natural for special occasions, given seasonally inspired creations like carrot–goat cheese mousse; luxurious paprika lobster quenelle with smoked almonds, red onions, snap peas, and mint in vanilla-carrot jus; and a dish of caper-studded, roasted Mediterranean grouper with olive potatoes, fennel, cherry tomatoes, and tarragon sauce. Consider the prix-fixe menu, and take time to explore the extensive wine list.

Fasano's Pizza, 8351 S. Roberts Rd., Justice, IL 60458; (708) 598-6971; fasanospizza.com; Pizza; $$. Everything a good pizza should be—crisp-crusted, cheesy, and sauced with tang—this longtime pizza counter has stood head and shoulders above most since opening in 1972. There are a handful of Italian dishes on offer—veal Parm, a meatball sandwich—but, really, it's all about the 'za. You can get pizzas shipped or pick one up frozen for baking at home. Admittedly, though, nothing compares one turned fresh from the oven and sealed in a paper sleeve.

Fox's, 9655 W. 143rd St., Orland Park, IL 60462; (708) 349-2111; foxsrestaurantsandpub.com; Pizza; $$. Although it serves other slices of Americana (prime rib, chopped sirloin beneath a blanket of mushrooms and onions), this vaguely castlelike haunt is best-known for its super-thin-crust, top-of-the-heap pizzas, which sport the perfect savory sauce-to-cheese ratio. Live entertainment takes place on weekends. **Additional locations:** 11247 W. 187th St., Mokena, (708) 478-8888; 31 N. River St., Batavia, (630) 326-9355.

Hog Wild, 14933 S. Pulaski Rd., Midlothian, IL 60445; (708) 371-9005; originalhogwild.com; Barbecue; $$. It's billed as a sandwich, but the juicy, monster pork chop that made a name for this cabinlike, cash-only place is more akin to fork-and-knife eating. Other slim-wallet specialties include boneless rib, Cajun chicken, or filet sandwiches and rib tips.

Jack Gibbons Gardens, 14700 Oak Park Ave., Oak Forest, IL 60452; (708) 687-2331; jackgibbonsgarden.com; Steak House; $$$. A dimly lit mainstay since 1922, this vintage steak house is a worthy small-town alternative to big-box meateries—especially since its aged steaks, too, arrive sizzling in butter. Get au gratin potatoes on the side, and end with the Irish cream cheesecake for a solid meal.

Krapils the Great Steak, 6600 W. 111th St., Worth, IL 60482; (708) 448-2012; krapilssteakhouse.com; Steak House; $$$. Don't let them sit you in the bar—or the expanded, enclosed patio. To get the real experience, you want to sip your pink squirrel before one of three roaring fireplaces in the darkish, main dining rooms. There, hunter's trophies—largemouth bass, deer and fox heads, and a hornet's nest—adorn the walls in supper club fashion. Chummy service complements the menu of simply prepared, dry-aged steaks, which arrive after metal trays of fresh veggies and marinated cucumbers and tomatoes. House soups are of note (get the baked potato with hunks of ham if you can), and splurge on lemony, garlicky shrimp de Jonghe, which does the bread crumb–laden Chicago original proud.

Mabenka, 7844 S. Cicero Ave., Burbank, IL 60459; (708) 423-7679; mabenka.com; Polish/Lithuanian/Eastern European; $$. One thing is for sure—you won't leave this home-baked hybrid hungry. It specializes in rib-sticking Polish and Lithuanian fare, including a solo meal that could feed the masses: a combo of roast beef, roast pork, Polish and Lithuanian sausages, a meat-filled blintz, a chicken breast, a veal cutlet, and a pork chop with a bounty of sides. Don't ignore tasty apple or potato pancakes or the dumplings. Come on polka nights, when the scene gets raucous. Frozen dumplings may be purchased to cook at home.

The Patio, 9100 S. Harlem Ave., Bridgeview, IL 60455; (708) 598-2099; patioribs.com; Barbecue/American; $$. Casual with a counter-service approach, this barbecue joint makes celebrated racks of baby backs. Offering just enough resistance, these slabs don't fall off the bone and are coated in tangy, sticky, lightly spicy sauce. The other pit preparations are fine enough, but better is the double-decker burger cluttered with 'shrooms, grilled onions, green peppers, and gooey, melted American cheese. **Additional locations:** Orland Park, 7830 W. 159th St., (708) 429-7575; Darien, 7440 S. Kingery Hwy., (630) 920-0211;

Bolingbrook, 151 S. Weber Rd., (630) 226-9696; and Lombard, 2780 S. Highland Ave., (630) 627-2600.

Petey's Bungalow Lounge, 4401 W. 95th St., Oak Lawn, IL 60453; (708) 424-8210; peteysbungalow.com; Steak House; $$$. A vintage fluorescent sign marks the location of this treasure, where career servers present relish trays and meat-centric dinners, followed by sherbet for dessert. Tackle the juicy, Greek-style pork chops, zippy chicken Vesuvio, or any of the properly cooked steaks. The hand-packed burger is a thing of beauty as well. There is another Petey's at 15900 S. La Grange Rd., Orland Park, (708) 349-2820.

Rosangela's Pizza, 2807 W. 95th St., Evergreen Park, IL 60805; (708) 422-2041; Pizza; $$. Get your wafer-thin, tavern-style pizza topped with big hunks of sausage, giving thanks that this generations-old institution remains untouched by time. Also storied are its sand-wiches, especially the Italian beef. Do yourself a solid, though, and don't mention the Cubs—this is Sox country after all.

Schoop's Hamburgers, 695 Torrence Ave., Calumet City, IL 60409; (708) 891-4270; schoophamburgers.com; Burgers; $$. This Indiana import with many area locations turns out lacy-edged two-slice cheeseburgers, topped with relish, onion, mustard, and "catsup" in old-fashioned environs. Bringing the retro diner experience full circle are happy endings, like chocolate sundaes and Green River milk shakes as well as sodas and floats. **Additional locations:** Bourbonnais, 515 S. Main St., (815) 936-9090; Orland Park, Orland Square, 348 Orland Square Dr., (708) 873-9933 ; Chicago Heights, 700 W. 14th St., (708) 748-7580; and Monee, 5701 Monee Manhattan Rd., (708) 534-6000.

Siam Marina, 16846 S. Oak Park Ave., Tinley Park, IL 60409; (708) 862-3438; siammarina.com; Asian; $$. Upscale-casual Thai and Asian fusion goes beyond the basics to include avocado crispy rolls, banana curry duck, and sizzling chicken in a tangle of pliant, brightly hued vegetables. All the handy Thai standbys, like pad Thai and basil fried rice, are available, too.

Tallgrass, 1006 S. State St., Lockport, IL 60441; (815) 838-5566; tallgrassrestaurant.com; New American; $$$$. Recalling a time when dining out was an affair, this jackets-requested sophisticate is worth the drive. And while the reservations-required, wood-paneled opulence suggests stodginess, there's plenty to leave you surprised. Diners mix and match three-, four-, or five-course meals. Look to the reliably intriguing soup trio; it may include squash-leek, eggplant–red pepper, and parsnip-apple. From pork tenderloin with prosciutto, Stilton polenta, pear chutney, and port wine syrup to butter-poached prawns strewn with shishito peppers, the classiness continues. For dessert, the pineapple Foster with pecan brittle and coconut glacé won't disappoint. Be sure to explore the carefully cultivated wine list, which is strong on Russian River Valley and Oregon Pinot Noirs.

Tin Fish, 18201 S. Harlem Ave., Tinley Park, IL 60477; (708) 532-0200; tinfishrestaurant.com; Seafood; $$$. Colin Turner's boisterous, clubby catch keeps the maritime spirit alive with seafaring touches and a design-your-own menu of creatively plated, super-sauced fish. Start with selections from the raw bar (oyster shooters, fresh-shucked oysters, and clams), a half-pound of uncommonly good buffalo shrimp, or lime-licked Asian tuna tartare. Then, start devising the main event, choosing your protein preparation and accompaniments. Birthday dish–worthy is the cornmeal-crusted Lake Superior whitefish on a mound of mashed potatoes bathed in sherry vinegar–pickled giardiniera. Alternately, try the halibut with bashed spuds, roasted tomatoes, prosciutto, and lemon-balsamic butter. Cooking classes are hosted regularly.

White Fence Farm, 1376 Joliet Rd., Romeoville, IL 60446; (630) 739-1720; whitefencefarm-il.com; American; $$. An on-site petting zoo and antiques museum help pass the time when waiting for a table at this always-clucking fried chicken farm, set in a labyrinth of ancient-feeling rooms. Served family-style with bowls of sweet beets, tangy slaw, and kidney-bean salads; powdered sugar–dusted corn fritters; cottage cheese; and mashed potatoes with highlighter-hued gravy, the moist mound of fried chicken retains its charm. Cheap cocktails are poured with a generous hand, a fact that shows in the bitingly boozy brandy ice dessert. Come early on Sunday, or expect to hold court with the after-church crowd.

Outlying

Bianchi's Pizza, 607 LaSalle St., Ottawa, IL 61350; (815) 434-6884; Pizza; $. Nestled into a vintage ice-cream parlor, this super-dark off-kilter pizza joint turns out an admirable sausage pie. It's a boon when you're staying at Starved Rock; if you plan on grabbing yours to go, know you'll be standing in the back kitchen with a shot of the action while you wait.

The Brat Stop, 12304 75th St., Kenosha, WI 53142; (262) 857-2011; bratstop.com; American; $. This ramshackle restaurant just off the highway does its namesake proud. Ask for it grilled, and order the cheese soup as well. Affordable tap beer, live entertainment, a small cheese store, and a game room that contains a vintage Showbiz ride-on truck are finishing touches.

Cavalier Inn, 735 Gostlin St., Hammond, IN 46327; (219) 933-9314; cavalierinn.net; Polish; $$. Paneled walls and pierogi are the name of the game at this jovial, family-run institution dating back to

1949. Many come for the fried chicken livers with onions, the meat-heavy Polish platter, and the *golabki* (stuffed cabbage), though picky eaters are easily sated with American standbys.

Fred's, 596 N. Pine St., Burlington, WI 53105; (262) 763-8370; frp .tripod.com; American; $. There's nothing quite like a burger from Fred's—provided you get past the ordering system. Jot down what you want—a burger topped with cheddar sauce and grilled onions—plus crazy-good house-made chips showered with Parmesan cheese. Then, bring it to the bar and place your order, counting down until the blissful moment it arrives. Afterward, head down the road for a creamy treat from Adrian's Frozen Custard, 572 Bridge St., Burlington, WI, (262) 763-8370, noting the vanilla with sprinkles and, when available, butter pecan.

Freddy's Steakhouse, 6442 Kennedy Ave., Hammond, IN 46323; (219) 844-1500; freddyssteakhouse.net/html/welcome_page .html; Steak House; $$$. Come for the prime rib, the battered lake perch, and the broiled, massive cowboy steak, served in a time-trap setting by servers who know their stuff. Dinners come with a relish tray and all the fixings, including a fab double-baked potato.

Green Gables, 17485 E. 2500 North Rd., Hudson, IL 61748; (309) 747-2496; Burgers; $. The unassuming tackle shop–meets–grocer, bar, and grill is known for its greasy griddled burgers, battered corn bites, and fried cheese cubes. According to lore, the simply sublime meat owes credit to the sizzling, seasoned grill, where the beef simmers in its own juices.

Jake's Delicatessen, 1634 W. North Ave., Milwaukee, WI 53205; (414) 562-1272; jakes-deli.com; Deli; $. The hand-sliced corned beef on seeded rye from this divine deli is insanely good—a fact that accounts for the crowds at this spot that does a brisk business at lunch. Zap it with mustard, don't ignore the pickle, and a get a Stewart's orange or Dr. Brown's black cherry soda to go with.

John's Pizzeria, 247 Ridge Rd., Munster, IN 46321; (219) 836-8536; theoriginaljohns.com; Pizza; $$. With a history that dates back to 1943, the original pizzeria in Calumet City no longer stands. However, its predecessor warrants a trip due east. Sure, you'll have to eat in your car, but such indulgences are worth the fuss. What sets this place apart? The robust tomato sauce, the mid-weight, cornmeal-dusted crust, and—above all—the house-ground, crumbled fennel sausage coating the whole thing.

June, Heritage Square, 4450 N. Prospect Rd., Ste. S1, Peoria Heights, IL 61616; (309) 682-5863; junerestaurant.com; New American; $$$. Emphasizing fresh, organic cuisine—the fruit of area farms—this Modern American from rising chef and owner Josh Adams has its own geothermal greenhouse brimming with fresh produce year-round. Everything here is handcrafted, from the maple tables made by a neighboring artisan to the house-made smoked pork dumpling with steelhead roe and hon-shimeji in a pool of charred ginger dashi. Butchering is done in-house; the wine list leans organic and biodynamic; and the cocktails are inspired by the seasons.

Karl Ratzsch's, 320 E. Mason St., Milwaukee, WI 53202; (414) 276-2720; karlratzsch.com; German; $$. This landmark serves solid sauerbraten and goose worth gobbling—not to mention hearty Hungarian goulash and an over-the-top Usinger sampler. The throwback setting, adorned with European steins, has a charm of its own.

Lincoln's O, 2813 Highway Ave., Highland, IN 46322; (219) 923-4144; Sandwiches; $. There's nothing to the setting, mind you. But you'll swoon over the homespun subs from this simple, delicious stand. Top billing goes to the Bunny Girl with ham and Swiss, the roast beef–packed US Steel Special, and everything-but-the-kitchen-sink Dagwood. Just as rewarding is its homey pie, especially when blueberry, cherry, or apple are thrown into the mix.

Miner-Dunn Hamburgers, 8940 Indianapolis Blvd., Highland, IN 46322; (219) 923-3311; Burgers; $. Smashed, griddled burgers with crisp edges are the claim to fame at this show-stopping, atmospheric diner, where a great meal is made even better with helpings of fries and orange sherbet.

Ridott Corners, 1862 S. Rock City Rd., Ridott, IL 61067; (815) 235-2451; ridottcorners.com; Burgers; $. This biker-friendly tap—located on the way in or out of town—serves one of the best burgers you ever will find. While you wait—the bartender also handles the small, gleaming grill—make haste with bags of Freeport, IL–bred Mrs. Mike's potato chips or cheese popcorn, the latter a finger-staining delight.

Rip's Tavern, 311 N. Main Ave., Ladd, IL 61329; (815) 894-3051; ripschicken.com; American; $. Folks line up for the juicy, crunchy fried chicken—light or dark. It's for good reason. Carving its niche, sour pickles and sides of fried batter bits come with. This is no-frills dining with a consortium of kindred folks, done the Illinois Valley way.

Ron's Cajun Connection, 897 US 6, Utica, IL 61373; (815) 667-9855; ronscajunconnection.com; Cajun; $$. There's no better way to end a day at the state parks than over a meal at this ragin' Cajun, a destination-worthy dining room for plump, blackened Gulf shrimp, warming jambalaya, and brooding crawfish étouffée. Fried gator and boudin balls—battered sausage balls—may as well be required additions.

Take a Jaunt

Whether you grab fresh-made pastas and sauces, a wedge of cheese from the massive selection, or canned goods—from sliced peperoncini to giardiniera and marinated eggplant salad—you really must visit **Tenuta's**, 3203 52nd St., Kenosha, WI 53144; (262) 657-9001; tenutasdeli.com. This institution of an Italian grocer, which has a street-side sausage stand, adds up quick. However, the amazing selection of house-label pantry items, imported finds, and pizzas with singular crust is staggering. When it's warm, a grill stand opens for on-site enjoyment; most any time, a musician holds court in the entryway of the store.

Schooner's, 810 E. Grove St., Bloomington, IL 61701; (309) 829-6841; American; $. Crisp, breaded pork tenderloin is popular in these parts. For an unparalleled, if peculiar, taste, head here. Arriving ridiculously large atop a pizza pan mounded with tomato sauce, cheese, sausage, lettuce, tomatoes, and onions, it gets cut into wedges and stuffed into buns (ask for extras, as a solo, standard-size bun won't cut it). This welcoming watering hole has a likeable dive vibe; as such, it's frequented by college kids, who also favor the wings and rings.

Smitty's Bar & Grill, 950th Road at Walnut St., Leonore, IL 61332; (815) 856-2030; American; $. If you have a stomach of steel, order the touted, platter-size pork tenderloin sandwich and perfectly crisped wings, or detour toward the broasted (fried) chicken, which is head and shoulders above most.

The Spot Drive-In, 2117 75th St., Kenosha, WI 53143; (262) 654-9294; spotdrivein.com; American; $. Words like "whoa" get attached to the house root beer and orange soda that arrive in frosted glass mugs at this iconic throwback, one that's everything—and then some—a drive-in should be. Cherished cheeseburgers topped with thick-cut bacon, golden onion rings, and fried cheese squares also lead the pack. Just remember you'll need to bring cash.

Stop 50 Wood-Fired Pizzeria, 500 S. El Portal Dr., Michiana Shores, IN 46360; (219) 879-8777; stop50woodfiredpizzeria.com; Pizza; $$. Plan a road trip to this Neapolitan-style pizzeria for slightly charred, fire-blazed pies laden with fresh, high-quality ingredients. Start with the smoky, fire-roasted seasonal vegetables or wood-roasted, sausage-stuffed Italian peppers. There's no wrong choice to be had among 'zas, though the Parmigiano graced with red onion, nutty cheese, pistachios, and rosemary offers chewiness of the most satisfying kind. Finish with house-made s'mores.

Teibel's Restaurant, 1775 US 41, Schererville, IN 46375; (219) 865-2000; teibels.com; American; $$. Seniors favor this Indiana holdout for its granny-style fried chicken, hassle-free roast turkey dinner, and fabled buttered, deep-fried pike with sides of coleslaw, beets, and cottage cheese, presented within these charmingly old-fashioned, hallowed walls since 1929.

Wells Bros., 2148 Mead St., Racine, WI 53403; (262) 632-4408; wellsbrosracine.com; Pizza; $$. Don't let the dark, dated interior (or shady surroundings) of this 1921 timepiece deter you from ordering impossibly thin, tavern-style pizza; chock-full, cheesy antipasti salad; and homemade Italian specialties (chicken cacciatore, eggplant parmigiana) within.

Cocktail Culture

Chicago hits the bottles with the best of 'em. Whether you favor craft beer bars and microbreweries (we have tons), prefer kitchen cocktails (have your pick!), or value fruits of the vine, a pick of potables is yours to be had.

Hops Havens

Argus Brewery, 11314 S. Front Ave., Roseland, Chicago, IL 60628; (773) 941-4050; argusbrewery.com. Take a 90-minute Saturday tour of Bob and Patrick Jensen's brewery, sampling Holsteiner, California Steam, and Pegasus IPA along the way. Set within a historic building, it started out brewing for suburban restaurants. Now, you can score the good stuff at well-stocked liquor stores, such as Binny's.

Atlas Brewing Company, 2747 N. Lincoln Ave., Lincoln Park, Chicago, IL 60614; (773) 295-1270; atlasbeer.com. Beer-serious Lincoln Parkers come for the house-brewed pale ale and milk stout—not to mention limited-edition finds like whiskey barrel–aged Obfuscation Imperial Stout or hibiscus-infused cask Saison, pairing them with chef-driven pub grub, like mussels steeped in coconut curry vindaloo, duck confit pizza, and a beer-braised beef panini with apple slaw and tomato aioli.

Begyle Brewing Co., 1800 W. Cuyler, Roavenswood, Chicago, IL 60613; (773) 661-6963; begylebrewing.com. Launched via Kickstarter, this community-supported brewery is situated in an industrial corridor and offers a monthly CSA-type beer subscription. Customers may also fill growlers or procure kegs and bottles on-site.

Clark Street Ale House, 742 N. Clark St., River North, Chicago, IL 60654; (312) 642-9253; clarkstreetalehouse.com. Spacious and convivial, this watering hole is marked by a sign encouraging you, logically, to STOP & DRINK. It's not a bad proposition, considering the reward: 100 beers, plenty of them specialty craft and many on draft, as well as a hefty selection of scotches and cognacs.

Edgewater Lounge, 5600 N. Ashland Ave., Andersonville, Chicago, IL 60660; (773) 878-3343; edgewaterlounge.com. Light filters through stained-glass windows at this friendly neighborhood tap with a thoughtful accrual of independent American and import beers, like Scrimshaw Pilsner from California. The grub is hardly an afterthought, though: Smoked-pepper brisket and grilled ham and cheddar on caraway-studded rye are fine foils.

Emmett's Ale House, 128 W. Main St., West Dundee, IL 60018; (847) 428-4500; emmettsalehouse.com. The Burns family conceived this handcrafted microbrewery in the 1870s-era Hunt's Block building, listed on the National Register of Historic Places. Known for its traditional water-, malt-, hops-, and yeast-based classically crafted beers, it furnishes everything from English-style A.M. Ale to jet-black Double Barrel Oatmeal Stout. Upscale bar fare—beer-battered walleye bites, cheddar-ale soup, shrimp Boursin pasta—buffer debauchery. **Additional locations:** 5200 Main St., Downers Grove, (630) 434-8500; 110 N. Brockway St., Palatine, (847) 359-1533.

Finch's Beer Company, 4565 N. Elston Ave., Mayfair, Chicago, IL 60630; (773) 283-4839; finchbeer.com. Look for the signature tallboys—Threadless IPA, Cut Throat Pale Ale—from this craft brewer, the brainchild of Benjamin Finch and his father, Paul, along with **Flossmoor Station** (p. 211) vet Richard Grant.

Fischman Liquors & Tavern, 4780 N. Milwaukee Ave., Portage Park, Chicago, IL 60630; (773) 545-0123; fischmanliquors.com. Head to this craft beer "slashie" for an impressive selection to enjoy on-site or off, as all selections are sold at an attached liquor store. Live music, regular food truck appearances, and a soon-to-debut restaurant further its crowd appeal.

5 Rabbit Cerveceria, 6398 W. 74th St., Bedford Park, IL 60638; (305) 878-5664; 5rabbitbrewery.com. Lauded Latin-inspired craft beers are the focus at this Bedford Park microbrewery, which sells its wares locally at **Whole Foods** (p. 261) and Andersonville Liquors as well as several bars and restaurants. Learn the story behind amber-hued, chile-spiked 5 Vulture; bright, hoppy 5 Grass; and hibiscus-laced Huitzi during periodic brewery tours.

Flossmoor Station Restaurant & Brewery, 1035 Sterling Ave., Flossmoor, IL 60422; (708) 957-2739; flossmoorstation.com. This boisterous brewpub, residing in the historic Flossmoor train station, made a name for itself with festival-winning takes on tradition. Cases in point range from orange blossom honey–scented Gandy Dancer Honey Ale to lightly spicy Station Master Wheat Ale. The menu goes beyond dressed-down basics to include tempura Zephyr Golden Ale–battered green beans and house beer–spiked teriyaki chicken. Brewery tours are offered, and kegs may be purchased on-site.

Fountainhead, 1970 W. Montrose Ave., Ravenswood, Chicago, IL 60613; (773) 697-8204; fountainheadchicago.com. After closing City Provisions, Cleetus Friedman resurfaced at this tap, already admired for its carefully culled beer and whiskey lists—the former with a dizzying 200-plus choices. But these days it's the hyper-local menu that gets buzz, starting with Bill Kim's Belly Fire–sauced chicken wings with yogurty ranch; mussels vindaloo, steeped in Half Acre ale; and beer-braised beef with onion frizzles and apple cider drizzle. When weather allows, ask to be seated in the rooftop garden, where a dedicated menu features house pickles, salsa and parsnip guacamole, and a proper Caesar salad. Farm dinners, cask and beer events, and various collaborations keep things interesting.

Four Paws Brewing, 5435 N. Wolcott Ave., Andersonville, Chicago, IL 60640; pawsbrewing.com. Passion flows at this in-the-works venture from husband-and-wife team Matt and Meghan Gebhardt, home brewers–turned–entrepreneurs who donate part of profits to animal charities and have a dog (Sadie) as their official mascot. Also of note are the bicycle-based microbrewery tours it hosts.

Goose Island, 1800 N. Clybourn Ave., Lincoln Park, Chicago, IL 60614; (312) 915-0071; gooseisland.com. Standing proud as Chicago's

BLOGGING ABOUT BEER

There's no denying that Chicago's beer culture has grown exponentially in the last few years. So has the number of people keeping tabs on the scene.

Launched in 2010, **Guys Drinking Beer,** guysdrinking beer.com, is a Chicago beer blog featuring beer, cellared beer, and vertical tasting reviews by Karl Klockars, Ryan Hermes, and Andrew Flach. It's also a source for beer news and advocacy awareness.

Also worth noting is **Good Beer Hunting,** goodbeer hunting.com, a labor of love from Chicago-based writer and photographer Michael Kiser, a grad of the School of the Art Institute of Chicago. He chats with brewers, barkeeps, drinkers, and farmers both locally and the world over and shares his insights online.

most widely recognized brewpub, the original location isn't without its rewards—there are seasonal brews you won't find elsewhere. A regular rotation of 20 drafts is available, plus brewmaster Nick Barron (formerly of **Flossmoor Station,** p. 211) collaborates with local chefs to make limited-edition labels; he also presides over bourbon barrel–aged and cask creations. Watch, too, for Fulton & Wood, a series of separate small-batch brews available only in Chicago for a limited time. Goose Island brewery tours and tastings take place on Saturday and Sunday. Its sibling is at 3535 N. Clark St., (773) 832-9040, near Wrigley Field.

The Grafton, 4530 N. Lincoln Ave., Lincoln Square, Chicago, IL 60625; (773) 271-9000; thegrafton.com. Craft beer and Irish comfort food define this popular Lincoln Square pad, which stocks a hefty selection of Emerald Isle brews and whiskeys, plus plenty of other European and American beers. Come on Sundays for toe-tapping, live Irish acts.

Half Acre Beer Company, 4257 N. Lincoln Ave., North Center, Chicago, IL 60618; (773) 248-4038; halfacrebeer.com. Gabriel Magliaro founded this company in 2006, initially creating beers on a contract basis at Wisconsin's Sand Creek Brewery. Years later, he moved the brewing operation to Chicago, opening an on-site retail store and taproom in its wake. Stop in for bottles and growlers of aromatic Gossamer Golden Ale and bold Baumé, and keep your eyes peeled for the tastings that occasionally take place. The shop also stocks a selection of other local brews and spirits, including potables from **Koval Distillery** (p. 228).

Haymarket Pub & Brewery, 737 W. Randolph St., West Loop, Chicago, IL 60661; (312) 638-0700; haymarketbrewing.com. Sure, the house-made sausages, rotisserie chicken, and other workingman's favorites are put to good use. But since this pub and brewery—located near the site of the Haymarket Riot—comes from former **Rock Bottom** (p. 217) brewer Pete Crowley, it's the Belgian-focused beers that command the utmost attention. Make a point to check out the brewhouse and fermentation room, made visible within the century-old building.

Hopleaf, 5148 N. Clark St., Andersonville, Chicago, IL 60640; (773) 334-9851; hopleaf.com. This tavern is tops among hops heads, who revel in its 200-strong craft suds selection that emphasizes Belgian-style brews. Food is a big part of the equation, too, with plump thyme, shallot, and bay leaf–scented, Wittekerke white ale–steamed mussels for two leading the way. Other upscale, beer-appropriate bites include a sausage plate with bourbon-pancetta white beans as well as cherry-glazed, St. Bernardus–braised venison ribs with cranberry beans alongside pumpkin, fennel, and celery-root slaw and dried-cherry-walnut-sage pesto.

Jerry's, 1938 W. Division St., Wicker Park, Chicago, IL 60622; (773) 235-1006; jerryssandwiches.com. Near-endless craft beers, lots o' whiskey, and 100-plus sandwiches go hand-in-hand at this friendly find, which regularly hosts beer dinners and tastings. Another location is at 5419 N. Clark St., (773) 796-3777.

Local Option, 1102 W. Webster Ave., Lincoln Park, Chicago, IL 60614; (773) 348-2008; localoptionbier.com. Taps flow with 30-plus rare beers at this convivial Creole, which leans heavy metal and is set off the beaten path on a residential street. Peruse the encyclopedic bottle list at this virtual unknown, soaking up the suds with jambalaya or a muffaletta sandwich, sidled by beer-battered fries.

The Map Room, 1949 N. Hoyne Ave., Bucktown, Chicago, IL 60647; (773) 252-7636; maproom.com. A staggering beer list is the draw at this friendly neighborhood tavern, known for its vast array of specialty and limited-release selections, cultivated by its resident cicerone. By day, it's a coffeehouse serving pastries from Bennison's Bakery. Want to decipher aromas and flavors? Sign up for its informative beer school series, hosted by local brewers.

Maria's Packaged Goods & Community Bar, 960 W. 31st St., Bridgeport, Chicago, IL 60608; (773) 890-0588; community-bar .com. The Sazerac set descends on this artsy slashie, a drinking den and liquor store from *Lumpen* editor and publisher Ed Marszewski. Local artwork decks the walls; musicians and DJs hail from the 'hood; and a cache of whiskey cocktails—like a tongue-in-cheek Old Grand-Dad number inspired by "the Stockyards' drainage canal"— give the place its semblance of collective cool. But the real hype revolves around the hundreds-strong, always-in-flux craft

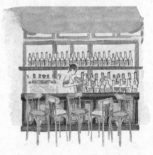

beer list. On warm summer nights, brother Mike Marszewski may fire up the grill. Also of note, the Bridgeport-based Marz Community Brewing company is in the works.

Metropolitan Brewing, 5121 N. Ravenswood Ave., Ravenswood, Chicago, IL 60640; metrobrewing.com. There's no public phone number (reach them via minion@metrobrewing.com), but this small-production brewery from husband-and-wife team Doug and Tracy Hurst is the talk of the town. Legendary suds include seasonal numbers and flagships like Kölsch-style Krankshaft and German-inspired Flywheel. You'll find their suds at neighborhood bars and specialty stores, and they may be purchased online. Public tours of the facility are offered on a semi-regular basis by reservation.

Moonshine Brewing Company, 1824 W. Division St., Wicker Park, Chicago, IL 60622; (773) 862-8686; moonshinechicago.com. Chill and inviting, this regional American brewhouse features a Southwestern-inflected menu (cast iron–singed shrimp with fire-roasted jalapeños and avocado, a three-pepper burger with habanero aioli, ancho-marinated rib eye) and a unique, changing 10-barrel selection of house-brewed beer, courtesy of brewer JD McCormick. Don't overlook the Bloody Mary bar on weekends—it's loaded with boutique hot sauces for heating things up.

Owen & Engine, 2700 N. Western Ave., Logan Square, Chicago, IL 60647; (773) 235-2930; owenengine.com. This boisterous, dimly lit pub is a date-appropriate, Brit-inspired hang that's heavy on surprises. Among its seductions is the lengthy, rotating selection of cask and craft beers overseen by a certified cicerone; house-cured sausages and char-cuterie with homemade pickles; and beyond-basic bar bites like Amish chicken wings with *piment d'espelette* and crème fraîche. The bangers-and-mash and fish-and-chips, too, are a step above most.

DIY Brewing

Home-brew club **Square Kegs** is a beer geek's best friend. Open to brewers of all skill levels, this educational, beer-minded forum and think tank meets the last Thursday of each month at various Lincoln Square establishments, giving experts and enthusiasts a change to drink and talk shop. Watch for events on its Facebook page or at lincolnsquare.org/pages/SquareKegsHomeBrewClub.

Piece Brewery & Pizzeria, 1927 W. North Ave., Wicker Park, Chicago, IL 60622; (773) 772-4422; piecechicago.com. Crisp, red or barbecue-sauced, garlicky "plain," and white New Haven–style pizzas have their share of enthusiasts, though it's Jonathan Cutler's painstakingly crafted, small-batch brews—The Weight American Pale Ale, Top Heavy Hefeweizen, Dark & Curvy Dunkelweizen—that accrue the awards. Enjoy cold ones in-house, or grab them by growler with a pie on the fly.

Pipeworks Brewing Co., 1675 N. Western Ave., Wicker Park, Chicago, IL 60647; (773) 698-6154; pipeworksbrewing.com. Made possible by Kickstarter, this collab between head brewmaster Beejay Oslon and partner Gerrit Lewis dispenses beer to major hops spots—from **Maria's Packaged Goods & Community Bar** (p. 214) to Binny's—with the hope of having a tasting room soon.

The Publican, 837 W. Fulton Market, West Loop, Chicago, IL 60607; (312) 733-9555; thepublicanrestaurant.com. This pad is as much about beer as it is pork and sustainable seafood. The list of amber-hued libations features coveted Trappist and Abbey-style Belgian ales, Flemish finds, lambics, and much more. And although it changes often, it remains cutting edge.

RAM Restaurant & Brewery, 1901 McConnor Pkwy., Scha-umburg, IL 60173; (847) 517-8791; theram.com. This gregarious, Washington-based brewpub has chains in several states. Don't rule it out, since you imbibe locally brewed but nationally honored suds, like Total Disorder Porter and Big Horn Blonde, while attacking loaded waffle fries, buffalo wings, or beer-bread pizza. Additional local outposts are at 9520 Higgins Rd., Rosemont, (847) 692-4426, and 700 N. Milwaukee Ave., Wheeling, (847) 520-1222.

Revolution Brewing, 2323 N. Milwaukee Ave., Logan Square, Chicago, IL 60647; (773) 227-2739; revbrew.com. Handlebar's Josh Deth is the man with the plan, and his serious gastropub is centered on signature fist-pump taps, replenished with the lifeblood of brewer Jim Cibak. Toss them back with orders of bacon-fat popcorn with crispy sage or curry-spiced sweet-potato cakes with red-pepper cream. Then, grab a to-go growler before hitting the road. You can also visit its nearby taproom and brewing facility, which is open Wednesday through Saturday and offers complimentary guided tours; it's located at 3340 N. Kedzie Ave., (773) 588-2267.

Rock Bottom Brewery, 1 W. Grand Ave., River North, Chicago, IL 60654; (312) 755-9339; rockbottom.com. Although its home base is in Colorado, this popular brewery and restaurant holds its own among local microbreweries, thanks to signatures like Chicago Gold, an American-style pale ale, and Terminal Stout, which appears as dry Irish, oatmeal, or imperial in style throughout the year. Expect a lineup of crispy salt-and-pepper shrimp with Thai chile sauce, slow-braised short ribs, and chicken-fried chicken with white-cheddar mashed potatoes as complements. **Additional locations:** in Lombard, 94 Yorktown Center, (630) 424-1550; Orland Park, 16156 S. La Grange Rd., (708) 226-0021; and Warrenville, 28256 Diehl Rd., (630) 836-1380.

Solemn Oath Brewery, 1661 Quincy Ave., #179, Naperville, IL 60540; (630) 995-3062; solemnoathbrewery.com. Located in the west suburbs, this craft brewery and taproom specializes in Belgian-inspired and barrel-aged brews. It also does collabs, like the chai-spiced porter it did for Terra Spice Company.

Spiteful Brewing, 1815 W. Berteau Ave., #15, Ravenswood, Chicago, IL 60613; facebook.com/spitefulbrewing. This small, start-up nanobrewery dispenses liquid gold to a handful of area bars, like Four Moon Tavern. But when it's gone, it's gone.

Three Aces, 1321 W. Taylor St., Little Italy, Chicago, IL 60607; (312) 243-1577; threeaceschicago.com. A rock-and-roll edge pervades at this loud, Italian-bent, small-plates spot where duck-fat potato chips gilded with fennel powder and pillowy rye gnocchi with braised oxtail, smoked pecorino, parsnips, and mushrooms are fashioned by Matt Troost (ex-Fianco). Amid big flavors and light fixtures obtained from Joliet's prison, it'd be easy to ignore the massive, carefully selected beer list. How-ever, options like Lagunitas Brewing Co.'s Maximus and Great Lakes Brewing Co.'s Burning River are worth paying mind.

Three Floyds Brewing, 9750 Indiana Pkwy., Munster, IN 46321; (219) 922-3565; 3floyds.com. Demanding a short jog out of town, especially on Saturday when free brewery tours are offered, this artisanal Alpha King has its own brewpub, serving a sausage-encased Scotch egg with garlic mayo, braised chicken leg with greens in bacon broth with fried chicken skin, and house-made tagliatelle with fennel sausage and tomatoes. Plan ahead and attend its annual Dark Lord Day, an over-the-top beer fest.

Two Brothers Brewing Company, 30W315 Calumet Ave., Warrenville, IL 60555; (630) 393-2337; twobrosbrew.com. Big ideas benchmark this operation from real-life bros Jim and Jason Ebel, whose warehouse opens for tours on Saturday. Of course, there's no need to plan ahead when devouring Cane & Ebel–battered Holland sole or dry-rubbed pulled pork at its companion restaurant, Two Brothers Tap House. While you're there, throw back ultra-fresh, cask-conditioned ales and drafts that are only available on site. Beer tastings and dinners often take place.

Two Brothers Roundhouse, 205 N. Broadway, Aurora, IL 60505; (630) 264-2739; twobrothersroundhouse.com. First of all, the structure—a historic roundhouse adjacent to the Aurora Transportation Center—is quite a sight. But it's what comes from the gleaming brew-tanks that earn a fan base, thanks to brothers Jim and Jason Ebel. That includes everything from oak-aged ales, limited-run seasonal beers, and anybody's guess artisan sips. The kitchen is ambitious, too, turning out hops-bent bites, like game sausage with beer mustard, Cane & Ebel–braised Duroc pork belly tacos, and bison meat loaf with chipotle-beer glaze. Consider visiting its sister pub and brewing facility (see listing above), where tours are offered every Saturday. Each June, the Roundhouse hosts a summer beer festival and home-brewer's competition. Live entertainment occurs regularly.

Vino Venues

avec, 615 W. Randolph St., West Loop, Chicago, IL 60606; (312) 377-2002; avecrestaurant.com. Blackbird's (p. 98) kin remains a frequented destination for small plates inspired by the seasons. It also has a worldly wine list that's appealing (and relatively affordable) to the food-loving masses. Whether it's a glass of 2010 Henri de Richemer

Terre & Mer Sec or 2010 Tasca D'Almerita Regaleali you seek, unearth it amid a list loaded with lesser-knowns.

Bar Ombra, 5310 N. Clark St., Andersonville, Chicago, IL 60640; (773) 506-8600; barombra.com; $$. The owners of **Acre** (p. 2) conceived of this *cicchetti* spot, a sepia-toned Venetian-style bar serving crustless *tramezzini* (tea sandwiches) and *baccala mantecato* alongside pastas and comforting mains, like spicy pork *arrabiatta* with chard and cannellini beans. Just as many grazers go for the salumi, focaccia, and bruschetta, all built for pairing with cocktails and wines that lean Northern Italian.

Bar Pastoral, 2947 N. Broadway, Lakeview, Chicago, IL 60657; (773) 472-4781; pastoralartisan.com/bar-pastoral. Cheese store **Pastoral** (p. 242) is the proud owner of this welcoming wine bar with an impressive, budget-friendly vino list, great cheese and charcuterie selections (don't miss the duck rillettes parfait), and an edited array of small and large plates, including pizza nuts and cheddar mac and cheese, from Chrissy Camba.

Beviamo Wine Bar, 1358 W. Taylor St., Little Italy, Chicago, IL 60607; (312) 455-8255. This canoodler's paradise is romantic, stylish, and global—not to mention a welcome, wine-centric relief amid Taylor Street's sauce-saturated scene. The fabric-draped, loungelike vibe extends to the DJ-curated beats and lineup of live piano.

Bin 36, 339 N. Dearborn St., River North, Chicago, IL 60654; (312) 755-9463; bin36.com. This popular spot serves great food, though plenty consider the approachable wine list a true come-on. Fruits of the vine are proposed as pairings with dishes. Many by-the-glass, flight, and bottle options—each with engaging, easy-to-relate-to descriptors—complement Wine Director Brian Duncan's endlessly sippable,

Chicago-conceived California wines, which may be enjoyed on-site, purchased, or shipped.

Blue Star Wine Bar, 1209 N. Noble St., Noble Square, Chicago, IL 60642; (773) 278-2233; bluestarbistroandwinebar.com. Sample mostly familiar flights and a small selection of by-the-glass and bottled wines at the granite-topped bar, weighted by Mediterranean small plates such as blue corn grits with blackened jumbo shrimp, Manchego cheese, and roasted garlic.

The Bluebird, 1749 N. Damen Ave., Wicker Park, Chicago, IL 60647; (773) 486-2473; bluebirdchicago.com. Emphasizing wine and beer in equal measure, this exposed-brick haunt from the owners of **Webster's Wine Bar** (p. 226) is also serious about its plates, from an impressive, artisanal cheese selection to shareable selections and more substantial mains, such as smoked, beer-brined chicken thighs. The beer-steamed mussels are most worth revisiting.

Davanti Enoteca, 1359 W. Taylor St., Little Italy, Chicago, IL 60607; (312) 226-5550; davantichicago.com. Scott Harris's red-hot spot hits the right notes with an Italian menu of polenta boards, Mason jar smears, and antipasti. However, thrifty, boot-based grapes—poured by the glass, bottle, and quartino and also available for purchase—offer perks beyond chow.

D.O.C. Wine Bar, 2602 N. Clark St., Lincoln Park, Chicago, IL 60614; (773) 883-5101; docwinebarchicago .com. Named for the Italian wine designation, this down-to-earth vino bar—a sibling of **Frasca Pizzeria & Wine Bar** (p. 36)— pours globe-trotting *vins* alongside bacon-wrapped, chorizo-stuffed dates; meat and cheese platters with apricot-Merlot jam; and a chocolate chip cookie skillet. It—and its mall-centered counterpart at 326 Yorktown Center, Lombard, (630) 627-6666—often host tastings.

ENO, **Intercontinental Chicago, 505 N. Michigan Ave., Gold Coast, Chicago, IL 60611; (312) 321-8738; enowinerooms.com.** Wine, cheese, and chocolate—that pretty much sums up the sins at this hotel-centered wine bar that manages to be esoteric without a trace of snootiness. (Sign up for its Eno-versity classes to experience firsthand.) Ask about featured, handcrafted wines, which are sometimes highlighted by flight, and do visit the tap vinos—one white, one red—blended by Wine Director Scott Harney. **Additional location:** Fairmont Chicago, 200 N. Columbus Dr., (312) 946-7000.

Enoteca Roma, **2146 W. Division St., Ukrainian Village, Chicago, IL 60622; (773) 342-1011; enotecaroma.com.** This is an intimate option for Italian eats, though it's the international wine list, featuring more than two-dozen options by the glass and many more by the bottle, that leaves budget-minded oenophiles aflutter.

Fion Wine & Spirits, **426 W. Diversey Pkwy., Lincoln Park, Chicago, IL 60614; (773) 549-5400; fion wineandspirits.com.** A step up for aging Duffy's and McGee's rabble-rousers, this marble bar disburses martinis, classic cocktails, and, notably, more than a dozen wines from an airtight system.

404 Wine Bar, **2856 N. Southport Ave., Lakeview, Chicago, IL 60657; (773) 404-5886; 404winebarchicago.com.** Warmed by a fireplace, this global addendum to Jack's Bar & Grill pours flights, glasses, and bottles, serving cheese and charcuterie plates, house-made tapenade, steak frites, and flatbread alongside.

Frasca Pizzeria & Wine Bar, 3358 N. Paulina St., Lakeview, Chicago, IL 60657; (773) 248-5222; frascapizzeria.com. More than a place for Italian-bent fare, this is also a sensible, jovial joint where you may swirl flights, clink glasses of sparkling wine, and idle over house-made sangrias.

Joie de Vine, 1744 W. Balmoral Ave., Andersonville, Chicago, IL 60640; (773) 989-6846; joiedevine.com. There's a hidden charm to this quiet, narrow wine establishment on a residential street, its long wood bar turning out more than two-dozen by-the-glass vintages. Take in its ambient, jazzy soundtrack, and nibble on small plates and cheese platters.

LUSH Wine and Spirits, 1257 S. Halsted St., University Village, Chicago, IL 60607; (312) 738-1900; lushwineandspirits.com. It started as a funky wine shop in 2006, rapidly expanding its offbeat beer, spirit, and wine selection. Come on Sunday afternoon from 2 to 5 p.m. for complimentary wine geek–guided tastings or stop by—pretty much whenever—when samples are uncorked for sheer fun. **Additional locations:** 2232 W. Roscoe St., (773) 281-8888; 1412 W. Chicago Ave., (312) 666-6900.

Pops for Champagne, 601 N. State St., River North, Chicago, IL 60610; (312) 266-7677; popsforchampagne.com. Expect swanky, bubbly-minded plates that don't take a backseat to the nearly 200-strong Champagne and sparkling-wine list. Then again, the still-wine, beer, and cocktail offerings are every bit as splendiferous.

Quartino, 626 N. State St., River North, Chicago, IL 60656; (312) 698-5000; quartinochicago.com. This late-night Italian kitchen features over 30 Italian wines by the carafe, which are natural bedfellows for John Coletta's house salumi, Neapolitan pizzas, and fresh pasta. Large-format wines are also available on the easy-to-navigate list, and a surfeit of cocktails—some utilizing house-made "grapefruitcello"—satisfy spirit-seekers.

RM Champagne Salon, 16 N. Green St., West Loop, Chicago, IL 60607; (312) 243-1199; rmchampagnesalon.com. Situated behind sibling **Nellcôte** (p. 119), this elegant hideaway is more than a pretty face: Jared Van Camp's lobster deviled eggs and trout meunière stand up to the posh, offbeat bubbles on offer. Of course, you can always start with oysters and end with *mignardises* (bite-size desserts), and wind up happy just the same.

Rootstock, 954 N. California Ave., Humboldt Park, Chicago, IL 60622; (773) 292-1616; rootstockbar.com. The brainchild of **Webster's Wine Bar** (p. 226) veterans, this unfussy boutique hang has judicious wine, bubbly, and beer lists, along with a menu—served until 1 a.m. nightly—of note. Chef Duncan Biddulph's sustainable, locally driven, shareable plates range from nibbles (fried quail eggs with hen-of-the-woods mushrooms and pumpkin gremolata) to anchoring fare like hanger steak with watercress, charred onions, baby turnips, and piquillo peppers. There's a nice selection of cheese and charcuterie, too.

The Stained Glass Wine Bar, 1735 Benson Ave., Evanston, IL 60201; (847) 864-8600; thestainedglass.com. The cubbies filled with wine—32 of them available by the glass and many more by the bottle—are offset by a *foie gras* BLT on toasted brioche; pork belly with chilled coconut custard, spicy tamarind-curry barbecue, and hearts of palm salad; and miso-glazed salmon with bamboo rice, baby bok choy, and lobster-uni emulsion. Ask about wine classes.

The Tasting Room, 1415 W. Randolph St., West Loop, Chicago, IL 60607; (312) 942-1313; thetastingroomchicago.com. For over a decade this loftlike wine bar has been a go-to for fruit-forward finds, available as taste-size pours and flights based on region, season, or varietal. Artisan cheese plates, tweaked American comfort food—like duck *arancini* with walnut pesto—and market cocktails round out the experience.

Telegraph Restaurant and Wine Bar, 2601 N. **Milwaukee Ave., Logan Square, Chicago, IL 60647; (773) 292-9463; telegraph chicago.com.** The folks behind **Webster's Wine Bar** (p. 226) and **The Bluebird** (p. 221) emphasize naturally produced "new Old World" wines, culled by Jeremy Quinn, at this Logan Square wine bar. Sit at the communal chef's table or settle in for charcuterie, cheeses, and hand-cut tagliatelle with yellow-foot mushrooms, olives, tomatoes, and ramp vinaigrette.

The 3rd Coast Cafe & Wine Bar, 1260 N. Dearborn St., **Gold Coast, Chicago, IL 60610; (312) 649-0730; 3rdcoastcafe.com.** Breakfast is served all day at this trim cafe and wine bar with a menu from sandwiches to steaks. However, the main event is the easily deciphered vinos, categorized by price (under $25, $40, and $70).

Vintage 338, 338 W. **Armitage Ave., Lincoln Park, Chicago, IL 60614; (773) 525-0521; vintage338.com.** The wine-producing regions of Spain, Italy, and France largely inform the edited list at this attainable, intimate wine bar with mosaic tile details. Almost all are available by the glass or bottle and may be paired with foods of southern Europe, such as crostini and meat and cheese platters.

Volo, 2008 W. Roscoe St., Roscoe Village, Chicago, IL 60618; (773) **348-4600; volorestaurant.com.** While an enjoyable place to savor wine year-round, it is particularly pleasant when the hidden cabana patio is swept by balmy breezes. Grab a seat there and pore over its descriptive wine list, decanted by the two-ounce taste, glass, mini-carafe, or bottle. Specials, perhaps half-price bottles on a designated day, are an additional enticement.

Webster's Wine Bar, 1480 W. Webster Ave., Lincoln Park, Chicago, IL 60614; (773) 868-0608; websterwinebar.com. The snoot-factor is nil at this friendly, affordable vino 'veyor from the folks behind **The Bluebird** (p. 221). Global small plates couple with an assemblage of cheese, cured meat, and more substantial (and traditional) large plates, like peppery pan-seared scallops with bitter greens, fennel salad, and grilled navel orange. The wine list—featuring many selections by the glass, bottle, and flight—is top-notch.

Cocktails

The Aviary, 955 W. Fulton Market, West Loop, Chicago, IL 60607; (312) 226-0868; theaviary.com. High-concept, theatrically prepared and presented cocktails from Charles Joly inform this Grant Achatz and Nick Kokonas (**Alinea** [p. 56], **Next** [p. 120]) venture, which has tipplers clamoring for more. The plush, neutral-hued dining room has a special-occasion feel. Small bites and more substantial eats from storied chef Andrew Brochu lend credence to coming for dates.

Bar DeVille, 701 N. Damen Ave., Ukrainian Village, Chicago, IL 60622; (312) 929-2349; bardeville.com. Matt Eisler (Empire Liquors, Angels & Kings) is behind this spot with a French name and decidedly low-key aura. Then there's perfectly balanced cocktails, created by Brad Bolt (an alum of **The Violet Hour,** p. 237). Get your pic taken in the vintage photo booth, shoot some pool, and stay for a couple more rounds before hailing a cab.

Barrelhouse Flat, 2624 N. Lincoln Ave., Lincoln Park, Chicago, IL 60614; (773) 857-0421; barrelhouseflat.com. Complex craft cocktails, both shaken and stirred, come courtesy of Stephen Cole, a **Violet Hour** (p. 237) vet. Ask to be seated in the upstairs salon, a moody perch when tipping back a frothy whiskey Pink Lady or effervescent French 75. Food is far from an afterthought, as evidenced by the confit chicken *bahn mi* with turnip slaw, red pepper jelly, and *togarashi* frites and the indulgent sugar-glazed bacon beignet.

Bernard's Bar, Waldorf Astoria, 11 E. Walton St., 2nd Fl., Gold Coast, Chicago, IL 60611; (312) 646-1300; elysianhotels.com. You don't have to shop until you drop to appreciate the tranquil sophistication of this haute haunt just off the Mag Mile. Whether you sit at the marble bar or plop down at a plush, pin-tucked velvet banquette, you get what you pay for: flawless Negronis, Sidecars, and cultured craft beers—not to mention luxury morsels.

Billy Sunday, 3143 W. Logan Blvd., Logan Square, Chicago, IL 60647; (773) 661-2485; billy-sunday.com. Named for an evangelist and Prohibition advocate, this Logan Square boîte from Matthias Merges (**Yusho,** p. 54) offers up intriguing, balanced cocktails using unconventional ingredients (wormwood bitters, dandelion, wild cherry bark). Not surprisingly, nibbles play a prominent role, be it quark with giardiniera, jarred chicken liver with curried raisin mostarda, or malt vinegar pig's ear with cornichon aioli. Finish with ethereal banana budding with whipped honeycomb.

The California Clipper, 1002 N. California Ave., Humboldt Park, Chicago, IL 60622; (773) 384-2547; californiaclipper.com. Linger over a board game or take in the tunes at this vintage-chic tap with an Art Deco bar readying cocktail classics, like venerable Rob Roys and Rusty Nails. More contemporary, though, is the Purple Martin, a lip-smacking coconut rum, lemon, and grape-soda libation.

Getting in the Spirit

Chicago has seen an influx of home-grown, artisanal distilleries, making it easier—not to mention more interesting—than ever to get your drink on.

CH Distillery, 564 W. Randolph St., West Loop, Chicago, IL 60661; chdistillery.com. Premium vodka is the focus of this distillery and cocktail bar, which makes the spirit from scratch using Illinois grain. It also has plans to make a juniper-light gin, unaged whiskey, and rum as well. Enjoy your ultra-chilly sips with small plates from Jesse Katzman (**avec,** p. 95).

Few Spirits, 918 Chicago Ave., Evanston, IL 60202; (847) 920-8628; fewspirits.com. Set in the midst of where the temperance movement began, this handcrafted distillery turns out new, spirited classics, including charred oak barrel–aged bourbon, lemon peel and vanilla-scented gin, and white and rye whiskeys. Watch, too, for its barrel-aged gin. Visit the tasting room for a glimpse into the process.

Jeppson's Malört, jeppsonsmalort.com, is an extra-bitter (some would say brutal) indigenous Chicago spirit distilled by Carl Jeppson Co. Its roots, however, date back to Swedes in the 1400s. During Prohibition, Jeppson, a Swedish immigrant, whipped up a home-made version. The rest, as they say, is history.

Koval Distillery, 5121 N. Ravenswood Ave., Andersonville, Chicago, IL 60640; (312) 878-7988; kovaldistillery.com. Chicago's first boutique distillery was created by former academics Robert and Sonat Birnecker. Both organic and kosher, its Lion's Pride whiskey is made from 100 percent grain bills and is available in oat, dark oat, rye, and dark rye varieties. Other potables include vodka distilled from rye;

liqueurs from rose hip to jasmine; pear brandy; and Bierbrand, a hoppy number produced in conjunction with **Metropolitan Brewing** (p. 215). Whiskey workshops occur from time to time, and distillery tours are available on Wednesdays, Saturdays, and Sundays.

Letherbee Distillers, 1815 W. Berteau, Ravenswood, Chicago, IL 60613; (217) 741-0392; letherbee.com. Brenton Engel turned a bootleg operation into a bona fide micro-distillery, one he operates with Miriam Matasar (the two met while working at **Lula Cafe** [p. 41]). The bourgeoning biz now produces original-label gin and barrel-aged absinthe. Collaborations are taking place, too, including coffee liqueur in conjunction with Dark Matter, malort for Violet Hour's Robby Haynes and, possibly, blue curaçao for Paul McGee's tiki bar, **Three Dots and a Dash** (p. 236).

North Shore Distillery, 28913 N. Herky Dr., #308, Lake Bluff, IL 60044; (847) 574-2499; northshoredistillery .com. This Lake Bluff distillery is behind some seriously smooth, small-batch vodka and chamomile citrus vodka as well as modern, dry botanical gin and gins that feature ginger, locally grown rhubarb, or exotic Medjool dates. It also turns out annual single-batch productions, such as 90-proof Mole Poblano and limited edition CR2, a cocktail-in-a-bottle containing gin, orange liqueur, Lillet Blanc, lemon juice, and absinthe. Plus, the distillery produces Aquavit and Sirène Absinthe as well as Silver Lining, a take on traditional German *kräuter* (herbal) liqueur, for Metropolis Coffee Co. Stop by the distillery store to see what's in stock; check out the tasting room when it's open on Friday and Saturday; and take a tour on Saturday afternoons.

Double A, 108 W. Kinzie St., River North, Chicago, IL 60654; (312) 329-9555; doubleachicago.com. Located beneath **Mercadito** (p. 117), this spot specializes in custom, made-to-order cocktails—like the Daisy Lightning, with Death's Door white whiskey, curaçao, hibiscus, lemon, and egg white—made before revelers' eyes at posh banquettes. Not surprisingly, cocktail connoisseurs the Tippling Bros. have something to do with the interactive experience.

The Drawing Room, 937 N. Rush St., Gold Coast, Chicago, IL 60611; (312) 266-2694; thedrchicago.com. Chef Rodney Staton conceives the progressive New American plates at this sultry boîte, where choices may include peekytoe crab with preserved lemon, pea purée, and pickled chile. But come for mixologist Cristiana DeLucca's seasonal, culinary cocktails, too, like the O'Leary's Cow, built from Old Weller 107, Campari, Coffee Heering, Fernet, and a Laphroaig rinse.

The Drinkingbird, 2201 N. Clybourn Ave., Lincoln Park, Chicago, IL 60614; (773) 472-9920; drinkingbirdchicago.com. For retro imbibing, it's hard to beat this Lincoln Park gem, a swanky, Old Vegas–inspired spot for Zombies and Negronis as well as craft beers. Soak up the booze with pigs in a blanket and steak Diane sliders.

Drumbar, Raffaello Hotel, 201 E. Delaware Pl., Gold Coast, Chicago, IL 60611; (312) 943-5000; drumbar.com. Perched atop the 18th floor of the Raffaello Hotel, find this low-lit, mahogany-swathed pad. When it's cold, sink into tufted leather banquettes beneath vaulted ceilings; come summer, score low-slung seats on the firepit-strewn terrace. All the while, sip Craig Schoettler–designed cocktails, with light bites from **Pelago Ristorante** (p. 81) chef Mauro Mafrici.

Elixir, 3452 N. Halsted St., Lakeview, Chicago, IL 60657; (773) 975-9244; elixirchicago.com. Properly prepared libations come from this pint-size, gay-friendly Boystown bar, a more hushed, adult alternative to Hydrate next door. Kick back in the neutral-hued space for an array of Prohibition-era and modern cocktails, top-tier accompaniments to cheese and charcuterie from neighbor **Pastoral Artisan Cheese, Bread & Wine** (p. 242).

The Exchange, 1270 N. Milwaukee Ave., Wicker Park, Chicago, IL 60622; (773) 342-5282; theexchangebar.com. Sepia (p. 127) vet Peter Vestinos masterminded the potables at this sleek, dimly lit, and conversation-friendly Wicker Park bar, serving punch bowls and a tequila cocktail infused with Lapsang souchong tea. Located in the intimate former home of Lava Lounge, it's now adorned with cool orbs of light and has (quietly) pulsing DJ beats.

Gilt Bar, 230 W. Kinzie St., River North, Chicago, IL 60654; (312) 464-9544; giltbarchicago.com. Brendan Sodikoff may have worked with Thomas Keller and Alain Ducasse in the past, but his lounge-y boîte favors simple preparations. Scenesters are attracted to the sleek, low-lit space, breaking the ice over smearable, roasted bone marrow and red-onion jam. Elevated American dishes—perhaps grilled pork belly with persimmons and farro—favor what's local. Most interesting, though, are libations—like the minty, gin-based Southside—designed by Paul McGee (**The Whistler**, p. 237). Also, visit Sodikoff's **Maude's Liquor Bar** (p. 233), **Au Cheval** (p. 95), **Bavette's Bar & Boeuf** (p. 96), and **The Doughnut Vault** (p. 276).

The J Parker, Hotel Lincoln, 1816 N. Clark St., Lincoln Park, Chicago, IL 60616; (312) 254-4747; jparkerchicago.com. Gaze at amazing skyline, park, and lake views at this laid-back Lincoln Park restau-bar, a welcome break from the throngs. The panoramic 13-story views are gleaned from plentiful outdoor seating—just the place to sip globally inspired cocktails with pickled-centric fare from Paul Virant at adjacent **Perennial Virant** (p. 82).

Rare Botanical Bitters

Mixologist extraordinaire Adam Seger (hum Botanical Spirit) partnered with Rodrick Markus (**Rare Tea Cellar,** p. 257) to launch Chicago-based **Rare Botanical Bitters,** (773) 561-3000, rarebotanicalbitters.com, a source for spendy, singular bitters, like Truffe Amere made with hand-sliced truffles. The crew is also working with Boyd & Blair Distillery to "deconstruct" vermouth by way of Balsam, a spirit made from a botanical infusion sans vino. It's then meant to be added to wine to fashion fresh-made vermouth. Incidentally, Seger is also behind hum botanical spirit, amaro and French Carribbean-inspired hooch, infused with green cardamom, ginger, Kaffir lime, and hibiscus.

Longman & Eagle, 2657 N. Kedzie Ave., Logan Square, Chicago, IL 60647; (773) 276-7110; longmanandeagle.com. People go gaga for this gastropub, and it's got little to do with the rooms available for overnight stays. Jared Wentworth's dishes—iconic wild-boar sloppy joes, buffalo frog legs—meet a liquor list that's 30 whiskeys strong. Not to be outdone, the extensive beer and biodynamic, boutique wine lists and the house cocktails—including an eponymous Manhattan with Italian Punt e Mes—are lounge-lovers' delights. Plan on overindulging? Reserve a room: There are six available upstairs. Visit on Saturdays, when there's a weekly pop-up sausage shop. The team also owns hotspot **Parson's Chicken & Fish** (p. 45).

The Matchbox, 770 N. Milwaukee Ave., River West, Chicago, IL 60642; (312) 666-9292. If there's one thing most every cocktailer agrees on, it's that the Matchbox is close-quarters-classic, a place where all types can—and should—sip handcrafted cocktails with house-infused spirits. Can't cram inside? Consider owner David Gevercer's other spot, train car–centered Silver Palm, 768 N. Milwaukee Ave., (312) 666-9322.

Maude's Liquor Bar, 840 W. Randolph St., West Loop, Chicago, IL 60607; (312) 243-9712; maudesliquorbar.com. Brendan Sodikoff (**Gilt Bar** [p. 231]) reimagined the Parisian dive bar, which serves rustic French fare such as escargot and tenderloin steak tartare. While a lot of the menu skews classic, dishes like French onion fondue take a slight detour. The sultry, loungelike setting is complemented by fancy smashes, handcrafted cocktails like the floral Smokey Violet. Check out the candlelit, sofa-laden upstairs lounge.

Nacional 27, 325 W. Huron St., River North, Chicago, IL 60654; (312) 664-2727; n27chicago.com. This hub is beloved for many reasons, not the least of which is its cocktails. Belly up for a 10 Cane mojito, muddled with mint, lime, pomegranate, ginger, and habanero, or an El Corazon margarita with El Jimador blanco, pomegranate, passion fruit, and blood orange with a salt-and-pepper rim before salsa dancing ensues. And do tackle the modern Latin menu, which trots from ceviche to Brazilian barbecue, paella, and sultry seafood and steak.

The Office, 955 W. Fulton Market, West Loop, Chicago, IL 60607; (312) 226-0868; theaviary.com. Grant Achatz's lower-level lounge is an invitation-only experience swathed in wood and period paintings beneath **The Aviary** (p. 226). Tony, painstakingly prepared tipples, rare spirits, and posh bites like steak tartare and oysters with atypical accoutrements are joined by make-your-own ice-cream sundaes.

Old Town Social, 455 W. North Ave., Old Town, Chicago, IL 60610; (312) 266-2277; oldtownsocial.com. There's really no 'tude at this gussied-up nightspot, where cocktails are crafted by hand and a house butcher shop induces herbivore fright. Snack on Chef Jared Van Camp's chorizo-stuffed shishitos and grilled smoked sausage and cornmeal-bacon waffles. Or make a meal of the house-made salted, smoked, and cured meats made from local heritage-breed pork and grass-fed beef. Then, linger over rounds of seasonal sips, like the Bramble #2, Grey Goose, and Crème Yvette with fresh lemon and blackberries.

Potter's Lounge, Palmer House Hilton, 17 E. Monroe St., Loop, Chicago, IL 60603; (312) 917-4933; potterschicago.com. When you're looking for a good, centrally located place to kick back over a well-executed cocktail, succumb to this bi-level spot—located in the city's most historic hotel. While lounging, order the VeeV Açaí–based Treetini (it helps save rain forests, after all).

ROOF, theWit, 201 N. State St., Loop, Chicago, IL 60601; (312) 239-9502; roofonthewit.com. Provided you don't mind a good, long wait, you'll dig this hot-spot, perched 27 floors up with glass-enclosed private table. Snag a Spicy Cubano, Pyray Rum with mint, lime, ginger-mango purée, and sliced serranos. Thankfully, an offering of upscale small plates means there's no reason to relinquish your seat when hunger strikes.

Sable Kitchen & Bar, Hotel Palomar, 505 N. State St., River North, Chicago, IL 60654; (312) 755-9704; sablechicago.com. Expect not only great food but also a lineup of liquids that live up to the promise of its radiant, quartz light-box illuminated bar, thanks to Head Bartender Mike Ryan and Master Sommelier Emily Wines. From the encyclopedic list of Prohibition-inspired cocktails, try the Fantasy Island—a beauty crafted from Letherbee's Gin, fresh pineapple, lime, green Chartreuse, and edible flowers—pairing it with stellar plates from Executive Chef Heather Terhune.

Scofflaw, 3201 W. Armitage Ave., Logan Square, Chicago, IL 60647; (773) 252-9700; scofflawchicago.com. Make no mistake: This partnership between **The Whistler** (p. 237) and Boiler Room vets is a dark, intimate cocktail lounge through and through, one with salvaged decor; free, warm chocolate chip cookies at midnight; and a lineup of perfectly balanced, way-affordable gin drinks. But it's also a great source for comfort food, like sheep's milk gnudi, chile-flecked Brussels sprouts with lemon, and pork belly confit.

Simone's Bar, 960 W. 18th St., Pilsen, Chicago, IL 60608; (312) 666-8601; simonesbar.com. Loaded with refurbished fixtures—bowling alley parts, vintage pinball machines—this joint from the North Side crew specializes in kitschy cocktails like the Give Inn, Tullamore Dew with butterscotch schnapps, brown sugar, strawberries, and ginger ale. There is tweaked bar fare, some of it Latin-tinged, to go with.

The Southern, 1840 W. North Ave., Wicker Park, Chicago, IL 60622; (773) 342-1840; thesouthernchicago.com. This Southern watering hole with a rustic timber bar, steel and wood details, and a lovely patio showcases soulful American updates from Executive Chef Cary Taylor, like battered andouille corn dogs with Creole mustard and a sandwich of slow-roasted, sliced Slagel beef, dunked in chow-chow and gravy. Thankfully, they help soak up booze-infused punch bowls and Georgia juleps with Bulleit Bourbon, peach schnapps, bitters, and mint. Taylor also mans mobile The Southern Mac & Cheese Truck, @thesouthernmac.

The Terrace at Trump, Sixteen, Trump International Hotel & Tower, 401 N. Wabash Ave, 16th Fl., River North, Chicago, IL 60611; (312) 588-8000; sixteenchicago.com. This sweeping, seasonal outdoor patio serves sparkling and still cocktails. Meanwhile, year-round Rebar—located on the mezzanine level of the hotel—is a sushi-focused sophisticate, with classy cocktails like the refreshing Sakezana, a muddled green-apple libation shaken with sake and vodka.

Three Dots and a Dash, 435 N. Clark St., River North, Chicago, IL 60653; (312) 610-4220; threedotschicago.com. Score Paul McGee's hyped hooch at this moody tiki bar, tucked into an alley, a stylin' entrant backed by Lettuce Entertain You with whimsical, shareable cocktails and a lineup of updated, throwback island eats (pork belly buns, curry chicken skewers) below **Bub City** (p. 100).

Untitled, 111 W. Kinzie St., River North, Chicago, IL 60654; untitledchicago.com. Head to this vast, underground speakeasy for intimate cocktailing, live entertainment, and, as it turns out, usually impressive, seasonally inspired dining on shared plates, like black walnut–date focaccia with caramelized onions and Gorgonzola; duck sausage with *foie gras* gravy; and pan-roasted skate in pancetta-clam broth. As is custom, there's cheese and charcuterie, too. If all else fails, the availability of over 300 whiskeys delights.

Vertigo Sky Lounge, dana hotel and spa, 660 N. State St., River North, Chicago, IL 60654; (312) 202-6050; vertigoskylounge.com. Located on the penthouse level of the dana hotel and spa, this sultry spot features a firepit and modern, modular furniture indoors and out. (Don't rule it out during winter, though—there's a solid-ice bar proffering cold-weather comfort). But whether you have a hot toddy or citrusy summer cocktail in hand, it's safe to assume the 26th-floor panoramic views get top billing.

The Violet Hour, 1520 N. Damen Ave., Chicago, IL 60622; (773) 252-1500; theviolethour.com. Named for a line in T. S. Eliot's "The Waste Land," this urbane cocktail collaborative involves many types of ice. Savor a Juliet and Romeo—Beefeater Gin with mint, cucumber, and rosewater—in a regal, high-backed chair. Edibles like frites and lemon aioli; fried, paprika-smoked garbanzos and Marcona almonds; and grilled ham and cheese on Pullman bread play the role of alcohol sponge. There's a no–cell phone policy, so turn your ringer off.

Watershed, 601 N. State St., River North, Chicago, IL 60610; (312) 266-7677; watershedbar.com. Since it's dedicated to regional craft beers and quite-cool liquid creations (a departure from **Pops for Champagne,** p. 223), you can look to the likes of an Italian Hurricane with hum, Campari, Del Maguey mezcal, lime, and ginger beer. The extensive selection of artisanal spirits is built for aficionados, who take time to examine them in detail while waiting for lamb pâté with violet mustard to arrive.

Weegee's Lounge, 3659 W. Armitage Ave., Logan Square, Chicago, IL 60647; (773) 384-0707; weegeeslounge.com. Soak up the classic cocktails—like the Delmonico and Knickerbocker—and a nostalgic feel at this understatedly cool neighborhood tavern named for crime-scene photog Arthur Fellig (Weegee was his pseudonym), whose prints adorn the walls.

The Whistler, 2421 N. Milwaukee Ave., Logan Square, Chicago, IL 60647; (773) 227-3530; whistlerchicago.com. Part art gallery, live music venue, and record label, this loftlike den fashions an ever-changing array of rapturous classic cocktails. Get with the program over a spicy herbal Verdita, cilantro-mint-laced pineapple juice with a hint of jalapeño, served alongside a shot of 100-proof tequila. By then you'll hear the Rosemary Collins calling your name.

Specialty Stores, Gourmet Shops & Purveyors

Are you a compulsive food shopper? Do you stock your pantry and refrigerator with edibles to endure many rainy days? You're not alone, and Chicago answers the call with plenty of food for thought. From intriguing ethnic grocers to niche boutiques, fishmongers, and butchers, the enticements are endless.

Specialty Stores & Grocers

A&G International Fresh Market, 5630 W. Belmont Ave., Portage Park, Chicago, IL 60634; (773) 777-4480; agfreshmarket .com; Grocery. This sprawling grocery store is destination-worthy for its multiculti baked goods alone. And although the owners are Italian, the space—at home in the former Goldblatt's department store—houses one of the most diverse selections of exotic produce, many fetas, olive oils from around the globe, and deli meats galore.

Al Khyam, 4738 N. Kedzie Ave., Albany Park, Chicago, IL 60625; (773) 583-3077; alkhyam.com; **Middle Eastern.** This market and bakery brims with temptations, from hot, just-baked pita and baklava to falafel, Middle Eastern cheeses, bulk legumes, pickles, and massive vats of olive oil. Its close proximity to several other specialty stores is another plus.

Andy's Deli, 5442 N. Milwaukee Ave., Jefferson Park, Chicago, IL 60630; (773) 631-7304; andysdeli.com; **Polish.** Although the original location on Division Street is no more, thank your lucky stars for what is in store at this address: fantastic Polish sausage, country-style bacon, grill-ready meats, and imported pantry items, such as red borscht starters, sauerkraut, and sour-cherry syrup. But that's not to say the delish pierogi and cheeses are something to overlook, nor is the fact that its meats and sausages can be shipped throughout the US.

Andy's Fruit Ranch, 4733 N. Kedzie Ave., Albany Park, Chicago, IL 60625; (773) 583-2322; andysfruitranch.com; **Grocery.** This standout has a vast selection of multiethnic produce (including less familiar varieties) as well as canned and dry goods and an impressive meat and seafood counter. Filled with the requisites for an Asian meal, it also stocks Polish faves, tons of cured meat, and plenty of Middle Eastern necessities, from imported olive oil to *labna*.

Angelo Caputo's Fresh Markets, 2400 N. Harlem Ave., Elmwood Park, IL 60607; (708) 453-0155; caputomarkets.com; **Grocery.** Come during off-hours to avoid a perpetual mob scene, and explore hundreds of varieties of fruits and vegetables, row upon row of sweet panettone, a dizzying number of olive oils, and countless pasta cuts. The fine meat, seafood, cheese, cured meat, and bakery counters have plenty of wow-factor, too. There are also locations in Addison, 510 W. Lake St., (630) 543-0151; Bloomingdale, 166 E. Lake St., (630) 924-0900;

To the Market

It could be argued that the **Maxwell Street Market,** maxwell
streetmarket.com, is less about wares and more about Mexican
street food. Its flea market, which takes place on Des Plaines
Avenue between Roosevelt Road and Harrison Street, is a lively
scene wafting with good scents. Wander its stalls in search of
pineapple-laced *atole*; rarely seen Mexican fare (pig esophagus
tacos stippled with onion and cilantro); produce from nopales
to hibiscus; and humble, heartwarming tamales. Then, move on
to pork in green mole, *huitlacoche* (corn smut) tacos on fresh-
made tortillas, and grilled corn *elotes* spurted with lime.

Hanover Park, 1250 Lake St., (630) 372-2800; South Elgin, 622 Randall
Rd., (847) 289-0600; and Naperville, 3115 111th St., (630) 579-3300.

Bari Foods, 1120 W. Grand Ave., West Loop, Chicago, IL 60622;
(312) 666-0730; bariitaliansubs.com; Italian. There's a not-to-be-
missed deli inside this old-world Italian grocer, where from-scratch
sandwiches—the Italian sub especially—are masterpieces. While
you're there, wander down the handful of aisles, which are
jammed with imported oils, pasta, and jarred sauces as well as
other requisites to culinary wizardry. Incidentally, specialty and
custom cuts of meat may be ordered from its butcher.

Bobak's Sausage Company, 5275 S. Archer Ave., Garfield
Ridge, Chicago, IL 60632; (773) 735-5334; bobak.com; Polish. Seekers of smoked sausage and ham, potato pancakes, and pierogi find
inspiration at this institution, which dates back to 1967. Anchored by
an expansive deli with private-label products, it also features an on-site
Polish bakery and hot-food island wafting with scents of anticipated
faves.

Brookhaven Marketplace, 100 Burr Ridge Pkwy., Burr Ridge, IL 60527; (630) 908-3180; brookhavenmarket.com; Grocery. Standing as the better of its locations—the others at 7516 S. Cass Ave., Darien, (630) 512-0600, and 19818 S. La Grange Rd., Mokena, (708) 479-7171—this multiculti grocer leans Greek, with offerings that include house-made avgolemono soup, seven-layer feta dip, and pastitsio. Fresh, affordably priced meat and out-of-this-world, fresh-squeezed OJ are other trip-worthy finds.

Caputo Cheese Market, 1931 N. 15th Ave., Melrose Park, IL 60160; (708) 450-0469; caputocheese.com; Cheese. The retail arm of family-owned manufacturing and processing company Wiscon Corporation sports upward of 1,000 cheeses from the world over as well as fresh, house-made sausage, deli meats, and prepared salads and sandwiches alongside aisles of imported olives, orecchiette, and spices, plus a bakery counter doling out Italian cookies. There is also a location at 231 E. Wisconsin Ave., Lake Forest, (847) 482-0100.

Carniceria Jimenez, 3850 W. North Ave., Logan Square, Chicago, IL 60647; (773) 235-3637; carniceriasjimenez.com; Mexican. Boasting several locations in the city and suburbs, this well-stocked grocer has all the makings of a good Mexican meal: a meat counter with choice cuts, fresh masa, and way-affordable produce, on top of an in-house taqueria that prepares above-average, cheap *tortas* and tacos.

Chinatown Market, 2121 S. Archer Ave., Chinatown, Chicago, IL 60616; (312) 881-0068; Chinese. Buy whatever you need to prepare an authentic Chinese meal at this bustling grocery store with a free parking lot in back. Score enoki, bitter melon, and tofu for less than you'd imagine, along with fresh finds from the seafood and butcher counters. Just be sure to come during off-hours since the narrow aisles are hard to navigate when the throngs descend.

INDOOR EATS

Sometimes, the weather just won't cooperate. That's when it's nice to know indoor options like these exist.

Chicago French Market, 131 N. Clinton St., West Loop, Chicago, IL 60661; (312) 575-0306; frenchmarketchicago.com. This market continues to step up its game. Featuring a collection of 30-plus specialty vendors, it's stocked with grab-and-go options and umpteen ingredients for the home cook. Be sure to check out these standouts while you're there:

> **Fumare Meats** (312-930-4220) earns accolades for its sold-by-the-pound, house-smoked pastrami, which also comes tucked between slices of Red Hen bread.

> **Lillie's Q** (773-772-5500) hawks Charlie McKenna's brand of smoky BBQ classics, including pulled pork, tri-tip, and hot links in sandwich form. His sauces are knockouts, too.

Pastoral Artisan Cheese, Bread & Wine (312-454-2200) is an offshoot of the Lakeview and Loop stores. It dispenses an abbreviated-but-awesome selection of cheeses, charcuterie, and picnic-ready nibbles.

Saigon Sisters (312-496-0094), from Mary Nguyen Aregoni and Theresa Nguyen, serves up tangy, crunchy, chewy *banh mi*. (Also located at 567 W. Lake St., 312-496-0090.)

City Fresh Market, 3201 W. Devon Ave., Rogers Park, Chicago, IL 60659; (773) 681-8600; cityfreshmarket.com; Grocery. Located at the corner of Devon and Kedzie Avenues, this reasonable ethnic grocer is filled with Eastern European and Balkan essentials like ajvar as well as cheese and meat pies, glorious cakes, feast breads, and cevapcici. There is also an offshoot at the **Chicago French Market** (p. 242).

Vanille Patisserie (312-575-9963) is the work of World Pastry Champion Dimitri Fayard, whose handmade chocolates, tarts, and mousse cakes are more than just eye candy.

Wisma (312-382-1805) offers John des Rosiers's ready-made salads, sandwiches, and spreads—without the need for a trip to the original Lake Bluff store.

If you're willing to embark on a brief drive north, **Milwaukee Public Market,** 400 N. Water St., Milwaukee, WI 53202; (414) 336-1111; milwaukeepublicmarket.org; awaits with a bevy of local, artisanal products and tasty, multiculti eats. Open early on Saturdays, it's a great place to stop for a cup of joe at Cedarburg Coffee Roastery. Even more thrilling, though, are vendors such as St. Paul Fish Company, which allows you to select iced, fresh catches to be prepared to your specifications on-site. Love goes to the meat counter at Nehring's Family Market, too, which prepares panini. Then, there are eats from Middle Eastern deli Aladdin, and primo, fresh-ground blends and rubs from **The Spice House** (p. 243). As if that's not already reason enough to come, cooking classes often take place in a demo kitchen upstairs, and there's a seasonal outdoor market as well.

City Olive, 5408 N. Clark St., Edgewater, Chicago, IL 60640; (773) 878-5408; cityolive.com; **Specialty.** Olive aficionados will swoon over the tapenades, nearly four-dozen olive oils, and jarred olives at this schmancy boutique gourmet. You'll also find an array of seasonings and spices as well as an abundance of imported goods, such as honey, canned tuna, vinegar, sauces, and rice. Come hungry—a tasting bar allows you to sample before you buy. Another location is at 5644 N. Clark St., (773) 942-6424.

Dill Pickle Co-op, 3039 W. Fullerton Ave., Logan Square, Chicago, IL 60647; (773) 252-2667; dillpicklefoodcoop.org; Grocery. You don't have to be a member to shop at the petite, community-owned place, but chances are—if you live nearby—you'll want to take part. Brimming with amazing edibles, its selection of locally sourced meat, produce, and dairy is teamed with an array of prepared refrigerated and frozen meals, dry goods, and personal care products, including basil-scented cleaners from Mrs. Meyer's Clean Day. The emphasis is on vendors adhering to sustainable, organic practices. Therefore, visits may yield Kishu mandarins and romanesco, calling from farmers' market–type wooden baskets, or Justin's peanut butter cups and pork tenderloin from Twin Oak Meats. Even in the dead of winter, bursts of flavor can be found on its wire shelves (look for Tomato Mountain Sun Gold preserves from Madison, WI, or dried herbs and spices from Frontier Natural Products Co-op).

Fox & Obel, 401 E. Illinois St., Chicago, IL 60611; (312) 410-7301; fox-obel.com; Grocery. There's much to adore about this luxury grocer and cafe with an adjunct wine bar—starting with its perfect, crisp-chewy, fresh-baked baguettes. The fromagerie, charcuterie, butcher, and prepared-foods counters lead to impulse shopping of the worthwhile variety. The wine-and-spirits department is top-tier, too, further necessitating visits. Produce—though not its strong suit—may include less-common heirloom and out-there finds, like rambutans. Validated garage parking at Illinois and Peshtigo is free for two hours with a $20 purchase. When hunger strikes, check out the on-site bistro and cafe.

Fresh Farms International Market, 2626 W. Devon Ave., Rogers Park, Chicago, IL 60659; (773) 764-3557; myfreshfarms.com; Grocery. The produce selection is jaw-dropping—that's for sure—but easily navigated aisles crammed with chutneys; cheeses from Bulgaria, Finland, Hungary, and Russia; and bakery items that include naan, *chapatti,* and French and ciabatta breads are sure to leave you enamored.

There's also a full-service deli and quality meat and seafood department, the latter with live, fresh, smoked, frozen, and dried options. There is another location at 5740 W. Touhy Ave., Niles, (847) 779-7343.

Gene's Sausage Shop & Delicatessen, 4750 N. Lincoln Ave., Lincoln Square, Chicago, IL 60625; (773) 728-7243; genes sausageshop.com; European. Fans of food may find themselves overwhelmed by the selection at this two-story specialty store in the old Meyer Delicatessen. Featuring a full-service butcher shop with second-to-none, smoked-on-site sausage, it's also rife with packaged edibles and liquors. When it's warm, the rooftop beer and wine garden is a prime perch for scarfing down those house-made sausages—cooked over an open wood grill—and small plates. Decked in steel, wood, and stone with looming chandeliers, the sleek space—owned by the Luszcz family—has a less glossy (but every bit as tasty) sib at 5330 W. Belmont Ave., (773) 777-6322.

The Goddess and Grocer, 1646 N. Damen Ave., Bucktown, Chicago, IL 60647; (773) 342-3200; goddessandgrocer.com; Specialty. Stocked with essentials for romantic picnics, many prepared, this grocer begins days with muffin sandwiches, moving on to matzoh-ball soup, sweet-potato fries with sage mayo, and drunken chicken salads as well as deluxe hot and cold sandwiches and desserts (cupcakes, chocolate ganache cheesecake). Owner Debra Sharpe delivers, too, in addition to selling fancy gift baskets bursting with tasty treats. **Additional locations:** 25 E. Delaware Pl., (312) 896-2600; 901 N. Larabee Ave., (312) 988-9870; 2222 N. Elston Ave., (773) 292-7100.

Golden Pacific Market, 5353 N. Broadway, Edgewater, Chicago, IL 60640; (773) 334-6688; Southeast Asian. This bright, approachable, and tidy market is a treasure trove bursting with

Go Local

Locally crafted, artisanal products are musts for your own pantry. Plus they make fantastic signature-Chicago souvenirs.

Birchwood Kitchen, 2211 W. North Ave.,Wicker Park, Chicago, (773) 276-2100, birchwoodkitchen.com, stocks Jesse Williams's lovingly crafted pickles—dilly wax beans, giardiniera—for at-home enjoyment.

Breslin Farms, 1700 Champlain St., Ottawa, breslinfarms.com, is a father-daughter-run farm emphasizing heirloom small grains and dry beans. Find them—and whole-wheat flour—at farmers' markets and specialty stores like **Dill Pickle Co-op** (p. 244).

Co-op Sauce, coopsauce.com, began as a fund-raising venture for a kids' art organization. Now a legit operation, you can procure its small-batch ramp finishing sauce, pickles, and grapefruit-ghost hot sauce online, at farmers' markets, and at offshoot Sauce and Bread Kitchen, a cafe at 6338-40 N. Clark St., Edgewater; (773) 942 6384; coopsauce.com/supper-club.

Lillie's Q Sauces & Rubs, lilliesq.com/store.htm, are available for purchase, both individually and as three- or six-bottle gift sets. Running faves: the tangy, vinegary Carolina Gold and the lime-laced, mayonnaise-based Ivory, which is a perfect foil for frites.

Rare Bird Preserves, rarebirdpreserves.com, is a suburban Oak Park venture that specializes in seasonal, local, and sustainable versions of its namesake jams. Leading the pack are fig–Earl Grey preserves, Meyer lemon curd, and chocolate-raspberry spread, available at the Andersonville and  Logan Square farmers' markets as well as at specialty stores such as **Publican Quality Meats** (p. 267).

The Flavor, theflavorbystephanieizard.com, is Stephanie Izard's (Girl & the Goat) boldly nuanced sauce and rub collection that makes marinating, grilling and sautéing an explosively flavorful, special occasion thing.

The Scrumptious Pantry, scrumptiouspantry.com, offers a monthly pantry subscription service and sells its delightful local, sustainable ketchup, oils, vinegars, and pickles at specialty stores throughout the city and suburbs.

Smoking Goose, 407 N. Dorman St., Indianapolis, (317) 638-6328, is a charcuterie biz from Chris Elay, who clocked kitchen time with Chicago chefs Jared Van Camp and Chris Pandel. Get these riches—black truffle bologna, Pekin duck prosciutto—on-site or at shops like **Fox & Obel** (p. 244).

Southport Grocery, 3552 N. Southport Ave., Lakeview, Chicago, (773) 665-0100, southportgrocery.com, sells tart, crisp, house-label "living" kraut, made from shaved local cabbage. There's a jalapeño-mustard version, too.

Spices of Lezzet, lezzetspices.com, specializes in atypical global spices, sourced from a select group of farmers and brokers. Among them, find brooding isot pepper; dried, sweet purple basil; and grassy, peppery nigella seeds in addition to herbal salts and energizing Spicewater.

urbanbelly, 3053 N. California Ave., Avondale, Chicago, (773) 583-0500, urbanbellychicago.com, bottles its excellent sauces, among which *sambal* and *nuoc cham*–spiked Belly Fire are boss. Buy them at the restaurant and at well-stocked grocers, such as **Standard Market** (p. 258).

insanely cheap Asian produce, imported dry goods, sauces, and super-fresh seafood. Frankly, it's packed to the hilt with everything the home cook could possibly crave (lotus root, soy sauces, curries, and big bags of rice) or fear (water beetles). There's also a freezer section with a generous smattering of finned finds.

Green Grocer Chicago, 1402 W. Grand Ave., West Town, Chicago, IL 60642; (312) 624-9508; greengrocerchicago.com; Grocery. Local and organic—that's the thrust at this neighborhood grocer specializing in sustainable ingredients that have been produced and grown in the Midwest. Turn to goodies from Bennison's Bakery in Evanston, artisan Potter's Crackers, and beer from **Metropolitan Brewing** (p. 215). Free classes, talks, and tastings regularly take place.

Half Italian Grocer, 2643 N. Milwaukee Ave., Logan Square, Chicago, IL 60647; (773) 227-5600; halfitaliangrocer.com; Italian. Load up on Mediterranean musts at this grocer, cafe, and espresso bar. While exploring the selection of house-made cannoli, European imports, and fresh linguine from Chicago's Perfect Pasta, stave off hunger pangs with a Creminelli prosciutto sandwich on D'Amato's bread.

HarvesTime Foods, 2632 W. Lawrence Ave., Lincoln Square, Chicago, IL 60625; (773) 989-4400; harvestimefoods.com; Grocery. In one fell swoop, supply stir-frys with fresh produce and noodles from Chicago-based Rock 'n Roll Noodle Company, then move on to Middle Eastern, Mexican, and Eastern European mainstays. There's a nice selection of gluten-free items, too.

Hyde Park Produce, 1226 E. 53rd St., Hyde Park, Chicago, IL 60615; (773) 324-7100; hydeparkproduce.com; Grocery. Affordable,

Eat Local

It's easier than ever to procure fresh fare, thanks to local food-delivery services like these.

Artizone, artizone.com, is a grocery delivery godsend, featuring fruit pies from **Bang Bang Pie Shop** (p. 273), ultra-fresh whitefish from **Hagen's Fish Market** (p. 158), and Seedling Farms' lush pear butter. Need something sweet? **Black Dog Gelato** (p. 291) is the perfect fix.

Irv & Shelly's Fresh Picks, freshpicks.com, brings organic food to your doorstep. Order single, double, or family-size boxes brimming with produce, humanely raised meat, dairy, and eggs.

New Leaf Natural Grocery Chicago, newleafnatural.net, offers seasonally changing, organic produce boxes stocked with the likes of clingstone Lady peaches and Delicata squash for pickup or delivery.

quality produce gives way to a deli scented with mushroom bisque soup, snacks, and prepared grub such as jerk chicken, guac, and mac and cheese. Tasty deli sandwiches and vegan, gluten-free, and organic items—not to mention a parking lot—seal its wide-reaching appeal.

J.P. Graziano Grocery, 901 W. Randolph St., West Loop, Chicago, IL 60607; (312) 666-4587; jpgraziano.com; Italian. This warm, generations-old mom-and-pop Italian grocer stocks high-end, small-production cheeses, whole-bean coffee, lardo, olives aplenty, and Sardinian bottarga. But the in-house sub shop—serving cheap, amazing sandwiches, stuffed with quality meats and cheeses—is a feather in its cap.

Joong Boo Market, 3333 N. Kimball Ave., Avondale, Chicago, IL 60618; (773) 478-0100; **Korean.** Often referred to as "Chicago Food Corp.," this import emporium—okay, warehouse—is one of Chicago's best spots to score specialty Asian items, be it sashimi-grade seafood, downright cheap kitchen necessities (stockpots, sake sets, rice cookers), and more ramen varieties than you imagined existed. Make time for a meal at the restaurant in back, which serves rousing renditions of bibimbap, Korean fried chicken, and fiery *kimchi jjigae.*

Kamdar Plaza, 2646 W. Devon Ave., Rogers Park, Chicago, IL 60659; (773) 338-8100; **kamdarplaza.com; Indian/Pakistani.** A Devon Avenue fixture since the 1970s, this joint is jammed with aromatic spices, dals, and beans, as well as chutneys, sauces, dried fruits, and nuts. Pickles, many types of flour, and a broad array of teas are found here, too. While in the store, do grab a bite (or a few) from the vegetarian snack bar. Items may also be purchased and shipped from its online store.

La Casa Del Pueblo, 1810 S. Blue Island Ave., Pilsen, Chicago, IL 60608; (312) 421-4640; **lacasadelpueblo.com; Mexican.** This friendly, family-owned *supermercado* leans Mexican, though it also has a large Middle Eastern section and imports from Thailand, Italy, India, and beyond. Housewares—including *molcajetes* and tortilla presses— make it a bit of a destination, as do the fresh, quality produce and availability of organic ingredients.

Lemon Tree Grocer, 5101 Mochel Dr., Downers Grove, IL 60515; (630) 969-9869; **lemontreegrocer.com; Grocery.** Hit this small, artisanal market for an edited selection of pantry items from local producers, responsibly raised and produced meat and seafood, and fresh-baked pastry. It hosts beer and cheese clubs, too. While you're exploring, pause for a meal at Zest, its bistro within, for sushi, burgers, and seasonally inspired libations.

Lindo Michoacan, 3142 W. Lawrence Ave., Albany Park, Chicago, IL 60625; (773) 279-8834; lindomichoacansupermarket.com; Mexican. Check out this Mexican market with an attached restaurant for fresh, affordable produce; prepared Mexican meals; and a nice array of bottled soda as well as sweeter-than-sweet Mexican pastries. But first, start with a bowl of restorative *posole* from next door—it'll limit the likelihood of a hunger-induced shopping spree.

Mama's Nuts!, mamasnuts.com; Nuts. Get your snack on with handmade garam masala walnuts, mocha stout almonds, and spicy Szechuan peanuts produced by this online Chicago venture. Or grab them—and spicy, creamy peanut sauce—from its booth at the Logan Square farmers' market.

Mariano's Fresh Market, 802 E. Northwest Hwy., Arlington Heights, IL 60004; (847) 253-5439; marianosfreshmarket.com; Grocery. Food-enthused shoppers gush over Roundy's rapidly expanding upscale grocery empire for endless reasons, among them house-label pastas, cheeses, and olive oil; exotic and essential produce; and authentic Sicilian pastries. You'll also have to contend with its sandwich station, hot bar stocked with global eats, and hand-pulled, wood oven–fired pizzas. There are ten other locations in the suburbs and Chicago proper; check the website for info.

Middle East Bakery & Grocery, 1512 W. Foster Ave., Uptown, Chicago, IL 60640; (773) 561-2224; middleeastbakeryand grocery.com; Middle Eastern. House-made *za'atar* pita; parsley, olive, and cheese pie; and falafel fragrance this fanatically fresh Middle Eastern and Mediterranean market. Hummus of many stripes, pickled vegetables, imported Turkish cheeses, and citrusy salads have the makings of impromptu gatherings, all of which should be capped off with a spread of fresh-made, pistachio-and-walnut-dotted baklava, *maamoul,* and semolina honey cake.

Mitsuwa Marketplace, 100 E. Algonquin Rd., Arlington Heights, IL 60005; (847) 956-6699; mitsuwa.com; Japanese. 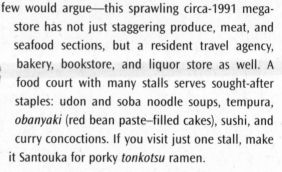 Regarded as the Midwest's largest Japanese grocery store—a claim few would argue—this sprawling circa-1991 mega-store has not just staggering produce, meat, and seafood sections, but a resident travel agency, bakery, bookstore, and liquor store as well. A food court with many stalls serves sought-after staples: udon and soba noodle soups, tempura, *obanyaki* (red bean paste–filled cakes), sushi, and curry concoctions. If you visit just one stall, make it Santouka for porky *tonkotsu* ramen.

Morse Fresh Market, 1430 W. Morse Ave., Rogers Park, Chicago, IL 60626; (773) 973-3765; Grocery. Don't let the unassuming exterior fool you: Inside is an expansive produce department, organic-leaning butcher shop, and impressive collection of import goods from Mexico, India, and Europe.

Mother Butter's Popcorn & Confectionary, 17 W. 35th St., Ste. B, Bronzeville, Chicago, IL 60616; (773) 548-7677; mother butterspopcorn.com; Popcorn/Candy. Whether you favor the classics (white cheddar or the venerable Chicago mix) or jazzier options (pesto-Parmesan or truffle salted), this family-owned popcorn purveyor never cuts corners. The result is sublime coconut oil–popped snacking, in the shadows of U.S. Cellular Field.

Nottoli & Son, 7652 W. Belmont Ave., Northwest Side, Chicago, IL 60634; (773) 589-1010; nottoli.com; Specialty. Head straight for the sausage display at this Italian deli, knowing the fennel-flecked hot Italian is what you want. Crave-worthy subs, messy meatball sandwiches, and house-brand giardiniera are other musts.

Nuts on Clark, 3830 N. Clark St., Lakeview, Chicago, IL 60613; (773) 549-6622; nutsonclark.com; **Popcorn.** If there's one thing you get from this iconic popcorn purveyor, make it the finger-staining cheese variety, which also stars in classic salty-meets-sweet Chicago mix (cheese corn and caramel corn). There are locations at O'Hare and Midway Airports, Union Station, and Soldier Field (during Bears games).

Old Town Oil, 1520 N. Wells St., Old Town, Chicago, IL 60610; (312) 787-9595; oldtownoil.com; **Specialty.** Nestled into a small storefront in a vintage building, this niche purveyor specializes in extra-virgin olive oil from around the world, some infused naturally with fruit, herbs, or citrus. There's also an ample selection of aged and white balsamic vinegars as well as reserve sherry and red-wine vinegars. Best of all is the fact that tasting is encouraged, and the availability of recipes ensures shoppers make the most of their buys. A second outpost is at 1924 Central St., Evanston, (847) 864-0487.

Olivia's Market, 2014 W. Wabansia Ave., Wicker Park, Chicago, IL 60647; (773) 227-4220; oliviasmarket.com; **Grocery.** Check out this cheery neighborhood market on rotation for small-batch chocolates, homemade soup, and fragrant, fresh-cut flowers. A nice selection of cheeses, ready-made meals, and ultra-fresh produce further its welcoming feel.

Panozzo's Italian Market, 1303 S. Michigan Ave., South Loop, Chicago, IL 60605; (312) 356-9966; panozzos.com; **Italian.** Swing by this Italian deli pre- or post-museum for swoon-inducing sausage and pepper sandwiches topped with house giardiniera or impressive cured porchetta stuffed with sage pesto–rubbed loin—it gets tucked into yeasty bread and topped with pickled fennel. Also memorable is its by-the-pound lasagna, citrus-mint roasted cauliflower, and locally sourced house-roasted, braised, or fried meats. Be on the lookout for themed food workshops and special dinners as well.

Pasta Fresh, 3418 N. Harlem Ave., Dunning, Chicago, IL 60634; (773) 745-5888; pastafreshco.com; Italian. As its name implies, this pasta shop specializes in fresh-made pasta—not the least of which is its touted ravioli—and toppings of garlicky house-made marinara and vodka sauce.

Pasta Puttana, 1407 W. Grand Ave., Noble Square, Chicago, IL 60642; (773) 439-9623; pastaputtana.com; Italian. Jessica Volpe learned to roll pasta at the Cooking and Hospitality Institute of Chicago. "Thank goodness she did" is the refrain upon snagging ramp ravioli; coarse-textured, golden egg noodles; and fiery red chile linguine, all shipped domestically on request. By the way, her semolina pizza dough is amazing, too.

Pastoral Artisan Cheese, Bread & Wine, 2945 N. Broadway, Lakeview, Chicago, IL 60657; (773) 472-4781; pastoralartisan .com; Specialty. Add charcuterie to the name and you get this gist of this European-inspired shop, stocked with picnic-appropriate essentials from purveyors near and far. Wine and cheese of the month clubs are on offer, and you can attend classes on cheese, wine, and craft beer on-site. Also watch for its annual artisan producer festival, a chance to meet the makers firsthand. Additional locations are at 53 E. Lake St., (312) 658-1250, and in the **Chicago French Market** (p. 242). Also, check out bistro-inspired **Bar Pastoral** (p. 220).

Patel Brothers, 2610 W. Devon Ave., Rogers Park, Chicago, IL 60659; (773) 262-7777; patelbros.com; Indian/Pakistani. This popular, family-owned grocery chain originated in Chicago in 1974, and it remains a go-to for ready-to-eat Swad brand foods, bulk spices, and rarely seen fruits (look for Alphonse mangoes and fenugreek greens). There is also an ample selection of herbs, Ayurvedic products, henna, naan, and roti as well as pickles and chutneys of all sorts. You'll also find kitchen basics—*tava* griddles, steel *masala dabba* spice boxes, pressure cookers—and baking requisites such as chapati flour, along with snacks and sweets. **Additional locations:** 2410 Army Trail Rd., Hanover Park, (630) 213-2222; 873 E. Schaumburg Rd., Schaumburg, (847) 524-1111.

Penzeys Spices, 1138 W. Lake St., Oak Park, IL 60301; (708) 848-7772; penzeys.com; Specialty. This mail-order business originating in Brookfield, WI, now has stores spread throughout the country. The spice specialist extraordinaire, owned by a member of **The Spice House** (p. 243) clan, stocks items—be it Ceylon cinnamon, annatto seed, or Maharaja curry—in several sizes. Its rubs, salt-free seasoning blends, and chile peppers from Dundicut to Sanaam and Tien Tsin likewise make meal-making a thing of bliss. Extracts, salad dressing mixes, and corned-beef spices are available, too. **Additional location:** 235 S. Washington St., Naperville, (630) 355-7677.

Pete's Fresh Market, 4700 S. Kedzie Ave., Brighton Park, Chicago, IL 60632; (773) 523-4600; petesfresh.com; Grocery. This excellent grocery chain with many area locations is a sparkling-clean, one-stop shop for affordable necessities and global fare. Stacks of bright, fresh produce give way to house salsas, just-baked cookies, and rotisserie-cooked meats. A gelato bar houses familiar and unusual (think lime–black pepper) flavors. The butcher turns out other interesting options, like grill-ready chorizo-stuffed jalapeños and *loukaniko* stippled with orange zest.

Pinch Spice Market, 1913 N. Milwaukee Ave., Bucktown, Chicago, IL 60647; (773) 360-8708; pinchspicemarket.com; Specialty.

FOOD (AND DESIGN) GALAS

Not everyone has the time (or inclination) to run around town. Fortunately, Chicago-based food bazaars do the legwork for you.

Dose Market, dosemarket.com, is a year-round, curated, by-ticket food and fashion market held in the River East Art Center. It's the perfect place to grab La Femme du Coupe syrups, Next Star vodka, and sweets from ByMDesserts.

Fête Chicago, comefete.com, is a pop-up Chicago and Midwestern festival conceived by Tasting Table's Heather Sperling, Daily Candy's Emily Fiffer, and freelance writer Jessica Herman, the former Dose crew. Featuring talks, tastings, and tours, the event emphasizes the work of chefs and artisans of food and design. While you're there, indulge in savory pies and heritage-bred pork bangers from **Pleasant House Bakery** (p. 286); sip Bridgeport-produced ginger ale from **Maria's Packaged Goods & Community Bar** (p. 214); and snack on brittle made from **Mama's Nuts!** (p. 251).

Ms. Mint, msmint.com, produces artisanal gift baskets and grassroots gatherings that connect rural, suburban, and urban communities to Chicago and Midwest edibles. Its annual holiday bazaar is a festive, locally driven shopping and tasting event. Consider joining its taste-of-the-month club, which emphasizes a regional producer, be it a purveyor of nuts, syrup, or grains.

Private-label, organic whole and ground spices inspire awe at this cute shop, where procurements include orange peel–infused Toast Crack, spicy Ethiopian berbere, *kala namak* (black mineral salt), and habanero sugar.

Produce World, 8325 W. Lawrence Ave., Norridge, IL 60706; (708) 452-7400; produceworldinc.com; Grocery. Veg-lovers will find it hard to tear themselves away from this world-wise market and deli. A vast, multiethnic selection of fruits and veggies is offset by scores of imported sweets, cheeses, and Balkan, Polish, and Italian goodies. There's a butcher and stellar deli as well. A second location is at 8800 Waukegan Rd., Morton Grove, (847) 581-1029.

Provenance Food & Wine, 2528 N. California Ave., Logan Square, Chicago, IL 60647; (773) 384-0699; provenancefoodandwine .com; Specialty. Housing needs (and even more wants) for special-occasion soirees and personal indulgences, Tracy Kellner's upscale wine and cheese shop is worth experiencing. Walk away with a bottle of Tempranillo, olive oil from Oleum Vitae, or La Mancha Oro saffron in reward. It also sells gift baskets filled with locally made items, plus there is a vino club showcasing its biodynamically focused sips. There is another location at 2312 N. Leland Ave., (773) 784-2314.

Rare Tea Cellar, rareteacellar.com; Specialty. This culinary importer and distributor overseen by Rodrick Markus is beloved for his dizzying selection of off-kilter and artisanal teas (including an oolong) Amazonian guayusa blend, vintage pu-erh, and blooming moonlight jasmine varietals. Markus has also teamed with Steve Smith of Portland's Smith Teas for a specialty line, which includes Willet Rye barrel-aged Forbidden Forest Lapsang souchong. Plus he stocks Jean-Marc Montegottero's small-batch oils as well as truffles, French flavor pearls, and Okinawan sea grapes, all of which are available for purchase online.

Sanabel Bakery & Grocery, 4213 N. Kedzie Ave., Albany Park, Chicago, IL 60686; (773) 539-5409; Middle Eastern. Piping-hot spinach and cheese pies, Middle Eastern sweets (try the glistening coconut macaroons), and *za'atar* flatbread are among the things you'll be plied with, right along with super-cheap, house-made pita, halal meats, and essential dry goods.

The Spice House, 1512 N. Wells St., Old Town, Chicago, IL 60610; (312) 274-0378; thespicehouse.com; Specialty. This Milwaukee-based merchant imports its aromatics from their countries of origin, showcasing a collection of salad seasonings, straight-up spices, spice blends, and herbs, along with stock-starting demi-glaces, lecithin, and rubs. A seasonal garden in back often hosts lectures, book signings, and events. **Additional locations:** 1941 Central St., Evanston, (847) 328-3711; and 577 S. Third St., Geneva, (630) 262-1777.

Standard Market, 333 E. Ogden Ave., Westmont, IL 60559; (630) 366-7030; standardmarket.com; Grocery. Answering the question "What's for dinner?" this impressive undertaking dry-ages meat in-house and whips up homey prepared meals (pot roast, turkey tetrazzini) and fresh-squeezed juices. It also houses a cheese and wine bar and American restaurant within. Meanwhile, its pantry shelves are stocked with an array of local sauces, condiments, and confections, and the meat, seafood, and sushi departments have everything you could ever need or want. Keep your eyes peeled for

hyper-seasonal, local finds, like foraged ramps, fiddlehead ferns, and morels. The market is also responsible for Bakersfield Restaurant, 330 E. Ogden Ave., (630) 568-3615, located across the street. Soon, Standard Market Grill, 444 W. Fullerton Pkwy., will be added to the mix.

Stanley's Fruit & Vegetable, 1558 N. Elston Ave., Noble Square, Chicago, IL 60642; (773) 276-8050; Grocery. This beacon is situated along an otherwise dreary stretch, so it's easily overlooked. Don't make that mistake, since cheap, super-fresh fruits and vegetables are the reward within. The decent selection of organic foods is another draw.

Super H-Mart, 801 Civic Center Dr., Niles, IL 60714; (847) 581-1212; hmart.com; Asian. Part of a chain, this expansive grocer is chock-full of intriguing Asian ingredients, a lot of Korean ones in particular. In addition to displaying a large selection of seafood, this one-stop shop brims with fresh produce, baked goods, and frozen fare. An inexpensive food court provides a place to recharge. **Additional location:** 1295 E. Ogden Ave., Naperville, (630) 778-9800.

Tai Nam Food Market, 4925 N. Broadway, Ste. J, Uptown, Chicago, IL 60640; (773) 275-5666; tainammarket.com; Southeast Asian. Find fixings for *pho* and much more at this well-stocked Asian supermarket deemed worthy of a detour. Wonder at the live lobsters and crabs as well as the plentiful array of fresh-baked bread, marinated and butchered meat, and dim-sum preparations—dumplings included. You'll also spy a fair number of Cambodian and Indonesian items, plus seemingly endless dry goods sold at rock-bottom prices.

Three Sisters Delicatessen, 2854 W. Devon Ave., Rogers Park, Chicago, IL 60659; (773) 973-1919; Russian. Outstanding smoked and cured meats (note the salami), plus herring, caviar by the

ounce, a bounty of rarely seen imported ingredients, and whimsical cakes attract loyalists to this established Russian deli, which also features relishes and jams easily put to good use.

Uni-Mart, 5845 N. Clark St., Edgewater, Chicago, IL 60660; (773) 271-8676; unimaronestop.com; Filipino. Ready-made *lumpia* and *pancit* give way to an atypical meat counter, candies, and canned goods at this definitive market. No visit is complete without stopping at its snack-centric, in-house Filipino carryout operation. There are locations in Niles, 7315 Dempster St., (847) 663-8388; Hoffman Estates, 1038 Golf Rd., (847) 755-1082; and Woodridge, 2457 W. 75th St., (630) 910-6386, as well.

Viet Hoa Plaza, 1051 W. Argyle St., Uptown, Chicago, IL 60640; (773) 334-1028; Southeast Asian. Durian, fragrant herbs, packaged noodles, curry pastes, and pickled veggies commingle at this Southeast Asian grocery store and meat market, which also features kitchen tools and an extensive selection of live fish. Marvel over the sauces, and delve into the cross-cultural Asian ingredients, including many Filipino items.

Whole Foods, 1550 N. Kingsbury St., Lincoln Park, Chicago, IL 60642; (312) 587-0648; wholefoodsmarket.com; Grocery. Standing proud as one of the biggest Whole Foods period, this expansive outpost houses a bakery, coffee roaster, wine lounge, and several food venues, and it prepares gelato on-site, scooping it up alongside locally sourced items not found at other outposts. There's also a music stage and a rooftop, where seasonal food and wellness events take place. There are a slew of other locations in the Chicago area—visit the website for info.

Whole Grain Fresh Market, 665 Pasquinelli Dr., Westmont, IL 60559; (630) 323-8180; Asian. Emphasizing Chinese and Southeast Asian ingredients, this large, well-stocked grocery store has all the pantry standbys, but also less-common produce—like the occasional lily bulb. Shaved beef may leave you longing for sukiyaki. Meanwhile, a large selection of fresh and dry noodles and frozen bao leaves carts loaded and wallets lighter.

Winston's Sausage, 4701 W. 63rd St., Midway, Chicago, IL 60629; (773) 767-4353; winstonsmarket.net; Irish. Founded in 1967 by Michael Winston Sr., a former stockyards meat cutter, this gem offers up house-made bangers and black-and-white pudding (sausages) as well as its own corned beef and smoked butt. Love Irish soda bread? You'll find that here, too. You'll also encounter enough European imports, including oats, Weetabix, and candy. Another market is at 7959 159th St., Tinley Park, (708) 633-7600, adjacent to adjunct Gaelic restaurant, The Ashford House.

Wisma, 24 E. Scranton Ave., Lake Bluff, IL 60044; (847) 234-1805; wisma.us; Specialty. Skip the trip to the grocery store in favor of this John des Rosiers (**Inovasi**, p. 172) gem, stocked with chef-driven, prepared fare using local, sustainable ingredients. Whether you warm them for enjoyment in-house, choose delivery, or take them to go, the ease and enjoyment of semolina shells carbonara, chicken jambalaya,

and shrimp and grits runs deep. House-label bacon, sausage, and barbecue heritage pork are other boons. Small production wines and craft
beers, plus charcuterie, house-made soups, and snacks, round out the
experience. A second location is in the **Chicago French Market** (p. 242).

Butchers

**Bende, Inc., 925 Corporate Woods Pkwy., Vernon Hills, IL 60061;
(847) 913-0306; bende.com.** When you have a hankering for salami,
head to this longtime sausage-maker to acquire its equally excellent
mild Teli and Hungarian paprika–infused Csabai varieties. You'll also
find packaged goods, such as *ajvar*, liver pâté, sour-cherry syrup, and
noodles both fine and broad. There is another location at 444 Roosevelt
Rd., Glen Ellyn, (630) 469-6525.

**Beograd Meat Market, 2937 W. Irving Park Rd., Irving Park,
Chicago, IL 60618; (773) 478-7575; beogradmarket.net.** Sniff out the
cevapcici, smoky *ajvar* (red pepper–eggplant spread), and savory *burek*
at this bustling Balkan. Afterward, mosey over to the adjunct cafe for
comforting cabbage-type fare.

**The Butcher & Larder, 1026 N. Milwaukee Ave., Ukrainian
Village, Chicago, IL 60642; (773) 687-8280; thebutcherandlarder
.com.** This humanely raised, locally sourced, whole-animal butcher
comes from snout-to-tail chef and modern meat-cutter Rob Levitt,
who offers a regular rotation of butchering classes alongside
the bounty of carved carcasses, house-smoked bacon, sausages, charcuterie, and corned beef. The meat is custom
cut; whole pigs, ducks, rabbits, goats, and turkeys
are available with advance notice. Additionally, there's an edited lunch menu available,

with the exception of Sunday, and family dinners are hosted each month. Craving his wife, Allie's, sweets? A selection of them—including her famed Migas Bark—are on hand.

Butcher & the Burger, 1021 W. Armitage Ave., Lincoln Park, Chicago, IL 60614; (773) 697-3735; butcherandtheburger.com. Part burger joint, part meat locker, this quaint counter lets you choose your own patty (from naturally raised turkey or local, all-natural beef); select spices, like Sonoran chile or onion soup; have your pick of buns; and finish with toppings both classic (ketchup, barbecue) and creative (black truffle aioli). After indulging on-site, take home uncooked burgers, meatballs, and meat loaf for a rainy day. Also, sign up for the ongoing, BYOB hog, beef, pheasant, and duck butchery classes.

Casey's Market, 915 Burlington Ave., Western Springs, IL 60558; (708) 246-0380; caseysmarketonline.com. It's spendy, quaint, and crowded, but this neighborhood butcher does deliver. Ogle bourbon-marinated strip steak; plump, stuffed chicken breast; and salty *queso* dip sold by the pound, but don't depart without asking for a roll of its comforting cream sausage, which is pulled from the freezer on request. Counterpart Mike's Market is at 32 S. Villa Ave., Villa Park, (630) 832-1760.

Columbus Meat Market, 906 W. Randolph St., West Loop, Chicago, IL 60607; (312) 829-2480. This small retail store is an arm of the hopping wholesale biz, which affords not just a friendly shopping experience but access to hard-to-find cuts, quality prime meats for the grill, and drool-inducing sausages.

Dreymiller & Kray, 140 S. State St., Hampshire, IL 60140; (847) 683-2271. It's all about the hickory- and applewood-smoked bacon at this old-fashioned artisan butcher, where edibles are turned from a signature brick smokehouse dating back to 1941. Mind you, the cured ham and smoked turkey breast are also of note. Look for its products at **Fox & Obel** (p. 244) and Sunset Foods, as well as at some orchards in northern Illinois.

Gepperth's Market, 1964 N. Halsted St., Lincoln Park, Chicago, IL 60614; (773) 549-3883; gepperthsmarket.com. Top-tier cuts, both exotic and trusty, are the thrust of Otto Demke's meatery, taunting passersby with crown roasts of lamb and pork, house-made sausages (try the jalapeño brats), and thick-cut steaks. Alligator, venison, elk, bison, and wild boar are regularly available, and specialty cuts may be procured with an advance phone call. An added boon: Items may be FedExed.

Grant Park Packing Co., 842 W. Lake St., West Loop, Chicago, IL 60607; (312) 421-4096; grantparkpacking.com. Come on Saturday mornings (the only time it's open to the public), and grab fine Italian sausages and economical cuts of pork, which are its true area of expertise. But skirt steak and less common options, such as goose neck and beef feet and head, aren't something to scoff at.

Halsted Packing House, 445 N. Halsted St., River West, Chicago, IL 60654; (312) 421-5147. The Davoses' generations-old butcher shop specializes in high-end small animals, slaughtering them on-site—a fact that impacts both the shop's aroma and the pleasing end results. Put on a brave face, as the lamb, goat, and pork are hyped for good reason.

Harrison's Poultry Farm, 1201 Waukegan Rd., Glenview, IL 60025; (847) 724-0132; harrisonspoultryfarm.com. Supplying to many area restaurants, this retail store and butcher sells crazy-fresh fowl—chicken, turkey, duck—that's no more than a day old, resulting in revelatory eating experiences. Come here to pick up eggs and butter as well.

Joseph's Finest Meats, 7101 W. Addison St., Dunning, Chicago, IL 60634; (773) 736-3766. A small but inviting butcher, this neighborhood joint is a must for prime dry-aged beef as well as wonderful Italian sausage and homemade giardiniera. Call ahead for custom cuts, and they'll be waiting upon arrival.

Koenemann Sausage Company, 27090 Volo Village Rd., Volo, IL 60073; (815) 385-6260; koenemannsausage.com. Enjoy a taste of Germany, choosing between 60-plus sausages, super-smoky ham, and cold cuts as well as imported spaetzle, sauces, and candy. The old-timer ships nationwide.

Kurowski's Sausage Shop, 2976 N. Milwaukee Ave., Avondale, Chicago, IL 60618; (773) 645-1692. A stunning selection of smoked sausages entice (and potentially intimidate the uninitiated) at this charming Polish market. Make it easy on yourself and order the juniper berry–scented *jałowcowa,* garlicky *kiełbasa weselna,* and *kabanosy pikantne,* spicy stick sausage seasoned with peppers. Pick up fresh rye bread and pickles to go with.

Lincoln Quality Meat Market, 4661 N. Lincoln Ave., Lincoln Square, Chicago, IL 60625; (773) 561-4570; lincolnqualitymeat market.com. This family-run operation is known for its homemade Italian, German, Bulgarian, Polish, Hungarian, and Romanian and sausages; imported and house-made deli meats and cheeses; and made-to-order sandwiches, all offered up by friendly butchers who know their stuff.

Olympia Meat Packers, 810 W. Randolph St., West Loop, Chicago, IL 60607; (312) 666-2222. Don't be shy: Stock up on the basics from this reliable meat market, be it lamb, sausages, or meaty ribs. Of course, the marbled prime steaks alone—when available—won't leave you disappointed, especially since the prices are quite low.

P. & E. Mullins: Local, 424 E. Buffalo St., New Buffalo, MI 49117; (269) 231-5138; localnewbuffalo.com. Day trip–worthy sustainable cured meats and cheeses from the Midwest join signature, spreadable bacon jam, fresh sausages, and farm-fresh meat as well as pantry items from local artisans at this quaint butcher shop, set within a cute-as-a-button converted house.

Paulina Market, 3501 N. Lincoln Ave., Lakeview, Chicago, IL 60657; (773) 248-6272; paulinameatmarket.com. Meat-eaters are in hog heaven at this standby, known for its extensive selection of sausages —turducken brats, chubby knackwurst, Serbian cevapcici—as well as stuffed veal breast, a plethora of Swedish specialties, handmade garlic salami studded with peppercorns, and fleshy, vibrant steaks. It's also a go-to for wild game—ostrich filet, guinea fowl, and pheasant—as well as offal. Purchases up to 30 pounds may be shipped, flash-frozen, via FedEx.

Peoria Packing Butcher Shop, 1300 W. Lake St., West Loop, Chicago, IL 60607; (312) 738-1800; peoriapacking.com. This wholesaler does a brisk business among retail connoisseurs, who don plastic gloves while meandering down aisle after aisle of fresh-cut beef, sausage, and seafood, displayed without flourish—openly—in bins. To the joy of loyal patrons, the availability of less-frequented bits and pieces means little gets ignored within the refrigerated, lockerlike space. Custom butchering and whole-animal purchases are options as well.

Prime "N" Tender, 777 N. York Rd., Hinsdale, IL 60521; (630) 887-0088; primentendermeats.com. You'll pay up the wazoo for everything at this tucked-away, neighborhood butcher shop that's popular with the well-to-do. The quality prime beef is what really sets the place apart, though the custom-made sandwiches with Boar's Head meats and edited selection of specialty products—peach applesauce from the Elegant Farmer, Peter Luger steak sauce—hardly hurt the cause.

Publican Quality Meats, 825 W. Fulton Market, West Loop, Chicago, IL 60607; (312) 445-8977; publicanqualitymeats .com. Paul Kahan's butcher shop, cafe, and deli draws the masses for pork belly and muffaletta sandwiches, locally sourced meats, house-made charcuterie, and curated pantry items, all divvied up in close confines. Beer and champagne dinners, mixology classes, and a parking lot– situated summer barbecue series showcasing guest chefs keep things interesting.

Ream's Elburn Market, 128 N. Main St., Elburn, IL 60119; (630) 365-6461; elburnmarket.com. Located about 45 miles west of Chicago, this family-owned shop is a standout for house-smoked bacon and encased meats, including garlic wieners, brats, Portuguese *linguiça*, and beer salami, not to mention bone-in ham and dried beef and jerky of many kinds.

Romanian Kosher Sausage Co., 7200 N. Clark St., Rogers Park, Chicago, IL 60626; (773) 761-4141; romaniankoshersausage .com. Love goes to the garlic-spiced hot dogs, tubs of chopped liver, and variably sized salamis—provided you're willing to look past the stark, fluorescent-lit setting of this encased-meat expert.

Rosario's Italian Sausage, 8611 S. Pulaski Rd., Ashburn, Chicago, IL 60652; (773) 585-0660. You can't miss this butcher's iconic neon sign, which depicts a pig hopping into a meat grinder. Porky tchotckes continue the whimsical tone at this porcine palace, which turns out some of, if not *the* best sausage in town. Excellent Italian beef and meatball sandwiches warrant a stop, as do the pizza setups, which contain everything you need to bake at home.

Schmeisser's Sausage, 7649 N. Milwaukee Ave., Niles, IL 60714; (847) 967-8995. Established in 1951, this is a deservedly popular, personable destination for prime meat and coils of house-made sausage. Plan on paying cash or by check, and be on the lookout for specialty finds, like pork and goose lard.

Spencer's Jolly Posh Foods, 1405 W. Irving Park Rd., Lakeview, Chicago, IL 60613; (312) 415-6919; spencerfoods.com. British and Irish classics are on tap at this across-the-pond ode, offering bangers, dry-cured bacon, and black and white puddings. Stay for a sandwich, then pick out imported beans, mustard, and HP sauce for added at-home authenticity.

Zier's Prime Meats & Poultry, 813 Ridge Rd., Wilmette, IL 60091; (847) 251-4000; ziersprime.com. Cut-to-order prime, dry-aged beef is the cornerstone of this old-fashioned North Shore butcher shop, which sells heritage birds during the holidays. The house-cured charcuterie is worth a look, too, as is the house-smoked ham and bacon.

Fishmongers

Burhop's Seafood, Plaza del Lago, 1515 Sheridan Rd., Wilmette, IL 60091; (847) 256-6400; burhops.com. Fin enthusiasts find the freshest of catches at this upscale shop, which stocks everything from striped bass and Atlantic char to turbot, clams, and scallops. Frozen preparations are eye-catching, too, as they may include wonton-crusted shrimp; cooked, flash-frozen lobster meat; and house-made soups. You can also find Homer's Ice Cream, pies, sauces, and seasonings that make meal preparation a cinch.

Dicola's Seafood, 10754 S. Western Ave., Beverly, Chicago, IL 60643; (773) 238-7071; dicolasseafoodbeverly.com. A mainstay for fresh sea fare, this South Side institution bakes, fries, or grills fillets and also allows customers to select them fresh and frozen to take home. All the basics—catfish, smelt, colossal shrimp, and Alaskan whitefish—are at the ready. Hot preparations, ranging from New England clam chowder to Maryland blue-crab cakes, are available along with other fixings for feasts at home.

Dirk's Fish & Gourmet Shop, 2070 N. Clybourn Ave., Lincoln Park, Chicago, IL 60614; (773) 404-3475; dirksfish.com. This sustainably minded place sells the city's best seafood, from farm-raised Laughing Bird shrimp and grouper to Petrale sole, mild Patagonian toothfish, shucked East Coast oysters, and live lobster. With one-day notice, options like corvina, opah, onaga, and hamachi may be available (season willing). Frozen frog's legs, conch, and crayfish also can be yours. Then again, garlicky, prepared escargots and smoked selections—think Finnan haddie, sable, trout, and salmon—aren't afterthoughts. There's sushi, too. Parties and cooking classes are hosted on-site.

The Fish Guy Market, 4423 N. Elston Ave., Albany Park, Chicago, IL 60630; (773) 283-7400; fishguy.com. Bill Dugan's retail operation is a top-tier choice for sushi-grade fish and seasonal seafood as well as some of the area's tastiest smoked fish (try the pecan wood–smoked trout). He also hosts caviar tastings and BYO dinners (see fishguy.com/dinners.html); the relaxed, multicourse meals take place in its Wellfleet dining room, where lunch is now served weekdays.

Isaacson & Stein Fish Co., 800 W. Fulton Market, West Loop, Chicago, IL 60607; (312) 421-2444; isaacsonandsteinfishcompany .com. An old-time feel, very fresh fare at reasonable prices, and a chance to don gloves and pick your next meal are the benchmarks of this seafood market. Though potentially overwhelming to newbies, row after row of mahimahi, tilapia, and Copper River salmon—also sold to the city's top chefs—are easily navigated with help from the friendly staff.

Market Fisheries, 7129 S. State St., Greater Grand Crossing, Chicago, IL 60619; (773) 483-3233. Super-fresh seafood—live blue crab, crawfish, lobster—are the draw at this no-frills, family-run operation. Upward of two-dozen species of fresh fish are joined by unexpected finds such as turtle and gator.

Mercato del Pesce, 2623 N. Harlem Ave., Montclare, Chicago, IL 60607; (773) 622-7503. This family-owned Italian seafood specialist jams its cases with slippery catches such as spigola, massive octopi, and sardines as well as beauteous bivalves. Fortunately, prices are poised for the budget-crunched, and the service is welcoming as can be.

New England Seafood Company Fish Market, 3341 N. Lincoln Ave., Lakeview, Chicago, IL 60657; (773) 871-3474; neseafoodcompany.com. Brothers Jeffrey and Robert Mazza are behind this retail and wholesale operation with a small adjunct restaurant serving unadulterated lobster rolls drizzled with drawn butter, rich lobster bisque, fried clams, and pan-seared haddock for enjoyment at quintessential red-and-white-checkered tables. Post-meal, grab all the fixings you need for an at-home, Northeastern-style feast, including oysters, live whole lobster, and scallops,

Rubino's Seafood, 735 W. Lake St., West Loop, Chicago, IL 60661; (312) 258-0020; rubinosseafood.com. This primo purveyor boasts an extensive seafood selection, including outstanding shellfish. The knowledgeable staff is more than willing to walk customers though the attributes of halibut, whiting, lake perch, and sea bass—among many other varieties—which are flown in fresh daily and sold at wholesale prices.

Sea Ranch, 3217 Lake Ave., Wilmette, IL 60091; (847) 256-4404; searanchwilmette.com. Lush, sushi-grade fish may be purchased here

THE FRESHEST OF CATCHES

Perhaps you prefer a hands-on approach. That's just what you'll get at **Rushing Waters Fisheries**, N301 CR H, Palmyra, WI 53156; (800) 378-7088; rushingwaters.net. Located within Kettle Morraine State Forest, visitors can rent equipment to catch—and cook—rainbow trout on the premises. (Come on Wednesdays, when pole rental is free.) Its pros will clean and fillet the fish for you, leaving you to throw it on the smoldering grill situated in front of the on-site store. The retail operation also sells its sublime smoked fish and accoutrements such as rubs and planks.

and prepared at home. However, this Japanese market also has a massive maki, sushi, and sashimi menu as well as a spread of sundries.

Supreme Lobster, 220 E. North Ave., Villa Park, IL 60181; (630) 834-3474; supremelobster.com. Its fleet of refrigerated vehicles is seen rambling around town, delivering more than 3,000 types of high-quality catches throughout Illinois, Wisconsin, Michigan, and Indiana. The retail store, brimming with lanky Alaskan king crab legs, a bevy of fillets, and namesake crustaceans, also ships selections throughout the US.

Tensuke Market, 3 S. Arlington Heights Rd., Elk Grove Village, IL 60007; (847) 806-1200; tensuke-chicago.com. Folks flock to this Japanese fish market for pristine pink snapper, black tiger shrimp, and flounder as well as grocery necessities, stopping by its small food court for prepared fare, such as beef sukiyaki, noodle soups, and maki.

Wagner Seafood, 9626 S. Pulaski Rd., Oak Lawn, IL 60453; (708) 636-2646. Make fast tracks for this mom-and-pop seafood shop, a south suburban beacon for home-style fillet-o'-fish. It's also a go-to for fresh catches, butchered and sold for cooking at home.

Sweet Treats

Chicago has a longstanding history with sweets—even Andes Mints got its start here. These days, the tradition lives on at throwback confectionaries and bakeries. Meanwhile, modern-day pastry chefs and artisanal ice-cream purveyors elevate finales to new, unexpected heights.

Bakeries

Abundance Bakery, 105 E. 47th St., Bronzeville, Chicago, IL 60653; (773) 373-1971; Bakery; $. Way-affordable and incredibly satisfying, this Far South Side bakery makes only a handful of coveted, massive, fruit-dappled apple fritters daily. When you can't get your hands on them, or the caramel upside-down cakes, the bread puddings and tasty doughnuts—chocolate-glazed long johns among them—are good stand-ins.

Argo Georgian Bakery, 2812 W. Devon Ave., Rogers Park, Chicago, IL 60659; (773) 764-6322; Bakery; $. Piping hot, crisp-crusted flatbreads, pastries, and flaky mozzarella- and feta-filled *hachapuri* are the draw at this simple, honest Georgian bakery, where delights are turned out from domed ovens. Time things just right, though: Bites are extra-ethereal when sampled fresh. Sweet tooths should finish with a *tapluna*—a sweet honey-nut pie.

Austrian Bakery & Deli (Cafe Vienna), 2523 N. Clark St., Lincoln Park, Chicago, IL 60614; (773) 244-9922; austrianbakery .com; Bakery/Austrian; $$. Michael Mikusch may be known for his flaky, cinnamon-scented *apfelstrudel,* but the custom cakes, Austrian butter cookies, and buttery croissants he doles out at his sweet cafe are every bit as sweet.

Baker & Nosh, 1303 W. Wilson Ave., Uptown, Chicago, IL 60640; (773) 989-7393; bakerandnosh.com; Bakery/Specialty; $. Bill Mill-holland, a former cooking-school instructor, serves satisfying pastries (coffee cake, muffins), sandwiches on house-made bread, and La Colombe coffee by day. Come evening, salumi and artisan cheeses take the stage. Want to learn the craft? Bread basics and croissant classes are offered on Monday and Tuesday nights for groups of up to six.

Bang Bang Pie Shop, 2051 N. California Ave., Logan Square, Chicago, IL 60647; (773) 276-8888; bangbangpie.com; Bakery; $. Although you wouldn't know it from the name, crusty outside, plush-within biscuits are the hook at this bustling bakery. Slather them with black-pepper butter and cherry preserves, or get them with addictive candied bacon, alongside jolt-ing coffee brewed from house-roasted beans. Of course, the sea-salted chocolate pie and Kentucky mud pie are nearly as hard to deny, whether sliced or bought whole.

Beurrage, 1248 W. 18th St., Pilsen, Chicago, IL 60608; (773) 998-2371; beurrage.com; Bakery; $. Bread, pastry, and *viennoiserie:* These disciplines achieve perfection at this small-scale Pilsen bakery, which sells wholesale and to the public via the Pilsen Community Market. Watch for its in-the-works storefront, which will make buying orange-curd tartlets, buttery pretzel croissants, and apple-pistachio frangipane tarts a cinch.

Bittersweet Pastry Shop, 1114 W. Belmont Ave., Lakeview, Chicago IL 60657; (773) 929-1100; bittersweetpastry.com; Bakery; **$.** Equal parts indulgent and inviting, Judy Contino's patisserie is a go-to for brides-to-be. It's also destination-worthy for casual sweet-seekers, its cases brimming with oversize chocolate-dipped cookies, scones, and lemon bars. Pair them with a steaming cup of hot chocolate, or enjoy them after light, cafe-style bites.

Bridgeport Bakery, 2907 S. Archer Ave., Bridgeport, Chicago, IL 60608; (773) 523-1121; Bakery; **$.** Fans of the other white meat savor the plush, insanely cheap, and routinely sold-out bacon buns—come early and get them while they're warm. Other morning wake-up calls include hot cross buns, crullers, and *paczkis*. Meanwhile, cheese- or fruit-filled *kolacky* are a wonderful midday pick-me-up.

Brown Sugar Bakery, 328 E. 75th St., Greater Grand Crossing, Chicago, IL 60619; (773) 224-6262; Bakery; **$.** Dangerously delicious when calories are a matter of concern, Stephanie Hart's sweet tooth haven has cobblers—peach, pear, apple, sweet potato—down pat. Be sure to get a slice of her storied caramel cake, keeping in mind the cookies, brownies, and banana pudding—available by the serving, half pan, and full pan—are contenders, too.

Chimney Cake Island, 1445 W. Devon Ave., Edgewater, Chicago, IL 60660; (773) 856-0919; chimneycakeisland.com; Bakery; **$.** Cozy up to this Transylvanian treasure, a singular spot for chewy *kurtoskalacs* (signature, cylindrical chimney cakes), finished with the likes of Nutella, cinnamon, or coconut. Get yours hot from the oven (that's when they're best), washed down with a piping hot cup of Lavazza coffee.

Chiu Quon Bakery, 2242 S. Wentworth Ave., Chinatown, Chicago, IL 60616; (312) 225-6608; chiuquonbakery.com; Bakery; **$.**

Chinatown's oldest and most beloved bakery turns out the flakiest barbecue pork buns, rivaled only by its piping-hot sesame balls filled with sweet red-bean paste, killer shrimp-pork turnovers, and tender rice crepes. A sister location is in Uptown at 1127 W. Argyle St., (773) 907-8888.

D'Amato's Bakery, 1124 W. Grand Ave., West Loop, Chicago, IL 60642; (312) 733-5456; damatobakery.com; Bakery/Deli; $. Known for many things—not the least of which are doughy Sicilian-style sheet pizza squares, exceptional Italian cookies, and decadent cannoli—this institution now serves prepared lasagna and fettuccine Bolognese for at-home pleasure. But back to that pizza, it's perfection, topped with just-spicy-enough pepperoni or sausage from **Bari Foods** (p. 240) next door.

Dat Donut, 8249 S. Cottage Grove Ave., Greater Grand Crossing, Chicago, IL 60619; (773) 723-1002; Doughnuts; $. This homespun, handcrafted doughnut shop, located in the same building as Leon's Bar-B-Q, makes its fresh-glazed and buttermilk cake creations—both types feather-light—24 hours a day. When you're really hungry, order the Big Dat—a supersize version of its signature sweet treat.

Dinkel's Bakery, 3329 N. Lincoln Ave., Lakeview, Chicago, IL 60657; (773) 281-7300; dinkels.com; Bakery; $$. Sating sweet tooths since 1922, this beloved bakery makes amazing cinnamon-sugar doughnuts, colorful cookies, and beyond-delicious cakes as well as the signature, focaccialike Burglaur, a savory breakfast poof filled with the likes of Asiago, cheddar, broccoli, and egg.

Do-Rite Donuts, 50 W. Randolph St., Loop, Chicago, IL 60601; (312) 488-2483; doritedonuts.com; Doughnuts; $. A pint-size, morning-only option for its yeasty namesake, this doughnut shop keeps candied maple bacon, traditional Valrhona chocolate, and old-fashioned lemon-glazed buttermilk versions at the ready—that is, until they're no more.

The Doughnut Vault, 401 1/2 N. Franklin St., River North, Chicago, IL 60654; thedoughnutvault.tumblr .com; Doughnuts; $. This River North doughnut shop from restaurateur Brendan Sodikoff really launched the city's doughnut craze, what with its chestnut-glazed, old-fashioned strawberry shortcake and birthday cake kinds. Look for it in the building that houses sib **Gilt Bar** (p. 231).

Ferrara Original Bakery, 2210 W. Taylor St., Little Italy, Chicago, IL 60612; (312) 666-2200; ferrarabakery.com; Bakery; $. The cannoli is every bit as good as the hype suggests, though the gratifying selection of other sweets—including tiramisu, éclairs, pignoli cookies, and *baba au rhum*—are distractions of note. This standby also serves sandwiches, salads, and pastas.

Firecakes Donuts, 68 W. Hubbard St., River North, Chicago, IL 60654; (312) 329-6500; firecakesdonuts.com; Doughnuts; $. Jonathan Fox (**La Madia**, p. 114) tweaked his great-grandfather's recipe, using it as inspiration for doughnut offerings like lemon verbena meringue, triple Valrhona chocolate cake, and butterscotch praline, all perfect companions for La Colombe coffee.

First Slice Pie Cafe, 4401 N. Ravenswood Ave., Ravenswood, Chicago, IL 60640; (773) 506-7380; firstslice.org; Bakery/ Cafe; $. Dine for a cause at this nonprofit eatery from l'École des Arts Culinaires–trained Mary Ellen Diaz (**North Pond**, p. 79). Located in the Lillstreet Art Center, proceeds from its menu selections—whether chocolate–peanut butter pie, chopped salad, or fancified lasagna—go to community kitchens, which in turn prepare quality meals for families in need. There's also a shareholder program, for which subscribers receive weekly meals while contributing the same quality fare to the hungry. **Additional locations:** 4664 N. Manor Ave., (773) 267-0169; and 5357 N. Ashland Ave., (773) 275-4297.

Floriole Cafe & Bakery, 1220 W. Webster Ave., Lincoln Park, Chicago, IL 60614; (773) 883-1313; floriole.com; Bakery/Cafe; $$. What began as a stand at Green City Market is now a bi-level Lincoln Park sweet spot serving all things amazing: plush, flaky almond crème croissants, seasonal clafoutis, and—quite possibly the feather in its cap—the B.A.D., a bacon and arugula sandwich with almond date spread and creamy goat cheese on yeasty corn bread.

Gingersnap Sweets & Such, 1416 W. Irving Park Rd., Lakeview, Chicago, IL 60613; (773) 697-8529; gingersnapsweets.com; Bakery; $. Trained at the French Pastry School, Jen Templeton knows her way around the oven, a fact that can't be denied upon trying savory (red pepper–feta) or sweet (chocolate) whirlaways, peach-packed scones, passion-fruit tarts, and savory hand pies. On weekends, make fast tracks for soon-to-sell-out hamburger buns.

Glazed & Infused, 1553 N. Milwaukee Ave., Wicker Park, Chicago, IL 60622; (312) 226-5556; goglazed.com; Doughnuts; $. Handcrafted doughnuts from Scott Harris—what's not to love? That goes double for the cakey, cream cheese–frosted banana that's drizzled with salted caramel and showered with candied walnuts; the maple-glazed long john with peppered caramel bacon; and the vanilla cream and strawberry lavender compote–filled "shortcake," under a poof of powdered sugar. This operation is tucked within Francesca's Forno; additional outposts are at 813 W. Fulton Market; 30 E. Hubbard St.; the Raffaello Hotel, 201 E. Delaware Pl.; and 939 W. Armitage Ave., all of them reachable at (312) 226-5556.

COFFEE AND PASTRY

Coffee and pastry go hand in hand. The good news is, Chicago has you covered on both fronts. In the caffeine department, you can start with the obvious (and certainly beloved): Intelligensia, intelligentsia coffee.com. Or, you can look beyond to find boutique operations of note. While you're at it, fuel your passion at chicagocoffeescene .com, a site dedicated to the local bean scene.

Asado Coffee, 1432 W. Irving Park Rd., Lakeview, Chicago, IL 60613; (773) 413-9454; asadocoffee.com. Made to order from house-roasted, family-farmed, sustainable beans, this one-cup-at-a-time operation has an additional outpost at 22 E. Jackson Blvd., (773) 703-3658, as well as a soon-to-open one at 1651 W. Chicago Ave.

Bow Truss Coffee Roasters, 2934 N. Broadway, Lakeview, Chicago, IL 60647; (773) 857-1361; bowtruss.com. Dollop founder Philip Tadros is behind the minimalist roaster with an industrial-feeling space. A second location is at 406 N. Wells St., (312) 222-1306. Incidentally, both host periodic pop-ups and CSAlike pickups from Rustic Tart, rustictart.net, a seasonal pie subscription service from Stephanie Lock.

Dark Matter Coffee, 738 N. Western Ave., Humboldt Park, Chicago, IL 60622, (773) 697-8472; dark mattercoffee.com. Enjoy a frothy cup of joe at Jesse Diaz's roasting facility or at this artisan's Star Lounge coffee bar, 2521 W. Chicago Ave., (773) 384-7827.

Hendrickx, 100 E. Walton St., Gold Coast, Chicago, IL 60611; (312) 649-6717; Bakery/Belgian; $. Carefully crafted Belgian bread is the specialty at this small bakery, which is worth a detour for the Belgian dark chocolate croissants alone. But behold the signature country loaf, available by the eighth, quarter, half, or whole loaf; the ethereal *liège* waffles; and the goat cheese sandwich with hints of honey, pistachios,

Gaslight Coffee Roasters, 2385 N. Milwaukee Ave, Logan Square, Chicago IL 60647; gaslightcoffee roasters.com. Metropolis vets Zak Rye and Tristan Coulter pair their house-roasted wares with Smoking Goose charcuterie at this cute cafe.

HalfWit Coffee Roasters at The Wormhole, 1462 N. Milwaukee Ave., Chicago, IL 60622; (773) 661-2468; halfwitcoffee.com. Choose from the likes of balanced Finca Santana, Peruvian Puno Lot 86, and demure Dukunde Kawa, sourced by this unpretentious roaster.

Ipsento, 2035 N. Western Ave., Logan Square, Chicago, IL 60647; (773) 904-8177; ipsento.com. Look to this direct-trade importer and roaster for straight-up beans and eye-opening espresso, served alongside pastries and sandwiches. Get the Garrison Keillor—turkey, cheddar, apple, avocado, greens, and honey mustard on multigrain—if you're wise.

La Colombe, 955 W. Randolph St., West Town, Chicago, IL 60607; (312) 733-0707; lacolombe.com. Look to this Philadelphia-based small-batch roaster for classic and reserve blends, plus cold-pressed, bottled coffee that's meant to be served over ice. A second location is slotted for the Bucktown neighborhood.

Metropolis Coffee Company, 1039 W. Granville Ave., Edgewater, Chicago, IL 60660; (773) 764-0400; metropoliscoffee.com. For a top-tier espresso and latte, caffeine-cravers consider this java-scented Loyola hang and small-batch roastery a go-to.

and thyme. Pause for a spell over made-to-order, Belgian-style coffee as well.

Hoosier Mama Pie Co., 1618 ½ W. Chicago Ave., West Town, Chicago, IL 60622; (312) 243-4846; hoosiermamapie.com; Bakery; **$.** Paula Haney has rocked the dessert scene with her buttery, lovingly

made double-crust apple, lemon chess, and sugar cream pies. The peanut butter and orange cream versions? Uh-huh, they really are all that. Even those preferring the savory side can get their fix with chicken potpie and creamy bacon, onion, and cheddar quiche. Friday nights usher in three-pie flights.

Huck Finn Restaurant, 10501 S. Cicero Ave., Oak Lawn, IL 60453; (708) 499-1112; huckfinnrestaurant.com; Doughnuts/American; $$. Ice cream and doughnuts—that's why everyone comes to this charming threesome. Get the best of both worlds by ordering your yeasty treat topped with ice cream and whipped cream. If you need sustenance of another sort, perfectly serviceable options like cream-of-chicken soup and burgers exist. **Additional locations:** 3414 S. Archer Ave., (773) 247-5515; 6650 S. Pulaski Ave., (773) 581-4285.

Interurban Cafe & Pastry Shop, 2008 N. Halsted St., Lincoln Park, Chicago, IL 60614; (773) 698-7739; facebook.com/ interurbanchicago; Bakery; $. Locate the carryout window, tucked down an alley off of Armitage Avenue, and reap the rewards: sticky maple-bacon buns, red velvet cake bites, and peanut butter–chocolate crispy bars from a Charlie Trotter's vet. There are some savories, too, like a salad of brown rice, kale, currants, sunflower seeds, and scallions in cumin-sherry vinaigrette, and chili with quinoa, sweet potatoes, and chipotle cream.

Jarosch Bakery, 35 Arlington Heights Rd., Elk Grove Village, IL 60007; (847) 437-1234; jaroschbakery.com; Bakery; $. Everyone falls hard for this uncommonly good, decades-old spot, serving smiley face and sprinkle cookies with the best of 'em. Still, real bliss arrives in the form of cheese strudel, custard rings drizzled with icing, and strawberry shortcake enveloped in a cloud of whipped cream.

Jimmy Jamm Sweet Potato Pies, 1844 W. 95th St., Beverly. Chicago, IL 60643; (773) 779-9105; Bakery; $. A specialist if there ever was one, this sweet spot focuses on spud-based confections. The result is fantastic sweet pies and cookies as well as muffins, ice cream, and sandwiches on sweet-potato bread, all of them deserving of a trek.

Julius Meinl, 3601 N. Southport Ave., Lakeview, Chicago, IL 60613; (773) 868-1857; northamerica.meinl.com; Bakery/Austrian; $$. The Viennese pastries—from apple strudel to a flourless chocolate-almond torte and six-layered, fondant-covered hazelnut dacquoise—enjoy a loyal following. They, as well as cafe-type fare, pair with stellar French-press coffee, espresso, and cappuccino. **Additional locations:** 4363 N. Lincoln Ave., (773) 868-1876; 4115 N. Ravenswood Ave., (773) 883-1862.

Kristoffer's Cafe & Bakery, 1733 S. Halsted St., Pilsen, Chicago, IL 60608; (312) 829-4150; kristofferscafe.com; Bakery; $. You can nibble on egg preparations (breakfast burritos; a sausage, scrambled egg, and cheese bagel) as well as standard ham and roast beef sandwiches. Not to discourage it, but it is in the moist *tres leches* cake that you'll find devotion. Whether you choose the classic version or one where creative liberties are taken (eggnog, *cajeta,* Kahlúa), be assured it—as well as the magically delicious chocoflan—warrants indulgence.

La Fournette, 1547 N. Wells St., Old Town, Chicago, IL 60610; (312) 624-943; lafournette.com; Bakery; $. Pierre Zimmermann, a French Pastry School vet, mans this slim, family-run bakery, a go-to for crackly baguettes, almond croissants, and cloud-like macaroons. One the savory side, look to smoked bacon and ham crepes and the pork rillette pâté or tart flambée sandwiches.

Little Goat Bread, 820 W. Randolph St., West Loop, Chicago, IL 60607; (312) 888-3455; littlegoatchicago.com/bread; Bakery; $. Stephanie Izard knows her way around loaves, but hers include "fat bread" with smoked duck fat, beer, and pickled mustard seed; crusty, dark tortone with garlic and mashed potatoes; and carrot, cumin, and walnut bread. Bagels share the same sensibility, creative schmears like tarragon-chile butter and kimchi cream cheese. Soups (tomato-apple), sandwiches, and pastries (fig–black pepper scones, apple cider cake) play an admirable supporting role.

Lovely: A Bake Shop, 1130 N. Milwaukee Ave., Noble Square, Chicago, IL 60622; (773) 572-4766; lovelybakeshop.com; Bakery; $. Cute seasonal mini-pies, sticky buns, airy *pain au chocolat*: They're worth every calorie. Thank Bob and Gina Hartwig (also of Bakin' & Eggs) for that. Sweets aside, don't overlook the house-made soups (apple-fennel, red pepper, minted split pea) and grainy mustard–smeared salami sandwich, which you can enjoy in full amid a collection of vintage aprons and kitchen accessories.

Lucila's Homemade, (773) 354-3830; lucilashomemade.com; Bakery/Argentine; $. Lucila Giagrande's Argentine *alfajores*—dulce de leche sandwich cookies—are the main event, and they're available online, at markets like Dose, and during pop-up events that occur around town. Adding to the indulgence, dark chocolate–swathed and guava- and caramel-filled versions are also on offer.

Lutz Continental Cafe & Pastry Shop, 2458 W. Montrose Ave., Ravenswood, Chicago, IL 60618; (773) 478-7785; lutzbakery .com; Bakery/German; $$. You'll be tempted by the pastry case—as well you should. It's the flaky strudels; towering, multilayered cakes and tortes; marzipan; and delicate pastries that incite satisfied sighs. So, as passable as the butter-crusted quiche Lorraine, goulash, and senior citizen–style sandwiches may be, it's a slice of chocolate-strawberry whipped-cream cake—accompanied by Viennese-style coffee—that's divine. In summer, seats in the flower-filled outdoor garden are prime real estate.

Maria's Bakery, 530 Sheridan Rd., Highwood, IL 60040; (847) 266-0811; Bakery/Italian; $. Savory and sweet Italian nibbles made con amore—that's what you get at this quaint North Shore bakery. Whether you settle on a roll of sugared raisin bread, layer-laden *sfogliatelle* dusted with powdered sugar, or *arancini,* you're in good hands at this superior Sicilian. Rather than grab and go, get a cup of joe and a cannoli—which is filled to order—eating at one of two tables in-house.

Mekato's Colombian Bakery, 5423 N. Lincoln Ave., Lincoln Square, Chicago, IL 60625; (773) 784-5181; mekatos.com; Colombian/Bakery; $. Customers—many Colombian—file in to procure house-made electric-yellow empanadas, *chicharrones,* and arepas with savory chorizo from this inviting bakery-cafe. Those in the know also save room for dulce de leche–laced sweets. Juices—from passion fruit to oatmeal—and imported dry goods such as guava paste, flour, and candy fill a need.

Molly's Cupcakes, 2536 N. Clark St., Lincoln Park, Chicago, IL 60614; (773) 883-7220; mollyscupcakes.com; Bakery; $. John Nicolaides named his sugar shack after his cupcake-baking grade-school teacher. If you get one thing, make it the Ron Bennington, peanut butter–filled chocolate cake, topped with chocolate ganache and butterscotch crumbles. If you get two, the carrot with cream-cheese frosting is a must. All cupcakes can also be made into cakes. A portion of proceeds benefit Chicago schools, a fact that only sweetens the deal.

More Cupcakes, 1 E. Delaware Pl., Gold Coast, Chicago, IL 60611; (312) 951-0001; morecupcakes.com; Bakery; $$. Excelling at both sweet and savory cupcakes, Patty Rothman's creations range from obvious (milk chocolate–frosted vanilla, red velvet with cream-cheese topping) to kooky (maple-bacon) and just plain  indulgent (salted caramel). The bottom line is these moist, crumby numbers are plain good. They're also available by mobile truck; follow it @themoremobile.

Naples Bakery, 3705 W. 95th St., Evergreen Park, IL 60805; (708) 424-1810; Bakery; $. Fine cannoli, cakes, cookies, and pastries come from this longstanding neighborhood shop and wedding cake specialist. But whether you settle on cream horns, brandy bites, or *sfogliatelle,* most assuredly waist expansion ensues.

Nazareth Sweets, 4638 N. Kedzie Ave., Albany Park, Chicago, IL 60625; (773) 463-2457; nazarethsweets.com; Bakery/Middle Eastern; $. Find Middle Eastern and Mediterranean treats—baklava, harissa semolina cake, honey-laced sesame brittle, and syrupy *awameh*—at this much-loved mainstay in Albany Park.

New York Bagel & Bialy, 4714 W. Touhy Ave., Lincolnwood, IL 60712; (847) 677-9388; newyork-bagelandbialy.com; Bagels/Deli; $. Offering the best local example of what a bagel should be, this brusque beacon beckons with chewy salt and poppy and mish-mosh creations. Bring cash, and get yours piled high with pastrami, chicken salad, or a simple slather of house-label cream cheese.

Nhu Lan Bakery, 2612 W. Lawrence Ave., Ravenswood, Chicago, IL 60625; (773) 878-9898; nhulansbakery.com; Vietnamese/Bakery; $. It doesn't get much better than the *banh mi* from this mostly carry-out bakery, where crusty loaves are made in-house and finished with texturally triumphant cilantro-flecked daikon, carrot, and jalapeño "slaw." (Try the pork belly and pâté or grilled pork versions.) Veering in a different though no less satisfying direction is its sticky rice with Chinese sausage, spring rolls, and the array of fresh-fruit smoothies dotted with tapioca pearls. Sister property Nhu Lan Saigon Subs is at 602 .W Belmont Ave., (773) 857-6868.

Oak Mill Bakery, 8012 N. Milwaukee Ave., Niles, IL 60714; (847) 318-6400; oakmillbakery.com; Bakery/Polish; $. There are several locations of this Polish baker, all of them dispensing plush *paczki,* rum balls, and petits fours, plus crazy-popular mini cheese flakies. Ogleworthy wedding cakes are a specialty as well. **Additional locations:** Chicago, 5753 W. Belmont Ave., (773) 237-5799, 5747 S. Harlem Ave., (773) 788-9800, and 2204 W. North Ave., (773) 252-4400; as well as Harwood Heights, 4747 N. Harlem Ave., (708) 867-9400; and Arlington Heights, 2314 E. Rand Rd., (847) 454-0139

Old Fashioned Donuts, 11248 S. Michigan Ave., Roseland, Chicago, IL 60628; (773) 995-7420; Doughnuts; $. A thing of great worth is Old Fashioned's iced, apple-packed fritter. The same is true of the real blueberry-dotted doughnuts, offered seasonally, as well as caramel- and pineapple-frosted sweet things. Greedily indulge in them—and quick-serve burgers and fries—while sitting in the diner-style digs.

Pan Hellenic Pastry Shop, 322 S. Halsted St., Greektown, Chicago, IL 60661; (312) 454-1886; panhellenicpastryshop.com; Bakery/Greek; $. Get your Greek on at this understated family-run bakery, a baklava expert with excellent alternates, like *galaktobureko* (milk custard); *kataifi,* which resembles shredded wheat; and *karidopita,* honey-walnut cake scented with cloves and cinnamon.

Peerless Bread & Jam, peerlessbreadandjam.com; Bakery; $.
Lauren Bushnell's coveted loaves include peasant wheat and country levain. She also turns out super rye-flour pretzels spiked with Two Brothers Country Ale and focaccia topped with ramps and roasted tomatoes or Swiss chard and onions. Find the ever-changing offerings at Green City Market on Saturdays. A production space is also in the works at The Plant, a hub for sustainable food in the Back-of-the-Yards neighborhood.

Pleasant House Bakery, 964 W. 31st St., Bridgeport, Chicago, IL 60608; (773) 523-7437; pleasanthousebakery.com; Bakery; $$.
For those who lean savory, not sweet, this excellent entrant has your back. BYO and order house-made soda mixers to go with flaky, individual mushroom-and-kale and steak-and-ale British "royal pies." The dedication and attention to detail is great, so much so husband-and-wife team Art Jackson and Chelsea Kalberloh Jackson grow much of their own produce at adjunct, urban Pleasant Farms. Come on Sunday for high tea and on Wednesday for house-made bangers.

Swedish Bakery, 5348 N. Clark St., Andersonville, Chicago, IL 60640; (773) 561-8919; swedishbakery.com; Bakery/Swedish; $.
It's always crowded at this 1929 fixture, where generations of sweet tooths succumb to Swedish treats. Expect an incomparable collection of cardamom-scented breads, chocolate-custard cake rolls, and ganache treasures as well as marzipan-enrobed slices, Bundts, cookies, coffee cakes, and tortes. This cavity-inducing destination is a favorite among brides-to-be.

Sweet Mandy B's, 1208 W. Webster Ave., Lincoln Park, Chicago IL 60614; (773) 244-1174; sweetmandybs.com; Bakery; $. The cupcakes draw you in to this cutesy Lincoln Park bake shop, but it may just be the seasonal fruit pies, oversize cookies, and butterscotch puddings that leave you clamoring for more.

Swirlz Cupcakes, 705 W. Belden Ave., Lincoln Park, Chicago, IL 60614; (773) 404-2253; swirlzcupcakes.com; Bakery; $. The crowds swoon over the cupcake-only menu at this takeaway bakery, where ever-present red velvet joins vegan and gluten-free options as well as versions topped with chocolate-covered espresso beans or vibrantly coated sunflower seeds. Pick up a fresh-baked sugar-free "pupcake" for Fido, too.

Toni Patisserie and Cafe, 51 S. Washington St., Hinsdale, IL 60521; (630) 789-2020; tonipatisserie.com; Bakery/Cafe; $. European-inspired white-chocolate mousse cake and salted caramel chocolate tarts are worth the indulgence, but this cheery little bakery also makes a mighty fine croque-monsieur. And the *pan bagnat*? The pork rillettes? *Mais oui.* A second location is in the Loop at 65 E. Washington St., (312) 726-2020.

Weber's Bakery, 7055 W. Archer Ave., Garfield Ridge, Chicago, IL 60638; (773) 586-1234; webersbakery.com; Bakery; $. Family-run and adored since 1930, this sweet staple whips up dense, cream cheese–frosted carrot cake, buttery *kolacky,* and out-of-this-world banana split cake, layered with fresh bananas, whipped cream, and strawberries. Come, too, for caraway-studded rye bread and cylindrical cinnamon-raisin loaves.

Confectionaries

Amy's Candy Bar, 4704 N. Damen Ave., Lincoln Square, Chicago, IL 60625; (773) 942-6386; Candy/Bakery; $. Amy Hansen, a

French Pastry School grad, stocks jar after jar with colorful retro and new candies, among them Jelly Babies made famous by Dr. Who, melt-in-your-mouth UFOs, and liquid-filled wax soda bottles. House-made sea-salt caramels, turtles, and nougat hold court with cupcakes, iced sugar cookies, and seasonal selections like chocolate bunnies at Easter.

Blommer Chocolate Company, 600 W. Kinzie St., River West, Chicago, IL 60654; (312) 226-7700; blommer.com; Candy; $. They don't make 'em like this home-grown chocolate company anymore, but it has been perfuming the neighbor-hood with an intoxicating scent since 1939. Stop by the factory storefront for bags of the sweet stuff, plus chocolate-covered rai-sins and fabled cocoa powder.

Candyality, The Shops at North Bridge, 520 N. Michigan Ave., Gold Coast, Chicago, IL 60611; (312) 527-1010; candyality.com; Candy; $. This trio tempts with a selection of retro candy, like Necco wafers, as well as by-the-pound gummies and fudge. Other outposts are at 3425 N. Southport Ave., (773) 472-7800, and in Water Tower Place, 835 N. Michigan Ave., (312) 867-5500, the latter featuring a candy art and artifacts museum within.

Dulcelandia Del Sol, 4616 S. Kedzie Ave., Brighton Park, Chicago, IL 60632; (773) 247-4355; dulcelandia.com; Candy/Mexican; $. Piñata-adorned, packed with party favors, and popular as all get-out, this Mexican candy shop imports an impressive array of sweet and spicy treats, among them giant bonbons, marzipan, and dulce de leche wafers. There are several locations scattered throughout the city. **Additional locations:** Chicago, 3300 W. 26th St., (773) 522-3816, 3411 W. Irving Park Rd., (773) 279-9762, and 3855 W. Fullerton Ave., (773) 235-7825; as well as in Aurora, 700 E. New York St., (630) 585-9330; and Melrose Park, 2009 W. Lake St., (708) 681-2946.

The Fudge Pot, 1532 N. Wells St., Old Town, Chicago, IL 60610; (312) 943-1777; fudgepotchicago.net; Candy; $$. These fresh-made confections—butter toffee, chocolate-covered strawberries, caramel apples—come from fourth-generation candy-makers, who make nearly a dozen fudge flavors daily, in addition to dark, white, and milk chocolate candies in every imaginable shape.

Katherine Anne Confections, 2745 W. Armitage Ave., Logan Square, Chicago, IL 60647; (773) 772-1330; Candy; $. Creative chocolates are the name of the game at Katherine Duncan's hot-spot, featuring a roster of 175 seasonal flavors, including olive oil truffles made from Scrumptious Pantry's single-grove olive oil, lavender-lemon caramels, and loose-leaf black tea and butter-cookie marshmallows. However, all of them are possibly outshone by thick, rich hot chocolate.

Long Grove Confectionery, 220 Robert Parker Coffin Rd., Long Grove, IL 60047; (847) 634-0080; longgrove.com; Candy; $$. Embark on a tour of the factory, 333 Lexington Dr., Buffalo Grove, (847) 459-0269, or relive childhood memories at the store, choosing from pecan myrtles, sprinkle-topped crispie pops, and hand-dipped chocolate-covered strawberries. Pay mind to the brown bag–baked apple pie as well.

Margie's Candies, 1960 N. Western Ave., Bucktown, Chicago, IL 60647; (773) 384-1035; margiescandies.com; Candy/Ice Cream; $.

This vintage soda fountain, which opened its doors in 1921, is a place where nostalgia meets a new generation of sundae slicker. Spiked with wafer cookies, the candy-colored creations arrive in clamshell-like bowls with hot fudge on the side, and they're churned out until quite late. Signature chocolate confections (and rather forgettable sandwiches) may be procured here and at its North Center offshoot, 1813 W. Montrose Ave., (773) 348-0400.

Mr. Kite's Chocolate, 6 W. Maple St., Gold Coast, Chicago, IL 60610; (312) 664-7270; Candy; $. Take a break from the Rush Street crush for Dominick Kite's massive caramel apples, sublime s'mores, and chocolaty sponge candy, all made on-site. Custom creations are an option as well, provided you plan in advance.

Old Fashioned Candies, 6210 Cermak Rd., Berwyn, IL 60402; (708) 788-6669; oldfashionedcandiesinc.com; Candy; $$. Family-owned and frequented for more than four decades, this nostalgic candy store specializes in chocolate-covered strawberries, French creams, and green, milk, and dark chocolate mint fluffs that put more-recognized Frangos to shame.

Sea + Cane Sweets, seaandcane.com; Candy; $$. Seek out this small-batch, sister-run operation for hazelnut-stuffed chocolate salami inspired by Italy's *salame al cioccolato*; "blue cheese" truffles made from blueberry-stippled white chocolate; and "hotties," hot chocolate spoons in orange spice, chipotle cinnamon, and strawberry–pink pepper flavors.

Terry's Toffee, 1117 W. Grand Ave., Near West Side, Chicago, IL 60642; (312) 733-2700; terrystoffee.com; Candy; $. The English toffee from Michael Frontier and Terry Opalek makes a regular appearance in Academy Awards gift bags. Here, it's joined by Grandma McCall's other fabled recipe—Wackerpop, toffee-covered popcorn that's drizzled with chocolate. Find, too, biscotti blanketed in toffee and chocolate and toffee ice cream that's only available on-site.

Vosges Haut-Chocolat, 520 N. Michigan Ave., Gold Coast, Chicago, IL 60611; (312) 644-9450; vosgeschocolate.com; Candy; $$. Experimental chocolates made a name for this artisan chocolatier selling chocolate-bacon truffles, stout-caramel bars, and balsamico beauties to the masses, here and in Northbridge Mall, 951 W. Armitage Ave., (773) 296-9866, and in O'Hare terminals one and three.

Windy City Sweets, 3308 N. Broadway, Lakeview, Chicago, IL 60657; (773) 477-6100; windycitysweets.com; Candy; $. Blueberry cheesecake ice cream, chocolate-covered nuts, and boxed chocolates give way to chocolate-dipped oranges and apricots, chocolate-covered cherries, and candy-coated pretzels at this endearing indulgence.

Ice Cream, Ice, Custard & Gelato

Black Dog Gelato, 859 N. Damen Ave., Wicker Park, Chicago, IL 60622; (773) 235-3116; blackdogchicago.com; Gelato; $. Dessert darling Jessica Oloroso, who earned chops as the pastry chef at Stephanie Izard's Scylla, started supplying her atypical, amazing gelato to the city's best restaurants. These days, her hot-pink storefront also dispenses the inventive, ever-changing flavors. Not to be denied is the allure of zippy, goat cheese–caramel–cashew and salty peanut flavors. A good case can be made for the smoky, creamy, bacon-dipped whiskey gelato bar, too. Creative sodas and gelato cookie sandwiches are also available. It's also at 1955 W. Belmont Ave., (773) 235-3116.

Bobtail Ice Cream, 2951 N. Broadway, Lakeview, Chicago, IL 60657; (773) 880-7372; bobtailicecream.com; Ice Cream; $. There's a nostalgic feel to this home-grown soda fountain with house-made ice cream. Signature Sunset (Merlot with dark chocolate chips) and Daley Addiction (vanilla with butter-fudge swirl) are standouts. Even Sox fans may succumb to the Cubby Crunch, vanilla rife with toffee, Oreo chips, and sprinkles. Design-your-own sundaes allow for self-expression, while coffee concoctions provide a cool weather warm-up. You'll also find it at 1114 Central Ave., Wilmette, (847) 251-0174.

Capannari Ice Cream, 10 S. Pine St., Mount Prospect, IL 60056; (847) 392-2277; capannaris.com; Ice Cream; $. Nestled in a historic general store, this quaint parlor makes its own frozen treats, including scoops of rich hazelnut ganache. Expect over-the-top creamy, standard flavors like chocolate, cake batter, and cookie dough, but don't shy away from lesser-knowns, such as lavender-honey, Nestlé-inspired Drumstick, or chocolate chile pepper. Ice-cream samplers, packed in dry ice, may be shipped.

Cunis Candies, 1030 E. 162nd St., South Holland, IL 60473; (708) 596-2440; Ice Cream; $. The homemade ice cream—including first-rate, seasonal peach and blueberry—comes with a dose of nostalgia at this South Suburban super scooper. Whatever the time of year, real-deal sundaes—topped with a gorgeous goo of chocolate fudge—do more than fill a void. The hand-dipped chocolates are knock-outs, too.

Gayety's Chocolates & Ice Cream Co., 3306 Ridge Rd., Lansing, IL 60438; (800) 491-0755; gayetys.com; Ice Cream; $. Scoops, ice-cream pies, and old-fashioned sundaes—as well as shippable, hand-dipped chocolates—define this South Suburban icon. The dense, hand-churned ice cream—rich with 14 percent butterfat—includes flavors from tropical banana, strawberry cream, and vanilla bean to seasonal peach or coconut during summer. Its candies are available here and at other area locations, including Horseshoe Casino in Hammond, IN, and the gift shop of the Fairmont Chicago.

Highland Queen Drive-In, 1511 W. 55th St., La Grange Highlands, IL 60525; (708) 246-1846; Ice Cream; $. Those who grew up in these 'burbs encountered this institution; others should seek it out. The old-time not-so-quick-serve is hopping during summer—and after Little League games—so expect a wait for your cherry-dipped soft-serve cone, pineapple shake, and chocolate malt. The cooked fare is passable at best.

The Jam House, 1854 W. 18th St., Pilsen, Chicago, IL 60608; (312) 243-5745; Shaved Ice; $. *Raspados* (shaved ice), popular in Jalisco, Mexico, have a cooling effect at this Pilsen storefront from a husband-and-wife team. Mix and match flavors—mango and pineapple, perhaps—layering them with house-made jams, such as guava, kiwi, or mamey. Fresh-squeezed fruit and vegetable juices and smoothies are among the other quenchers. Lovely *tortas,* avocado wraps, and *molletes* (bean-slathered, open-face sandwiches) offer sustenance.

Lagomarcino's, 1422 Fifth Ave., Moline, IL 61265; (309) 764-1814; lagomarcinos.com; Ice Cream; $. This quaint parlor and soda fountain enjoys a generations-old reputation for its fine, bittersweet hot fudge sundae and hand-made confections, dating back to 1908. Although it also serves sandwiches and salads, don't bother with that. Another one is at 2132 E. 11th St., Davenport, (563) 324-6137.

Lickity Split Frozen Custard & Sweets, 6056 N. Broadway, Edgewater,

Chicago, IL 60660; (773) 274-0830; lickitysplitchicago.com; Custard; $. Build malts, shakes, and concrete concoctions from the fresh, house-made custard—vanilla, chocolate, seasonal lemon—at this Edgewater shop with checked floors and a retro feel. Brownies, scones, pies, and cupcakes from local bakers are other perks.

Mario's Italian Lemonade, 1068 W. Taylor St., Little Italy, Chicago, IL 60607; No phone; Italian Ice; $. It's possible to mark the seasons by the operation of this 1954 family-run fixture, turning out the best lemony, slushy, zest-specked Italian ice early May through September 15. (Needless to say, the other fruit-based creations—watermelon, straw-berry, tutti frutti, cantaloupe—are equally sublime.) This place embodies Chicago in so many ways; to this day, a cross-section of Chicago floods it on hot summer nights. Some advice: Skip dessert elsewhere, choosing this as your nightcap when meals at *cucinas* wind down.

Miko's Italian Ice/Mike's Flipside, 3000 W. Lyndale St., Logan Square, Chicago, IL 60647; (773) 645-9664; mikositalianice .com; Italian Ice; $. Enjoy Italian ice in a rainbow of flavors—from grapefruit and orangezilla to green tea, tamarind, and cherry—at this family-run, seasonal operation, which closed up shop when it's cold. A second address—1846 N. Damen Ave., (773) 645-9664, flipsidechicago .com—morphs into Mike's Flipside when it's cold. That's when its chalkboard menu hosts hand-poured coffee, grilled cheese on home-made bread, and kale burgers.

Original Rainbow Cone, 9233 S. Western Ave., Beverly, Chi-cago, IL 60643; (773) 238-7075; rainbowcone.com; Ice Cream; $. You don't have to wait for its appearance at the Taste of Chicago to enjoy treasured chocolate, strawberry, Palmer House (cherry), pista-chio, and orange-sherbet beauties, served seasonally from March to

November in a vintage soda-shop setting. Cakes and a handful of other scoops are available as well.

The Original Scoops, 608 W. 31st St., Bridgeport, Chicago, IL 60616; (312) 842-3300; scoops1.com; Ice Cream; $. Tap your inner child (or glutton) with classic cones, sundaes, and gut-busting banana splits, crafted from 32 flavors of hand-packed ice cream. When in need of a warm-up, turn to the array of coffee concoctions.

The Plush Horse, 12301 S. 86th Ave., Palos Park, IL 60464; (708) 448-0550; theplushhorse.com; Ice Cream; $. Truth be told, the cones at this 1937 parlor are excessively large, but the cases filled with homemade, candy-colored 'screams—rum raisin, blue moon, black cherry, cake batter—simply can't be denied. You'll also find gelato, shakes, malts, and other sweet treats. When it's warm, get your licks in on the quaint patio, as the nostalgic interior is usually jam-packed.

Scooter's Frozen Custard, 1658 W. Belmont Ave., Roscoe Village, Chicago, IL 60657; (773) 244-6415; scootersfrozencustard.com; Custard; $. Old-fashioned in feel, this custard shop with a walk-up window serves thick, slick chocolate, vanilla, and specialty flavors (like Reese's). They're also employed in a host of blended concretes, shakes, brownie and turtle sundaes, and malts. You know what? The hot dogs are darn good, too.

Snookelfritz Ice Cream, PO Box 146536, Chicago, IL 60614; (773) 575-4449. German for "ice cream," Nancy Silver's chef-driven certified-organic retail operation arose after graduating from the Culinary Institute of America. She also makes her own waffle cones as vessels for maple-candied pecan, salted caramel–apple, strawberry-honey nougat, rhubarb–crème fraîche, and rosemary–honey–goat cheese scoops, which may be sampled, purchased by the pint, or enjoyed in sandwich form at Green City Market.

Village Creamery, 4558 Oakton St., Skokie, IL 60076; (847) 982-1720; villagecreamery.com; Ice Cream; $$. The creative scoops never cease to amaze at this Far East–inspired ice-cream parlor from Lito Valeroso. Go on an adventure with varieties such as *buko*, purple yam, or avocado with sweetened young coconut. Or play it safe with mint chip or orange sherbet. Also of note are the bubble teas, shaved ice, and jolting cappuccino with tapioca pearls. There is a second installment at 8000 Waukegan Rd., Niles, (847) 965-9805.

Farm Fresh

Eating locally isn't always easy to do in Chicago—the weather poses a challenge for at least half the year. The good news is many small family farms share a deep-seated belief: Delicious, wholesome edibles are tantamount to a healthy future. These farmers are busy cultivating a rich food culture; meanwhile, restaurant menus read like a who's who, upending the notion of chefs-as-rock-stars and putting more focus where it belongs: on producers.

Learn more about area options at **The Local Beet,** the localbeet .com, a source for practical sustainably minded outlets and advice.

Local Farms

Arnolds Farm, 997 N. Salem Rd., Elizabeth, IL 61028; (815) 858-2407; arnoldsfarm.com. This hilly, family-run farm is located in the picturesque Apple River Valley en route to Galena. It offers pasture-raised, grass-fed, and grain-finished beef; Duroc, Berkshire, and Chester White–bred pork; and all-natural lamb and poultry. All of the meat is free of chemicals, hormones, and antibiotics and is sold by the whole animal, side, mixed package, and individual cut.

Caveny Farm, 1999 N. 935 East Rd., Monticello, IL 61856; (217) 762-7767; cavenyfarm.com. The bird is the word at this poultry farm, which is dedicated to raising heritage-breed Bourbon Red turkeys—sold straight-up or smoked—as well as Rouen ducks and American Buff geese. The juicy, rich poultry is typically sold in advance of slaughter and delivered to pickup points in Chicago. Alternately, poultry may be grabbed directly from the farm.

Cedar Valley Sustainable Farm, 1985 N. 3609th Rd., Ottawa, IL 61350; (815) 431-9544; cedarvalleysustainable.com. Jody and Beth Osmund are behind this idyllic, old-timey plot. Consider signing up for its affordable CSA meat-share program, which includes a mixture of fresh, farm-raised eggs and hormone- and antibiotic-free beef, pork, and chicken. And plan on visiting when field days, festivals, cookouts, and tours are scheduled. Sometimes there are hayrides and bonfires on the farm, too.

Dietzler Farms, W4222 CR A, Elkhorn, WI 53121; (262) 642-7665; dietzlerbeef.com. Some of the area's most coveted beef comes from here. The face behind this family-owned specialty beef ranch—located about 90 miles northwest of the city—is Michelle Dietzler, a spa-journalist-turned-farmhand. Call in advance to arrange a visit, and keep your eyes peeled for beef-centric farm dinners, which feature fare prepped by top Chicago restaurateurs. They're held during summer in a light-strung former dairy barn.

Epiphany Farms Enterprise, 23676 800 North Rd., Downs, IL 61736; (309) 378-2403; epiphanyfarms.com. Farm-to-fork is the mantra at this labor of love, owned by Culinary Institute of America grad Ken Myszka and his wife, Nanam Yoon Myszka. Ken worked under Thomas Keller and Guy Savoy in Las Vegas before having, well, an epiphany. Joined by Stu Hummel, who worked under Joël Robuchon, the crew now presides over Station Two Twenty, 220 E. Front St., Bloomington; (309) 828-2323. The sustainable farm also welcomes visitors, the more hard-core of whom may spend the day doing a hands-on, work-and-learn experience.

ILLINOIS HONEY

Beehives are abuzz all over town. Those interested in how-tos can find information on classes, events, webinars, and seminars by contacting the Cook-DuPage Beekeepers Association (cookdupagebeekeepers.com). You can also score some pretty sweet stuff from these ventures.

Belfry Bees & Honey, belfrybees.com, is a collection of honeybee apiaries scattered throughout Illinois's Fox River Valley. Score the sweet nectar or find out about educational programming online.

Chicago Honey Co-op, chicagohoneycoop.com, is an urban beekeeping cooperative with an apiary in the North Lawndale community. It employs sustainable practices, while offering job training for the underemployed. Its products—which include everything from honey to lip balm and candles—are sold at Green City Market, by CSA, and online. It also holds beekeeping classes.

Heritage Prairie Farm, heritageprariefarm.com, produces several varieties of Bron's Bee Company all-natural honey, including versions laced with lavender, cinnamon, or rosemary.

HoneyGirl Honey, honeygirlhoney.com, produces honey bears, containers of honey, and honey straws in Fullton, IL.

Genesis Growers, 8373 E. 3000 South Rd., St. Anne, IL 60964; (815) 953-1512; genesis-growers.com. Vicki Westerhoff's heirloom vegetable–driven, direct-market farm hosts an April through December CSA program, using hoop houses to extend the growing season. Drop-offs of everything from sunchokes and daikon to Asian greens, dry beans, and eggs take place throughout Chicago and the suburbs; produce from the north-central Illinois farm is also sold at farmers' markets.

Grazin' Acres, 29493 E. 400 North Rd., Strawn, IL 61775; (815) 688-3486; grazinacres.com. Terry and Judy Bachtold raise a small herd of grass-fed cattle without the use of hormones, antibiotics, or steroids. The result is deeply flavorful, lean beef with an appealing minerality. Call ahead to visit the property, where you'll learn about the labor-intensive rotational grazing process, importance of a stress-free environment for animals, and the family's steadfast commitment to sustainable agriculture. The meat is sold in advance of butchering by the whole animal, side, quarter side, and individual cut.

Green Earth Farm, 8308 Barnard Mill Rd., Richmond, IL 60071; (815) 403-7735; greenearth farm.org. Fans of heritage-breed meat will have a field day at this spot, which raises Narragansett, Royal Palm, and Bourbon Red turkeys, plus pasture-raised, heritage-breed chickens and eggs listed on the American Livestock Conservancy breed list. Heritage ducks (Rouens, Swedish, and Pekin) and geese are available, too. Its CSA is offered on a first-come, first-served basis.

Growing Power, 2215 W. North Ave., Chicago, IL 60647; (773) 486-6005; growingpower.org. It may be headquartered in Milwaukee, but Growing Power has a significant presence in Chicago proper. Local projects range from a community garden at 3333 S. Iron St. in the Bridgeport neighborhood to an urban agriculture *potager* at Grant Park and a half-acre farm in Jackson Park utilizing a biological worm system approach. The latter is also the site of a community garden, where workshops educate the farm-curious about composting, vermicomposting, and vegetable growing. Check out its "market basket" program to get a taste.

Harvest Moon Farms, PO Box 302, Viroqua, WI 54665; (773) 472-7950; harvestmoonorganics.com. This 20-acre, certified organic farm is located in west-central Wisconsin's driftless region, at the South Fork of the Bad Axe River. Beginning in November, it offers a CSA of cellar crops, such as potatoes and winter squash, bolstered by homemade egg noodles, beans, and eggs. It also provides 12-week home delivery in summer through Peapod. Its produce emphasizes Ark varieties, endangered fare identified by Slow Food International. Beyond that, its farm-to-school programs teach kids about the benefits of working the land.

Heartland Meats, 204 E. US 52, Mendota, IL 61342; (815) 538-5326; heartlandmeats.com. This specialist raises long-lashed, black-nosed Piedmontese cattle. The resulting meat from Pat and John Sondgeroth's humanely run farm appears at Green City Market and the Evanston Farmers' Market. Its products are also sold at **Hyde Park Produce** (p. 248).

Henry's Farm, 432 Grimm Rd., Congerville, IL 61729; (309) 965-2771; henrysfarm.com. This petite heavyweight grows 688 types of vegetables—many of them heirloom—on a small, sustainable plot in the Mackinaw River Valley of central Illinois. Its CSA program consists of fresh-picked finery—cabbages, sweet corn, mizuna—that's free of GMOs, pesticides, herbicides, and synthetic fertilizers. Its grub also makes the rounds at markets, such as the Evanston Farmers' Market. Watch for its annual potluck and tour, held in early fall.

Kinnikinnick Farm, 21123 Grade School Rd., Caledonia, IL 61011; (815) 292-3288; kinnikinnickfarm.com. A powerhouse on 40 acres of certified organic land, Kinnikinnick is situated 80 miles northwest of Chicago. Its ingredients run rampant on Chicago restaurant menus and appear at farmers' markets citywide. Growing everything from Minestra Nera greens to purslane, Helios Gold radishes, and Cherokee Purple tomatoes, it also hosts occasional events at the farm. Incidentally, many of its seeds have been sourced from small companies in Italy.

Living Water Farms, 29695 E. 100 North Rd., Strawn, IL 61775; (815) 848-2316; livingwaterfarms.net. This small family farm is run by the Kilgus and Schneider families, and it's anchored by a geo-thermal greenhouse that makes grown-year-round, chemical-free produce possible. Advance orders can be made for its unusual salad greens (Red Lollo Rosa, Bronze Arrowhead), watercress, daikon, pea shoots, and cucumbers—not to mention borage, edible violets, and anise hyssop. Farm tours are sometimes offered; farm fans also may call ahead to arrange a visit.

Mint Creek Farm, 1693 E. 3800 North Rd., Stelle, IL 60919; (815) 256-2202; mintcreekfarm.com. Consider Harry and Gwen Carr's 220-acre farm your go-to for grass-fed lamb. It utilizes traditional, rotational grazing techniques on lush prairie pastures, resulting in incomparable lamb shank, luxe legs, and sultry stews. The eastcentral Illinois farm has a CSA, appears at several markets, and ships meat nationally. Organically fed veal, beef, pork, and goat are options as well.

Moore Family Farm, 2013 N. 1950 East Rd., Watseka, IL 60970; (815) 432-6238; moorefamilyfarm.com. Grass-fed beef, veal, and lamb as well as pastured pork, duck, turkey, and chicken is the focus at this pesticide-free plot. Pork and veggies as well as Pekin ducks are finds, too, and may be picked up at the farm by appointment.

Nichols Farm & Orchard, 2602 Hawthorn Rd., Marengo, IL 60152; (815) 568-6782; nicholsfarm.com. Practically a household name around these parts, Nichols is a champion on the farmers' market scene. The 250-acre fruit and vegetable farm propagates a staggering array of unique varieties, such as tangy Black Pineapple tomatoes, Rat Tail radishes, and Fordhook lima beans. It is known to host farm dinners, too.

Making Connections

Not-for-profit **FamilyFarmed.org,** 7115 W. North Ave., #504, Oak Park, IL 60302; (708) 763-9920; is making a difference in Chicagoland by connecting local food producers with regional buyers and consumers. It also developed a Buy Local campaign and the Local Organic Initiative, along with the FamilyFarmed EXPO, a grower gathering that takes place annually. Visit its website (familyfarmed.org) to find local foods and CSAs and to learn about local family farms. And be sure to save the date for the Good Food Festival & Conference, goodfoodfestivals.com, a springtime symposium and workshop in one.

Oriana's Oriental Orchard, 8429 N. Harding Ave., Skokie, IL 60076; (847) 673-9175; asianpearfarm.com. Oriana Kruszewski grows over a dozen varieties of Asian, Japanese, and Korean pears—plus pawpaws, persimmons, and Chinese medicinal greens—on her plot. She also harvests walnuts and sells dried fruits, and you can buy fruit trees directly from her.

Phoenix Bean Tofu, 5438 N. Broadway, Chicago, IL 60640; (773) 784-2503. Jenny Yang makes small-batch silky, cholesterol- and gluten-free tofu from Illinois-grown soybeans. She also produces soy milk and bean sprouts. Find her products seasonally at Green City Market.

Plapp Family Organics, 23544 McQueen Rd., Malta, IL 60150; (815) 825-2589. Over a century old, this farm raises ducks, chickens, pigs, and sheep, producing most of its own soy, wheat, barley, oats, and corn to feed livestock. Look for its grains, popcorn, meat, and poultry at Green City Market.

Prairie Fruits Farm and Creamery, 4410 N. Lincoln Ave., **Champaign, IL 61822; (217) 643-2314; prairiefruits.com.** Illinois's first farmstead cheese-making facility fashions fluffy, fresh chèvre and gooey, bloomy-rind goat cheeses as well as Camembert-style creations from the milk of Nubian and La Mancha goats, which thrive on a foraged diet. It also grows seasonal fruits and berries, including white-fleshed peaches and black currants, in a certified organic orchard. Plan to attend one of its idyllic farm breakfasts and dinners from May through November—overseen by on-farm chef Alisa DeMarco, a Culinary Institute of America grad. Goats are available for purchase as well.

Prairie Pure Cheese, PO Box 805, Belvidere, IL 61008; (815) **568-5000; prairiepurecheese.com.** This cooperative between a small dairy and its veterinarian produces artisan cheeses, its specialty being Butterkäse (sample it in crepes and paninis at Green City Market). It also produces mild, aged cheddar, feta, blue, and Swiss cheeses.

Q7 Ranch, 22106 Anthony Rd., Marengo, IL 60152; (815) 219-**9356; q7ranch.com.** Family-run Quarter Seven Ranch (aka Q7) specializes in grass-fed beef from cattle that roam and graze on 1,000 acres of native grass pastures, less than 60 miles from the Loop. Purchase meat online for delivery, or find it on menus all over town, including at **Girl & the Goat** (p. 106) and **The Butcher & Larder** (p. 262). FYI: It sells all-natural pet food, too.

Radical Root Farm, 147 Westerfield Pl., Apt. C, Grayslake, IL **60030; (815) 830-6653; radicalrootfarm.com.** Responsible for growing over 50 kinds of vegetables throughout the spring, summer, and fall, this heirloom-centric offering has a CSA. Plus, it cultivates and sells medicinal herbs.

Seedling Orchard, 6717 111th Ave., South Haven, MI 49090; (269) 227-3958; seedlingfruit.com. A staple growing more than 75 types of fruit, including many heirloom varieties, century-old Seedling brims with apples, peaches, pears, plums, and nectarines. Its cider—which may be purchased at the Green City, Lincoln Square, and Wicker Park farmers' markets—is fantastic. Seedling is also a working dairy, one that makes cheese from the milk of its Nubian and La Mancha goats, plus pints of gelati and sorbetti, too. Come for educational farm tours in season, and consider signing up for its diverse CSA.

Spence Farm, 2959 N. 2060 East Rd., Fairbury, IL 61739; (815) 692-3336; thespencefarm.com. Marty and Chris Travis's influence on local food culture is far-reaching. In addition to running the oldest family farm in Livingston County, IL, they raise heritage-breed animals (Jacob's sheep, Dexter cows, Black Cayuga ducks); grow crops in two hoop houses on the farm; and reintroduce rare produce—such as roasted, milled Iroquois White Corn—for consumption. Meanwhile, their son, Will, makes maple syrup in a sugarhouse built with a grant from the Frontera Farmer Foundation. The inspiring farmstead also holds educational programs at a facility on-site.

Tempel Farm Organics, 17970 W. Millburn Rd., Old Mill Creek, IL 60083; (847) 244-5330; tempelfarmsorganics.com. Sustainable, organic agriculture is key at this diversified, 65-acre farm, where pros grow vegetables, fruits, and cut flowers as well as produce pasture-raised poultry, honey, eggs, and all the feed grain for livestock. A roadside store is in the works; a CSA program is offered at present; and its grub appears at area farmers' markets, such as the one held in Logan Square.

Three Sisters Garden, (312) 399-5585. Tracey Vowell (**Frontera Grill** [p. 105], **Topolobampo** [p. 133]) and Kathe Roybal, restaurant industry veterans, changed career paths to run this sustainable

AN EPICENTER OF EDIBLES

Situated about two hours southwest of Chicago, rural Livingston County is home to something hidden in plain view: more than two-dozen small family farms doing curious things.

From entrepreneurial 11- and 13-year-old children growing their own chemical-free kohlrabi to farmers reviving lost heirloom seeds, raising heritage animals, and procuring wild pawpaws, nettles, and ramps coveted by chefs, many are members of the not-for-profit **Stewards of the Land,** thestewardsoftheland .com. Suffice it to say, they are a force to be reckoned with.

Members, residing within a 50-mile radius of Fairbury, IL, sell their crops to food enthusiasts, farmers' markets, and celebrity chefs. They also stock the produce section of **Dave's Supermarket,** 120 S. Third St., Fairbury, IL 61739; (815) 692-2822; davessupermarket.com; a quaint grocer with a fried chicken and pizza counter in back.

You can really immerse yourself in it all with events offered by the **Spence Farm Foundation,** spencefarmfoundation.org. It hosts everything from a chef camp to an intensive, hands-on foodie boot camp and "crop mob," when folks come to farms to till, plant, cultivate, weed, and harvest. Additionally, you can learn about the farm during periodic Chores and S'mores farm tours and beehive tours and workshops.

Kankakee farm, named for the Native American practice of growing corn, beans and squash simultaneously. They focus on specialty veg, like microgreens, heirloom tomatoes, and shelled-at-market beans. They're a source for *huitlacoche,* too. They sell their produce—and legendary oats, cornmeal, and dried beans—at Green City Market.

TJ's Pasture Free-Range Poultry, 2773 N. 1500 East Rd., Piper City, IL 60959; (815) 686-9200. Consider buying broad-breasted white turkeys from this pleasant, central Illinois poultry farm. Given plenty of room to roam, these birds are raised on a natural diet of chemical-free grass, and one free of animal by-products and antibiotics.

Triple S Farm, RR #1, Box 122A, Stewardson, IL 62463; (217) 343-4740; triplesfarms.com. It's a family affair at this all-natural, chemical-free, certified organic farm in east-central Illinois. In addition to growing veggies, it sells pork, poultry, and beef as well as beef sticks and free-range eggs via a home-delivery and pickup program.

Wettstein Organic Farm, 2100 US 150, Carlock, IL 61725; (309) 376-7291; wettsteinorganicfarm.wordpress.com. Located on 140 acres of certified organic land in central Illinois, this farm—which grows its own combination of soybeans, corn, and other grains as feed—provides poultry, pork, beef, and eggs directly to customers, all the while maintaining a low carbon footprint.

Farm Stands & Farms with Stands

Big John's Farm Stand & Greenhouse, 1754 E. Joe Orr Rd., Chicago Heights, IL 60411; (708) 758-2711; bigjohnsfarmmarket .com. Find quality plants and produce—from shelly beans and purple hull peas to garlic, onions, and okra—at this family-owned farm market. You may also pick your own beets, cabbage, tomatoes, and crowder peas, among other edibles, from July through October.

Bultema's Farmstand & U-Pick, 2785 E. Lincoln Hwy., Lynwood, IL 60411; (708) 758-1565; bultemasfarm standandgreenhouse.com. Whether

SUSTAINABLE FOOD FOR ALL

Situated in the Back-of-the-Yards neighborhood in a former meat-processing facility, **The Plant,** 1400 W. 46th St., Chicago, IL 60609; (773) 847-5523; plantchicago.com; is part aquaponic, outdoor, and mushroom farm. It also hosts a fish hatchery, shared kitchen, and food education facility. Attend a public tour on Thursday or Saturday at 2 p.m. or on Friday at 3 p.m. It'll explain how the zero-waste, closed loop system works. Also, consider attending workshops about hoop-house growing and home weatherization.

you're seeking winter cabbage, cauliflower, or beets, you'll find them here from May through October. In turn, vegetables may also be picked by the pound, half bushel, or full bushel beginning around the third week of May.

City Farm, 1204 N. Clybourn Ave., Chicago, IL 60610; (773) 821-1351; cityfarmchicago.org. This sustainable farm is perched between disparate neighborhoods: Cabrini-Green and the Gold Coast. It turns out over two-dozen varieties of vegetables and herbs, growing them in composted soil made from Chicago restaurant trimmings. A model for urban farming, it welcomes individuals and groups to its once-vacant lot as volunteers. Take a tour of the facility, which creates jobs and propagates the future of sustainable agriculture. Its riches appear on many Chicago menus. It also has a small on-site market stand that is open to the public. Another stand is in the works at the Washington Park Consortium, 57th Place and Perry Street.

Chicago High School for Agricultural Sciences, 3857 W. 111th St., Chicago, IL 60655; (773) 535-2788; chicagoagr.org. The Chicago Board of Education launched the school as part of a nationwide endeavor to foster jobs in the fields of agribusiness and agriscience. It offers classes on animal science, agricultural mechanics, food science, horticulture, landscape design, and farm finance. The student-run stand also sells what it grows, be it fresh, hand-picked sweet corn, pickles, or peppers.

Garden Patch Farms & Orchard, 14154 W. 159th St., Homer Glen, IL 60491; (708) 301-7720; gardenpatchfarms.com. Pick an extensive selection of fruits and vegetables when weather allows—typically June through October—at this farm. Fronted by a stand selling pre-picked potatoes, blackberries, gooseberries, and tomatoes, its garden and orchard stretch far behind. You may also buy feed for its chickens.

Goebbert's Pumpkin Farm & Garden Center, 40 W. Higgins Rd., South Barrington, IL 60010; (847) 428-6727; pumpkin farms.com. Keep your eyes peeled for the pumpkin silo—it'll guide you to a large selection of annuals and perennials, plus sweet corn, peppers, melons, and stone fruit. You can also pick up soil, compost, and mulch. The farm has an adjunct pumpkin patch at Route 47 and Reinking Road in Hampshire, where a roadside stand is open mid-July through October.

Heritage Prairie, 2N308 Brundige Rd., La Fox, IL 60119; (630) 443-8253; hpmfarm.com. A rarity in these parts, four-season growing takes place at this small farm. Come to its store for everything from beets and celeriac to summer squash, tomatillos, and turnips as well as year-round micro-greens, such as pac choi, pea tendrils, and shungiku. Its CSA is an option, too, and there is an apiary on-site. Also, it hosts farm dinners and serves as an idyllic wedding venue.

Ho-Ka Turkey Farm, 8519 Leland Rd., Waterman, IL 60556; (815) 264-3470; hokaturkeys.com. The Kauffman family has been raising turkeys since 1933 on green-minded land. Buy fresh birds in person Monday through Saturday at its store.

Kilgus Dairy, 21471 E. 670 North Rd., Fairbury, IL 61739; (815) 692-6080; kilgusfarmstead.com. Make a point to stop at this family-run, single-source Jersey cow dairy farm. Arranging tours of its farmstead is possible, and seeing the cows milked is quite something. While you're there, step inside the self-service country store for a lush, soft-serve ice-cream cone, viewing the bottling process through a large picture window between licks. You can also pluck wholesome, insanely rich, all-natural milk, chocolate milk, half-and-half, heavy cream, and drinkable yogurt from its coolers. Local cheese and meat are stocked in the refrigerator and small freezer as well. Pay is by the honor system; cash or personal checks are accepted.

McCarthy Farms, 10301 W. 159th St., Orland Park, IL 60462; (708) 349-2158; mccarthy farmstands.com. For Athena muskmelon, bicolored corn, and crisp orchard apples, pay an in-season visit to this farm. Come fall, you'll also find Howden Biggie pumpkins.

North Chicago Green Youth Farm, Greenbelt Forest Preserve, 2 miles north of Green Bay Road past Pulaski Memorial Drive/14th Street, Waukegan, IL 60085; (847) 835-8352; chicagobotanic.org/greenyouth farm. Support the student agriculture program of the Chicago Botanic Garden, which hosts a seasonal U-pick farmstand on Wednesday and Saturday from mid-July through early October. Produce is also sold at the Chicago Botanic Garden's farmers' market the first and third Sunday from early June through mid-October as well as a handful of stands around town.

Puckerville Pumpkins, 13332 Bell Rd., Lemont, IL 60439; (708) 508-0906; puckervillefarms.webs.com. In fall, blue and white pumpkins—as well as mini and giant varieties—abound at this picturesque patch.

R Family Farm, 6501 N. Boone School Rd., Poplar Grove, IL 61065; (815) 519-4341; r-family-farm.com. For traditional broad-breasted white and heritage-breed Bourbon Red turkeys, sniff out this poultry specialist. Cornish Cross broilers, goat, and Berkshire pork are options as well and may be picked up from the on-farm store, by CSA, or at area farmers' markets, such as the suburban Woodstock and Belvidere markets.

Random Acres Garden Center, corner of Roselle and Central Roads, Schaumburg, IL 60194; (847) 524-5296; randomacres .com. You'll find a bevy of locally grown produce—including green beans, corn, onions, and zucchini—at this family-run garden center and farm market. There's also a selection of pickled and canned fruits and vegetables from Door County, WI–based Wienke's.

River Valley Mushroom Ranch, 39900 60th St., Burlington, WI 53105; (262) 539-3555; rivervalleykitchens.com. You can't be beat this farm store and market for button, cremini, shiitake, portobello, and oyster mushrooms—they're grown on-site, along with locally foraged morels; imperfectly shaped, multicolored farm-fresh eggs; local produce; and fresh-baked bread. Be sure to peruse the house-label salsas, extra-garlicky bread spread, and handcrafted foods. Grow-at-home mushroom kits and mushroom compost are also available.

Slagel Family Farm, 23601 E. 600 North Rd., Fairbury, IL 61739; (815) 848-9385; slagelfamilyfarm.com. The bucolic locale is known for naturally raising and processing beef, veal, goat, rabbit, turkey, pork, and lamb at its own facility. The high-quality, USDA-inspected products, which are additive-, hormone-, and steroid-free, may be sampled via a CSA or picked up at its retail butcher shop, located 5 miles from the farm at 103 E. Krack St., Forrest, IL 61741. Farm eggs and pet food are available, too.

Smits Farms, 3437 E. Sauk Trail, Chicago Heights, IL 60411; (708) 758-3838; smitsfarms.com. From mid-June through October, load up on sweet and hot peppers, summer and winter squash, melons, and leeks. Late-season gourds and pumpkins are available, too. You'll also find its produce and herbs—such as lemongrass, lavender, and lovage—at farmers' market locations like Daley Plaza, Lincoln Park, and Green City Market.

South Pork Ranch, 32796 E. 750 North Rd., Chatsworth, IL 60921; (815) 635-3414; south-pork-ranch.com. In addition to raising critically endangered Red Wattle hogs, Donna OShaughnessy and Keith Parrish's farm sells unpasteurized, non-homogenized raw milk direct to customers, who appreciate its purity and the presence of body-beneficial bacteria. (Find it at the farm proper.) Meanwhile, procure its antibiotic-, hormone-, and steroid-free, pasture-raised beef and pork from livestock that has been fed certified organic hay.

Twin Oak Meats, 11197 N. 2300 East Rd., Fairbury, IL 61739; (815) 692-4215; twinoakmeats.com. Gaining a reputation for its Duroc boar and Yorkshire Gilt hogs, crossbred and fed without by-products, this farm features a retail store chock-full of loin cuts, hickory-smoked bacon, and honey-glazed, spiral-sliced ham as well as roasts, brats, and country-style ribs. While you're at it, pick up some pig's ears and fresh-frozen femur bones for pets. Some items, like crown roast of pork and baby-back ribs, must be special-ordered a few weeks in advance.

GROWING GREATS

Nothing beats padding out to your backyard, barefoot, to pluck tomatoes, peppers, and lettuce for a fresh-as-can-be salad. Thankfully, there are amazing spots to purchase fruit and vegetable plants, both individually and by the flat.

Worthy of a day trip: **Woldhuis Farms Sunrise Greenhouse,** 10300 E. 9000 North Rd., Grant Park, IL 60940; (815) 465-6310; woldhuisfarms.com. Featuring a labyrinth of interconnected, fragranced greenhouses flush with bright, unique annuals, it also grows from seed a stunning selection of unusual heirloom and hybrid vegetables and herbs. Sure, you'll find Sugar Baby watermelons, bush pickles, and collards, but you'll also unearth scorching Bhut Jolokia peppers, Green Sausage and Great White tomatoes, and herbs from rue to costmary, comfrey, and epazote. Come early (it gets crowded) and grab a map, then fortify on hot dogs topped with sour-pickle relish and lemon shakeups from the snack stand.

Provided you need a quicker fix for your perennials, vegetable and herb plants, cacti, and succulents, however, head to **Ted's Greenhouse,** 16930 S. 84th Ave., Tinley Park, IL 60487; (708) 532-3575; tedsgreenhouse.com. You'll find potted chervil and curry leaf, borage and burnet as well as moujean tea, cardoons, and artichokes for planting in plots.

Van Kalker Farms & Greenhouses, 1808 E. Joe Orr Rd., Chicago Heights, IL 60411; (708) 758-1732; vankalkerfarms.com. Filled with vibrant begonias, dahlias, impatiens, aromatic verbena, and annual grasses, you'll also find an array of tomatoes, peppers, and other veggies for sale during the growing season. Its produce also appears at the Park Forest and Oak Lawn farmers' markets—as well as at its sister location at 13169 E. 10500 North Rd., Grant Park, (815) 466-0234.

Countless farmers' markets operate throughout Chicago and its suburbs starting in May; note, though, that run dates and days of operation may vary by season. A good resource for tracking them down, using the event-search tool, is chicagofarmersmarkets.us. You may also call (312) 744-0565 or visit cityofchicago.org for location information. The majority of them run though October or November. Increasingly, some continue year-round indoors.

Bronzeville Community Market, 4400 S. Cottage Grove Ave., Bronzeville, Chicago, IL 60653. It may be small, but this Saturday market packs a punch. You'll find produce from nearby Washington Park/Dyett Green Youth Farm, baked items, and perfect little multicolored potatoes from Kap Farms.

Daley Plaza Farmers' Market, 50 W. Washington St., Loop, Chicago, IL 60602. It runs on Thursday from mid-May through mid-October in the heart of the Loop. This is a favorite among lunch-breakers, who seek respite from the workaday world by ogling vendors' flowers, meat, and produce, as well as baked goods, honey, and jarred treats.

Evanston Farmers' Market, University Place and Oak Avenue, Evanston, IL 60201; (847) 448-8138; cityofevanston.org. The festive gathering operates on Saturday from early May through early November. Pick out meat, milk, eggs, and Brunkow cheese, as well as kaleidoscopic produce, while listening to live musical acts.

Federal Plaza Farmers' Market, Adams and Dearborn Streets, Loop, Chicago, IL 60606. Operating on Tuesday mid-May

WINTER WARRIORS

Let's face it: Chicago winters are dreary at best, bone-chilling at worst. Fortunately, the edible movement assures we no longer live without green things half of the year. A handful of indoor markets help tide us over until spring.

Evanston Indoor Farmers' Market, Evanston Ecology Center, 2024 McCormick Blvd., Evanston; evanstonfarmersmarkets.org; allows you to score fresh mushrooms from River Valley Ranch and Sheekar Delights' baklava on Saturdays, early December through late April, indoors.

Faith in Place, faithinplace.org, and the Churches' Center for Land and People (CCLP), cclpmidwest.org, are behind a series of indoor winter farmers' markets, featuring provisions from small, local producers. The gatherings offer fresh produce as well as cheese, honey, syrup, meat, poultry, and canned goods. Watch, too, for brunches and other gatherings highlighting food made with local ingredients. The markets typically take place November through April and are held at various locations.

The Glenwood Sunday Market, The Glenwood Bar, 6962 N. Glenwood Ave.; glenwoodsundaymarket.org; moves indoors from early November to late May, featuring a bumper crop of root vegetables, baked goods, eggs, and grass-fed beef.

Green City Market, Peggy Notebaert Nature Museum, 2430 N. Cannon Dr., Chicago; (773) 880-1266; chicagogreencity market.org; moves inside on Saturdays from early November through late April, with cheese from Nordic Creamery, local cold-weather produce, and countless events—including a soul-warming soup series—featuring Chicago chefs.

through late October, you'll find fruits, veggies, plants, and flowers galore—all surrounded by the towering skyline.

Green City Market, Clark Street and Stockton Drive, Lincoln Park, Chicago, IL 60614; (773) 880-1266; chicagogreencitymarket .org. This is the granddaddy of local, organic, sustainable markets in Chicago, held Wednesdays and Saturdays from early May through October. In addition to having the largest selection of fresh-picked, unique produce, it hosts ongoing chef demonstrations, a farmer scholarship program, and a heritage and heirloom project. Its annual Locavore Challenge is celebrated, as is its beloved chef's barbecue, when nearly 100 restaurants band together to highlight farm-fresh products each July. During winter, Green City is held on Saturdays only, when it moves inside of the Peggy Notebaert Nature Museum, 2430 N. Cannon Dr.

Hyde Park Farmers' Market, cul-de-sac at 52nd Place and Harper Court, Hyde Park, Chicago, IL 60602; (312) 744-3315. It runs on Thursday from June through October. For fresh fare on the South Side, head to see these vendors, who sell the stalwarts as well as herbs, cut flowers, and preservative-free baked goods.

Logan Square Farmers' Market, 3111 W. Logan Blvd., Logan Square, Chicago, IL 60647; (773) 489-3222; logansquarefarmers market.org. There's a decidedly hip vibe at the Sunday market. It's smaller than many of the city markets but has the basics well covered. It's also a great spot to score morning bites, like pastries from **Cook Au Vin** (p. 320). Logan Square now operates an indoor winter market as well; it takes place at the Congress Theater, 2135 N. Milwaukee Ave., Sundays through late March.

Oak Park Farmers' Market, 460 Lake St, Oak Park, IL 60302; (708) 358-5780; oak-park.us/farmersmarket. Enter the parking lot

ROADTRIP-WORTHY PRODUCE

Worthy of a day trip is Madison's **Dane County Farmers' Market,** Madison, WI 53701; (608) 455-1999; dcfm.org; held Wednesdays around Capitol Square mid-April through early November. The year-round market moves indoors for the winter, while an additional Wednesday market takes place in the 200 block of Martin Luther King Jr. Boulevard mid-April through early November. Check the website for up-to-date info and special events, and don't rule it out in the winter, as non-stop growing takes place in hoop houses throughout the area. Plan ahead and attend the winter market breakfast, when $7 buys you a meal made from local farmers' market products, live music, and something to sip.

next to Pilgrim Church on the last Saturday of the month, May though October, and feel as though times are simpler. Swelling with fresh familiar and atypical produce, this weekly gathering has a following for its piping-hot doughnuts, passed though the church window and coated in powder or cinnamon sugars. Browse stalls offering artisan cheeses, canned goods, and honey, and linger over live music between bites of purchased produce.

Wicker Park and Bucktown Farmers' Market, 1500 N. Damen Ave., Wicker Park, Chicago, IL 60622; (773) 384-2672; wickerparkbucktown.com. On Sundays from early June through late October, you'll find a smallish selection of must-have produce, including apples and heirloom tomatoes, as well as baked goods and pretty, affordable fresh-cut flowers.

Culinary
Instruction

Some people want to sit and be served; others like to play with their food. For the latter, hands-on culinary instruction—from basic to specialized and advanced—is offered at formal institutions, restaurant kitchens, or cultural centers. If you endeavor to roll sushi, want to whip up an exotic company-appropriate curry—heck, even butcher a whole hog—there is a pro with expertise to impart.

Cooking Classes

Alliance Française de Chicago, 810 N. Dearborn St., Gold Coast, Chicago, IL 60654; (312) 337-1070; af-chicago.org. This cultural center is dedicated to fostering French relations, language, and cuisine, while offering a regular roster of wine- and gastronomy-related classes (cassoulet-concocting, wine and cheese pairings) and demonstrations for Francophiles, including those of the pint-size variety.

Bespoke Cuisine, 1358 W. Randolph St., West Loop, Chicago, IL 60607; (312) 455-8400; bespokecuisine.com. A full-fledged boutique caterer at heart, this culinary hub also hosts hands-on cooking classes and parties for singles, couples, and small groups with varying themes—be it bourbon-based, backyard barbecue–themed, or comfort food–centric. Classes may be customized, namely for private events for 15 or more.

Cakewalk Chicago, 1741 W. 99th St., Beverly, Chicago, IL 60643; (773) 233-7335; cakewalkchicago.com. If you come to stock up on pineapple pastry filling, Guittard chocolates, and luster dust, you may be lured into signing up for a sugar-sculpting or cupcake-making course at this sweet spot. Professional diploma courses are taught, too.

Calphalon Culinary Center, 1000 W. Washington Blvd., West Loop, Chicago, IL 60607; (312) 529-0100; calphalonculinarycenter .com. Both novices and experts plan private and corporate events amid sleek environs, where namesake cookware serves as backdrop decor and a chef's kitchen—in which more intimate, multicourse, customized menus are prepared—mimics the experience of cooking like pros.

Chez Madeline Cooking School, 425 Woodside Ave., Hinsdale, IL 60521; (630) 655-0355; chezm.com. A labor of love from cookbook author Madelaine Bullwinkel, who has taught the techniques of French cooking for more than three decades, this haven hosts classes on day-to-day cooking, coupled with topical gatherings and food tours to far-reaching destinations like the Côte d'Azur.

The Chopping Block, 222 Merchandise Mart Plaza, River North, Chicago, IL 60654; (312) 644-6360; thechoppingblock.net. Interactive, engaging options for the home cook abound at Shelley Young's state-of-the-art culinary confines. Offering everything from demos to hands-on instruction and wine classes with laid-back and boot-camp bents, classes are both traditional (knife skills) and more complex (pasta workshops, sushi). Themes for children, couples, and gals' nights out are furthered by affairs like a Sunday supper club. There is a second location at 4747 N. Lincoln Ave., (773) 472-6700.

Cook Au Vin, 2256 N. Elston Ave., Bucktown, Chicago, IL 60614; (773) 489-3141; cook-au-vin.com. This French portal features an on-site bakery and creperie turning out custom-made, Black Dog gelato–filled cakes and crackly baguettes. To the point, it also holds four-course, BYOB cooking classes revolving around seven themed menus. Custom catering is offered as well, and this kitchen may be reserved for parties and events.

Cooking Fools, 1916 W. North Ave., Bucktown, Chicago, IL 60622; (773) 276-5565; cookingfools.net. Head to this gourmet kitchen for takeout when you're too lazy to cook, and sign on to learn the art of fish, rice, or dumpling cookery when you're not. There's also a nice selection of specialty goods for sale, such as Tupelo honey, global wines, and sauces from La Cocina.

Cooking with the Best Chefs, Various, (224) 353-3300; bestchefs.com. An ongoing catalog of classes, demonstrations, and events—offered at many locations by countless chefs throughout northern Illinois—is met by restaurant tours, day trips, and local and regional food forays at this one-stop spot. Online registration is required.

Flavour Cooking School, 7401 W. Madison St., Forest Park, IL 60130; (708) 488-0808; flavourcookingschool.com. Whether you're a seasoned cook or just starting out, Denise Norton's approachable mealmaker educates on seasonal topics and ethnic cuisines, and simply offers fun. Subjects, while ever changing, may include noodles, grilling, and chicken 101. Also, boot camps, couples classes, and instruction for kids as young as 4 are provided.

Give Me Some Sugar, 2205 W. Belmont Ave., Roscoe Village, Chicago, IL 60618; (773) 281-3154; givesugar.com. Alessandra Sweeney reveals the sweeter side of life during once-monthly classes at TipsyCake, while offering private cake-decorating and candy-making instruction in-home. During the latter, participants can fancify a fondant cake.

Green City Market, Clark Street and Stockton Drive, Lincoln Park, Chicago, IL 60614; (773) 880-1266; chicagogreencitymarket .org. This indoor and outdoor farmers' market is the biggest and best in the city, and it features an endless array of culinary events. Demonstrations—hosted by top toques—cover topics such as snout-to-tail cooking and the making of manly meat and potatoes–type dishes.

A Kid's Kitchen, 1603 N. Aurora Rd., Naperville, IL 60563; (630) 983-3663; akidskitchen.com. Little chefs get their cook on at this peanut- and tree nut–free facility, hosting private and group lessons as well as birthday parties for those as young as age 3. Kid-size, professional-looking embroidered aprons and hats are available for purchase.

The Kids' Table, 2337 W. North Ave., Wicker Park, Chicago, IL 60647; (773) 235-2665; kids-table.com. Parents and kids find common ground at this family-friendly, health-minded locale, which offers a workshop for picky eaters, plus tutelage for tots, teens, grown-ups, and families. It also hosts parties and events.

Macy's on State Street, 111 N. State St., Loop, Chicago, IL 60602; (800) 329-8667; macys.com/culinarycouncil. The food-related activities are abundant at this spot with its own culinary council of big-name chefs. Workshops as well as tastings, food-and-wine pairings, and cookbook signings attract food fanatics to these digs. Afterward, stop at Seven on State—an upscale food court with celebs' quick-serve joints from Rick Bayless (Frontera Fresco), Takashi Yagihashi (Noodles by Takashi), and Marcus Samuelsson (Marc Burger). Macy's has several locations in the Chicago area.

Parties That Cook, Various; (888) 907-2665; partiesthatcook .com. Recognized for its corporate team-building events, this festive spot provides instruction in homes or at venues preordained by food-loving groups of families and friends. Additionally, hands-on cooking classes—some with a date-night focus—are hosted at spots like Charlie Baggs in the Belden.

The Second Floor, Fuller's Home & Hardware, 35 E. First St., Hinsdale, IL 60521; (630) 323-7750; fullerssecondfloor.com. Sign up for a range of educational classes—from family-style fêtes to lunch-and-learn, pizza- and bunch-based gatherings—held at the upper-level chef's studio of this upscale, West Suburban hardware store.

Sur la Table, 755 W. North Ave., Lincoln Park, Chicago, IL 60610; (312) 787-5111; surlatable.com. Those into cooking will be tempted by the electric gadgets, cutlery, and cooks' tools from this kitchen expert. Some advice: Avert your eyes and sign up for the Saveur cooking series instead. Additional classes cover everything from global cuisine to stylish entertaining. Consider the kids' camps as well. **Additional locations:** 55 S. Main St., Naperville, (630) 428-1110; 100 W. Higgins Rd., South Barrington, (847) 551-1090.

The Wooden Spoon, 5047 N. Clark St. Uptown, Chicago, IL 60640; (773) 293-3190; woodenspoonchicago.com. Come to eye cookware from Lodge, Le Creuset, and All-Clad, but stay for the vary-ing how-tos, which may include schooling in Latin, Caribbean, and mom-type cuisines. Private events may be arranged, and next-day knife sharpening is provided for a nominal, per utensil fee.

Young Chef's Academy, Glenbrook Market Place, 2825A Pfing-sten Rd., Glenview, IL 60026; (847) 715-9474; youngchefsacademy .com. It's never too soon to start wee ones on a culinary regimen—especially when it's as fun as the classes, kids' nights out, birthday parties, and summer camps offered here. They'll learn about kitchen safety, food preparation, and cooking and baking techniques. Best of all, they won't leave feeling duped into hard work. Kitchens may be kept peanut-free.

Cooking Schools

Chicago's Community Kitchens, Greater Chicago Food Depository, 4100 W. Ann Lurie Pl., Archer Heights, Chicago, IL 60632; (773) 843-5414; chicagosfoodbank.org. Teaching career-building kitchen skills since 1998, this food-service job-training center assists unemployed and underemployed Cook County residents. Its students make over 2,000 meals daily for after-school Chicago Food Depository Kids Cafes and the elderly. Guest chefs and presenters are a source of inspiration.

The French Pastry School, City Colleges of Chicago, 226 W. Jackson Blvd., Loop, Chicago, IL 60606; (312) 726-2419; frenchpastry school.com. Expect upper-crust pastry instruction—including full-time certificate programs like L'Art de la Pâtisserie—and continuing-education courses from this cooking school, which opens its doors for tours with advance registration.

The International Culinary School, Illinois Institute of Art–Chicago, 350 N. Orleans St., Near North Side, Chicago, IL 60654; (312) 280-3500; artinstitutes.edu/chicago. Degree, diploma, and certificate programs—including an Associate of Applied Science in Culinary Arts—are part of the curriculum at this hands-on learning environment. Visit its BackStage Bistro, (312) 777-7800, a student-operated restaurant, at which reservations are recommended.

Kendall College, 900 N. North Branch St., Goose Island, Chicago, IL 60642; (888) 905-3632; kendall.edu. Many a serious student gravitates to this culinary college, with schools of business, hospitality management, culinary arts, and early-childhood education. Its culinary instructors—who preside over degreed and certificate programs in 12 commercial kitchens and at 3 open-to-the-public dining rooms—have at least a decade of real-world managerial experience.

Le Cordon Bleu College of Culinary Arts, 361 W. Chestnut St., River North, Chicago, IL 60610; (888) 295-7222; chefs.edu/Chicago. Culinary students secure degrees and certificates adhering to European and North American culinary traditions, methods, and present-day cooking technologies at this educator.

Washburne Culinary Institute, City Colleges of Chicago, 740 W. 63rd St., Greater Grand Crossing, Chicago, IL 60621; (773) 602-5487; kennedyking.ccc.edu/washburne. Degree and certificate programs give graduates the skills they need to advance in the culinary and hospitality industries. Taste the fruits of their labor at the sedate **Parrot Cage** (p. 155) and Sikia in the Englewood neighborhood.

Wilton School of Cake Decorating & Confectionery Art, Chestnut Court Shopping Center, 7511 Lemont Rd., Darien, IL 60561; (630) 810-2888; wilton.com/classes. Providing instruction for professionals and nonprofessionals, this spot specializes in courses like artisan gelatin and fondant modeling as well as half-day workshops on starting your own cake biz. Also, check out its decorating camps for kids.

Bev Art Brewer & Winemaker Supply, 10033 S. Western Ave., Beverly, Chicago, IL 60643; (773) 233-7579; bev-art.com. Learn how to brew beer and make wine—or pick up the supplies needed to do it at home—at this spirited address. Its regularly offered, step-by-step classes yield batches of custom-labeled bottles (about 6 gallons for hops heads and 28 bottles for winos).

DANKhaus German Cultural Center, 4740 N. Western Ave., Lincoln Square, Chicago, IL 60625; (773) 561-9181; dankhaus .com. You needn't yodel to appreciate the definitive demonstrations—be it sausage-making or schnitzel, *krapfen,* or *rouladen* preparation—offered at this Deutsche destination, during which participants eat, drink, and receive recipes to take home.

The Glass Rooster, Various; info@ theGlassRooster.com; theglassrooster.com. Specializing in an age-old—if initially intimidating—culinary tradition, Laura McLaughlin comes to homes to teach the art of canning and preserving, bringing with her all the necessary produce and equipment, including jars, rings, lids, and cleaning supplies.

Green Spirit, 551 N. Ridge Blvd., Rogers Park, Chicago IL 60645; (773) 484-093; greenspiritliving.com. Check notions of raw-food-as-tree-bark at the door when attending the global raw-food workshops at this healthy hub from Living Light Culinary Arts Institute grad Linda Szarkowski. Instead, walk away with heat-free know-how, including the preparation of decadent desserts and Latin American and Italian fare.

Go, Go Gadget

As any good cook knows, using quality tools makes all the difference in the world. Thankfully, you can fulfill your needs (and wants) at these spots around town.

The Chopping Block, (312) 644-6360, thechoppingblock.net, for stainless-steel All-Clad pans, baking dishes, and gourmet goodies like saffron salt.

Northwestern Cutlery Supply, (312) 421-3666, northwestern cutlery.net, sells everything from two-handled cheese knives to extra-fine strainers, cast-iron cookware from Le Creuset, and Vitamix blenders. Knife-sharpening services are provided as well.

P.O.S.H., (312) 280-1602, poshchicago.com, stocks everything from vintage hotel silver to flea-market finds. Visits may yield a floral ashtray from Belgium, nostalgic Schweppes "Indian tonic" nut dishes from France, or mouth-blown Italian Army carafes.

1730 Outlet Company, (773) 871-4331, 1730outlet.com, has two Chicago-area locations selling TAG products, such as cake stands, chip-and-dip sets, kitchen towels, and dishes, at rock-bottom prices.

Woks 'n' Things, (312) 842-0701, a Chinatown treasure trove, sells not only its namesake implements, but also professional-grade cookware, chopsticks, sushi-making supplies, and pre-seasoned woks.

Naveen's Cuisine, 2325 W. North Ave., Wicker Park, Chicago, IL 60647; (773) 661-2696; naveenscuisine.com. Traveler, cook, and photographer Naveen Sachar teaches the techniques of Indian and Thai cuisines, while imparting the ins and outs of aromatic spices and cultural cooking techniques. Leave knowing how to create everything from madras murgh curry to vegetable *korma* and juicy kebabs.

Ranjana's Indian Cooking Class, 6730 S. Euclid Ave., South Shore, Chicago, IL 60649; (773) 355-9559; indiancookingclass.com. Unleash the bold flavors of Indian cuisine under the deft hand of Ranjana Bhargava, who hosts three-hour vegetarian classes for all skill sets in her home. Opt to take single classes or a more in-depth, four-class series. Or, arrange a custom, spice-centric dinner party based on Indian tapas or eggplant, prepared six ways.

Rebecca Wheeler, (773) 368-1336, rebeccawheeler.com. Rebecca hosts ethnic and regional classes, which trot from Chinese, Punjab, and Southern Indian–style vegetarian to the cuisines of Italy, France, and Southeast Asia. In addition to stints at Trotter's to Go and Trio, Wheeler has taught classes at Williams-Sonoma and is a staff member of **The Wooden Spoon** (p. 322). Be sure to inquire about her market and neighborhood food tours as well.

Food Fests &
Events

Some are charitable or themed; others prove downright strange. But
whether in deference to desserts or in reverence of ribs, food gatherings
are a way to unite bons vivants, uncover indigenous eats, and—often—
revel in seasonal delights. That's true in Chicago proper—and beyond.

February

Chicago Restaurant Week, choosechicago.com, is an annual
10-day restaurant "week" that takes place at more than 200 restaurants.
Expect specially designed, deeply discounted two- to four-course, fixed-
price meals during lunch. Some spots even throw in bottles of vino.

March

Chicago Chef Week, chicagochefweek.com, makes a case for
overindulgence. Special three-course lunch and dinner menus are
available at dozens of restaurants at cut-rate prices.

The Good Food Festival and Conference, goodfood festivals.com, is a gathering of food enthusiasts that features DIY workshops, artisan vendors, and a local food court. All sorts of events are held in conjunction with its occurrence, perhaps a kimchi challenge or urban farm tour by bus.

Localicious, goodfoodfestivals.com, is a food fête held in tandem with the Good Food Festival. Featuring food and drinks from top Chicago chefs, it also hosts musical acts.

April

Baconfest, (773) 257-3378, baconfestchicago.com, is a crazy-popular porcine party, dedicated to cured meat and featuring a who's who of Chicago chefs. During the event, pros whip up enough bacon-based foods, spirits, and desserts to, frankly, stuff a pig. For those who can't leave well enough alone, there are bacon-themed crafts on hand, too.

May

Chicago Craft Beer Week, chibeerweek .com, celebrates Chicago's burgeoning beer culture. Held in May during American Craft Beer Week, the citywide bash features tastings at bars, shops, and restaurants, plus beer dinners, brewery tours, book signings, and a slew of limited-release beers. There are pub crawls and drink specials aplenty, too.

Day and Night of the Living Ales, chibeer.org, is an annual, walk-around tasting featuring craft and cask-conditioned ales from Chicago breweries.

The Morel Mushroom Festival, (608) 739-3182, **muscoda .com,** takes place in the Dairy State's morel capital, Muscoda, a town situated along the winding Wisconsin River. Folks may sell or buy elusive morels around town from early to mid May. Then, during a mid-month festival, there's a carnival, horseshoe tournament, and helicopter rides as well as fried morels at its "mushroom headquarters."

The World's Largest Brat Festival, bratfest.com, takes places in Madison, WI, each Memorial Day weekend. In addition to lots o' brats, you'll find classic takes and veggie takes, plus plenty of milk, ice-cold soda, and brewskis to wash them down. The fête features bands, brat-themed souvenirs, an ice-cream booth, and fireworks as well.

June

Harvard Milk Days, (815) 943-4614, **milkdays.com,** takes place in Harvard, IL. It began with a small hay-wagon stage and street dancing. Now, it's a bona-fide bovine tribute, complete with a milk-drinking contest, pancake breakfast, and grilling competition as well as an endless spread of dairy-based food. Hop atop a camel for a ride, and check out the reptile exhibit, too.

Pretzel City Fest, (815) 232-2121, **pretzelcityusa.org,** arose after the circa-1869 Billerbeck Bakery brought pretzels to the town of Freeport, IL. (Its high school athletic team is even named for the salty snack.) During the event, merrymaking includes tractor and pony rides, food galore, and a pretzel-themed recipe contest.

The Rhubarb Festival, aledomainstreet.com, is a June extravaganza in Aledo, IL, during which over 12,000 rhubarb seeds are gifted; more than 20,000 pies filled with the stalky staple may be purchased; and samples of the sweet-tart perennial abound. Meanwhile, live music offers a diversion.

Ribfest Chicago, (773) 525-3609, ribfest-chicago.com, is a popular North Center jubilee that takes places each summer. Young and old converge over tangy, sauced ribs, prepared by 'cue restaurants citywide. Nearly two-dozen bands keep the vibe light, and a cook-off puts amateur grillers to the coals.

SausageFest Chicago, sausagekingchicago.com, showcases some of Chicago's tastiest encased meats. It's presided over by a Sausage King.

The Strawberry Festival, visitlonggrove.com, is a weekend affair, taking place in the city of Long Grove. Sample everything from strawberry doughnuts and drinks to chocolate-covered strawberries. There's live music, too, plus a pie-eating contest.

Taste of Randolph Street, (312) 666-1991, **westloop.org,** is in equal parts about cuisine from West Loop restaurants—including **bellyQ** (p. 96) and **Publican Quality Meats** (p. 267)—and indie rock. Dishes and beats usually drop mid-month.

July

The Green City Market Chef BBQ Benefit, (773) 880-1266, greencitymarket.org, is a popular, perpetually sold-out picnic showcasing farm-fresh food sizzled up by Chicago chefs. In addition to grilled grub, there's plenty of locally made beer, wine, and handcrafted cocktails. Profits support programming for the sustainable farmers' market.

National Cherry Festival, (231) 947-4230, cherry festival.org, is a weeklong event honoring Traverse City's famous fruit. In addition to parades and entertainment along Lake Michigan's shores, you can sample the bounty in every which way.

Pierogi Fest, (219) 659-0292, pierogifest.net, takes place in Whiting, IN, midsummer. Rife with walking, talking pastries and booty-shaking dumplings, it's presided over by a Polish princess, a dozen Rockette-esque Pieroguettes, and a Polish ambassador dubbed Polka-hontas. In other words, if you own a babushka, wear it.

Ribfest (Naperville), (630) 259-1129, ribfest.net, is a showcase of national pitmasters in suburban Naperville, luring thousands to gnaw on vendors' baby backs, tip back suds in strategically placed beer tents, and listen to live acts.

Roscoe Village Burger Fest, (773) 327-5123, rvcc.biz, is a patty-themed gathering featuring handhelds prepared by popular restaurants. There's live music, too.

Taste of Chicago, (312) 744-3315, tasteofchicago.us, is the city's signature crowd-thronged food festival, where sample portions of food are bought with tickets. There's also music from major acts, held on multiple stages.

Taste of Wisconsin, (262) 654-7307, tasteofwi.com, is an option for near-endless Dairy State nibbles and sips, in addition to garden workshops, cooking demonstrations, and nutritional seminars.

Windy City Ribfest, (312) 799-0354, is a gathering of ribbers, who compete for the title of tastiest racks in the Uptown neighborhood.

Brat Days, brat-days.com, pays homage to the encased sausage Sheboygan, WI, is known for. While munching on the snappy snacks, listen to live tunes, plenty of them nodding to eras past.

Burger Fest, homeofthehamburger.org, honors the "birthplace" of the burger in Seymour, WI. An idyllic town of 3,000 situated 15 miles west of Green Bay, it's where an 8,266-pounder was grilled. Besides mouthfuls of meat, the bash features hot-air balloon ascensions as well as a run, pony rides, a hamburger-themed parade, and an eating contest.

DeKalb Corn Fest, (815) 748-2676, cornfest.com, is among the state's oldest and last remaining free music festivals, making it a favorite among students from nearby Northern Illinois University. Come for the inflatables, carnival, and craft show, and stay for the beer garden and sweet corn boil, yielding free cobs during a specified time. Helicopter and biplane rides up the ante during the late-summer event.

The Mendota Sweet Corn Festival, (815) 539-6507, sweet cornfestival.com, is a butter-spiked ode to Del Monte sweet corn, which is cooked with the help of a vintage steam engine in the north-central Illinois town of Mendota. During it, festival-goers consume more than 50 tons' worth of ears. There's also a beer garden and flea market jam-packed with crafts.

National Blueberry Festival, blueberryfestival
.com, is an annual event honoring its namesake in
South Haven, MI. Come for the blueberry pancake
breakfast, and stay for the fish boil. There's also
a parade, arts and crafts show, and blueberry
bake-off.

The Rutabaga Festival, cumberland-wisconsin.com, is the
pride and joy of Cumberland, WI, come late summer. Curiously, it
includes an annual hot pepper–eating contest, too. Plus, a fly-, drive-,
or walk-in all-you-can-eat pancake breakfast takes place at the Cumberland Municipal Airport. The veg that inspires the gathering can be
found at a concurrent farmers' market.

Taste of the Nation, (800) 969-4767, ce.strength.org/chicago,
is Share Our Strength's culinary benefit, which aims to end childhood
hunger. Locally, the gathering culls Chicago's top chefs, pastry chefs,
and mixologists, who donate their time to prepare a belly-busting array
of edibles. Ticket sales, in their entirety, support Share Our Strength's
efforts.

The Urbana Sweet Corn Festival, (217) 344-3872, urbana
illinois.us/Sweetcorn_Festival, warrants a weekend getaway. In addition to an endless supply of hot, butter-soused corn, it features local
and national acts and a wrestling show.

Veggie Fest, (630) 955-1200, veggiefestchicago.org, is a veg-
focused food and music festival scheduled each August in Naperville.
Beyond health-conscious eats tinged with Thai, Indian, and kid-friendly
flavors, it welcomes speakers and lifestyle-oriented booths.

The Amish Cheese Country Festival, (800) 722-6474, arthurcheesefestival.com, takes place annually on Labor Day weekend in Arthur, IL. Festivities include a tractor pull, rat race, parade, and plenty of free cheese. It's also the site of a national cheese-eating competition and international cheese-curling championship, which involves scooting a cheese "stone" down a rink toward its target.

Apple Dumpling Days, elroylions.org, spur competition in the town of Elroy, WI. During the event, races take place on repurposed railroad beds. However, couch potatoes also are invited to gobble up its honorary treat.

Beef-a-Rama, beef-a-rama.com, is held each year in Minoqua, WI, complete with a Rump Roast Run, a beef-eating contest, and cooking competition featuring rare and well-done categories.

Cheese Days, (608) 325-7771, cheesedays.com, take place in Monroe, WI, each autumn. The event is loaded with family fun, beer, and—you guessed it—cheese, which appears in cream puffs, griddled sandwiches, and in cake form on a stick. Listening to polka bands, yodelers, and accordion players—or attending farm animal–related festivities—are all quintessential ways to pass time.

Chicago Gourmet, (312) 380-4128, illinoisrestaurants.org, is an extravaganza celebrating food and wine in Millennium Park each fall. In addition to the event proper—which features speakers, sommeliers, and demos—some area restaurants offer special menus, and there is a Hamburger Hop, during which Chicago chefs compete in a burger showdown.

The Fondue Festival, (920) 921-9500, fonduefest.com, celebrates the world's largest fondue pot in Fond du Lac, WI, each year. Tastes of fondue varieties are on hand. There's also a bicycle ride and plenty of cheesy gift baskets displayed at downtown shops.

The Pumpkin Festival, (309) 263-2491, pumpkincapital.com, is hosted annually in the town of Morton, IL. Indulge in squash-based cheesecake, ice cream, cookies, fudge, and pies. Other events include a parade, pageant, and decoration contest as well as live banjo music.

Warrens Cranberry Festival, (608) 378-4200, cranfest.com, in Warrens, WI, is said to be the largest gala of its kind worldwide. In addition to a lineup of marsh tours, more than 80 food vendors tempt with treats (try the pancakes topped with cranberry syrup). Biggest berry and recipe contests are scheduled, and a parade takes place.

The Watermelon Festival, (608) 697-6744, pardeeville watermelonfestival.com, puts the fruit in the limelight in Pardeeville, WI. An open-air market, free sliced watermelon, and a baked-goods auction are featured. There's a speed-eating and seed-spitting contest as well.

October

Apple Festival, visitlonggrove.com, is a longstanding event dedicated to its namesake fruit. Enjoy them by the bushel in pie, cider doughnut, and even martini form.

Fine Chocolate Show, (786) 558-5234, chicagochocolate festival.com, is the perfect excuse to eat some sweets at Navy Pier. Tastings from world-class chocolatiers are plentiful, and you may purchase sweet treats for the road.

The Turkey Testicle Festival, (815) 234-9910, **parksidepub huntley.com/ttf,** in Huntley, IL, is an adventure eater's paradise, featuring hundreds of pounds of "hot nuts."

November

The International Beer Tasting & Chili Cook-Off, (217) 344-3872, urbanabusiness.com, ushers in fall in Urbana, IL, with more than 150 specialty and import beers and all the chili you can eat.

The Wisconsin Cheese Originals Festival, (608) 358-7837, wicheesefest.com, takes place in Madison, WI, and highlights loads of painstakingly crafted artisan cheeses, plus tasting seminars, farm tours, and cheese-maker dinners.

Quick Index of Food Fests & Events

Recipes

Eating out is enjoyable. But sitting down to a home-cooked meal? That can be inspiring. In the pages that follow, Chicago chefs—not ones to be stingy with know-how—offer up recipes for beginners and vets, plate-sharers and sweet-tooths, using ingredients that embody the city's vibrant, seasonal sensibility and inventive spirit.

Chilled Cucumber Soup with Red Currants, Dill, and Gin Granita

This cold, refreshing soup appears in various incarnations at Lula Cafe, some-times with pickled honshimeji or chanterelle mushrooms.

Serves 4

For the Pickles

1 cup sliced cucumbers, using ¹⁄₁₆-inch rounds

½ teaspoon citric acid

2 teaspoons sugar

For the Granita

1 tablespoon chopped jalapeño

⅓ cup shishito peppers

7 juniper berries

⅔ cup fresh-squeezed lemon juice

⅓ tablespoon gin

2¼ cups peeled and chopped cucumber

1 cup water

¼ cup, plus 1 tablespoon sugar

For the Soup

½ cup chopped skin-on, non-waxy cucumbers

⅛ cup shishito peppers

¼ cup chopped spring onions

3 teaspoons chopped dill

2 teaspoons chopped mint

½ cup whole blanched almonds

1¾ cups yogurt

2 tablespoons extra-virgin olive oil

Additional Garnishes

⅛ cup fresh currants

¼ cup sliced almonds

¼ cup dill fronds

¼ cup crème fraîche

Make the pickles by tossing all the ingredients together. Place in the refrigerator to chill for at least 1 hour.

Prepare the granita by blending all the ingredients in a blender at high speed. Strain through cheese cloth. Freeze for 1 hour, then stir with a fork. Freeze for 40 minutes more, then rake with a fork every 30 minutes until granita is icy and slushy (about 3 hours total).

Blend all the soup ingredients in a high-speed blender. Strain through a fine-mesh strainer and refrigerate in a resealable container until ready to use.

When you're ready to serve, ladle the soup into individual bowls. Garnish each with a few pickles; a sprinkle of currants, almonds, and dill; a dollop of crème fraîche; and a scoop of "shaved ice" from the granita, achieved by using the side of a spoon.

Adapted recipe courtesy of Jason Hammel, Executive Chef and Owner of Lula Cafe (p. 41)

Wisconsin Trout Soup
with Bacon and Sour Cream

Nightwood's Jason Vincent uses trout from Wisconsin's Rushing Waters for this hearty soup with loaded baked potato flavors.

Serves 4

3 slices streaky bacon, minced
1 small onion, chopped
½ bulb fennel, chopped
1 rib celery, chopped
Kosher salt
Cracked black pepper
1 head garlic, peeled and sliced
½ teaspoon tomato paste
1 tablespoon fresh-squeezed orange juice
2 tablespoons apple cider
1 cup dry white wine
1 quart fish, chicken, or vegetable stock

1 cup heavy cream
1 large trout (12 to 14 ounces), filleted with head reserved and skin discarded
3 small, starchy potatoes, finely diced
4 sprigs thyme, plus 2 teaspoons minced thyme leaves
2 bay leaves
1 cup sour cream or crème fraîche
¼ cup minced fresh chives
½ cup cheddar cheese

Render out some of the bacon fat by cooking it in a sauté pan over medium-high heat until browned but not crisp, about 4 minutes. Remove the bacon pieces with a slotted spoon, placing them, covered, on a plate to keep warm.

Raise the heat slightly and sweat the onion, fennel, and celery in the remaining fat. Season with salt and pepper and cook, stirring continually with a wooden spoon. They should never sizzle or brown.

Once they are soft, reduce the heat to medium and add the garlic. Continue cooking for another 3 minutes, then add the tomato paste, orange juice, and cider. Cook until the mixture is completely dry.

Add the wine and bring to a boil, then simmer for 2 minutes. Add the stock, heavy cream, trout flesh, fish head, potatoes, thyme sprigs, and bay leaves, and turn the heat up slightly. Once the broth is simmering, it should be skimmed several times. Cook until the fish is no longer fleshy and flavors have had a chance to meld, about 15 minutes.

Season lightly, and reduce until it tastes like a good, fishy, slightly salty, soothing broth.

Whisk in the sour cream or crème fraîche and cook for a few more minutes. Taste and season as needed.

Remove and discard the head, thyme sprigs, and bay leaves. Puree the soup in small batches, adding minced thyme to each batch. Strain the soup several times through a very fine mesh strainer.

Divide the soup into 4 hot bowls, and garnish sour cream, warm bacon, chives, and cheddar.

Adapted recipe courtesy of Jason Vincent, Executive Chef of Nightwood (p. 154)

Mushroom Yaki Udon

This hearty dish is popular in Japanese izakayas. Takashi Yagihashi recommends making it in two batches when increasing the portion size.

Serves 2

- ¼ cup dried wood ear mushrooms
- 3 tablespoons vegetable oil
- 2 ounces pork belly, thinly sliced
- 6 large shrimp, peeled, deveined, and tails removed, cut into ½-inch pieces
- ¼ cup sliced lotus root (optional)
- ⅓ cup thinly sliced carrots
- 2 cups chopped napa cabbage
- ¼ cup thinly sliced onion
- ¼ cup sliced bamboo shoots
- ¼ cup each stemmed enoki and shimeji mushrooms
- ½ cup chicken broth
- 2 tablespoons soy sauce
- 1 teaspoon sesame oil
- 18 ounces fresh or frozen udon noodles, thawed if frozen
- Kosher salt
- Cracked black pepper
- ¼ cup finely shaved bonito flakes

Rehydrate the wood ear mushrooms by soaking in hot water for 10 minutes. Drain the liquid and set aside.

Set a large sauté pan over high heat. Add 2 tablespoons of the vegetable oil and heat just until the oil begins to smoke.

Add the pork and shrimp and cook for about 2 minutes, stirring often, until the shrimp just turn pink but neither is cooked through. Transfer to a plate, keeping the oil in the pan.

With the pan over high heat, add the lotus root, carrots, cabbage, onions, bamboo shoots, and wood ear, enoki, and shimeji mushrooms. Add the remaining 1 tablespoon of oil, if necessary. Cook until the vegetables are tender, 2 to 4 minutes.

Reduce the heat to medium and add the broth, soy sauce, and sesame oil to the vegetables. Cook for 2 minutes longer or until most of the liquid has evaporated.

Place a large pot of water over high heat and bring to a boil. Add the noodles and cook for 1 minute, just long enough to heat t. Drain well.

Add the noodles to the pan with the vegetables, along with the reserved pork and shrimp. Mix well and cook for 1 to 2 minutes longer, until the shrimp and pork are fully cooked and the vegetables are soft. Season with salt and black pepper.

To serve, divide the noodles between 2 plates. Garnish with the bonito flakes.

Recipe courtesy of Takashi Yagihashi, Chef/Owner of Takashi (p. 89), Slurping Turtle (p. 129), and Noodles by Takashi

Roasted Carrots with Hazelnut Brittle, Ricotta, and Kale

Chef Bryan Moscatello of Storefront Company prepares a version of this salad with chestnut brittle. Here, hazelnut brittle using standard grocery-store ingredients stands in its place.

Serves 4

For the Salad

1 ½ pounds baby carrots (preferably a mixture of colors), peeled

1 ½ tablespoons olive oil

Kosher salt

Cracked black pepper

1 bunch kale, such as Russian red, torn and tough stems discarded

1 cup hand-dipped or homemade ricotta

For the Brittle

1 cup sugar

½ cup light corn syrup

¼ teaspoon salt

¼ cup water

1 cup whole hazelnuts, crushed

2 tablespoons butter

1 teaspoon baking soda

Preheat oven to 400°F.

Place carrots in a medium bowl and toss with olive oil, salt, and pepper. Arrange in a single layer on a baking sheet and transfer to the oven, tossing periodically until tender and caramelized, about 20 minutes total.

Meanwhile, line a large cookie sheet with parchment paper and spray with cooking spray. Set aside.

To make the brittle, combine sugar, corn syrup, salt, and water in a medium saucepan outfitted with a candy thermometer over medium heat. Stir until sugar is dissolved. Add hazelnuts and stir frequently until temperature reaches 300°F. Remove from heat and immediately add butter and baking soda. Pour onto the prepared cookie sheet and cool completely. Remove from pan and break into small pieces.

When carrots are finished cooking, remove from the oven and place in a large bowl. Add kale and bits of brittle. Toss to combine. Garnish with dollops of ricotta and a light drizzle of vinaigrette or squirt of lemon (optional).

Adapted recipe courtesy of Bryan Moscatello, Chef/Partner of Storefront Company (p. 89)

Bread and Butter Pickles

Mark Steuer's house-made pickles are equally welcome as a snack as they are as a burger-topper.

Makes 4 quarts

- 6 small zucchini, cut into ⅛-inch rounds
- 3 Vidalia onions, thinly sliced
- 3 cups ice cubes
- ⅜ cup salt

- 6 cups distilled white vinegar
- 6 cups sugar
- 2 sprigs fresh dill
- 1 tablespoon mustard seeds

Combine zucchini, onions, ice cubes, and salt in a large bowl. Toss to combine and let stand at room temperature for 3 hours. Drain, rinse well, and drain again.

Add vinegar, sugar, dill, and mustard seeds to a large pot over medium-high heat. Bring to a boil. Add zucchini mixture and return to a boil, stirring occasionally until crisp-tender, about 3 minutes.

Remove from heat and bring to room temperature. Transfer to a large, resealable container and refrigerate for at least 1 day before serving.

Adapted recipe courtesy of Mark Steuer, Executive Chef of Carriage House (p. 65)

Olive Oil—Poached Octopus with Cannellini Bean Salad and Tabasco Sauce

Zoe Shor, chef at Ada St., uses tenderized baby octopus in this dish. Ask your fishmonger for a hand in cleaning and tenderizing it.

Serves 6

For the Salad

1 cup canned cannellini beans, drained and rinsed

¼ large red onion, julienned

Juice and zest of 2 lemons

1 canned, fire-roasted red bell pepper, seeded and julienned

¼ cup fresh flat-leaf parsley leaves, torn

2 cups, plus 1 tablespoon extra-virgin olive oil, divided use

Kosher salt

Cracked black pepper

2 pounds tenderized, cleaned baby octopus

1 tablespoon vegetable or grapeseed oil

For the Tabasco Sauce

2 tablespoons extra-virgin olive oil

½ large Spanish onion, thinly sliced

4 cloves garlic, chopped

¼ cup brown sugar

2 tablespoons tomato paste

1 (28-ounce) can fire-roasted tomatoes, such as Muir Glen

2 tablespoons bourbon

1 teaspoon Tabasco

⅛ cup apple cider vinegar

Combine beans, onion, lemon zest and juice, bell pepper, parsley, and 1 tablespoon olive oil in a medium bowl. Season generously with salt and pepper and stir to combine. Cover and refrigerate to marry flavors.

Submerge octopus in 2 cups olive oil in a medium pot, set over low heat. Bring it to a simmer and allow it to boil very gently until octopus is very tender, 45

minutes to 1½ hours, depending on size. Remove from oil using tongs and place on a cooling rack in the refrigerator.

While the beans are marinating and the octopus is cooling, prepare the Tabasco sauce by adding 2 tablespoons olive oil to a large, heavy-bottomed pot over medium-high heat. Add Spanish onions and cook, stirring periodically, until translucent, about 7 minutes.

Add garlic to the pot and continue cooking for 1 minute, then add the brown sugar and tomato paste. Stir to coat and allow to caramelize and achieve deep, complex flavor, about 3 minutes more. Add the remaining ingredients. Season with salt and pepper and simmer over low heat for 20 minutes.

Taste and season sauce, if necessary. Transfer to a blender and puree until completely smooth.

Cut the octopus into bits. Heat the vegetable or grapeseed oil in a large sauté pan until shimmering. Add octopus and season with salt and pepper. Stir periodically until it gets some color and texture, about 3 minutes.

Spread a generous amount of sauce on individual plates. Mound a few heaping spoons of bean salad on top, and top with octopus. Sprinkle with additional chopped parsley, a squirt of lemon juice, and a whirl of olive oil. Serve immediately.

Recipe courtesy of Zoe Shor, Chef at Ada St. (p. 55)

Crispy Carnaroli with Cheese Curds

At Perennial Virant, Paul Virant finishes this dish with pea shoots and smoked spring onion vinaigrette. Feel free to top it with pickled and smoked ingredients of your choosing.

Serves 8

- 2 tablespoons unsalted butter
- ½ cup sliced spring onions
- 2 cups carnaroli or arborio rice
- 2 cups white wine
- 4 cups water
- ¼ cup grated Parmesan cheese
- 2 pounds cheddar cheese curds
- Kosher salt
- Cracked black pepper
- 2 tablespoons clarified butter or ghee
- ½ cup rice flour

Melt butter in a large stockpot over medium heat. Add onions and sweat until slightly tender, about 3 minutes. Add rice and toast, stirring continuously. Wet with a bit of wine and stir until all liquid is absorbed. Add 1 cup of water and continue to stir, then alternate adding water and wine, stirring until rice is tender. Add Parmesan cheese and season with salt and pepper.

Allow to cool slightly, then fold in cheese curds. Spray an 8 x 8-inch pan with cooking spray. Pour rice into pan and press down so it's compacted into an even layer. Cool completely. Slice into ¾-inch-thick slabs.

Heat clarified butter in a large sauté pan over medium-high heat. Dust rice cakes in rice flour, taking care to shake off excess. When oil is hot, add rice and brown on all sides, about 6 minutes total. Remove from pan and top with a combination of pickled, smoky ingredients.

Recipe courtesy of Paul Virant,
Chef/Partner at Perennial Virant (p. 82) and Chef/Owner of Vie (p. 195)

Escalivada with Grilled Bread

This summery recipe from Ryan Poli is a great way to utilize a bumper crop of produce.

Serves 8

4 small eggplants, halved
4 small onions, halved
4 red bell peppers, seeded and halved
2 medium tomatoes
⅓ cup extra-virgin olive oil, plus additional for brushing

2 cloves garlic, minced
3 tablespoons sherry vinegar
Kosher salt
Cracked black pepper
¼ cup high-quality extra-virgin olive oil for finishing
1 loaf country bread, sliced and briefly grilled

Light a chimney full of charcoal. When all the charcoal is lit and covered with gray ash, pour out and arrange the coals in an even layer. Set cooking grate in place, cover grill, and allow to preheat for 5 minutes.

Brush the eggplant, onions, peppers, and tomatoes with the ⅓ cup of olive oil. Place the vegetables over the fire and grill until the skins blacken and the vegetables are tender.

Remove from the grill and transfer vegetables to a large, lidded container. Cover and steam for 10 to 15 minutes. When cool enough to handle, peel the charred outer skins of the eggplants, onions, peppers, and tomatoes. Discard skins.

Cut eggplant, onions and peppers lengthwise into 1½-inch-wide strips. Roughly chop tomatoes. Transfer to a bowl, and add the garlic and sherry vinegar. Season with salt and pepper, and stir to combine. Drizzle with the ¼ cup high-quality olive oil and serve at room temperature on grilled bread.

Recipe courtesy of Ryan Poli, Chef/Partner at Tavernita Restaurant (p. 131)
and Little Market Brasserie (p. 75)

Crab Cakes with Louis Dressing

If you dine at Big Jones during brunch, consider ordering Paul Fehribach's eggs New Orleans, a lush meal of crab cakes, poached eggs, and a popover blanketed in béarnaise. In the meantime, this one works as an appetizer—or as an entrée for four.

Serves 6

For the Crab Cakes

2 tablespoons minced carrot

4 tablespoons minced celery

2 tablespoons minced red bell pepper

1 clove garlic, mashed

1 pound fresh lump crabmeat, picked over for shells and chilled

2 teaspoons kosher salt

2 tablespoons Louisiana-style hot sauce

1 tablespoon prepared Creole, Dijon, or Dusseldorfer mustard

¼ cup mayonnaise

½ cup French bread crumbs or Japanese panko, plus extra for dredging

2 large eggs, lightly beaten

4 tablespoons minced onion

2 tablespoons vegetable oil

For the Louis Dressing

1 cup mayonnaise

2 tablespoons Louisiana-style hot sauce

1 fresh jalapeño, seeded and minced

1 tablespoon freshly grated horseradish

2 green onions, thinly sliced

2 tablespoons fresh-squeezed lemon juice

1 teaspoon kosher salt

To prepare the crab cakes, combine the onion, carrot, celery, red pepper, garlic, crabmeat, 2 teaspoons salt, 2 tablespoons hot sauce, mustard, ¼ cup mayonnaise, and bread crumbs. Add eggs and carefully toss again to combine. Refrigerate at least 1 hour.

While mixture is chilling, make the Louis dressing. Place 1 cup mayonnaise, 2 tablespoons hot sauce, jalapeño, horseradish, green onions, lemon juice, and 1 teaspoon salt in a medium bowl. Stir to combine and refrigerate until ready to use.

To cook the crab cakes, heat oil in a large skillet over medium heat. Scoop up ¼ cup of crab mixture at a time and shape into a ball. Roll in bread crumbs to lightly coat. Place cake in the oil and flatten slightly with the back of a spatula.

Working quickly and in batches, continue making more cakes until the skillet is full but not overcrowded, about 8 minutes on the first side. Reduce heat, if necessary, so they don't burn. Gently turn and cook another 4 minutes, turning up the heat on the second side if necessary to brown. The crab cakes are done when they're springy to the touch and not mushy, and a toothpick inserted in the center doesn't come out milky.

Serve immediately with Louis dressing.

Recipe courtesy of Paul Fehribach, Executive Chef and Co-Owner of Big Jones (p. 5)

Quiche Lorraine

Martial Noguier serves this simple-but-stunning quiche at Bistronomic, topped with a farm salad.

Makes 1 9-inch tart

For the Pâte Brisée

2 cups flour

10 tablespoons cold, unsalted
  butter, finely diced

Kosher salt

1 egg yolk

1 ounce very cold water

For the Filling

2 tablespoons olive oil

8 ounces bacon

2 egg yolks, plus 2 eggs

1 cup milk

1 cup heavy cream

⅓ teaspoon salt

¼ teaspoon cayenne pepper

⅓ teaspoon freshly grated
  nutmeg

⅓ cup grated Gruyère cheese

Toss flour, butter, and a pinch of salt into the bowl of a food processor. Whisk 1 egg yolk and water together in another small bowl. Pulse flour and butter until butter is pea-size. Add just enough egg mixture to make it come together. Turn out mixture onto a floured workspace and form into a round, flat disk. Refrigerate for 1 hour.

Preheat oven to 400°F.

Roll out dough to ¼-inch round, and line tart pan. Place a piece of parchment or foil on top of dough, and weight it with beans or pie weights

Bake for 20 minutes. Remove parchment and beans and bake an additional 5 minutes until dry and lightly browned. Cool crust completely.

Reduce oven temperature to 300°F.

Combine oil and bacon in a sauté pan over medium-high heat. Cook bacon until crisp and drain off fat.

Whisk together 2 egg yolks and 2 eggs in a large bowl. Add milk and heavy cream, along with ⅓ teaspoon salt, cayenne, and nutmeg, and stir to combine.

Scatter bacon and cheese evenly over baked crust. Pour filling on top. Transfer to the oven and bake until custard is just set, about 20 minutes

Recipe courtesy of Martial Noguier, Executive Chef/Owner of Bistronomic (p. 61)

Poached Salmon in Tarragon Broth

This simple salmon dish from Michael Kornick allows bright citrus-herb flavors to shine.

Serves 2

1 carrot, cut into matchsticks

1 rib celery, cut into matchsticks

1 small head fennel, cored and thinly sliced

2 green beans, cut into matchsticks

7 tablespoons butter, divided use

1 medium shallot, minced

2 5-ounce salmon fillets

Kosher salt

Cracked black pepper

¼ cup minced tarragon

¼ cup minced mint

1 lemon, zest and juiced

1 orange, zest and juiced

½ cup dry Riesling

3 scallions, finely sliced

Bring a medium stockpot filled with water to a boil. Individually blanch the carrot, celery, fennel, and green beans until slightly tender. Shock with cold water to stop the cooking process. Reserve.

Preheat oven to 450°F.

Rub 6 tablespoons of butter onto the bottom of a straight-sided, oven-safe pan. Julienne the shallot and scatter it atop the butter.

Season fish with salt and pepper and place it on top of the shallot. Sprinkle with tarragon, mint, and zests, and pour citrus juices and wine on top. Cover and transfer to the oven to cook for 6 to 8 minutes, until flaky but not fleshy.

Melt remaining 1 tablespoon of butter in a sauté pan over medium heat. Add the vegetables and toss to reheat. Add the scallions and continue cooking for another minute. Transfer to vegetables in equal portions to individual serving bowls.

When fish is done cooking, remove it from the oven place atop vegetables. Finish with pan sauce and serve immediately.

Recipe courtesy of Michael Kornick, Chef/Owner of mk (p. 118) and Co-Owner of Ada St., DMK Burger Bar, and Fish Bar (pp. 55, 34, and 35)

Baked Sriracha Ribs

These ribs are a go-to for the author, injecting a bit of warmth into meals when it's too cold to bust out the grill. A version of this recipe originally appeared in the author's column, Sunday Supper, on Serious Eats.

Serves 4

- ½ teaspoon ginger powder
- 2 teaspoons freshly ground black pepper
- 1½ teaspoons onion powder
- 1 tablespoon ground chili, such as ancho

- ½ teaspoon kosher salt
- ¼ cup packed brown sugar
- 2 racks baby back ribs
- 1 cup apple juice
- 1 (12-ounce) bottle light-flavored beer

For the Glaze

- ½ cup honey
- ½ cup Sriracha
- 1½ tablespoons Asian chili sauce (such as sambal oelek), divided

- ¼ cup brown sugar

Adjust oven rack to middle position and preheat oven to 275°F.

Combine ginger powder, black pepper, onion powder, chili powder, salt, and ¼ cup brown sugar in a small bowl. Mix thoroughly with fingertips.

Place ribs on a large, foil-lined baking sheet and coat with rub on all surfaces. Place in the oven to roast until fat begins to render and ribs are softened, 1½ to 2 hours. Meanwhile, lay two 12 x 24-inch sheets of heavy-duty aluminum foil out on the countertop and fold their edges tightly together to form one large sheet.

Remove ribs from the oven and set them on top of the foil. Return ribs to the rimmed baking sheet with the foil. Pour apple juice and beer on top of the ribs, then fold up foil

and seal tightly to create an enclosed package. Return to oven and continue cooking until ribs are completely tender, about 1 hour longer.

While the ribs are cooking, prepare the glaze by mixing honey, Sriracha, chili sauce, and ¼ cup brown sugar in a small bowl.

Remove ribs from oven and raise temperature to 375°F. Discard liquid, return ribs to baking sheet, and generously brush with glaze. Return to oven until glaze is burnished and sticky, 15 to 20 minutes longer.

Recipe courtesy of Jennifer Olvera

West Town Tavern Pot Roast
with Black Vinegar Sauce

Now-defunct (but sorely missed) West Town Tavern was known for its pot roast, which employed boneless beef short ribs instead of the usual beef chuck.

Serves 6

8 9-ounce square-cut, boneless beef short rib pieces

Kosher salt

Cracked black pepper

¼ cup canola oil

2 carrots, scrubbed and roughly chopped

2 ribs celery, roughly chopped

1 large red onion, peeled and cut into eighths

2 large bay leaves

10 sprigs flat-leaf parsley

1 bottle red Zinfandel wine

4 cups water or more to barely cover

For the Black Vinegar Sauce

4 cups red wine vinegar

1½ cups packed dark brown sugar

¾ cup dark raisins

Preheat oven to 325°F.

Season short ribs with salt and pepper. Heat the canola oil in a heavy pan over medium-high heat. The pan should be just large enough to hold the short ribs. Sear the beef on all sides until brown, about 8 minutes total.

Add the carrots, celery, onion, bay leaves, and parsley to the pan. Pour in the wine and just enough water to barely cover meat. Bring to a boil.

Remove pan from heat, cover with a lid or foil, and braise in the oven 1½ to 2 hours, or until meat is very tender.

While the meat is cooking, combine the vinegar and brown sugar in a heavy saucepan. Bring to a boil, reduce the heat, and simmer until liquid reduces to 2½ cups. Add the raisins. Continue to simmer the sauce and reduce to 2 cups. The sauce should appear black, syrupy, and glossy. Let sauce cool to room temperature.

When pot roast is done cooking, serve immediately, drizzled with sauce. Or, if not serving immediately, refrigerate and then reheat meat and bring sauce to room temperature.

Recipe courtesy of *West Town Tavern: Contemporary Comfort Food* (2010),
by Susan Goss with Drew Goss

Brioche-Crusted Halibut with Mustard-Chive Sauce

Elegant and approachable, Carrie Nahabedian's fish dish is a spring and summer fave at NAHA.

Serves 2

- ½ stick (4 tablespoons) unsalted butter
- 1 small kohlrabi, peeled and julienne-cut
- ½ pound asparagus, cleaned and tough ends removed
- ¼ pound sugar snap peas
- 2 Roma tomatoes
- 2 6-ounce wild Alaskan halibut fillets
- Kosher salt
- Cracked black pepper
- 2 cups pound fine brioche crumbs, dried in the oven
- 1 bunch pea shoots
- 2 tablespoons hazelnut oil
- 2 teaspoons sherry vinegar

For the Sauce

- ½ teaspoon olive oil
- 1 shallot, peeled and minced
- 1 cup white wine
- 1 cup heavy cream
- 1 tablespoon grainy mustard
- 1 small bunch chives, minced

Clarify the butter by melting it in a medium sauté pan over low heat. Skim off foam, remove the clear liquid, and discard the milk solids.

Drain kohlrabi on a paper towel to remove excess moisture. Blanch asparagus and snap peas in a pot of boiling, salted water until just starting to soften. Shock with water to stop the cooking process. Reserve. Cut an X in the bottom of the tomatoes. Using the same water, blanch tomatoes. Peel skin, discard seeds, and slice into thin strips.

To make the sauce, heat the olive oil in a heavy saucepan over medium heat, then add shallot and sauté until it starts to soften, about 3 minutes. Add wine and reduce by two-thirds. Pour in heavy cream and reduce by two-thirds again. Add mustard, remove from heat, season with salt and pepper, and add chives. Stir to combine, and cover to keep warm.

Heat half of the clarified butter in a large, nonstick or stainless steel sauté pan over medium-high heat. Season fish with salt and pepper. Dip into the remaining clarified butter, then dredge in the bread crumbs to coat. Reduce heat to medium, place halibut in the pan, and cook until golden brown, about 3 minutes per side. (If fillets are especially thick, you may need to finish them in a preheated 375°F oven for 5 minutes.)

Remove fish from pan, drain on paper towels, and place on individual plates.

Quickly place reserved kohlrabi, asparagus, tomatoes, and snap peas in a large bowl. Add pea shoots, season with salt and pepper, and dress with hazelnut oil and sherry vinegar. Top fish with vegetables and garnish plate with mustard-chive sauce.

Recipe courtesy of Carrie Nahabedian, Chef/Owner of Naha (p. 119) and Brindille (p. 100)

Lobster with Melted Leeks, Thai Chiles, and Toasted Garlic

Thai Dang, executive chef of Embeya, recommends serving this dish with a crisp, chilly Riesling or beer.

Serves 2

- 7 cloves garlic, minced
- 1 tablespoon minced ginger
- 2 quarts grape seed or vegetable oil, plus extra for sautéing
- 6 dried Thai chiles
- 3 shallots, diced
- 2 medium white onions, diced
- 2 jalapeños, minced
- 5 leeks, rinsed thoroughly and sliced thinly
- Kosher salt
- Cracked black pepper
- 2 1½- to 2-pound lobsters
- 1 cup rice flour
- 1 cup cornstarch

Add ginger and garlic to a cold pan, and pour in just enough oil to cover. Place on stovetop over medium heat and sauté until lightly toasted.

Add dry chiles, shallots, onions, jalapeños, and leeks. Season with salt and pepper, and stir to combine. Sauté until leeks are tender, about 8 minutes. Reserve.

Remove tail, claws, and knuckles from the lobster body, using heavy-duty scissors. Then, use scissors to split knuckles and expose claws and tail meat. Reserve other lobster parts for another use.

In a large, heavy-bottomed stockpot or countertop fryer, heat 2 quarts of oil to 340°F.

Combine rice flour and cornstarch on a plate. Season with salt and pepper. Dredge cleaned lobster in mixture.

Place lobster pieces in oil and fry until golden brown. You'll know they're done when lobster is no longer translucent and the crust is golden brown.

When lobster is finished cooking, remove from the oil, drain on paper towels, and finish with black pepper and warmed leek mixture.

Recipe courtesy of Thai Dang, Executive Chef of Embeya (p. 103)

Blueberry Pop Tart with Lemon Glaze

Gregory Ellis fuels the morning masses with this seasonally changing recipe at 2 Sparrows.

Makes 10 tarts

3 cups all-purpose flour

1 cup, plus 1 teaspoon sugar, divided use

1 teaspoon salt

2 sticks (1 cup) butter, cubed and chilled

¼ to ½ cup cold water

12 ounces fresh blueberries

½ cup fresh-squeezed lemon juice (from about 4 lemons), divided use

2 tablespoons sugar

1 egg, whisked

2 cups confectioners' sugar

Zest of ½ lemon

Mix flour, 1 teaspoon sugar, and salt together in bowl of an electric mixer fitted with a paddle. Add butter and mix on medium speed until the mixture makes way to pea-size chunks. With mixer running on low speed, slowly add ¼ to ½ cup water, just until dough comes together. Continue to mix dough at medium speed for 3 minutes.

Flatten dough and wrap in plastic wrap. Refrigerate for at least 2 hours before rolling out.

To make the filling, combine blueberries, ¼ cup lemon juice, and 1 cup sugar in a medium saucepan and bring to a boil over medium-high heat. Reduce heat to medium and cook 12 to 15 minutes or until blueberries give up their juices and reduce until no longer soupy. Remove from heat and cool completely until ready to use.

Preheat oven to 375°F.

Roll out dough to ⅛-inch thick. Cut dough into ten 6 x 5-inch rectangles. Poke each rectangle several times with the tines of a fork.

With the dough rectangles lying horizontal, spoon ⅓ cup of the filling on one half of the rectangle, leaving a ½-inch edge of dough around all sides. Brush egg wash around the filling and fold the other half of the dough on top. Press the dough down to seal edges. Using a fork, go around all edges, pressing down to make sure no filling leaks when the tarts bake.

Place pop tarts on a parchment-lined cookie sheet. Lightly score tops with an X so they do not balloon in the oven. Brush tart tops with egg wash and bake for 12 to 15 minutes or until golden brown on top.

While the pop tarts are in the oven, whisk powdered sugar, remaining ¼ cup lemon juice, and lemon zest in a small bowl until smooth.

Remove tarts from the oven, brush with glaze, and serve immediately.

Adapted recipe courtesy of Greg Ellis, Chef-Partner at 2 Sparrows (p. 92)

Niçoise Financier

Patrick Fahy, Executive Chef at Sixteen, surprises with this savory take on the classic French finale.

Serves 8

1 pound, plus 2 ounces butter
1 pound, plus 2 ounces egg whites
1 cup all-purpose flour
1 cup hazelnut flour
2½ cups powdered sugar

1 egg yolk
1 tablespoon kosher salt
½ cup granulated sugar
1 tablespoon lemon juice
1 cup black niçoise olives, minced

Brown the butter by melting it in a large pot over low heat for roughly 20 minutes. The butter will foam up when it comes to a boil, so make sure you use a pot that is twice the volume as the butter. The butter is ready when it is brown-hued and toasty. Remove from heat and place pot in the freezer or atop a bowl of ice water to stop the cooking process.

Preheat oven to 350°F.

Wisk the egg whites with the all-purpose flour, hazelnut flour, and powdered sugar in a large bowl until there are no lumps and it looks like a slurry. Add the egg yolk, salt, granulated sugar, and lemon juice. Whisk again. Slowing pour in the brown butter, whisking continuously until emulsified. Add the olives and stir to combine.

Spray a 10-inch springform pan with cooking spray. Pour batter into pan. Transfer to oven and bake until the cake is golden and a toothpick inserted into its center comes out clean, 15 to 30 minutes.

Remove from oven, allow to cool slightly, and serve warm with apricot or lemon preserves and a dollop of whipped cream.

Recipe courtesy of Patrick Fahy, Executive Chef at Sixteen (p. 129)

Sweet Corn Crème Brûlée

Sable's Heather Terhune is equally lauded for atypical-but-awesome endings as she is for updated American mains.

Serves 6

4 ears fresh sweet corn,
    shucked and kernels
    removed and reserved

4 cups heavy cream

8 egg yolks

¼ cup granulated sugar

1 teaspoon kosher salt

½ cup coarse raw sugar

French sea salt

Place cobs and cream in a stockpot over medium heat. (Reserve the kernels for a later step.) Cook, stirring occasionally, just until it comes to a boil. You need about 15 minutes to infuse the cream with corn flavor. Remove from heat and reserve.

Adjust oven rack to middle position and preheat oven to 300°F.

Whisk egg yolks, granulated sugar, and kosher salt in a large bowl. Whisking constantly, gradually pour in the hot cream mixture. Strain the mixture into a pitcher.

Divide the kernels evenly between six 8-ounce ovenproof rame-kins. Pour the cream mixture into the bowls and arrange in a hot water bath. Transfer to the oven and cook until almost set but still a bit soft in the center, 30 to 40 minutes. The custard should "shimmy" a bit when you shake the pan; it will firm up more as it cools.

Remove from the water bath and let cool 15 minutes. Tightly cover each bowl with plastic wrap, making sure the plastic does not touch the surface of the custard. Refrigerate at least 2 hours and up to 24 hours. Adjust oven rack to the upper position and preheat broiler.

Uncover the chilled custards. Pour as much raw sugar as will fit onto the top of one of the custards. Pour off the excess sugar onto the next custard. Repeat until all the custards are coated. Discard any remaining sugar.

Place the bowls on a baking sheet. Caramelize the sugar under a preheated broiler for 3 to 6 minutes or until a crackly, candy-sugar crust forms. Let cool for a minute, sprinkle with French sea salt, and serve.

Recipe courtesy of Heather Terhune, Executive Chef at Sable Kitchen & Bar (p. 127)

Appendix A: Eateries by Cuisine

Barbecue

Volare, 92

Tozi, 90

**Middle Eastern/Lebanese/
Assyrian/Israeli**

Original Gino's East Pizza, The, 80
Osteria Via Stato, 120
Parkers' Restaurant & Bar, 191
Piece Brewery & Pizzeria, 216
Pizzeria da Nella, 82
Pizzeria Uno, 123
Roots Handmade Pizza, 84
Rosangela's Pizza, 200
Sabatino's, 47
Sono Wood Fired, 88
Spacca Napoli, 22
Stop 50 Wood-Fired Pizzeria, 207
Union Pizzeria, 178
Villa Nova, 195
Vito & Nick's, 162
Wells Bros., 207

Polish
Cavalier Inn, 202
Flo & Santos, 145
Mabenka, 199
Oak Mill Bakery, 285
Pierogi Heaven, 123
Podhalanka, 83
Smak Tak, 22

Portuguese
Fat Rice, 35

Pub
Billy Goat Tavern, 98
Publican, The, 124

Puerto Rican
La Bomba, 39
Papa's Cache Sabroso, 81

Regional American
Big Jones, 5
Carriage House, 65
Chicago's Home of Chicken and
   Waffles, 142
Flo, 104
Masa Azul, 42
Pearl's Place, 155
Priscilla's Ultimate Soul Food, 192
Ruby's Restaurant, 126
TABLE fifty-two, 89
Wishbone, 136

Russian
Russian Tea Time, 126

Sandwiches
Lincoln's O, 204
Monti's, 17
Moon's Sandwich Shop, 118
Philly's Best, 122
Soulwich, 177
Zenwich, 196

Seafood
Calumet Fisheries, 158
Cape Cod Room, 65
Captain Porky's, 166
Chinn's 34th St. Fishery, 183

Appendix B:
Index of Purveyors

Organizations, Food Services & Learning Centers

Appendix C: Index of Cooking Classes, Schools, Clubs & Food Forays

Index

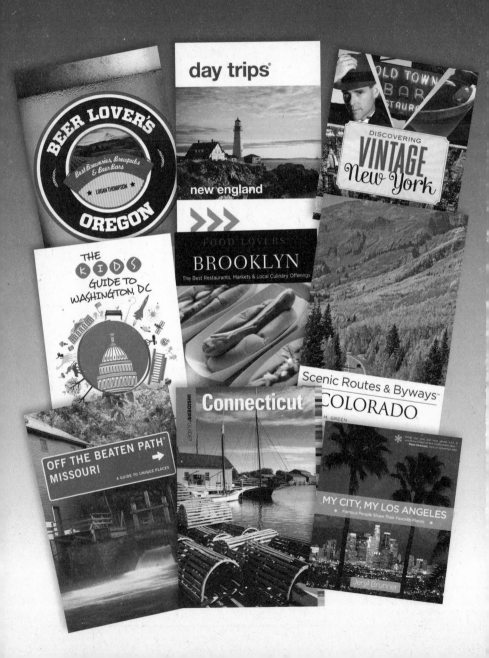